BTEC
NATIONAL
Sport

| Book 2 |

Development, Coaching and Fitness

Mike Hill
Olivia McLaughlin
Helen Moors
Andrew Procter
Kate Randerson

Nelson Thornes

First edition published in 2003

Second edition published in 2007 by:
Nelson Thornes Ltd
Delta Place
27 Bath Road
CHELTENHAM
GL53 7TH
United Kingdom

08 09 10 11 12 / 10 9 8 7 6 5 4 3 2 1

A catalogue record for this book is available from the British Library

ISBN 978 0 7487 8163 8

Page make-up by Pantek Arts Ltd, Maidstone, Kent

Printed in Great Britain by Scotprint

Contents

Introduction

Sport is such an important aspect in our world today. A significant number of people watch, take part in or work in sport. Millions of pairs of eyes will be on London in the summer of 2012, watching the Olympic Games. Thousands of people each week watch football, rugby and athletics events in the UK. Many compete in sports at different levels, from Sunday morning club games to the elite athletes who train many hours each day to achieve high standards in performance. There is a thriving industry supporting sport, with a range of related jobs from sports hall supervisors to events organisers, to top performance coaches. Should you want to be part of the sports industry, a BTEC National Diploma in Sport is an important step in your sports education.

How do you use this book?

Covering 8 specialist units of the new 2007 specification, this book has everything you need if you are studying BTEC National Certificate or Diploma in Sport (Development, Coaching and Fitness). Simple to use and understand, it is designed to provide you with the skills and knowledge you need to gain your qualification. We guide you step by step toward your qualification, through a range of features that are fully explained over the page.

Which units do you need to complete?

BTEC National Sport Book 2 provides coverage of 8 units for the BTEC National Diploma in Sport (Development, Coaching and Fitness). To achieve the Diploma, you are required to complete 7 core units plus 11 specialist units that provide for a combined total of 1080 guided learning hours (GLH). *BTEC National Sport Book 2* provides you with the following:

Specialist Units

Unit 10 **Sports Nutrition**

Unit 12 **Leadership in Sport**

Unit 13 **Exercise, Health and Lifestyle**

Unit 15 **Exercise for Specific Groups**

Unit 17 **Sports Injuries**

Unit 20 **Sport and Exercise Massage**

Unit 21 **Rules, Regulations and Officiating in Sport**

Unit 23 **Working with Children in Sport**

BTEC National Sport Book 1 offers coverage of all 8 core units and 2 further specialist units, providing the 1080 Guided Learning Hours required for the Diploma.

Is there anything else you need to do?

1 Find our about sport and leisure in your area – check local newspapers, TV and radio.

2 Get as much experience as you can in the sports industry, for example at local clubs or leisure centres.

3 Keep yourself fit and healthy by participating in sport

4 Read national newspapers, including the broadsheets, to gain a wider knowledge of sport.

5 Talk to people who are involved in the sports industry, as them how they got their position and what qualifications/experience they needed.

We hope you enjoy your BTEC course – Good Luck!

Turn over now for your guide to the features of this book.

Features of this book

UNIT 10

Sports Nutrition

This unit covers:

- The concepts of nutrition and digestion
- Energy intake and expenditure in sports performance
- The relationship between hydration and sports performance
- Plan a diet appropriate for a selected sports activity.

This unit aims to provide a broad understanding of the effects of nutrition and hydration on sports performance in a variety of sports. It includes the effects of digestion and how different sources of food are digested and then utilised by the body in order to promote or enhance exercise performance. The importance of a healthy diet will be investigated and the links between diet and health discussed. The energy requirements and body types of athletes involved in sports during training and competition will be considered. As a result, an outline dietary plan should give a clear indication of the need for individual nutritional and fluid requirements when linked to sport.

Learning Objectives

At the beginning of each Unit there will be a bulleted list letting you know what material is going to be covered. They specifically relate to the learning objectives within the specification.

Grading Criteria

The table of Grading Criteria at the beginning of each unit identifies achievement levels of pass, merit and distinction, as stated in the specification.

To achieve a **pass**, you must be able to match each of the 'P' criteria in turn.

To achieve **merit** or **distinction**, you must increase the level of evidence that you use in your work, using the 'M' and 'D' columns as reference. For example, to achieve a distinction you must fulfil all the criteria in the pass, merit and distinction columns.

grading criteria	To achieve a **Pass** grade the evidence must show that the learner is able to:	To achieve a **Merit** grade the evidence must show that the learner is able to:	To achieve a **Distinction** grade the evidence must show that the learner is able to:
	P1 describe nutrition, including nutritional requirements and common terminology associated with nutrition		
	P2 describe the structure and function of the digestive system		
	P3 describe energy intake and expenditure in sports performance	**M1** explain intake and expenditure in sports performance	
	P4 escribe energy balance and its importance in relation to sports performance	**M2** explain the importance of energy balance in relation to sports performance	**D1** analyse the effects of energy balance on sports performance
	P5 describe hydration and its effects on sports performance	**M3** explain the effects of hydration on sports performance	
	P6 describe the components of a balanced diet	**M4** explain the components of a balanced diet	
	P7 describe an appropriate two week diet plan for a selected sports performer for a selected sports activity	**M5** explain the two-week diet plan for a selected sports performer for a selected sports activity	**D2** analyse how the cardiovascular system responds to exercise

activity
GROUP WORK

P5

Design a poster that describes hydration and why it is important to sportsmen/women. Link your work to the different types of sports drinks that are available.

case study
10.1

Chris is a professional rower who has been advised to eat a diet totalling 3500 kcal per day, the breakdown of macro nutrients is Carbohydrates 61%; fats 20% and Proteins 19%.

activity
INDIVIDUAL WORK

1. List the different sources of proteins that Chris could eat
2. Decide which food sources would be better for him
3. Calculate the total number of grams of protein he will need each day

remember

Refuelling after exercise will enable the body to recover quickly, it can take up to 20 hours post exercise to replace used carbohydrate stores. Ideally 1 g carbohydrate per kg of body weight is needed within a 2 hour period, so a 70 kg athlete will need 70 g of carbohydrate.

Carbohydrate guidelines are usually calculated as a proportion of the total calorie intake, however for athletes it may be more relevant to consider the carbohydrate needed to be consumed per day (in grams) per kilogram of body weight.

Endurance trained athletes may range from between 8–10 grams per kg of body weight per day, compared to those who exercise less than five hours per week whose requirements may be set at 4–5 grams per kg of body weight.

 Link

For more information, see Unit XX page XX.

 i

The British Heart Foundation
www.bhf.org.uk

Progress Check

1. What are enzymes and why are they important?
2. What are the end products of digested
   (a) Proteins
   (b) Fats
   (c) Carbohydrates
3. What do we mean by the following terms:
   (a) Food.
   (b) Nutrition.
   (c) Diet.
4. Give an example of each of the major components of food.
5. What are amino acids?
6. What is meant by 'bad' cholesterol?
7. Why is water so valuable as part of a balanced diet?
   (a) Name three different vitamins.
   (b) State why each should be part of your diet.
8. Why is food labelling so important?
9. Name the different methods of measuring body composition
10. What steps can athletes follow to prevent dehydration?

Activities

are designed to help you understand the topics through answering questions or undertaking research, and are either *Group* or *Individual* work. They are linked to the grading criteria by application of the D, P, and M categories.

Case Studies

provide real life examples that relate to what is being discussed within the text. It provides an opportunity to demonstrate theory in practice.

An **Activity** that is linked to a case study helps you to apply your knowledge of the subject to real life situations.

Keywords

of specific importance are highlighted within the text, and then defined in the glossary at the end of the book.

Remember boxes

contain helpful hints, tips or advice.

Links

direct you to other parts of the book that relate to the subject currently being covered.

Information bars

point you towards resources for further reading and research (e.g. websites).

Progress Checks

provide a list of quick questions at the end of each Unit, designed to ensure that you have understood the most important aspects of each subject area.

Acknowledgements

The authors and publisher would like to thank the following organisations for permission to reproduce material:

Australian Sports Committee Table 21.3, p. 260; BabyFit Figure 15.2, p. 122; BAILI Case Study 17.4, p.174; BBC Case Studies 17.1, p. 165, 17.3, p. 170; Barrow Sports Council Case Study 15.6, p. 136; Crown copyright Figure 13.1, p. 78, Figure 13.3, p. 80, 13.5, p. 81; Bolton University Case Study 15.11, p. 147; East Riding of Yorkshire Council Case Study 15.8, p. 138; Food and Agriculture Organisation Figure 13.7, p. 83; Greater Glasgow NHS Board Case Study 15.4, p. 132; Saga Case Study 13.7, p. 118; Sport England Case Study 13.6, p. 104; Figure 13.16, p. 100, Figure 13.17, p. 101, Figure 13.19, p. 104; Ribble Valley Borough Council Case Study 15.9, p. 143 l; Rugby Football Union Figure 21.5, p. 248; *Runners World* text p. 160; *Sunday Times* Table 10.16, p. 34; Warwick District Council Figure 15.10; WHO Figure 13.10, p. 85; www.supersizeme.com Figure 13.13, p. 92; YWCA Case Study 15.7, p. 138..

Case Study 13.3 modified from Wikipedia – Copyright © 2008 NelsonThornes Ltd. Permission is granted to copy, distribute and/or modify this modified version under the terms of the GNU Free Documentation License, Version 1.2 or any later version published by the Free Software Foundation; with no invariant Sections, no Front-Cover Texts, and no Back-Cover Texts. A copy of the license is included in the section entitled 'GNU Free Documentation License'.

Photo credits

Alamy Figures 10.9 (p. 18) (Scott Camazine), 12.13, p. 60 (Les Gibbon), 13.4, p. 81 (Sally greenhamm), 13.6, p. 83 (Les Gibbon), 15.3, p. 123 (Andrew Fox), 17.1, 156 (Jennie Woodcock), 17.25, p. 188 (John T. Fowler), 17.27 (right) (Grant Pritchard), 17.28, p. 192 (IT Stock Free), 17.30, p. 196 (Popperfoto), 20.4, p. 205 (Lourens Smak), 20.11, p. 222 (Creatas Images), 21.11, p. 256 (Jeff Morgan sport), 23.1, p. 265 (Picture Partners), 23.2, p. 267 (Jack Sullivan), 23.4, p. 268 (Cade Martin), 23.6, p. 272 (Sally Greenhill), 23.7, p. 274 (Sally Greenhill), 23.8, p. 275 (PNC), 23.9, p. 278 (Adrian Sherratt), 23.10, p. 279 (Ian Miles-Flashpoint Pictures), 23.11, p. 281 (Bigshots), 23.15, 290 (Andrew Gilliver).

Corbis 15.4, p. 126, 17.10, p. 165.

Empics Figures 12.1, p. 39, 12.2, p. 42, 12.4, p. 45, 12.5, p. 47, 12.10, p. 54, 13.25, p. 115, 15.1, p. 121, 15.5, p. 129, 15.7, p. 135, 17.6, p. 161, 17.12, p. 167, 17.16, p. 175, 17.24, p. 187, 17.29, p. 193, 17.31, p. 196, 21.3, p. 244, 21.4, p. 246, 21.8, p. 252, 21.7, p. 250, 21.12, p. 259, 23.5, p. 270.

Getty Images Figures 1.2, p. 2, 12.3, p. 43, 12.17, p.17, 17.2, p. 157, 17.4, p. 159, 17.27 (left), p. 190, 21.1, p. 243

iStockphoto Figures 10.3, p. 5, 10.15, p. 25, 10.17, p. 35, 12.12, p. 58, 13.9, p. 85, 20.3, p. 204, 21.2, p. 243

NT Figures 10.14, 12.11, p. 57 Digital Vision 11 (NT), 12.14, p. 61, 13.23, p. 111.

Science Photo Library Figure 20.7, p. 211 (Gusto Images).

UNIT 10

Sports Nutrition

Kate Randerson

This unit covers:

- The concepts of nutrition and digestion
- Energy intake and expenditure in sports performance
- The relationship between hydration and sports performance
- How to plan a diet appropriate for a selected sports activity

This unit explains the effects of nutrition and hydration on performance in a variety of sports. It includes the effects of digestion and how different sources of food are digested and then used by the body to promote or enhance exercise performance. It investigates the importance of a healthy diet and the links between diet and health. It considers the energy requirements and body types of athletes involved in sports during training and competition. It shows how an outline dietary plan can give a clear indication of a sports performer's nutritional and fluid requirements.

grading criteria

To achieve a **Pass** grade the evidence must show that the learner is able to:	To achieve a **Merit** grade the evidence must show that the learner is able to:	To achieve a **Distinction** grade the evidence must show that the learner is able to:
P1 describe nutrition, including nutritional requirements and common terminology associated with nutrition Pg 13		
P2 describe the structure and function of the digestive system Pg 13		
P3 describe energy intake and expenditure in sports performance Pg 21	**M1** explain intake and expenditure in sports performance Pg 21	
P4 describe energy balance and its importance in relation to sports performance Pg 16	**M2** explain the importance of energy balance in relation to sports performance Pg 16	**D1** analyse the effects of energy balance on sports performance Pg 17

grading criteria

To achieve a **Pass** grade the evidence must show that the learner is able to:	To achieve a **Merit** grade the evidence must show that the learner is able to:	To achieve a **Distinction** grade the evidence must show that the learner is able to:
P5 describe hydration and its effects on sports performance Pg 26	**M3** explain the effects of hydration on sports performance Pg 26	
P6 describe the components of a balanced diet Pg 36	**M4** explain the components of a balanced diet Pg 36	
P7 describe an appropriate two-week diet plan for a selected sports performer for a selected sports activity Pg 36	**M5** explain the two-week diet plan for a selected sports performer for a selected sports activity Pg 36	**D2** justify the two-week diet plan for a selected sports performer for a selected sports activity Pg 37

The concepts of nutrition and digestion

Macronutrients such as fats, carbohydrates and proteins are needed in larger amounts. Micronutrients, such as vitamins and minerals are needed in much smaller amounts.

Macronutrients

Carbohydrates

Primarily involved in energy production, carbohydrates are made of three chemical elements: carbon, hydrogen and oxygen. They come in two forms: simple sugars and complex starches.

Simple sugars provide a quick energy source and are called monosaccharides. Commonly found in the diet, they include glucose, fructose and galactose (Figure 10.1). Fruits contain high levels of fructose and milk contains high levels of galactose.

Disaccharides are two simple sugars joined together. Examples are sucrose, lactose and maltose (Figure 10.2). Most monosaccharides and disaccharides are water soluble and readily absorbed to provide a sugar burst, hence energy. Insulin is released to lower blood sugar levels, and ultimately this can leave the athlete feeling fatigued.

Polysaccharides are polymers made from simple sugars. One example is glycogen, a chain of glucose molecules. Polysaccharides can be made from between 10 and several thousand units of simple sugars; such complex carbohydrates are digested through the small intestine, so they are a steadier source of energy for the athlete.

Carbohydrates are very important to the athlete, especially during intense exercise. They are also essential to the nervous system and fat metabolism.

Carbohydrates are stored in the muscles and the liver as glycogen but in limited amounts that need to be regularly replenished not just before exercise but also during and after exercise. The quantities vary according to a person's body weight and level of activity.

Figure 10.1 Glucose, fructose and galactose are monosaccharides

Glucose

Fructose

Galactose

Figure 10.2 Maltose, sucrose and lactose are disaccharides

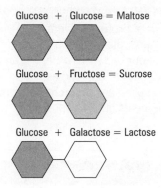

Glucose + Glucose = Maltose

Glucose + Fructose = Sucrose

Glucose + Galactose = Lactose

Research indicates that 2.5 g of carbohydrate per kilogram of body weight 3 h before exercise can help improve endurance running capacity (Chryssanthopoulos *et al.* 2002).

During exercise that lasts more than 60 min (moderate to high intensity) a pre-meal of complex carbohydrates will help to ensure that muscle glycogen levels are high, especially if they are supported by eating sufficient carbohydrates in the previous few days.

Refuelling should begin as soon as possible after exercise to ensure that glycogen storage is taken up quickly in the recovery period; this happens quickest during the first 2 h after exercise, then the uptake rates slows quite significantly, but it is still higher than normal for up to 4 h. The carbohydrates being eaten stimulates the release of insulin so that glucose is removed from the bloodstream and stored as glycogen in the muscles, replacing diminished levels. The suggested level is approximately 1 g of carbohydrate per kilogram of body weight for the first 2 h. For maximum refuelling and a speedier recovery, 50 g of the recommended carbohydrate intake is every couple of hours until the next main meal.

remember
- Carbohydrates should be a minimum of 47% of total daily calories; endurance athletes may find that their carbohydrate levels before an event are as high as 60% of their total dietary intake.
- The glycaemic index (GI) runs from 0 to 100; glucose is the highest at 100. It is based on a scale that ranks foods on the effects they have on blood sugar levels.
- Most carbohydrates should come from starches – 40 percentage points of the minimum 47% – and the rest can come from simple sugars.
- If exercise levels are below 95% of the athlete's V_{O_2max}, both carbohydrates and fats are used as fuels. Above this intensity, carbohydrates appear to be used exclusively; therefore, a fast pace in the early stages of exercise may lead to glycogen depletion and premature exhaustion.

 **Link**

See page 81 in Unit 3 in *BTEC National Sports Book 1* for more information on V_{O_2max}.

Sources of carbohydrates
- Complex – cereal, pasta, potatoes, bread, fruit.
- Simple – sugar, jam, confectionery, fruit juices.

Glycogen is broken down during exercise into the glucose that supplies muscles with energy. When glycogen stores are depleted, there is less energy available and the athlete will become fatigued. It is recommended that carbohydrates are about 60% of a sportsperson's diet.

Proteins

Proteins are chemical compounds that consist of **amino acids**, composed of carbon, hydrogen, oxygen and nitrogen; some contain minerals such as zinc. Proteins are the building blocks of body tissue and are essential for repair. They are also necessary for the production of **enzymes** and hormones. Proteins can be used as a source of energy but only if fats and carbohydrates are in very short supply.

Amino acids

Amino acids are the building blocks of proteins. There are 10 amino acids that we are unable to make for ourselves; they are called essential amino acids. We have to take in the essential amino acids as part of our diet. The other 12 amino acids are non-essential amino acids because we can make them in our bodies; two examples are glycine and glutamine. Leucine, isoleucine and valine are **branched-chain amino acids**; they help to reduce fatigue by protecting the heart and the muscles.

Table 10.1 Functions of the essential amino acids

Essential amino acid	Function
Arginine	Wound healing; enhances fat metabolism; insulin production; stimulates production of human growth hormone (HGH)
Histidine	Removal of toxic metals from the body; maintains myelin sheath around nerve fibres; stimulates production of red and white blood cells
Leucine and isoleucine	Branched-chain amino acids; useful in the formation of haemoglobin
Lysine	Helps in the formation of antibodies; enhances concentration
Methionine	An essential amino acid containing sulphur; powerful antioxidant; detoxifies heavy metals from the body; assists the gallbladder through bile salt synthesis
Phenylalinine	Needed for normal thyroid function; needs vitamin C to be metabolised; may improve memory, concentration and mental alertness
Threonine	Prevents accumulation of fats in the liver; needed for digestive and gastrointestinal tract function
Tryptophan	Acts as a mood adaptogen (calms agitation, stimulates depressed individuals); powerful painkilling effects; needed to synthesise vitamin B3
Valine	A branched-chain amino acid; normalises nitrogen in the body; vital for mental function, muscle coordination and neural function

Protein should account for approximately 15% of total calorific intake. There are some health risks from excessive protein intake, such as kidney damage due to excreting so many unused amino acids.

Sources of protein

Meat, fish and poultry are the three primary sources of complete proteins. The proteins obtained from vegetables and grains are called incomplete proteins because they do not supply all the essential amino acids; proteins obtained from quinoa and wheat are incomplete proteins as they do not contain lysine.

Athletes who take part in regular exercise may need twice as much protein as a sedentary individual, often 1.2–1.8 g protein per kilogram of body weight per day; this is necessary for tissue repair, to maintain muscle mass and to stimulate new tissue growth. If there is insufficient protein in the diet, it can lead to a reduction in muscle mass, a lack of tissue growth and ultimately a reduction in strength and body weight. An increase in protein intake should be proportionate to the total calorific intake, so the increase may be up to 20%, although studies suggest there is no benefit from increasing proteins above this level.

Weight trainers who wish to optimise their muscle bulk would need to increase their calories by 15% (eating an extra 300–500 kcal per day) by sourcing a mixture of high-carbohydrate and high-protein foods. A sprinter may need more protein than a long-distance runner to help ensure maximum speed, and this may be taken as a creatine supplement, whereas a cyclist would focus more on carbohydrate intake.

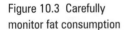

- Protein breaks down more readily during and immediately after exercise.
- The amount of protein broken down depends on the duration and intensity of the exercise.
- Increased protein intake may be needed in the early stages of training to support increases in muscle mass and myoglobin.
- Protein makes up 12–15% of the body mass.
- Elite athletes may eat small protein meals at regular in the day; some eat portions the size of a pack of cards.

Fats

Fats or lipids have essential roles in the diet:

- **Insulation** – around nerve fibres (myelin sheath) and to help conduct nerve impulses; subcutaneous fat also helps to maintain body temperature by preventing heat loss from the body.

- **Protection** – the heart and kidneys are embedded in fat to protect them in everyday activities; fat padding acts as a shock absorber.

- **Absorption** – the body needs fats so it can absorb and use vitamins A, D, E and K.

- **Energy source** – especially for athletes performing low-intensity endurance exercise.

Fats and lipids are made up of carbon, hydrogen and oxygen but in different proportions to carbohydrates. There are two types:

- **Triglycerides** – stored in the form of body fat.

- **Fatty acids** – used mainly as fuel for energy production; they are saturated or unsaturated.

- **Saturated fats** – usually solid (e.g. lard) and primarily from animal sources.

- **Unsaturated fats** – usually liquid (e.g. vegetable oil) and from plant sources.

When muscle cells are readily supplied with oxygen, fat is the usual fuel for energy production. This is because the body is trying to save the limited stores of glycogen for high-intensity exercise and delay the onset of fatigue. But the body cannot get its energy from fat alone, so muscle is fuelled by a combination of fat and glycogen.

Sources of fats

- **Saturated fats** – along with trans fats, they are the most damaging to health. They are usually solid at room temperature and are often called hidden fats as they are found in meat products, dairy products, cakes and confectionery.

- **Monounsaturated fats** – usually used in cooking, they are stable at high temperatures and are found in oily fish, nuts, margarine and olive oil.

Figure 10.3 Carefully monitor fat consumption

■ Polyunsaturated fats – also called **EFAs**, they are liquid at room temperature and have an anti-inflammatory action on the body. They can be eaten as oils and are usually used in salad dressings rather than cooking, e.g. walnut oil, corn oil and sesame oil. Polyunsaturated fats also include the omega-3 and omega-6 groups of fatty acids, which help to maintain a healthy heart and nervous system; they can be found in oily fish, seeds and oils.

remember

- The average fat reserve in competitive athletes is 10 kg (about 70 000 kcal), equivalent to 23 marathons.
- Adipose tissue is an efficient way to store extra energy in a small space.
- When a marathon runner hits the wall, their glycogen stores are depleted and the body attempts to metabolise fat, which is a slower way of producing energy. Therefore the athlete experiences extreme fatigue and the muscles struggle to contract.
- Generally, a maximum of 30% of total calories consumed should be from fatty foods.
- An ideal calorie intake is 10% saturated fats (butter, lard, margarine), 10% monounsaturated fats (olive oil) and 10% polyunsaturated fats (seeds, seed oils, oily fish).
- Trans fats are thought to be more harmful than saturated fats and are formed during hydrogenation – the conversion of oil to a solid fat.
- Fat consumption should be carefully monitored; too much can cause obesity.
- Essential fatty acids (EFAs) are not produced by the body and need to be eaten as part of a balanced diet, but foods high in EFAs are usually high in calories.

Cholesterol

Cholesterol is a type of fat that is actually essential to a healthy life. It is produced by the liver and taken in the diet. Cholesterol is carried around the body in the blood attached to lipoproteins, which come in two forms: low-density lipoprotein (LDL) and high-density lipoprotein (HDL). LDL is bad for you and HDL is good for you. LDL-carrying **cholesterol** is bad for you because it causes the accumulation of cholesterol in the vessel walls; HDL is good for you because it transports the cholesterol back to the liver for disposal.

British Heart Foundation

www.bhf.org.uk

case study 10.1 **Janet's fat intake**

Janet is concerned that her diet contains too much fat and would like to know how to eat a safe amount of fat.

activity
INDIVIDUAL WORK

1. List foods that contain good fats.
2. Research three different prepared meals that are low in fat. Suggest one that would be good for breakfast, one for lunch and one for a main evening meal.
3. State three examples of low-fat snacks that provide energy.

Micronutrients

Vitamins

Vitamins are chemical compounds that are needed by the body in small quantities. They are essential **micronutrients** because they are used in energy production, disease prevention, and metabolism. The body can produce vitamin D but it cannot produce any other vitamins. Vitamins A, D, E and K are fat-soluble vitamins. Vitamins B and C are water-soluble vitamins. Vitamins can be found in fresh fruit and vegetables.

Table 10.2 Functions of the major vitamins

Vitamin	Function
A	Good vision and healthy skin
B	Energy production, stress reduction
C	Fighting viruses, keeping skin and gums healthy, healing wounds
D	Helps to build bones and teeth
E	Protects cells, helps immune system, aids growth
K	Helps form blood clots

Antioxidant vitamins

Antioxidant vitamins are beta-carotene, vitamin C and vitamin E; they are sometimes known as the ACE vitamins. They can help prevent damage to muscles and reduce post-exercise muscle soreness.

Large doses

Extremely large doses of vitamins can be dangerous. For example, too much vitamin A can cause hair loss and enlargement of the liver. There is little evidence to suggest that supplementary vitamin pills can enhance performance and most excess vitamins are simply excreted in the urine. There is some evidence that hard exercise can deplete the body's stores of **antioxidant vitamins**.

Minerals

Minerals do not contain calories and are inorganic elements essential for our health. There are two types:

- Macrominerals are needed in large amounts, e.g. calcium, potassium and sodium.

- Trace elements are needed in very small amounts, e.g. iron, zinc and manganese.

Many minerals are dissolved in the body fluids as ions; they are called electrolytes. Electrolytes are essential for healthy cells, for the nervous system and for muscle contraction. Minerals can be lost through sweating, so people who exercise should replace them quickly to ensure good health.

Iron

Iron is an essential component of haemoglobin, which carries oxygen in the blood. Iron-deficiency anaemia can impair performance in endurance events. Research has shown that over 36% of female runners are anaemic and should eat iron-rich foods. Only a qualified medical doctor should prescribe iron supplements, because too much iron can be dangerous. Iron can be found in meat, fish, dairy products and green vegetables. Two main sources are red meat and offal.

Calcium

Calcium is essential for healthy bones and teeth. A person that has a calcium deficiency has an increased likelihood of bone fractures and osteoporosis. Calcium absorption requires sufficient vitamin D, which is produced by the body in response to sunlight. Calcium is found in milk and dairy products, green vegetables and nuts. Calcium deficiency can be found in females who are underweight as well as smokers, alcoholics, vegetarians and people who overdo training in sport.

Table 10.3 Functions of the major minerals

Mineral	Function
Calcium	Strengthens bones, helps blood to clot, strengthens muscles
Iodine	Helps the thyroid gland to promote normal growth and energy production
Iron	Aids production of red blood cells, creates good skin tone, prevents fatigue, helps resistance to disease
Potassium	Aids muscle contraction, promotes healthy skin, maintains normal blood pressure
Sodium	Maintains body fluid levels, aids muscle contractions

Water

Water is also crucial for good health, particularly for those who participate in sport. It carries nutrients in the body and helps with the removal of waste products. It is also very important in the regulation of body temperature. The body readily loses water through urine and sweat. The amount of water lost depends on the environment and the duration and intensity of exercise. On average, a person should drink about 2 litres of water per day. People involved in exercise should take more to ensure a good state of hydration.

Fibre

Fibre is also known as non-starch polysaccharide (NSP). It is found in the cell walls of vegetables fruits, pulses and cereal grains. A good diet should include soluble fibre and insoluble fibre.

Soluble fibre

Soluble fibre includes pectin, present in fruits such as apples and bananas and also found in vegetables such as carrots, turnips and sweet potatoes. Although water soluble, pectin is not fibrous and is completely digested. It has little effect on the faeces, but it has an important role in transporting cholesterol, bile acids and toxins out of the body.

Insoluble fibre

Cellulose is a fibre that is insoluble in water. It consists of thousands of glucose units and cannot be digested by humans. It is found in wholemeal flour, bran, cabbage, green beans and prunes. Cellulose helps to add bulk to the stools and assists in moving waste products through the large intestine, which prevents constipation. Research suggests a diet high in fibre may also prevent weight gain, colon cancer and gallstones. The recommended level of NSP is 12–18 g per day; more that 32 g per day is thought to have no extra benefits.

Foods Standards Agency

www.food.gov.uk

remember
- People who are dehydrated become intolerant to exercise and heat stress.
- The cardiovascular system becomes inefficient if a person is dehydrated and becomes unable to provide adequate blood flow to the skin, which may lead to heat exhaustion.
- Fluids must be taken in during prolonged exercise to minimise dehydration and slow the rise in body temperature.
- A number of sports drinks containing electrolytes and carbohydrates are available commercially but some of the claims that are made about these drinks have been misinterpreted. A single meal, for instance, can replace the minerals lost during exercise.
- Water is the primary need in any drink taken before, during and after exercise because it empties from the stomach extremely quickly and reduces the dehydration associated with sweating.
- Thirst is not a reliable indicator for fluid intake; if you are thirsty, you are already dehydrated. It is best to drink small amounts regularly even if you are not thirsty. Under cooler conditions, a carbohydrate drink may give the extra energy needed in events lasting over an hour.

Figure 10.4 Food labels tell you what's in the packet

Nutritional requirements

Food labelling

The amounts and proportions of nutrients vary enormously in different types of food. People need to know what nutrients are present in foods so they can make more informed choices based on health requirements. Since 1986 all UK foods that are processed and all non-alcoholic beverages must carry a label showing a list of ingredients. This list shows the ingredients in descending order of weight, so the first few ingredients make up most of the food. The additives are usually at the bottom of the list because they make up only a small proportion of the food. Many manufacturers also publish the nutritional value of the food on the labels.

The truth behind the labels

- **Low fat** – less than 5 g in 100 g. Note that labelling is based on percentage weight of fat in the product, not percentage of calories from fat.

- **Reduced fat** – at least 25% less fat than 'normal'.

- **Virtually fat free** – less than 0.3 g fat in 100 g.

- **Reduced sugar** – at least 25% less sugar than 'normal'.

- **Low sugar** – less than 5 g sugar in 100 g.

- **Sugar free** – no natural or added sugar.

- **Reduced calories** – at least 25% fewer calories than 'normal'.

- **Low calorie** – less than 40 calories in 100 g.

- **High fibre** – at least 6 g in 100 g.

Healthy eating

Healthy eating involves a daily calorie intake in the following proportions: 50% carbohydrate, 30–35% fat, 15–20% protein. The Health Development Agency (HDA), formerly known as the Health Education Authority, proposes these principles for making food choices:

- Enjoyment

- Not too much fat

- Not too many sugary foods

- Inclusion of vitamins and minerals

- Plenty of fibre

- Alcohol within prescribed limits

- A balance between intake and output

- Plenty of fruit and vegetables.

Figure 10.5 Food pyramid: eat more foods from the bottom, fewer from the top

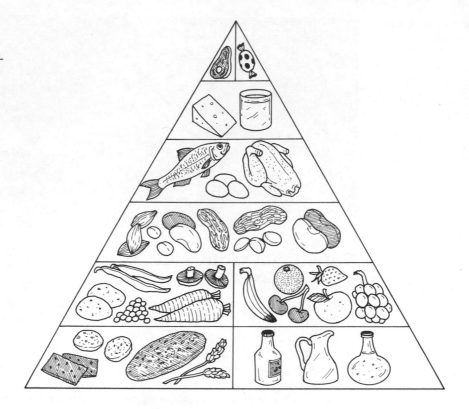

Alcohol consumption

Alcohol is a concentrated source of energy but the energy cannot be available during exercise for our working muscles. The HDA recommends the following maximum daily alcohol intakes for adults:.

- Men 3–4 units
- Women 2–3 units.

One unit

- Half a pint of 'ordinary strength' beer = 3.0–3.5% alcohol = 90 calories
- One standard glass of wine = 11% alcohol = 90 calories
- One measure of spirits = 38% alcohol = 50 calories.

Figure 10.6 Alcohol consumption is increasing among under-18s

Binge drinking, which is a growing habit among teenagers and young adults, is particularly bad for you. It is better to spread your alcohol consumption across the week and to leave some alcohol-free days.

A healthy diet

There are no healthy or unhealthy foods; there are only good or bad uses of food. The right balance in a diet is essential for health and fitness. Enjoyment is an important aspect of eating; a healthy diet does not mean that you have to give up all your favourite foods that are considered bad foods; it is the overall balance that counts. Balanced meals contain starchy foods, plenty of vegetables, salad and fruit. Your fat content should be kept to a minimum by using low-fat or lean ingredients.

Here are some other factors that affect foods choices:

- Culture, morals, ethics
- Family influences
- Peer group influences
- Nutrition and weight management in sport
- Lifestyle
- Finance.

The balance of good health model

The balance of good health model was designed by the HDA to show what healthy eating means. Eating sufficient fruit and vegetables is important for a healthy diet. It helps to reduce the likelihood of coronary heart disease and some cancers. Government guidelines suggest that you should eat at least five portions of fruit and vegetables each day.

What is a portion of fruit or vegetables?

- Two tablespoons of vegetables
- One dessert bowl of salad
- One apple, orange or banana
- Two plums
- One cup of grapes or cherries
- Two tablespoons of fresh fruit salad
- One tablespoon of dried fruit
- One glass of fruit juice.

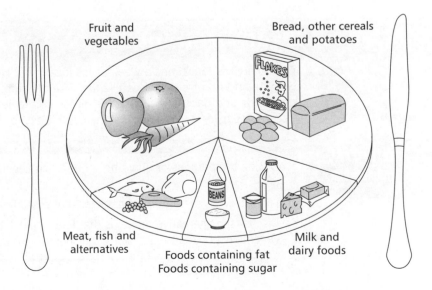

Figure 10.7 Eat a balanced diet

Fruit and vegetables

Bread, other cereals and potatoes

Meat, fish and alternatives

Foods containing fat
Foods containing sugar

Milk and dairy foods

What is too much salt?

Most healthy eating guidelines warn against eating too much salt. If your diet contains too much salt, your blood pressure may become too high, which can cause heart and kidney disease. Table 10.4 shows dietary values that are widely recognised as recommended nutrient intakes (RNIs).

Table 10.4 RDIs for males and females

	Male	Female
Energy (kcal)	2550	1940
Chloride (g)	2.5	2.5
Copper (mg)	1.2	1.2
Folate (mg)	200	200
Iodine (mg)	140	140
Iron (mg)	8.7	14.8
Magnesium (mg)	300	270
Niacin (mg)	17	13
Phosphorus (mg)	550	550
Potassium (g)	3.5	3.5
Protein (g)	55.5	45
Selenium (mg)	75	60
Sodium (g)	1.6	1.6
Vitamin A (mg)	700	600
Vitamin B1 (mg)	1.0	0.8
Vitamin B2 (mg)	1.3	1.1
Vitamin B6 (mg)	1.4	1.2
Vitamin B12 (mg)	1.5	1.5
Vitamin C (mg)	40	40
Zinc (mg)	9.5	7.0

case study 10.2 — Paul's fruit intake

Paul exercises four times a week at his local gym. He does a combination of weights and aerobic exercises. He has recently suffered from a lot of coughs and colds and has decided that his diet needs reviewing. He only eats fruit and vegetables twice a week because he cannot get to the shops every day.

activity
INDIVIDUAL WORK

1. Decide the portions or quantities of fruit and vegetables that Paul should eat per day.

2. List the types of fruit and vegetables that could help boost Paul's immune system.

3. Discuss the alternative methods that Paul could use to increase his fruit and vegetable intake without visiting the shops every day.

Table 10.5 Common abbreviations

Abbreviation	Stands for	Explanation
RDI	Recommended daily intake	The suggested daily levels of intake usually linked to micronutrients
RDA	Recommended daily allowance	EU regulations require RDAs to be shown on food labels and food supplement labels as an amount for an 'average' adult. It is only a rough guide
SI	Safe intake	The safe amount of nutrient where there is insufficient information to establish the DRV (below a level that would cause undesirable effects)
EAR	Estimated average requirement	An estimate of the average need for food energy or a nutrient. Some people may need more, some may need less. A man aged 19–51 needs 2550 kcal (10.60 MJ), used particularly for energy
RNI	Reference nutrient intake	The amount of a nutrient that is enough for almost every individual, even those with high needs. RNIs are not minimum targets
LRNI	Low reference nutrient intake	The amount of a nutrient considered sufficient for the small number of people with low nutrient needs
GDA	Guideline daily amount	Quantity recommended for adults of average weight
FSA	Food Standards Agency	Independent watchdog established to protect UK public health and consumer interests
AI	Adequate intake	A recommended average daily nutrient intake based on observed or experimentally determined estimates of nutrient intake by a group of healthy people
BMI	Body mass index	A measurement representing the ratio of a person's weight to the square of their height
TEF	Thermic effect of food	The energy expended as a result of processing food consumed
kJ	Kilojoule	A joule is the metric measurement of heat energy
cal	Calorie	The amount of energy released as heat when food is metabolised. 1 cal = 4.2 J
OL	Optimum level	Usually refers to food and food supplements; an OL can be 5–10 times higher than an RDI

Common terminology

activity
GROUP WORK
10.1

P1

Collect labels from a variety of foods then compare and contrast the terminology they use.

activity
INDIVIDUAL WORK
10.2

P2

Describe the structure and function of the digestive system.

Structure of the digestive system

The digestive system is designed to break down food into smaller chemical substances that can be easily absorbed by the intestines to provide energy and sustenance for the body. Digestion uses mechanical and chemical processes; it starts as soon as food enters the mouth, or buccal cavity. The digestive system is also called the alimentary canal or the gastrointestinal (GI) tract and includes the mouth, pharynx, oesophagus, stomach, small intestine, large intestine (colon) and the anus.

Although they are part of the excretory system, the kidneys work in conjunction with the digestive system to regulate fluid levels, and this is particularly important when water and salt balances are maintained during exercise.

Functions of the digestive system

- **Ingestion** – the voluntary action of putting food or drink in the mouth is called ingestion.

- **Propulsion** – this is the movement of food while it is being broken down so that it is shifted from one digestive area to another. In the oesophagus this strong involuntary contraction and relaxation is called **peristalsis**. In the small intestine it is called segmentation, because food moves forwards and backwards to ensure it is adequately mixed with digestive enzymes.

- **Mechanical digestion** – chewing of food in the mouth, churning of food in the stomach, and the forward and backward motion during segmentation are examples of mechanical digestion.

Figure 10.8 The human digestive system

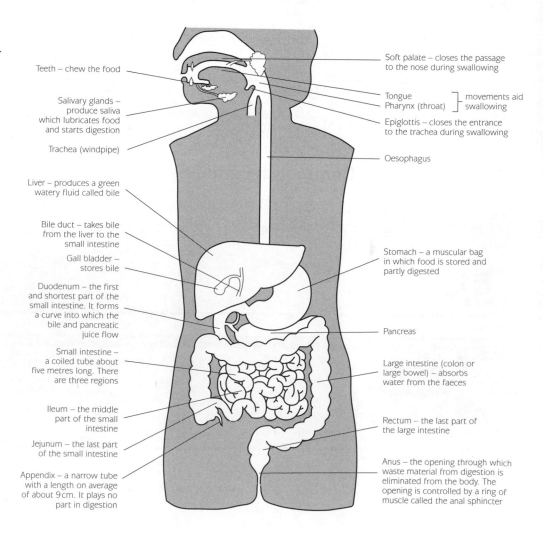

Teeth – chew the food

Salivary glands – produce saliva which lubricates food and starts digestion

Trachea (windpipe)

Liver – produces a green watery fluid called bile

Bile duct – takes bile from the liver to the small intestine

Gall bladder – stores bile

Duodenum – the first and shortest part of the small intestine. It forms a curve into which the bile and pancreatic juice flow

Small intestine – a coiled tube about five metres long. There are three regions

Ileum – the middle part of the small intestine

Jejunum – the last part of the small intestine

Appendix – a narrow tube with a length on average of about 9 cm. It plays no part in digestion

Soft palate – closes the passage to the nose during swallowing

Tongue
Pharynx (throat)   } movements aid swallowing

Epiglottis – closes the entrance to the trachea during swallowing

Oesophagus

Stomach – a muscular bag in which food is stored and partly digested

Pancreas

Large intestine (colon or large bowel) – absorbs water from the faeces

Rectum – the last part of the large intestine

Anus – the opening through which waste material from digestion is eliminated from the body. The opening is controlled by a ring of muscle called the anal sphincter

- **Chemical digestion** – the process of using enzymes to break down large molecules of food into smaller building blocks that are then easier to transport across the wall of the small and large intestines, ready for transport around the body.

- **Absorption** – digestion products are primarily absorbed in the small intestine, although there is some absorption in the large intestine. Most food is shifted by active transport across the intestinal membranes to the hepatic portal vein before going on to the liver.

- **Defecation** – expulsion of waste matter, the very end products of digestion, that is not required by the body.

Table 10.6 Digestive secretions

Enzyme	Action
The salivary glands secrete saliva, which contains water, mucus and bicarbonate	
Salivary amylase	Softens food; makes food slippery; saliva provides an almost neutral medium for salivary amylase; attacks bacteria
The gastric glands secrete gastric juice, which contains water, mucus and hydrochloric acid	
Pepsin, secreted as pepsinogen	Further softens food; prevents gastric juices from damaging the stomach wall
Gastric lipase	Stops the action of salivary amylase and allows pepsin to work; kills many germs; curdles milk; splits some proteins into proteases and peptones, i.e. shorter-chain polypeptides; curdles milk in adults
Renin	Curdles milk in many young mammals; presence in man doubtful; splits fats into fatty acids and glycerol
The pancreas secretes bile, which is produced by the liver, stored in the gallbladder and contains bicarbonate	
Pancreatic lipase	Splits fats into fatty acids and glycerol; acts more effectively than gastric lipase as fat is emulsified
Pancreatic amylase	Splits all forms of starch and dextrin into maltose
Trypsin, secreted as trypsinogen	Splits some proteins, proteases and peptones into shorter polypeptide chains and frees some amino acids
Chymotrypsin, secreted as chymotrypsinogen	Further softens food; prevents gastric juices from damaging the stomach wall
Elastin	
The duodenal glands secrete intestinal juice, which contains water and mucus	
Enterokinase	Protects the intestinal mucosa; activates trypsinogen forming trypsin; trypsin then activates more trypsinogen and chymotrypsinogen
Peptodase	Splits peptides into amino acids
Maltase	Splits maltose into sucrose
Sucrase	Splits sucrase into monosaccharides
Lactase	Splits lactose into monosaccharides
Lipase	Splits glycerides into fatty acids and glycerol

Adapted from Rowett (1988)

Energy intake and expenditure in sports performance

Energy measures

Table 10.7 Units of energy

Name	Definition
Calorie (cal)	The amount of energy needed to raise the temperature of 1 litre of water by 1°C
Kilocalorie (kcal)	1 Cal = 1 kcal = 1000 cal; kcal is more commonly used than Cal with a capital C
Joule (J)	A metric unit of energy intake and energy output
Kilojoule (kJ)	1000 joules, the amount of work needed to move 1 kg a distance of 1 m

Energy sources

To calculate the energy value of a food, find the number of grams of carbohydrate it contains then multiply by the number of kilocalories per gram; it is 4 kcal/g, as shown in Table 10.8. Do the same for protein and fat. Total the number of calories from carbohydrate, fat and protein to get the energy value of the food.

Table 10.8 Kilocalories per gram for macronutrients

	Kilocalories per gram
Carbohydrates	4
Protein	4
Fats	9

Example

Here is the energy value of one slice of wholemeal bread with 80 g of baked beans.

	Mass (g)	Multiplier (kcal/g)	Energy (kcal)
Carbohydrate	14	4	56
Protein	6	4	24
Fat	1	9	9
Total			89

activity **GROUP WORK 10.3**

P4

M2

You have been asked to devise a leaflet that can be given to athletes to inform them of the importance of refuelling.

1. Give specific examples of foods and their quantities.
2. Describe why energy balance is important to the sports performer.
3. Explain how sports performance can be affected by energy intake and expenditure.

To complete the leaflet you devised in Activity 10.3, analyse how sports performance can be affected by different levels of energy balance; you can name different sporting activities to support your answer.

Measuring requirements

Measuring an athlete's body composition can be very useful when linked to healthy eating and the requirements of exercise. Laboratory methods to assess body composition can be divided into direct measurements and indirect measurements:

- Direct measurement – analysis by chemical means on animal or human cadavers.

- Indirect measurement – by weighing or by simple **anthropometry**.

Table 10.9 Indirect methods for measuring body composition

Method	Advantages	Disadvantages
Skinfold analysis (measures fat)	Non-invasive method; calipers are inexpensive; easily repeatable in standardised conditions; immediate results	Accuracy depends on the operator's technique; ageing causes more fat to be deposited internally rather than subcutaneously
Bioelectric impedance (measures fat)	Non-invasive method; quick to implement; easily repeatable in standardised conditions; immediate results	Tends to overestimate body fat in athletes; tends to underestimate body fat in obese people
Hydrodensitometry (measures fat)	Repeatable procedure to ensure dependable score; immediate results	Residual lung volumes can give readings that make the athlete fatter; requires special equipment and a hydropool to submerse the subject
Direct calorimetry (measures energy expenditure)	Can focus on requirements at rest and during activity	Expensive, specialised equipment; staffing costs to operate and maintain; the subject is required to stay in the chamber for long periods; limited application for use; cannot be used effectively to yield data for exercise
Indirect calorimetry (measures energy expenditure)	Can focus on energy expenditure; simple to use; less expensive to maintain; various forms of spirometer and other equipment such as bag, portable and computerised methods	Some of the equipment may be bulky and inconvenient when performing activities

The resulting measurements can monitor desired weight gains or losses, identify health risks for athletes, provide an estimate of ideal body weight, and establish the necessary requirements for short- and long-term goals, especially for athletes taking part in sports that have weight classifications, such as horse racing and boxing.

Body mass is the total weight of a person, including their fat and lean tissue. Lean body mass, sometimes known as fat-free mass, excludes the fat and includes body components such as muscles, bones and organs.

Percentage body fat

Skinfold analysis

Skinfold analysis is frequently used to measure body fat. Skinfold calipers measure subcutaneous fat at predetermined sites on the body. With the index finger and thumb, grasp the area of skin and fat then lift it away from the body. Apply the calipers and

Figure 10.9 Skinfold calipers measure subcutaneous fat

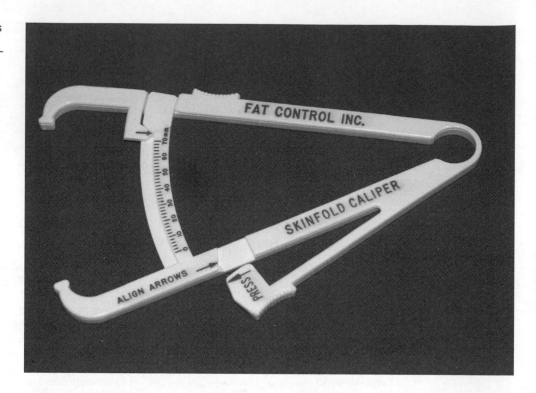

record the measurement on the digital readout. The sum total of the measurements can then be tabulated and matched against published categories or recorded and monitored to see if there are individual changes over a period of time. Some skinfold measurement sites are the triceps, the subscapular region, the iliac crest and the biceps brachii. Other areas are the front of the thigh and the abdomen.

See page 38 in Unit 1 in *BTEC National Sports Book 1* for more information on how energy sources are used during exercise.

Bioelectric impedance analysis

Bioelectric impedance analysis (BIA) establishes percentage body fat by using a small alternating current that flows between two electrodes. Current will pass more quickly through hydrated fat-free tissue because it has a lower electrical resistance. This resistance reveals the quantity of total water in the body and thus the fat-free body mass, the density of the body and the percentage body fat. Here are some factors that can affect the results:

■ Hydration levels of the body

■ Ambient temperature

■ Skin temperature.

The body fat percentage is put into a predefined category of low, medium or high.

Figure 10.10 The athlete is fully submerged for underwater weighing

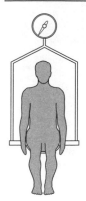

Hydrodensitometry

Hydrodensitometry, also called underwater weighing (UWW) or hydrostatic weighing, calculates the body fat from bone density, which is bone mass per unit bone volume. It was established from **Archimedes' principle** of water displacement, buoyancy and specific gravity, The athlete is fully submerged in a swimming pool or therapy pool using a specially designed cradle that has a weighing scale attached to it. The athlete forcefully exhales then lowers their head under the water so they are fully submersed. The athlete's weight on land is usually recorded before the hydrostatic weighing.

Figure 10.11 You need a
big bath for underwater
weighing

Energy expenditure

Calorimetry

Direct or indirect calorimetry is used to determine the rate of energy expenditure from the body.

Direct calorimetry

Direct calorimetry requires a specialised airtight chamber that circulates a predetermined volume of water at a given temperature; this water absorbs the heat produced from a subject and the resulting data is then used to determine the energy used, hence the calories required.

Indirect calorimetry

Indirect calorimetry focuses on the oxygen uptake, especially when completing aerobic exercise. This gives a more accurate estimate of energy expenditure.

- Closed-circuit spirometry – measures resting energy expenditure; the subject breathes in 100% pure oxygen from a prefilled spirometer.

- Open-circuit spirometry – can measure energy expenditure during physical activities with the subject breathing in a mixture of oxygen, carbon dioxide and nitrogen. The energy expenditure is calculated from the percentage changes in oxygen and carbon dioxide of the exhaled air along with the volume of air breathed over a specified time period. This method is more frequently used in sport.

Nutritional strategies in sport

Carbohydrates and fats are oxidised to release energy for body tissues; the amounts converted to energy will depend on the intensity of the exercise. Carbohydrate will generally release energy rapidly whereas fat will release energy slowly and steadily. Glycogen stores plus fat reserves are essential to the athlete as a form of fuel. If the exercise intensity is approximately 50% of $V_{O_2 max}$, then fat is the main fuel source; but as soon as the intensity is raised to 75% of $V_{O_2 max}$, then carbohydrate is the major fuel source. The higher the exercise intensity, the more the body will use carbohydrate as a fuel source.

It is essential that glycogen supplies are adequate for optimum energy supply. One method of increasing the glycogen available is through carboloading. The sportsperson depletes their stores of glycogen by cutting down on carbohydrates and keeping to a diet of protein and fat for 3 days. Light training follows, with a high-carbohydrate diet for the 3 days leading up to the event. This significantly increases the stores of glycogen and helps to offset fatigue. When an athlete is carboloading, their diet should consist mainly of foods such as pasta, bread, rice and fruit. A high-carbohydrate diet will generally ensure that glycogen will be replenished during exercise.

Other energy-giving strategies

- Consume carbohydrates 2–4 h before exercise.
- Consume a small amount of carbohydrate within the first 30 min of exercise to ensure refuelling of glycogen.
- Eat carbohydrates straight after exercise for up to 2 days to replenish stores.

Figure 10.12 Muscle glycogen versus time for high- and low-carbohydrate diets

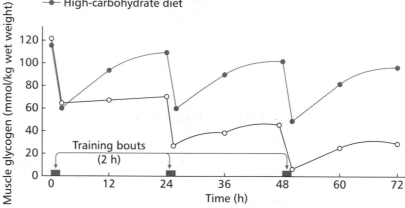

Energy balance

Basal metabolism

Whether or not you participate in sport, you need to eat enough food for energy. The basal metabolic rate (BMR) is a measure of the amount of energy needed at rest. Food intake needs to consider BMR and the energy to participate in sport. Men can consume 2800–3000 kcal per day and women 2000–2200 kcal per day without putting on weight (Honeybourne *et al.* 2000). Metabolic rates vary from person to person and get slower as a person ages. Energy is measured in kilocalories and kilojoules, 1 kcal = 4.2 kJ. Energy requirements differ according to the output of physical activity. A sedentary person and an active athlete will have different energy requirements.

Table 10.10 Energy requirements for five types of people

	Required energy per day (kcal)
Body builder	3000
Aerobic exercise class	2500
Male sedentary worker aged 19–50	2550
Female aged 15	2110
Female aged 65–74	1900

Energy expenditure

Resting metabolic rate

Resting metabolic rate (RMR) is influenced by body composition, age, gender and genetic predisposition. Muscle is more active metabolically than fat, so an increase in muscle mass produces an increase in RMR. On average, it is 60% of energy expenditure.

Thermic effect of feeding

The thermic effect of feeding is due to the effects of digestion, absorption and metabolism of food. It is largely influenced by the calorie content of food, especially the ratio of fat and carbohydrate. It is easier for the body to take on body fat from dietary fat than from dietary carbohydrate. On average, it is 10% of energy expenditure.

Thermic effect of activity

The thermic effect of activity is the energy expended in activity. It varies more than the other components and is far higher for active people than for sedentary people. This has implications for those who participate in sport. It also depends on the type of activity and the duration of the activity. On average, it is 20% of energy expenditure.

Adaptive thermogenesis

Adaptive thermogenesis is a response to changes in temperature and physiological stresses. The body may respond by shivering. On average, it is 10% of energy expenditure.

Factors that affect energy expenditure

- Frequency of exercise
- Intensity of exercise
- Type and duration of exercise
- Age, gender, body composition
- Available fuels
- Climate.

Available fuels

- Protein is used during prolonged exercise.
- Alcohol cannot be metabolised by working muscles.
- Glycogen stored in the liver is used to top up glucose levels in the blood.
- Glycogen in the muscles is made from fat and carbohydrates.
- Water.

Body mass index

A body mass index (BMI) greater than $25\,kg/m^2$ indicates that you are overweight. If it exceeds $35\,kg/m^2$, there is a severe health risk. A **BMI** over 30 for adults indicates obesity.

BMI indicators (kg/m^2)

- < 20 underweight
- 20 to 24.9 healthy weight
- 25 to 29.9 overweight
- 30 to 40 moderately obese
- > 40 severely obese.

BMI does not consider body composition, which means that someone with a high percentage of lean body tissue may well weigh the same as or more than someone else with an equally high percentage of body fat; the two people would not be equally obese.

activity
GROUP WORK
10.5

P3

M1

1. Form two groups. One group makes a list of energy intake in sports performance and the other group makes a list of energy expenditure in sports performance.
2. Each group describes its answers.

The relationship between hydration and sports performance

Hydration: signs and symptoms

The skin is an important temperature regulator through sweating, where water is evaporated from the skin surface. During activity, sweating begins after approximately 1.5 to 3 min, but will usually level off after 10–15 min. During sustained continuous activity, fluid loss can impair performance by up to 50% if the fluids are not replaced.

An athlete may lose up to 1 litre of water per hour during endurance exercise, so rehydration is essential, especially in a hot environment. By the time they become thirsty, an athlete is already dehydrated, so they need to drink plenty before, during and after exercise, even if they do not feel thirsty.

Dehydration is dangerous for everyone, not just athletes, because it places extra strain on the heart and lungs. This means they have to work much harder, which can decrease exercise performance. As the degree of dehydration increases, the effects on the body become more severe; the rate of dehydration will depend on the amount of water lost, the environmental conditions, the age and fitness level of the athlete, and the intensity of the exercise. Here are some of the effects:

- Thirst
- Decreased blood volume
- Concentrated urine
- Difficulty concentrating
- Dizziness
- Breathing difficulties
- Confusion and poor speech
- Muscle spasms
- Tingling and numbness of the limbs
- Renal failure
- Death.

Conditions caused by lack of fluids

Muscle cramps

Muscle cramps can occur in the legs, arms or abdomen after exercise of up to 2 h and are often the result of fluid loss or inadequate salt intake when sweating heavily. Body temperature will usually be normal but the skin may feel sweaty.

Heat exhaustion

Heat exhaustion is where the body loses its ability to cool down efficiently – it is overheating because sweating rates fall through lack of fluid intake. The athlete's skin will feel moist and clammy; they will have a fast, weak pulse and shallow breathing; they may look pale and feel tired, weak and dizzy. Some athletes may feel nauseous or vomit, others may feel dizzy or faint. Heat exhaustion can lead to heatstroke, which is more serious.

Heatstroke

Heatstroke occurs when the body cannot cool down and when the hypothalamus, which controls body temperature, is overwhelmed and loses the ability to monitor and control safe body temperature limits. The signs and symptoms of heatstroke are very similar to heat exhaustion, but are usually more pronounced. This is a dangerous condition that can cause death if not treated quickly and efficiently.

Hypohydration

Hypohydration describes voluntary dehydration. Athletes often hypohydrate to meet the needs of a competition, usually a competition that has a weight class, such as boxing, rowing and horse racing. The athlete may actually begin a competition event in a state of dehydration. The effects on performance are well known and well researched but severe cases can still lead to death.

Hyperhydration

Hyperhydration or superhydration is when extra fluid is ingested before exercising, especially in hot climates. It is thought to delay the effects of dehydration and so reduce the risks associated with overheating conditions. Water alone is not sufficient for hyperhydration; it merely leads to greater urine output. Water and glycerol are used to achieve the desired effects. Glycerol helps to get more water into cell fluids, which produces an overall increase in total body fluid.

The period of hyperhydration can be up to 1 week before competition, especially in athletes that are acclimatising to new environments. Alternatively, athletes can take on 400–600 ml of fluids 24 h before competition to maximise their performance and recovery. Research evidence suggests that athletes who are well hydrated function and perform better than dehydrated athletes, but this could have serious implications for any athletes who need to keep their weight to an optimum level during sports performance.

Hyponatraemia

Hyponatraemia is a result of overhydrating the body. It is not common but it can happen during activities where water is constantly drunk and there is excessive sweating. The effects are to dilute the blood salts, which is dangerous and results in lethargy, confusion and nausea.

Fluid intake

Fluid intake includes more than water intake. Other drinks such as tea and small amounts of coffee can also be included in daily consumption, but with exercise it may be appropriate to consider a sports drink. Most commercial drinks contain varying quantities of sucrose, glucose and fructose; some even include cornstarch or corn syrup. These sports drinks are generally designed to prevent dehydration and improve performance; it is the sugar content that determines their usefulness to the athlete.

Gastric emptying

The rate that food and drink leave the stomach will vary from person to person. This rate is important when hydrating the body, plus the fluid's temperature and its concentration (osmolality). Cooler drinks usually leave the stomach more rapidly than warmer drinks and can help prevent stomach cramps. Concentrated fluids with a high calorie content leave the stomach more slowly. The colour of urine is a good indicator of the body's degree of hydration. Dark-coloured urine indicates that more fluid is needed. Ideally, urine should be the same colour as straw.

How to prevent dehydration

- Schedule training to the cooler times of the day.
- Limit alcohol intake.
- Aim to drink up to 3 glasses of water (up to 600 ml) before exercise.
- Always carry water or diluted juice to sip or drink frequently.
- Drink before feeling thirsty.

remember

Hyperthermia, from the Greek *hypo* 'high' and *thermes* 'heat', describes several conditions relating to overheating such as muscle cramps, heatstroke and heat exhaustion.

Figure 10.13 Take fluid regularly during exercise

Figure 10.14 Do not become dehydrated

Rehydration

Water is an excellent medium to rehydrate the body; it is calorie free, it is cheap to buy and it has heat-stabilising qualities so it can absorb heat with only small changes in its temperature. Water is ideal for low- or moderate-intensity exercise that lasts less than 1 h, as fluid losses are likely to be small, but some athletes may prefer to add flavoured squashes or cordials to improve the taste and this can influence how much fluid is replaced during and after exercise.

A sports drink may be more appropriate when fluid losses increase due to the intensity and the timing of the exercise (longer than 1 h). The quantity and timing of the fluid intake are important, but so are the type of drink and the environmental conditions. Personal choice and taste preferences also have an effect on the consumption of sports drinks.

Table 10.11 Sports drinks and their carbohydrate content

Type of drink	Carbohydrate per 100 ml (g)	Effect
Isotonic	5–8	Rapidly absorbed; meets fluid and carbohydrate requirements
Hypertonic	> 8	Low water levels
Hypotonic	< 4	Little carbohydrate; quick fluid replacement

case study 10.3

Sports drinks for Ian the swimmer

Ian is a long-distance swimmer aged 19 and he regularly competes for his county. He is concerned that his fluid intake is not sufficient for his swimming activities. He has asked you to research three commercial sports drinks that may be suitable for him, especially when he competes at centres where only vending machines are available.

activity
INDIVIDUAL WORK

1. Design a chart that shows the contents of each drink.
2. Find out the cost of each drink.
3. Decide which type of drink is most suitable for Ian.
4. List the reasons for your choice.

Figure 10.15 Some athletes use sports drinks to replace lost fluids

How hydration affects sports performance

Diet alone cannot improve a person's ability to perform well at their chosen sport; many factors contribute to overall performance and success. The principles of training and fitness also include variance, or variety, and reversibility, which is a reduction in performance if training decreases or stops. Frequency is how often an activity is performed; it affects an athlete's nutritional requirements. Exercise intensity – how hard an exercise is performed – and exercise duration – how long it is performed for – will also affect an athlete's energy expenditure, hence their dietary, hydration and refuelling needs.

To be effective, a training regime should be designed for a specific sporting activity. Marathon runners are likely to do aerobic training over long distances, whereas a sprinter is likely to train anaerobically. The balanced diet of a marathon runner will differ greatly from the balanced diet of a sprinter in its calories of daily **macronutrients** such as carbohydrates, in how it speeds up the recovery process from exercise, and in how it replaces other nutrients such as proteins, fats, vitamins, minerals and water.

Effective exercise requires progression or the benefits of fitness will be lost. A gradual increase in the difficulty of exercise and training ensures that fitness is maintained and improved. To perform at optimum levels, an athlete requires sufficient levels and timescales of recovery, not only between exercises within a training session but also between each training session.

An athlete's training regime may change in preparation for competition. Often this involves a change in location, and possibly changes in time zone, environment and climate. These changes may alter the athlete's dietary requirements (Table 10.12).

remember

The duration of an activity will depend on its intensity. Usually, the greater the intensity, the lower the duration.

Table 10.12 How environment influences training and diet

Hot environment
Training environment temperatures of over 25°C require 2–3 days of adjustment
Temperatures over 30°C require up to 10 days of acclimatisation
Excessive sweating can cause loss of minerals
Energy consumption rises, so eat carbohydrates that are easy to digest
Cold environment
Increases energy use, so have a higher fraction of fat in the diet
Overall energy requirements can increase by approximately 10%
Eat complex carbohydrates to get a thicker layer of subcutaneous fat
High-altitude environment
Reduces glycogen stores and increases protein deficiency, so eat foods rich in carbohydrate and protein
Dehydration, so drink adequate amounts of fluid before and after training

Changes from existing time zones when training or competing can change the availability of specific foods the athlete requires. Changes in climate may mean that an existing diet needs to be reviewed, adapted and planned ahead of schedule. Time zone changes and jet lag can also produce temporary disruption to normal eating and refuelling times.

Figure 10.16 Performance falls with dehydration

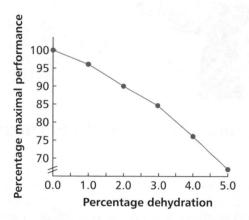

activity
GROUP WORK
10.6

P5

Design a poster that describes hydration and explains why it is important to sportspeople. Link your work to the different types of sports drinks that are available.

activity
INDIVIDUAL WORK
10.7

M3

Using a table format, explain the effects of hydration on sports performance and state the conditions that can result from excess fluids and inadequate fluids.

Planning a diet appropriate for a selected sports activity

A balanced diet

The quantities of fats, proteins, carbohydrates, fibre and vitamins vary from one athlete to another and from one exercise schedule to another. Remember that these requirements may differ considerably from the requirements for a non-active individual. Methods of preparing and cooking foods will also have a significant effect on the overall balance of the diet. Fresh food that is microwaved, steamed, baked, poached, grilled or stir-fried is, wherever possible, a better way to maintain a balanced approach. The quantities of the foods and their balance with each other will also have a big influence on the daily meal plan.

Fats

An athlete's dietary fat intake will be very individual and will be directly linked to the sport; for example, bodybuilders may have a very restricted fat intake to promote their lean physique. The proportions of fat to carbohydrates and proteins are important for achieving a balance.

Ideally 20–30% of fat should make up the diet, but the type of fat is also important for good health. Cheese, for example, is high in fat and is also an excellent source of calcium, so it may be more appropriate to choose a smaller piece of cheese or to eat low-fat cheese. Instead of butter, perhaps eat a spread based on olive oil – use it sparingly – or perhaps change from full-fat milk to skimmed or semi-skimmed milk.

Table 10.13 Daily fat intake

| | Fat intake per day (g) when | |
Required energy (kcal/day)	Fat is 20% of the diet	Fat is 30% of the diet
2500	55	75
3000	66	90
4000	88	120

Some endurance athletes use fat loading. They load up on fat so they will burn the fat instead of their more limited supplies of glycogen, but research suggests that a high-fat diet 3–5 days before competition actually lowers performance as it takes longer to digest.

Proteins

Protein may be used as an energy source in addition to carbohydrates and fats; this is particularly true for endurance sports. Using protein as an energy source is not ideal; it is the most expensive method for the body as it wastes the body's essential resources. Besides that, there is a danger that protein is lost from the liver and the muscles, which can have a significant effect on sporting performance.

At present, the recommendations are for 0.75 g of protein per kilogram of body weight, but this is based on a sedentary lifestyle; some athletes may benefit from greater amounts. Here is what Griffin (2001: 70) suggests:

> Strength or speed athletes should consume about 1.7 to 1.8 g protein per kg of body weight per day and endurance athletes about 1.2 to 1.4 g protein per kg body weight per day. Putting it into context, this is 100 to 212 per cent of the requirement of the average sedentary individual.

Why do athletes need more protein?

- To minimise protein breakdown.
- To maximise protein synthesis.
- The synthesis and breakdown of protein can occur not only during exercise, but also for several hours after training, especially for endurance activities.
- The level and intensity of training will affect protein synthesis and breakdown.
- To ensure that adequate levels are replenished to aid the recovery process.
- Protein is needed to make glucose and maintain adequate blood sugar levels.
- Regular exercise stimulates tissue growth and repair; proteins are the building blocks in this process.

High-protein diets are sometimes used by strength and power athletes, where the daily consumption can be 3–4 times higher than the recommended daily allowance (RDA). When such high levels are ingested, more water is required to prevent dehydration, and although there is a suggestion that kidney function is affected, there is little reliable data to confirm it.

The type of protein and how it is prepared will have an important effect on the overall balance of the diet. Some good sources are meats, eggs, dairy products, soy products, legumes, wholegrain foods and nuts. Be careful about eating animal proteins that may be high in saturated fats.

> **remember**
>
> The proteins found in meat and fish are quite similar to the proteins found in human skeletal muscle. Protein supplements should not be necessary if dietary protein levels are adequate.

case study 10.4

Protein for Chris the rower

Chris is a professional rower who has been advised to eat a diet totalling 3500 kcal per day. The breakdown of macronutrients is carbohydrates 61%, fats 20% and proteins 19%.

activity
INDIVIDUAL WORK

1. List the different sources of proteins that Chris could eat.
2. Decide which food sources would be better for him.
3. Calculate the total number of grams of protein he will need each day.

Carbohydrates

Carbohydrates are vital sources of energy for all athletes. In daily activity the body relies on carbohydrates and fat to provide energy, but the breakdown of fat is a much slower process and requires oxygen. The brain and red blood cells require a ready supply of glucose for normal functioning. During exercise the fuel requirements may sharply increase, but this will depend on several factors:

- The intensity of the activity
- The duration of the exercise
- The age of the athlete
- The training regime
- The fitness level of the athlete
- The current diet of the athlete.

For all activities and sport, an average intake of 60% of the diet should be derived from carbohydrates; in a sedentary person this requirement may fall to 50%. Carbohydrate guidelines are usually calculated as a proportion of the total calorie intake, but for athletes it may be more relevant to consider the required carbohydrate consumption per day in grams per kilogram of body weight. Endurance-trained athletes may require 8–10 g per kilogram of body weight per day. People who exercise less than 5 h per week may require 4–5 g per kilogram of body weight.

Carbohydrate as a fuel

- Carbohydrates provide the energy for contraction of skeletal muscle.
- Glycogen can be broken down very quickly to glucose, aerobically or anaerobically.
- Light-intensity exercise will rely on approximately 12.5% of fuel from carbohydrates.
- Medium-intensity exercise will rely on approximately 45% of fuel from carbohydrates.
- High-intensity exercise will rely on up to 67% of fuel from carbohydrates.
- Unrefined carbohydrates maintain higher levels of fibre and nutrients.
- Good examples of carbohydrate-containing foods are rice, pasta, cereals, muesli, potatoes and flapjack.

Water

The body consists of about 55–65% water (40 litres). Water has these important functions:

- Transporting nutrients around the body
- Removing waste products via the kidneys
- Keeping the body cool when sweating
- Keeping joints lubricated
- Maintaining blood volume
- Aiding digestion and chemical reactions with enzymes.

Ideally, adults should drink at least 2–3 litres of water per day, which replaces the amounts lost through normal activity and metabolism. Water cannot be stored in the same way as fat and carbohydrate, so regular intake is necessary, but all of this does not have to be from plain water. Some food sources plus beverages such as fruit juices, teas and coffee can also be included in the daily amount. Foods such as watermelon, cucumber, lettuce, white fish, yoghurt, milk and oranges all yield a high water content.

Fibre

The UK Department of Health recommends a daily fibre intake of 18–24 g to decrease blood lipids, to move food through the intestines and prevent constipation, and to modify the effects of food, especially its glycaemic values. Excessive amount of dietary fibre can prevent the normal absorption of some minerals such as calcium, iron and zinc, as well as causing flatulence or diarrhoea. Fibre intake should be adjusted according to the total amount of calories being consumed; it is the proportions and balances that are important.

Vitamin and mineral supplements

Regular intensive exercise increases the body's requirements for vitamins and minerals. An athlete needs more energy, so they will need to eat more food. This will mean that their body is receiving more vitamins and minerals. But large quantities of extra vitamins and minerals can damage health, so take care to monitor the intakes. Supplementing an athlete's diet can be beneficial in some circumstances.

Vitamin supplements

- Smokers should consider taking extra vitamin C.
- Supplements in low doses may be beneficial for athletes on a diet and consuming less than 1200 calories per day.
- Vegans or vegetarians on a limited diet should consider multivitamins and mineral supplements.
- Supplementation is best considered under medical supervision.

> **remember**
>
> Refuelling after exercise will enable the body to recover quickly. It can take up to 20 h following the end exercise to replace used carbohydrate stores. Ideally 1 g of carbohydrate per kilogram of body weight is needed in a 2 h period, so a 70 kg athlete will need 70 g of carbohydrate.

Other substances

Besides the well-known macro- and micronutrients, some athletes will use some food sources to boost their energy levels and perhaps improve their performance. They may use ergogenic aids or superfoods.

Ergogenic aids

Ergogenic aids are thought to enhance sporting performance above expected levels, unlike nutritional supplements that are designed to help the athlete meet the needs of training or competition. Here are some things an athlete should check carefully when using ergogenic aids:

- Is there clear evidence from trials and published results?

- Does it contravene any rules on doping?

- Is it safe to take?

- Does it meet their individual needs?

Here are some ergogenic aids or supplements that are currently available:

- Creatine

- Carnitine

- Caffeine

- Fat burners or thermogenics

- Glutamine.

Superfoods

Superfoods are some of the best-known nutritionally concentrated foods containing vitamins, minerals, enzymes and other nutrients. They are also described as having medicinal properties.

Table 10.14 Superfoods

Food	Effect	Content and eating
Alfalfa	Laxative, antidiuretic, detoxifies the liver, relieves fluid retention	A legume, the leaves contain eight essential amino acids; its sprouts can be eaten in place of lettuce
Algae	Antioxidant, boosts the immune system, stimulates red blood cell formation, assists weight control	Dried versions contain high levels of protein, iron and beta-carotene; it includes spirulina, chorella and blue-green algae; available from health food stores
Bee pollen	Builds the immune system, rich source of antioxidants, provides energy, can be used by athletes to recover from activity	Rich source of vitamins, minerals, enzymes and amino acids; available from health food stores
Cabbage	Antiviral, antibacterial, manages oestrogen levels, reduces the chances of colon cancer, heals gastric ulcers	High content of vitamins A, B, C, E and K plus potassium, copper and sulphur; eat as steamed cabbage, include in coleslaw, drink cabbage juice; Chinese cabbage is particularly beneficial
Honey	Antibacterial, antioxidant, stimulates the immune system, healing effects on skin wounds, burns and acne	Manuka honey is particularly high in antioxidants; the best type is cold-pressed raw honey that has not been subjected to heat
Nuts	Reduce LDL cholesterol, increase omega-3 fatty acids, rich sources of vitamins	Include brazil nuts, macadamia nuts, almonds, walnuts, chestnuts, peanuts. Shelled and unsalted nuts are useful for refuelling or as an energy-boosting snack
Yoghurts	Probiotics protect the gut from harmful bacteria; they help to prevent yeast infections, bloating, allergies and digestive imbalances	Include prebiotic and probiotic yoghurts; they are readily available in supermarkets and health food shops; probiotic yoghurt should be kept refrigerated

Probiotics work in the opposite way to antibiotics; 'pro' means 'for' and 'anti' means 'against'. Antibiotics can kill not only the harmful bacteria, but also the good bacteria in the gut. Probiotic yoghurt aims to provide an external source of good bacteria. Prebiotics encourage the body to stimulate the existing good bacteria found in the body. Considerable research is currently being done to evaluate the effectiveness of pre- and probiotic food sources on the human body.

Factors to consider

Sports performers, especially elite performers, have lifestyle characteristics that should be considered when planning nutritional intake:

- Meals need to be timed to fit around training and competition.
- The diet must be well balanced.
- Fluid intake should be adequate.
- Iron intake should be adequate.
- The diet should be suitable for very high workload (depending on the activity).
- Psychological well-being is important. If an athlete is unhappy with their diet, even if it's ideal for their physiology, the psychological effects could impair their performance.
- Coach, dietician and performer should work together to agree the best strategy to suit the athlete's needs and perceptions.
- Obsession with food is common in high-performance athletes and should be avoided.

Mark Foster is an Olympic and Commonwealth Games sprint swimmer. Here is what he says about his diet:

I weigh about 14 stone, but when it comes to competition, I aim to have lost half a stone. I eat a lot of protein food. Two hours of work in the gym burns off anything, but while I watch my diet, I have a lot of protein drinks after weight sessions and take supplements to make sure my body does not become broken down. (Adapted from the *Sunday Times*, 22 September 2002)

Aerobic and anaerobic activity

Aerobic and anaerobic activity draw on different energy systems during exercise. Every athlete should aim to have a balanced diet that will meet their individual requirements for exercise, training and competition. This can often mean continually adjusting the amounts of macro- and micronutrients according to their sport, training regime, personal preferences and responses as well as competition. Remember that each athlete has their own their nutritional needs and preferences.

Daily menu plans are available from registered nutritionists who can accurately detail all the requirements for each athlete and link this to the energy input and energy expenditure, age or special requirements. Marathon runners, who train for endurance, may have much higher carbohydrate intake than weightlifters, who focus on muscle strength and who may have more protein in their diet. Similarly, the dietician may recommend supplements such as glucosamine and chondroitin for gymnasts and long jumpers, who put great stresses and strains on their joints and ligaments.

Vegetarians, diabetics, teenagers, children and the elderly will also have very different nutritional requirements and meal plans to meet their specific needs.

Timing

Consider nutritional requirements throughout the sporting year, even when athletes are resting and recovering. An unbalanced diet during the quiet season will impair performance when the athlete returns to training. The demand of a sport may alter halfway through a season, so the emphasis on macro- and micronutrients will vary. The pre-season diet may be adjusted to meet the needs of the different training programmes; perhaps strength will be the focus for one session and endurance for another.

Pre-event training

Pre-event food intake needs to give sufficient energy stores for use during the activity; it's rather like putting petrol in a car before a journey. Table 10.15 offers a few simple guidelines.

Table 10.15 Activity and carbohydrate intake

Frequency of activity	Carbohydrate intake per kilogram of body weight (g)
3–5 h per week	4–5
5–7 h per week	5–6
1–2 h per day	6–7
2–4 h per day	7–8
> 4 h per day	8–10

Adapted from Bean (2003)

Ideally an athlete should eat 2–4 h before exercise and after eating they should not feel hungry or too full; avoid heavy meals. A low-fat, higher-carbohydrate meal will provide sufficient energy to prevent fatigue and will help to optimise performance. An ideal meal includes slow-release carbohydrates (or low-glycaemic carbohydrates); here are some examples:

- Wholegrain cereal
- Pasta
- Sandwich or bread roll with proteins such as chicken, fish and eggs.

Here some things that can go in a pre-event snack eaten 2–4 h before exercise:

- Yoghurt
- Fruit smoothies
- Sultana bread
- Cereal bars.

Inter-event training

Eating opportunities during exercise or training will depend on the type of activity, the time spent exercising, and the location and accessibility of food.

On average an athlete exercising for more than 60 min will need to ingest 30–60 g of carbohydrate per hour, but it is more appropriate to take on carbohydrates in smaller quantities. Staging the intake by eating every 20–30 min can meet the body's needs more rapidly. Fast-release carbohydrates are better choices during inter-event training or competition:

- Bananas
- Energy or cereal bars
- Low-fat biscuits (Jaffa cakes)
- Raisins or sultanas
- Chocolate buttons
- Jelly babies.

Post-event training

Do not underestimate the benefits of good nutritional intake after exercise. The nutrients in the food allow the body to replenish proteins, carbohydrates, fats, water and fluids, and electrolytes.

A combination of carbohydrate and protein aids recovery by stimulating the release of insulin from the pancreas; insulin promotes the uptake of glucose and amino acids from the bloodstream and into the muscles to replace the used stores.

Sometimes there is an opportunity to refuel immediately after exercise. Here are some good post-event snacks:

- Sandwich with a low-fat filling
- Scone with jam but no butter
- Jacket potato with a low-fat, high-protein topping
- Energy bars.

Some athletes prefer to eat a snack rather than a full meal immediately after exercise. All athletes should make some effort to eat after exercise.

Post-event meals can include a low-fat meal with moderate amounts of carbohydrate and protein. A regular intake every 2–4 h is an ideal way to refuel the body. One way to encourage eating is to prepare food before activity and take it with you. This food should be nutritionally sound and it should be appetising to the athlete.

---

case study 10.5 — A complete diet for Jennifer

Jennifer, aged 40, is a semi-professional golfer who practises or trains for up to 3 h five days per week. Two weeks from now, she will be competing in a five-day competition and would like some guidance on her diet for the week of the competition and the week before. She has noticed that her weight has increased 4 kg in the past 6 months and her BMI is now in the obese range.

activity
INDIVIDUAL WORK

1. Describe an appropriate diet for Jennifer over the two weeks she has requested.
2. Explain the aims of the diet.
3. Justify why Jennifer should follow this diet and what the benefits will be.

Planning diets

A diet must always meet the needs of an athlete. There is little point in providing detailed meal plans if they contain foods that the athlete does like or will not eat. The meals need to be appetising, affordable and, for some athletes, easy to prepare. Before the initial consultation, prepare detailed notes or prompts to remind you to ask about the athlete's lifestyle and current eating habits. To help you devise a diet, discuss the athlete's training and competition schedules.

Assessment of needs

Nutrition and weight management

Energy balance is realised when a person's food energy input equals their body's energy output. When input exceeds output, the excess energy is stored as fat. The simple way to lose weight is to eat less and exercise more. But problems can occur if energy intake is restricted over a long period of time or if exercise is excessive. Try to reach a healthy balance.

If too little energy is taken in, the body will lose other tissues as well as fat, particularly muscle, and this can slow down the rate at which the body burns its fat stores. Consequently, dieting can lead to more fat not less. Athletes need a ready supply of energy, so they need to maintain the correct energy input.

Body mass index
Body mass index (BMI) is calculated like this:

$$\text{BMI (kg/m}^2) = \frac{\text{body weight (kg)}}{\text{height}^2 \text{ (m}^2)}$$

Lifestyle
Weight is greatly influenced by lifestyle, although much depends on body type, age and genetic make-up. Athletes cannot change their genetic make-up but they do have some control over their lifestyle. It is crucial to balance energy input and energy output. If your energy input is just enough for your needs, your weight will remain fairly constant.

Energy consumption increases during exercise and stays high for some time after exercise. Exercise increases metabolic rate and burns up stored calories. Aerobic exercise, such as swimming, running and cycling, is most effective at burning up body fat. It has been calculated that an average adult must walk more than 48 km to burn up 3500 calories, which is the equivalent of 450 g of fat.

Exercise can also cause weight gain. Developed muscle weighs more than fat, so body composition measurements are far more accurate than BMI as an indicator of body fat.

Energy expenditure

Energy expenditure considerably influences the total amount of calories needed per day. It requires an index of calories matched against specific activities. Table 10.16 can give an accurate picture if the athlete keeps good records of their activities. Another way is to obtain the data from pedometers or activity monitors linked to computers.

Table 10.16 Energy expended in a variety of sports

	Energy expended in 30 min (kcal)	
	Man (175 lb, 79 kg)	Woman (135 lb, 61 kg)
Cycling	334	258
Hatha yoga	167	129
Dancing (general)	188	145
Gardening	209	161
Basketball	334	258
Frisbee	125	97
Horse riding	167	129
Skating	292	225
Soccer	292	225
Tennis	292	225
Hiking	251	193
Walking	146	113
Canoeing	292	225
Swimming	334	258

Reprinted, with permission, from the *Sunday Times*, 22 September 2002

Different activities will mean that an athlete's diet may need to be adjusted for their energy requirements and expenditure. Here are the factors to consider:

- Age
- Gender
- Current BMI
- Medical history
- Additional needs or requirements, such as **diabetes** and allergies
- Type of sport

Figure 10.17 Different activities require different diets

- Training regimes
- Assessment of needs
  - Weight gain or loss
  - Muscle gain or loss
  - Body fat gain or loss
- Existing diet
- Short-term goals
- Long-term goals.

Carefully consider how to prepare athletes at different points in the year and in their day-to-day activities. Always link it to the frequency, intensity and time spent doing the sport or activity.

---

case study 10.6 — Calories and grams for Doug the cyclist

Doug, aged 25, is an amateur cyclist who trains for 2 h each week at medium intensity. He has noticed that he has been losing weight since he increased the intensity of his training regime. He currently weighs 68 kg.

activity
INDIVIDUAL WORK

1. On a simple chart, show an estimate of the total number of calories he should be eating.

2. Use another simple chart to show the balance between fats, carbohydrates and proteins.

3. Devise a simple table to show the daily total number of grams of fats, carbohydrates and proteins he should be eating.

4. Give specific examples of foods that will meet the requirements. If you wish, you may use prepared meal sources.

Nutrition, food groups and sources

General nutrition will vary from activity to activity. Link the quantities and balances of each food group and the best sources to provide a holistic diet that is safe and balanced. Consider factors one at a time then consider the overall picture to provide an appealing and exciting diet. A good first step is a simple pie chart that shows the distribution and balance of nutrients in the total calorie intake. Then build up the picture using more details of specific food sources, fluid balances, treats and training schedules.

Availability

Food availability varies from athlete to athlete. Here are the factors that can influence food availability:

- Season, especially for fruit and vegetables
- Cost
- Accessibility of food and drink for purchase
- Availability and nutritional value of food and drink at sporting venues
- Storage and transport facilities of prepared breakfasts and lunches, especially in hot weather.

Athletes can make themselves more aware of their diet and control the type, quantity and quality of the food they take to training or competitions. To help them adhere to their diet plans, athletes need appetising and appealing food. Quick preparation may also be significant. Here are some good basic sources of macronutrients: sandwiches made with wholemeal bread, bagels, cooked chicken, turkey, ham, tuna, sweetcorn, baked potatoes, pasta, peanut butter, bananas, pears, apples and other fruits.

activity
INDIVIDUAL WORK 10.8

P6

M4

1. Use a large, simple diagram to describe the aspects of a balanced diet. You may want to use pictures, labels from foods or food supplements, or diagrams to indicate your food choices.

2. Give reasons for the choices you made in the overall balanced diet. You can include the reasons on your diagram.

activity
GROUP WORK 10.9

P7

M5

1. Describe a diet for a sportsperson in a named activity and include the different types of macro- and micronutrients, fluid intake and energy output. You can present it as a daily list for a 14 day period.

2. Explain the importance of each aspect of the diet.

For the diet devised in Activity 10.8, justify the way you have developed the diet for each of the components; consider the quantities and types of foods and fluids. You can indicate this on a table of strengths and weaknesses.

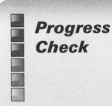

Progress Check

1. What are enzymes and why are they important?
2. What are the final digestion products of (a) proteins, (b) fats and (c) carbohydrates?
3. Define the following terms: (a) food, (b) nutrition, (c) diet.
4. Give an example of each of the major components of food.
5. What are amino acids?
6. What is 'bad cholesterol'?
7. (a) Why is water so valuable as part of a balanced diet?

   (b) Name three different vitamins.

   (c) State why each should be part of your diet.
8. Why is food labelling so important?
9. Name the different methods of measuring body composition.
10. What steps can athletes follow to prevent dehydration?
11. What is (a) a hypertonic drink, (b) a hypotonic drink, (c) an isotonic drink?
12. What is BMR?
13. What is carboloading?
14. Give four guidelines for healthy eating.
15. Why is it important to eat both carbohydrates and proteins after exercise?
16. Name four superfoods and state their beneficial effects.

UNIT 12

Leadership in Sport

Andrew Procter

This unit covers:

- The qualities, characteristics and roles of effective sports leaders
- The importance of psychological factors in leading sports activities
- The ability to plan sports activities
- The ability to effectively lead sports activities

More and more people are taking part in sport and good people are needed to lead sports activities. National governing bodies and the Youth Sport Trust help to train young people as sports leaders. There are many opportunities for qualified leaders, including after-school clubs, sports colleges and local sports teams. Opportunities in the community help to improve social interaction, reduce crime and give children an opportunity to express and develop themselves through sport and physical activity.

grading criteria	To achieve a **Pass** grade the evidence must show that the learner is able to:	To achieve a **Merit** grade the evidence must show that the learner is able to:	To achieve a **Distinction** grade the evidence must show that the learner is able to:
	P1 describe four qualities, four characteristics and four roles common to effective sports leaders, using examples of effective sports leaders Pg 46	**M1** explain four qualities, four characteristics and four roles common to effective sports leaders Pg 46	**D1** analyse four qualities, four characteristics and four roles common to effective sports leaders Pg 46
	P2 describe four psychological factors that are important in the leading of sports activities Pg 56	**M2** explain four psychological factors that are important in the leading of sports activities Pg 56	
	P3 produce a risk assessment for a selected sports activity Pg 66		
	P4 plan for leading a selected sports activity Pg 66		

grading criteria	To achieve a **Pass** grade the evidence must show that the learner is able to:	To achieve a **Merit** grade the evidence must show that the learner is able to:	To achieve a **Distinction** grade the evidence must show that the learner is able to:
	P5 lead a selected sports activity, with support Pg 71	**M3** lead a selected sports activity Pg 71	
	P6 review the performance of participants, within activity, identifying strengths and areas for improvement Pg 71	**M4** make suggestions relating to development of participants in identified areas for improvement Pg 71	**D2** justify suggestions made relating to development of participants Pg 74
	P7 review own performance in the planning and leading of the sports activity, identifying strengths and areas for improvement Pg 74	**M5** make suggestions relating to personal development in identified areas for improvement Pg 74	**D3** justify suggestions made relating to own development as a sports leader Pg 73

The qualities, characteristics and roles of effective sports leaders

Figure 12.1 Do you recognise these sports leaders?

Qualities

Effective sports leaders use sport as a vehicle to help develop individuals as participants and people. Not only do they lead the sport, but they also lead people. And to lead people, they need to help them develop in several ways:

- **Technically** – by developing good technique through the identification of areas for improvement and organising practices to learn new techniques and skills.

- **Physically** – by identifying the physical requirements of the sport and organising fitness-based practices to develop the physical condition of the body.

- **Socially** – by organising practices to allow for group interaction, problem solving and communication through cooperation and competition.

- **Psychologically** – by developing the ability to understand and interpret feelings and emotions associated with sport and by providing situations which enhance and develop self-esteem.

- **Personally** – by teaching sound values and attitudes towards officials, coaches, opposition and teammates by using sport to develop life skills.

Knowledge

Effective leaders are respected for their knowledge. However, this is not just knowledge of the sport's technical and tactical elements. The leader needs to have knowledge of their performers, what makes them tick, their reactions to specific situations, their personal strengths, areas for improvement, their stage of development and perhaps a little about their personal background.

Knowledge of the sport

Every sport has its own unique characteristics, including the skills required to perform, the strategies used to overcome the opposition and the rules to abide by. A thorough knowledge of all these characteristics will enable the leader to be more effective, but will also gain them the respect of participants.

Knowledge of techniques

The technical element of the sport can be practised in isolation, but the real skill comes when the correct technique is selected at the appropriate moment, such as selecting a good cricket stroke for a particular delivery. The effective leader will have that knowledge and will impart it to the participants as they practise.

Knowledge of strategies

The effective leader will know a number of strategies to help their performer overcome the opposition. They will be able to identify the strategy of the opposition and counteract it with one of their own. Football experts, for example, know a great deal about the formations of players on the pitch, such as 4-4-2 and 3-5-2.

Knowledge of rules and laws

remember

A good leader develops the person through the sport, not the sport through the person.

Rules of a sport define its unique characteristics and help people to participate safely. An effective leader will know all the rules of the sport, instil discipline and imbue participants with a sense of fair play. Some, however, may try to manipulate the rules to gain an advantage over the opposition.

Knowledge of the participants

To get the best out of a participant, it is important that the leader treats them as an individual. Each participant will have a unique personality. They will react differently to situations, progress at different rates and have different goals and aspirations.

remember

Participants will progress at different rates technically, physically and mentally.

- Athletes progress at different rates. If you provide the same training stimulus to each athlete, it will not elicit the same results.
- Some may pick up a skill quickly whereas others may take time then suddenly improve. Some may mature physically more quickly than others, especially during puberty.

Link

See Unit 23 for more information on working with children in sport

- An effective leader will understand the concept of **long-term athlete development (LTAD)** and adapt practices to suit the physical maturity of the individual. Some athletes may mature mentally more quickly than others, and the leader should understand how this affects an athlete's moods and their reactions to situations.

---

case study 12.1 — Extra fitness training

A team of under-14s had been losing games in the last ten minutes and the leader concluded that it was due to their lack of fitness. Hoping to halt the trend, the leader organised a programme of fitness sessions. All players were asked to do the same fitness programme and the leader began to see a difference in most of the players. But two players didn't seem to improve as much as the others and continued to struggle with their fitness. The leader kept them behind for extra sessions and made them work harder. Unfortunately, one player became injured and another left the team, upset at having to do the extra training.

activity
INDIVIDUAL WORK

1. What did the leader not consider when organising the training programme?
2. What knowledge did the leader require to improve the players' fitness?
3. The players who had not improved, how could the leader have dealt with them differently?

Knowledge of factors affecting performance

To plan safe and effective sessions, the leader needs to consider several factors that affect performance. They need to understand how the body responds to exercise in order to incorporate the right intensity of training and rest periods. They need to understand how to reduce situations that may lead to injuries and illness; this includes knowing about the rates of growth in children, the effect of ageing, the eating habits of performers and the symptoms of overtraining and competing. They need to be aware of how participants acquire skills and how they respond mentally to different situations, including how they interact with others. They should also be aware of technology to enhance the performance of participants and teams.

- **Body response to exercise** – an effective leader will know the short- and long-term effects of exercise on the body. They will understand the key principles of training and how they influence performance and training. Knowledge of work and rest intervals will allow the leader to organise sessions that challenge the performer and enable them to recover sufficiently to allow for adaptations and to avoid overtraining.

- **Reduction of injuries** – all participants and leaders fear injuries as they can disrupt training schedules or even ruin careers, so minimise any situations that may lead to injuries. This may be very difficult in rugby and other contact sports, but an effective leader will understand calculated risks and will have completed a risk assessment when the sessions were planned.

- **Technology** – the modern leader, especially at elite level, can use technology to enhance performance. Ultra slow motion cameras can now capture action from a variety of angles, and powerful computers can produce simulated and real-life images to identify areas of performance that require development. The effective leader knows about these advances and can use them to plan practices that meet specific needs of the participants.

Figure 12.2 Technology can help improve performance

Characteristics

Effective sports leaders come from a variety of backgrounds and use their qualities and experiences in different ways to develop participants. They use different leadership styles, have different values and beliefs and use a range of techniques to get their message across. However, all effective leaders require a number of characteristics.

Objective

Close relationships between leader and participant may affect the leader's judgement. An effective leader will maintain objectivity by using some form of criteria whenever judgements are made about a performance.

Patient

Learning new skills takes time and effort. The mastery of skills, techniques and tactical concepts comes much more easily to some participants than others. A leader has to remain patient and not become frustrated if their initial goals and ideas are not met immediately by all participants.

Persistent

A leader also has to be persistent in the pursuit of their goals. Setbacks in training and performance should not deter the leader from persevering with participants.

Empathetic

The psychological well-being of the participant is just as important to the leader as their physical ability. A participant who is unhappy generally doesn't perform at their best, so an effective leader will need to be a good listener and be able to empathise with the participant when necessary.

> **remember**
> About 10 000 h of practice are required to excel at anything.

Figure 12.3 A good leader listens and shows empathy

Approachable

To maintain good relationships with their participants, an effective leader will need to portray a friendly and open personality. This will enable the participants to feel comfortable if they wish to approach the leader about a personal matter.

Consistent

Participants perform at their best if the messages they receive from a leader are consistent, including instructions on techniques and tactics. The leader also needs to be consistent in their behaviour towards participants. They must not have favourites or appear to have favourites. Consistency with praise and discipline will help with this.

Goal focused

An effective leader will not be sidetracked in the pursuit of their overall goals. They will be able to remain focused on what they are trying to achieve, despite the many challenges they face each day.

Committed

A leader demands commitment from their participants by asking them to make sacrifices to train and compete for several hours a week, sometimes during unsocial hours and at a financial cost. If the participant is to make sacrifices in pursuit of excellence, then an effective leader should commit themselves to meeting the participant's needs.

Discreet

Just as a doctor has to respect patient confidentiality, a leader should be discreet with any personal information they have about their participants. The effective leader will ensure confidentiality, avoiding any loose words that could cause upset and decrease the self-esteem of a participant.

Forgiving

Making mistakes is part of the learning process. An effective leader remembers this when providing feedback to a participant. Blaming a person for a defeat or holding a grudge against a participant will not help with relationships and will have an adverse effect on performances.

Attentive

It is natural for leaders to pay attention to some participants at the expense of others. This may be because they are having more difficulties than others or because they are the most talented. An effective leader will give the same amount of time to all participants and be attentive to their needs.

Empowering

A good way to improve performance is to allow participants to take responsibility for their own learning. An effective leader will be able to create an environment where the participants can work independently to improve their own performances.

Roles

Organiser

A well-planned and well-organised session is vital to improving performance. A participant works best when they are challenged and provided with a variety of tasks where achievement is difficult but not impossible. Well-planned sessions can guide a leader and performer to monitor their progress and make changes where necessary. The leader may also have to organise fixtures, travel arrangements and facilities so that competitions and practices can occur. When several leaders work together effectively, they organise how they can cooperate for the benefit of the participants.

Motivator

Participants look to their leader to create a positive environment where they can perform. An effective leader will have strategies that provide the encouragement and support which motivate participants to do their best. A participant who is consistently criticised will soon lose interest and drop out of sport, whereas a participant who is praised, encouraged and supported for their efforts will remain **motivated**.

Guardian

Many participants spend more time with their leader than with their parents, so a leader may become a surrogate parent. They will need to provide a safe environment where the participant is protected from injury and harm. Leaders use sport as a tool for promoting health and well-being and teach life skills through sport's values and beliefs.

Teacher

Sports leaders often impart knowledge about new skills, techniques or strategies. They may also be required to teach emotional and social skills, particularly how to cope with winning and losing and how to work as part of a team.

---

case study 12.2 — Tearful athlete, busy leader

When the training was hard, one athlete regularly became upset and began to cry. The leader told the athlete that to become the best, they had to work harder and toughen up. At the end of the session, the upset athlete stayed behind to speak to the leader, but the leader was too busy and had to leave quickly.

activity
INDIVIDUAL WORK

1. What characteristics did the leader not show when dealing with the participant?
2. How would an effective leader deal with the situation?

Figure 12.4 A well-organised leader sets out on time

Instructor

Participants rely heavily on the leader to provide instruction. This may be to direct activities or produce practices for them to work on. It is usually the younger participants that require instruction. Older and more experienced participants often have a better idea of what is required.

Psychologist

Λ leader needs to understand a participant to optimise their performance. The leader needs to be able to control their emotions, cope with winning and losing, develop self-esteem and understand what makes each participant tick.

case study 12.3 — New boy not made welcome

A young boy joined a new football club for the first time. When he arrived, he was greeted by the sight of the other players chatting and laughing about their last match and how well they played. The leader pulled up in his car, gave the balls to the boys and ran to set up his cones on the field. When the session finally started, it was clear the boy was less skilled than the others and was beginning to feel uncomfortable. At the end of the session, the boys picked teams and played a game. The new boy was last to be picked and was put in goal by his teammates. After letting in three goals, he developed a stomach ache and asked to sit out. On the final whistle, he quickly packed his bags and left the club feeling very unhappy.

activity
INDIVIDUAL WORK

1. What roles did the leader not demonstrate that an effective leader would have?

2. What qualities could the leader have shown to make the experience more pleasant for the new boy?

3. What characteristics would have made the leader more effective in dealing with the new boy's experience?

Trainer

A leader has the role of trainer to develop a participant's physical condition. The leader must organise fitness activities to develop the participants so they can meet the physical demands of their sport.

Role model

A leader has an important responsibility to be someone worth imitating. They need to portray a positive image inside and outside the sporting environment. A leader that abuses officials and leads an unhealthy lifestyle away from their sport can have a serious effect on the behaviour of participants.

> **remember**
>
> Participants see their leaders as role models and seek to imitate their behaviour.

activity

INDIVIDUAL WORK 12.1

P1

1. Produce a poster or leaflet describing four qualities, four characteristics and four roles common to effective sports leaders; include examples.

activity

INDIVIDUAL WORK 12.2

M1

D1

1. Use the qualities, characteristics and roles described in Activity 12.1 to compose a presentation explaining how leaders use them effectively when leading sports activities.

2. In the presentation analyse the effectiveness of the qualities, characteristics and roles by comparing how leaders use them when leading sports activities.

The importance of psychological factors in leading sports activities

Psychological factors

A leader needs to be aware of how participants behave, what affects their confidence and **self-concept** and how their mood may change and affect their motivation. They need to be aware of what causes participants to get stressed or anxious before or during an activity and how they can manage those feelings to optimise performance and enjoyment of the sport.

A leader needs an awareness of how teams are formed and developed over time so that they can influence the **cohesiveness** of the team with their instruction and activities to get the best out of them individually and collectively. An understanding of these psychological factors will enable a leader to build relationships with participants and teams and to incorporate activities that will be enjoyable and successful.

When it is achieved, this task and social team cohesion leads to a satisfied team. Other factors may also influence team cohesion, including the size of the group, how long it has been together (its maturity), the similarity of its members and how much their sense of belonging to the team promotes effort and motivation.

> **remember**
>
> A successful group or team is not always determined by the results they produce. A group or team can be regarded as successful if all members contribute to a common goal or have good relationships with each other.

Group or team cohesion

Cohesiveness is the tendency of a group to stick together in the pursuit of a common goal while maintaining the satisfaction of its members. Team members need to feel supported and appreciated for their efforts while getting the job done. The team leader has a responsibility to provide an environment where this can happen.

Here are some possible ways to create team cohesion:

- Improve communication between team members.
- Recognise role behaviours that benefit the team rather than team members.
- Encourage fun activities outside of the practice sessions.
- Establish a positive feedback environment between team members.
- Provide clear roles for team members to increase the feeling of belonging.
- Create a feeling that the team is more important than the team members.

Group size

The size of the group will cause its own problems for the leader, particularly when trying to maintain group cohesion. As the group size increases, there will be more problems with coordination and **social loafing**. A small group will be easier to control and the relationships between group members and the leader will become very close. Larger groups may form subgroups or cliques and the relationships between members may not develop as well.

Group stability

As Tuckman's model describes, a group goes through development stages that will be unstable. Groups with the highest productivity usually have the lowest amount of disruption to group members, leader and situational characteristics.

Similarity

Groups are generally formed when people with similar interests and goals get together. The more productive the group, the more similar the characteristics, goals and interests of the group members in and out of the group environment.

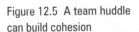

Figure 12.5 A team huddle can build cohesion

Membership

Being a member of a group increases a person's feeling of belonging. They enjoy the social contact and support that a group provides and the image it portrays to others outside the group. Most groups have a symbol their members can display to demonstrate their membership; it may be a badge, a colour scheme or a uniform.

Tuckman's stages of group development

Tuckman (1965) and Tuckman and Jensen (1977) described group development using four basic stages.

Forming

Forming is where the group goes through a stage of getting to know each other and is heavily reliant on the leader for guidance and direction. A 'telling' leadership style would be used. The leader would also need to provide an environment where all members can mix in a fun and informal environment where they will have confidence to communicate and get to know all members of the group.

Storming

Following the calm of the forming stage, there is a storming stage where there may be tension associated with establishing roles within the group and competition for status and influence. The leader has to manage this stage very carefully using a 'selling' leadership style. Strong personalities may clash and take over group decisions through their influence on others, and less confident members may get disillusioned and feel unwanted within the team structure. Some members will tend to establish subgroups or cliques based on similarities in personality, interests, living proximity, appearance, etc.

Norming

As the group develops, the members will establish their roles and positions within the group. They will have established rules and boundaries for behaviour. There will be a supportive network for all members. It is the responsibility of the coach to monitor the group and maintain harmony by policing the rules and making sure that each group member has a role and is supported by all the other group members.

Performing

The performing stage is when the group is performing at its potential. All group members will be aware of their roles and their contribution to the group's goals; they will work together to maintain harmony. Conflicts will be resolved within the group and the leader will act more like a delegator.

Adjourning

Ten years after his original work, Tuckman added the adjourning stage. This is where the group disbands, ideally after having achieved all its goals. This is a natural occurrence in most sporting activities, where participants move on to new challenges or are forced to retire.

The model

Although Tuckman's model follows five stages of group dynamics, sports activities tend to remain in the storming, norming and performing cycle as members join or leave the group on a regular basis. There are regular changes of goals and even changes of leadership that can keep the group from remaining at the performing stage.

Figure 12.6 Tuckman's stages of group development

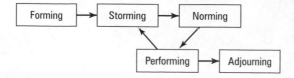

case study 12

Team cohesion

A leader took charge of a new team that had been selected from all the talented athletes in the area. At the first meeting, it was noticeable that some of the participants already knew each other and were very loud as they gathered their kit. Other participants sat quietly and looked nervous as the leader arrived to address them.

activity
INDIVIDUAL WORK

1. What stage of Tuckman's model is the team demonstrating?
2. What problems might the leader experience during the first few weeks?
3. How can the leader overcome the problems to create a cohesive team?

Development of cohesion

Carron (1982) suggested four primary factors that contribute to the development of a cohesive team:

- **Situational factors** – group size, geographic variables, contractual responsibilities, intergroup conflict.
- **Personal factors** – gender, maturity, personal attributes, shared perceptions, individual satisfaction, similarity.
- **Leadership factors** – leader behaviour and styles, communication, leader–participant relationship, decision-making style.
- **Team factors** – relationships, task characteristics, ability, achievement orientation, homogeneity, intragroup cooperation, experience, stability, team maturity.

Social loafing and the Ringelmann effect

Ringelmann (1913) discovered that one man pulling on a rope was likely to pull twice as hard (average 63 kg) than in a team of eight (31 kg). The reason for the difference could be associated with the coordination problems of working in a team of eight, but other simple coactive tasks (hand clapping) revealed that the gap between actual group performance and individual potential productivity was not fully explained by coordination problems.

Steiner's equation says that actual productivity equals potential productivity minus losses due to faulty group processes (Steiner 1972)

This effect is known as the **Ringelmann effect** and the reduction of effort is called social loafing. There are many factors that could contribute to the reduction in individual effort within a group, including group size, the ability to identify individual effort, the strength of group identity, the nature and attractiveness of the task, the degree of trust between group members, intergroup comparisons and personal responsibility.

The effective leader will be aware of this and be careful to avoid situations where social loafing may occur. Social loafing can be reduced by reducing group sizes, identifying individual contribution, and making everybody feel part of the group.

Personality

Effective leaders will spend time getting to know their participants in order to understand their behaviour when faced with different situations.

Figure 12.7 How many athletes are loafing here?

Sport attracts people with similar characteristics, but each of these similar people is a unique person with a unique blend of characteristics.

remember

Hollander's theory

According to Cox (1994: 21), in 1967 Hollander proposed this three-tier model of **personality**:

- **Psychological core** – this is the deepest component of personality, often called 'the real you'. It represents a participant's attitudes, values, interests, motives and beliefs about their self-worth.

- **Typical responses** – this is how the participant displays their personality through actions and behaviours when faced with situations. For example, if a participant responded to being fouled by retaliating, this would demonstrate an aggressive personality to the leader. But if their behaviour was not consistent, the leader would have a problem deciding whether or not this was a typical response.

- **Role-related behaviour** – this is where the participant will change their behaviour to meet the requirements of the role they are playing. An aggressive player may foul regularly in the sporting arena, but be polite and courteous when serving customers in a restaurant.

Figure 12.8 Hollander's three-tier model of personality

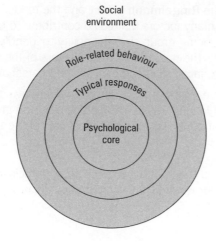

Social environment

Role-related behaviour

Typical responses

Psychological core

Trait theory

Early studies of personality proposed that the causes of behaviour rested with the individual. In the 1960s Eysenck called this trait personality, which led to the belief that people behaved in a particular way regardless of the situation. An example would be a person being aggressive to the opposition regardless of the score or who they were playing.

Situational theory

Situational theory builds on work by Bandura (1977). His social learning theory explained behaviour in terms of modelling (copying others) and feedback (reinforcement). Some participants behave aggressively on the field of play but are gentle and shy off it. The sport or situation requires them to behave aggressively and the reward or reinforcement encourages them to continue with the behaviour.

Interactional theory

Interactional theory proposes that traits and situations have equal influence on a participant's behaviour. A leader in this situation will be at an advantage if they know the personality traits of a participant and the situation in which the behaviour manifests itself. For example, if the leader knows that an aggressive participant will commit a foul if the referee gives a controversial decision against them, they could remove the participant from the situation before they commit the foul. It is also useful for the leader as it allows them to work on a strategy to control the behaviour of the participant by exposing them to situations that don't elicit the aggressive behaviour and that make it less likely to occur again.

Confidence

Confidence is a belief that you can be successful at performing a task. In sport, confidence might be scoring a basket, hitting a ball, running the marathon. A confident participant believes in their ability to complete any task that is set them, whereas a less confident participant will create a **self-fulfilling prophecy** that they will fail, and inevitably they do. This becomes a vicious cycle of failure, as confidence drops, anxiety increases and performance deteriorates.

Some participants become overconfident – their confidence is too great for their abilities. Their performances may decrease as they feel that they don't have to prepare as well or that they don't have to put in the effort because success will occur. An effective leader will monitor their participants and build confidence where it is lacking or temper confidence where it becomes exaggerated. Bandura (1997) brought together the concepts of confidence and expectations to formulate a model of **self-efficacy**, a situation-specific form of self-confidence. A leader could use this model to increase self-confidence.

Performance accomplishments

Participants need successful experiences in order to increase their self-confidence. The more successful a participant, the more they will believe their expectation of future success. Leaders need to provide situations where the participant experiences more success than failure.

Vicarious experiences

Watching others perform tasks and be successful increases self-confidence. Experience gained by watching someone else is called **vicarious experience**. However, this will only have the desired effect if the watcher perceives the performer's skills and abilities as similar to their own. If they are not matched, then confidence may not be enhanced.

Verbal persuasion

Leaders may use verbal cues to increase confidence by convincing the participant that they can complete the task. They may even resort to deception if the mental block is too great. Be careful not to lose the trust of the participant by lying to them. Verbal persuasion will only work when the participant receives it from someone they see as significant.

Emotional arousal

A positive emotional state improves confidence levels. A participant who is suffering from depression, anxiety or sadness will not perform as well as a participant who is happy and pleased to be performing.

Self-concept

Self-concept describes how we see ourselves and what value we place on ourselves in society. Exercise and increased levels of fitness have a positive relationship with self-concept, especially in people who already have low self-esteem. Changes in the body after physical activity training can alter a participant's body image – how they see themselves and how they believe others see them. Competence in achieving skills can also have a positive effect.

An effective leader will strive to improve a participant's self-concept by manipulating the environment to allow those with low self-concept to succeed. This might be by increasing their fitness and body shape or by providing situations where they are successful. Their success should also be celebrated among their peers as social approval can increase self-concept.

---

case study 12.5 — Confidence drop

A female gymnast fell in a recent competition and found it difficult to complete any moves she had previously been able to do. Back at training, the gymnast would not attempt any difficult moves and made excuses that they were too difficult and she couldn't do them. The leader recognised that the fall had affected the confidence of the gymnast and formulated a strategy to restore it.

activity
INDIVIDUAL WORK

1. What feelings might the gymnast be experiencing after the fall?
2. How can the leader increase the gymnast's confidence so she can return to competition?

Profile of mood states

Morgan (1979) developed a mental health model to predict athletic success. He based his theory on the shape of the pattern produced by plotting scores from the profile of mood states (POMS). Participants who scored below the norm on POMS subscales of tension, depression, anger, fatigue and confusion but above the norm on vigour produced an iceberg profile, or positive mental health. According to Morgan, these participants tended to be more successful than those with a flat profile.

However, insufficient evidence has led to the conclusion that although the iceberg profile is apparent in some successful participants and it is useful in determining mental states, it cannot be used to predict success and certainly not to identify talent.

Motivation

Motivation is defined by Sage (1974) as the direction and intensity of effort. The direction of effort refers to a participant being attracted to a sporting activity, and the intensity of effort refers to how much effort the participant is willing to put into the activity. The question which all leaders ask themselves is why some participants have high **motivation** and others have low motivation. The answer usually comes from participants being able to fulfil their needs.

The two most important needs of young participants are to have fun, which includes stimulation and excitement and to feel worthy, which includes the feeling of competence

remember
If the leader is able to identify the needs of each individual, they may possess the key to their motivation.

Figure 12.9 Athletes with an iceberg profile seem to be more successful. Adapted from Weinberg and Gould (2003)

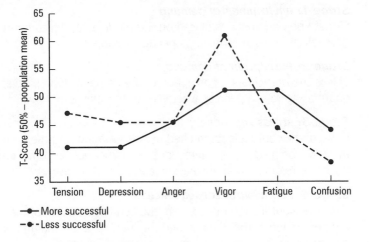

— ● — More successful
- ● - Less successful

and being successful. Older participants are motivated by the need to belong and the social aspects associated with participation in sport and physical activity.

A leader will need to match a participant's needs with the activities they provide. This can prove extremely difficult, particularly in a team situation. For example, some participants may want to play games whereas others may want to learn a new skill. The leader will have to separate the groups and give them their preferred activity (change the situation, the easier option) or find ways of changing the participants' motives by explaining that learning new skills will help in game situations and playing games will help enhance the newly learned skills (change the participant, the harder option).

Extrinsic

Sport regularly uses **extrinsic rewards**. At the end of each year, there is a prize-giving ceremony where participants are presented with trophies, medals, money and praise. Extrinsic motivation is only effective in the short term.

Intrinsic

Intrinsic rewards are those things that are internally satisfying. Fun, competence and personal achievement are good **intrinsic rewards**. They are usually the reason why participants take up a sporting activity in the first place.

Stress

Stress is an imbalance between the demands of an activity and how a person perceives their ability to meet those demands plus the importance they attach to the perceived consequences of failure. McGrath (1970) proposed a four-stage model.

remember

An effective leader aims to provide an environment where participants are motivated without using extrinsic rewards. If participants become reliant on extrinsic rewards, they will reduce their efforts when the rewards are removed and may even give up completely.

case study 12.6   # No more training rewards

A couple of weeks into the new season, the leader of a basketball team noticed the players were not motivated. They were turning up later than usual and were not working hard in training. After asking the players what the problem was, the leader was told that last year they received rewards for training performances but had not received anything this year.

activity
INDIVIDUAL WORK

1. Why might the players be demotivated during this year's training sessions?
2. What strategies could the leader use to overcome this problem with motivation?

Stage 1: environmental demand

Some type of demand is placed on the participant, which might be physical or psychological, such as taking a penalty in football.

Stage 2: perception of demand

This is the participant's perception of the demand. One participant may find it quite daunting to take a penalty, whereas another may look forward to it.

Stage 3: stress response

If the participant feels threatened by the situation and the demand of taking a penalty, there will be a physiological response – an increase in somatic state anxiety – and/or a cognitive response – an increase in cognitive state anxiety.

Stage 4: behavioural consequences

The behavioural consequences are the actual behaviour of the participant in response to the perception of the demand and the feelings and thoughts produced. They increase performance in some people and decrease it in others.

Stress management

If a participant's performance decreases due to the effects of **stress**, then it is the responsibility of the leader to help the participant explore different stress management techniques to find one that works best for them.

Progressive relaxation

Jacobson (1938) developed a technique where the participant tenses and relaxes their muscles alternately until a relaxed state is achieved.

Biofeedback

The key to controlling stress is to be aware of how the body responds to it. Biofeedback is the process of measuring physiological responses such as heart rate and skin temperature and training the participant to control them.

Figure 12.10 Relaxation helps athletes to cope with stress

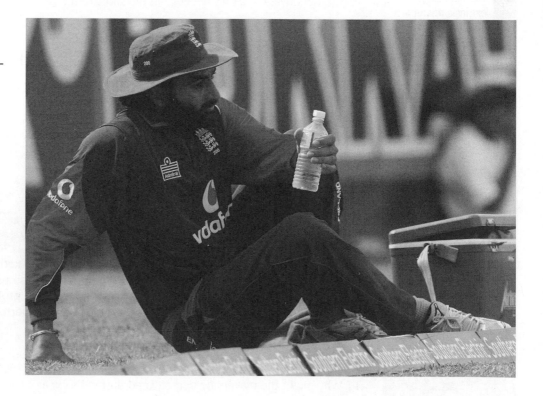

Breathing

Smooth, deep and rhythmical breathing are signs of a relaxed state. The participant should aim to control their breathing when under stress to achieve a relaxed state. Inhaling and exhaling while counting on a 1:2 ratio can help with this.

Autogenic training

Autogenic training is a series of exercises to produce a sensation of warmth and heaviness. It uses self-hypnosis where the participant's attention is focused on producing the desired sensations.

Stress inoculation training

Stress inoculation training gradually exposes the participant to the threat that is causing the stress. As the participant learns to cope with low-stress situations, they are gradually exposed to higher-stress situations until they can cope with full exposure.

Anxiety and arousal

Anxiety and arousal are sometimes used interchangeably, but **arousal** is a combination of physiological and psychological responses in a participant, usually associated with the intensity of motivation. It can vary in people from deep sleep (no arousal) to extreme frenzy (high arousal). **Anxiety** is a negative emotional state with characteristics of nervousness, worry and apprehension associated with arousal of the body.

Anxiety can be divided into a thought component, cognitive anxiety, and a physiological component, somatic anxiety. In **cognitive anxiety**, negative thoughts about performance manifest themselves in the participant, such as 'I can't do this, it's too difficult.' In **somatic anxiety**, the body responds by increasing heart rate, sweating, feeling sick, butterflies, etc. This can lead to decreases in performance due to muscle tension and coordination difficulties.

The leader will be able to identify participants who show the symptoms of anxiety while observing performance. However, some participants might be anxious in one situation but calm in another. This is called **state anxiety**, where anxiety changes depending on the situation faced by the participant. A participant that displays state anxiety in most situations is regarded as having **trait anxiety**, where anxiety is part of their personality or psychological core.

Many participants enjoy the feelings and thoughts associated with the three components and try to reproduce them to a particular level. This is known as the **individualised zone of optimum functioning (IZOF)**; see Hanin (1980: 236–249). Each individual will have their own zone and an effective leader will help the participant find their level to optimise performance.

> **remember**
>
> Not all stress, increased anxiety and arousal have a negative effect on performance.

case study 12.7 | Penalty kick

A player steps up to take a penalty in an important cup game and begins to think negatively about the outcome. They feel their heart start to beat faster and sweat poor down their forehead. As they place the ball on the spot, they notice their hands shaking.

activity
INDIVIDUAL WORK

1. Why is the player experiencing these symptoms?
2. How can the leader help the player cope with the situation better?

INDIVIDUAL WORK 12.3

P2

M2

1. Produce a poster describing the four psychological factors that are important when leading sports activities.

2. Choose one psychological aspect from each of the four factors – groups, motivation, personality, stress – and produce a presentation that explains where leaders have used the factors to demonstrate effective leadership.

Planning sports activities

Some leaders don't like to plan, they tend to be hands-on practical people who prefer to be active with their sessions and work with participants. However, good planning will allow the leader to make the most of the time available with the participants, which is usually not very long. They will be able to give the participants more time and therefore a greater chance of improving their performances. They will be able to make sure the sessions are safe and be prepared for all eventualities.

Risk assessment

One of the most important responsibilities of a leader is to ensure that activities are safe and that there is minimum risk to the participants.

When planning an activity, the leader should follow a few simple steps to make the session safe for the participants.

Know your activity

Each activity will have its own unique characteristics, whether it is indoor or outdoor, contact or non-contact, individual or team. It is the leader's responsibility to recognise the potential **hazards** of the activity and the risk associated with them. They are required to understand their responsibilities in maintaining the safety of the participant and themselves by identifying and managing the risks appropriately.

Hazard

A hazard is something that has the potential to cause harm and can be categorised in terms of the **risk** of it happening. An example is slipping on the tiles at the swimming pool or colliding with an object in the sports hall.

Risk

Risk is the likelihood and severity of the injury occurring.

- **Likelihood** – the probability the hazard will cause an injury to occur.
- **Severity** – the degree of injury the hazard can cause.

Table 12.1 Injuries of low, medium and high severity

Severity	Examples	Subsequent activity
Low	Scratch, bruise, minor cut	Activity can be resumed after first aid
Medium	Fracture, strain, sprain, burn	Activity may not be possible immediately
High	Fatality, disability, amputation	Activity may not be possible like before

> **remember**
>
> Physical activity is inherently risky and participation carries an element of danger, especially where contact is involved. However, good planning and risk management can reduce or eliminate the risk of injury occurring.

Figure 12.11 Sports performers face many hazards

Table 12.2 Injuries that are unlikely, possible and very likely

Likelihood	How often they occur
Unlikely	Very rarely
Possible	Sometimes
Very likely	Frequently

Tables 12.1 and 12.2 could be expanded to include more categories.

Risk rating

A leader should follow four simple steps to rate the risk:

- Identify the hazard.
- Evaluate the likelihood that the hazard will cause an injury and the severity of the injury.
- Produce a strategy to minimise or eliminate the risk.
- Plan for the worst eventuality.

Table 12.3 Risk assessment matrix

	Likelihood		
Severity	**Unlikely**	**Possible**	**Very likely**
Low	Very low risk	Low risk	Medium risk
Medium	Low risk	Medium risk	High risk
High	Medium risk	High risk	Very high risk

The strategies used to minimise or eliminate the risk will depend on the perceived risk produced in the risk assessment. This should be done by an experienced health and safety officer and most facilities will have documents on how to make risk assessments. Otherwise it will be up to the leader to take the appropriate action.

> **remember**
> Risk assessment is a priority. Leaders have a duty of care to give their participants a safe environment in which to work.

Very high risk and high risk

Very high risk and high-risk hazards should be eliminated by removing the hazard or by not doing the activity. If this is not possible, then warning signs should be clearly visible, backed up by verbal instruction. The leader should make sure they are covered by indemnity insurance and in some cases the participants should be insured as well. It is usual practice to transfer the risk by asking participants to sign a waiver where they accept the risks. A waiver does not eliminate the leader's duty of care. It should be checked by a legal expert as incorrect wordings in waivers can cause more problems.

Medium risk

Medium-risk hazards should be avoided or their likelihood should be reduced. This can be done through warning signs, safety instructions, padding of protruding objects, etc.

Low risk and very low risk

Low-risk and very low risk hazards can be accepted as long as the leader is aware of their potential risk and has warned the participants.

Planning for potential injuries

Planning for potential injuries and producing a risk assessment for the activity is very time-consuming and many leaders neglect their responsibilities in this area, hoping that the facility has the correct documentation or that the risk will not become a reality.

Simple ways to reduce risks

Facilities

Activities don't always take place in a purpose-built sports hall. Many take place in church halls, community centres and school halls that have hazards such as glass windows, radiators and other protruding objects. The leader needs to ensure that the hazards are covered or padded, that the participants are aware of the risks and that the activities are appropriate to the space.

> **remember**
> When you plan an activity, check the emergency procedures, first-aid provision and emergency equipment at all the facilities you are going to use.

The weather can pose problems for outdoor activities. Blinding sun and intense heat are a danger in the summer. Wind, rain and freezing conditions cause problems in the winter. Appropriate clothing and skin protection should help to minimise the risks. Entrances and exits should be checked at all venues as they could be required during an emergency. If you make regular use of a facility, rehearse the safety procedures there.

Figure 12.12 Activities don't always happen in purpose-built halls

Playing surfaces

Sporting activities take place on a variety of surfaces such as grass, concrete, wood and synthetic pitches. A leader has to be aware of the potential risks, particularly on outdoor surfaces, as the weather can affect their condition. Participants' footwear should be appropriate for the surface and its condition as this will also affect the potential risk of injury. There are risks from litter, glass and animal excrement at many outdoor venues with open access, so assess these risks before you begin an activity.

Equipment

Not all participants and organisations can afford the latest equipment and have it maintained regularly, so check that the equipment is appropriate for the activity and in good condition. All substandard equipment should be reported to the appropriate person; do not leave it for others to use.

Participants

Each participant should be regarded as an individual who has their own requirements and their own potential to experience harm. If they have a specific health or medical requirement, it should be known through medical screening or a questionnaire. Their age, gender, ability level, experience and specific needs should be known before the activity begins, so the activity can meet their needs in a safe and appropriate manner. Failing to plan for these factors could cause a participant to suffer serious injury.

Leaders

In recent years there has been a significant increase in the number of claims due to no-win, no-fee litigation. Many national governing bodies (NGBs) have some form of insurance scheme that covers public liability or professional indemnity insurance. Sporting activities are also risky for the leader. Demonstrating skills that were once easy to do may prove to be more dangerous as the leader gets older or is not properly warmed up, for instance.

> **remember**
> It is not a legal requirement, but it is strongly recommended that leaders have some form of liability insurance to cover themselves from claims by the public.

Activities

Once the leader has planned for a safe and secure session, they need to plan the activities they are going to deliver based on the requirements of the participants. This may be a general sports coaching or fitness session or one that includes a number of modified practices to meet the needs of special populations, including children of different ages, females, the elderly and participants with disabilities. Some participants may also have cultural and religious needs and these needs should be considered by the leader when planning the session's activities, particularly with a mixed group.

Basic sports coaching

Here are a few simple guidelines for leading a general sports coaching session.

> **remember**
> A general sports coaching session follows this sequence: warm-up, skill warm-up, technique development, skill development, modified game and cooldown.

Warm-up

A thorough warm-up is generally considered essential before any physical activity. It may include some form of aerobic activity to raise the heart rate, increase blood flow, lubricate the joints and increase body temperature. There should also be some form of stretching although there is a debate about the type of stretching: static, dynamic or **proprioceptive neuromuscular facilitation (PNF)**. The preferred option for most sports is to do limb movements similar to those experienced in the sport. Sports such as gymnastics and swimming may also include static and PNF stretching.

Skill-related warm-up

A popular method used to warm up is to include elements of skill in the warm-up activity. This is done for a number of reasons, including revisiting a learned skill from the previous session, switching on neural impulses and thought processes ready for the session, making the warm-up more fun and enjoyable, and saving time for other developments during the session.

Figure 12.13 A thorough warm-up is essential

Technique development

Technique development is where the leader divides the group into subgroups and the coaching area into practice zones. Usually the leader will introduce the technique and explain it, perhaps accompanied by a clear demonstration. The participants then perform drills to practise the technique in isolation while the leader observes and analyses the performance and offers coaching tips for improvement. The leader needs to plan for progression that suits each participant's rate of learning.

Skill development

Although the words 'skill' and 'technique' are used interchangeably, skill development is where the leader takes techniques that have been practised and puts them into a sports-related context. The participants then select the correct technique for that context. For example, in the context of basketball shooting, should a participant use a jump shot or a lay-up shot? The leader plans for progression to ensure all participants are working at the correct level.

Modified game

Most participants prefer playing to practice, so the session normally includes some form of game. But instead of performing the full version of the sport, most sports allow for some form of adapted game. An effective leader plans a game that incorporates all participants as much as possible and that incorporates the techniques used during the session. The leader may introduce rules that reward participants for using a particular technique, such as a bonus point for performing lay-ups correctly during a basketball game.

Cooldown

Cooldown tends to be neglected, often because the modified game is so enjoyable that it goes on to the session's end, followed by a rush to collect or dismantle equipment and get changed. An effective leader allows enough time to cool down after a modified game. Activities gradually get slower in intensity and include some form of static stretching, which has a greater effect after exercise. Here are some other benefits:

- It prevents injuries and muscle soreness.
- It is an opportunity to check participants' understanding.
- It allows the leader to see if the session met its aims and objectives.
- It is a moment to tell participants about future sessions and matches.
- It allows time to collect and dismantle equipment.

Figure 12.14 Never neglect a cooldown because you've let a game overrun

Modified activities

A leader needs to know the characteristics of the participants and needs to treat them as individual learners. The general sports coaching session may need to be modified for children, females, elderly people and people with disabilities.

Children

The leader needs to understand children's physical and mental maturity and children's goals when they do sport and physical activity. The leader needs to be aware of how they influence the lives of children – a bad experience could put a child off sport for life and a good experience could initiate the career of a gold medallist.

Figure 12.15 Know your participants

Very young children

Very young children, aged 0–5 years, learn through play and rely on regular positive feedback to know that what they are doing is correct. Activities should be fun and simple, including lots of movement and objects with different colours, shapes and sizes.

Young children

Young children, aged 6–10 years, begin to develop their skills and become very competitive. Most sports have developed some form of mini version where the playing area and number of participants are reduced and the size of the equipment is in proportion to the child. The leader should incorporate these activities in their sessions and should also plan to keep activity time short, as young children have not yet developed their attention span and physical abilities.

Older children

Older children, aged 11–16 years, experience puberty. The leader should be aware of this when they plan activities. Consider matching children by physical maturity rather than age. Activities and equipment should still remain in proportion to the child. As children get older, it is possible to increase the duration, intensity and complexity of the activities.

Table 12.4 Adapted games for children

Sport	Problem	Solution	Equipment
Rugby	Physical contact, too many players, rules, position-specific	Tag rugby	Tags, small area, small balls
Cricket	Ball too hard, difficult to bowl accurately over large distance	Kwik cricket	Plastic stumps, small plastic bats, short run-up, rubber ball
Tennis	Net too high, game too fast, difficult to keep a rally going	Short tennis	Small net and court, plastic bats and sponge balls

Females

At 10 years or under, there is very little difference between the physical maturation of males and females. But during puberty, which happens earlier in females than in males, the differences in physical and mental maturity are much greater. Females tend to have more body fat, lower aerobic power and less strength than their male counterparts, so the leader must be aware of this when planning sessions, particularly with mixed groups. The leader should also be careful not to discriminate against participants based on their gender. The same principle of matching participants appropriately still applies, regardless of their gender. Nowadays, football, cricket and rugby are regularly played by females.

Elderly people

Many diseases and physical problems associated with ageing can be prevented through continuation of physical activity. Many older participants are taking up physical activity but are unable to perform like their younger selves. The leader needs to understand the ageing process and adapt activities to meet their capabilities.

- Longer warm-ups and cooldowns are required to avoid injury and aid recovery.
- Weight-bearing exercises are excellent for reducing and preventing osteoporosis.
- Core strength work is excellent for postural problems.
- Light weight training with large repetitions is excellent for muscular strength and endurance.
- Flexibility exercises are excellent for maintaining and improving the range of motion at the joints.
- Aerobic activities prevent heart disease and improve social and psychological well-being.

People with disabilities

The key to leading sessions for people with disabilities is to understand quickly what they can and can't do and adapt the activities to meet those needs. A deaf participant may need to be close to the leader to be able to lip-read instructions. A wheelchair participant may not be able to use their legs but may have outstanding hand–eye coordination. Several activities have been developed for people with disabilities, including **boccia**, bowls, crab football and wheelchair rugby and basketball.

Religious and cultural differences

Some participants may have other needs the leader should consider when planning the activities, including cultural differences and religious beliefs. To avoid accusations of discrimination, it is essential that the leader knows the participants' needs before planning an activity.

Fitness sessions

The leader has a responsibility to develop a participant's fitness to meet the demands of their sport. During the planning stage, they must incorporate activities that place physiological demands on the participant. These may include activities such as circuit training, weight training, continuous and interval training, depending on the physiological requirements of the sport. With special populations the activities could be adapted to improve fitness for health reasons. Activities for elderly participants might include water aerobics or chairobics.

Plan

Once the leader has planned for the activity to take place in a safe environment and considered the welfare of the participants, they can concentrate on the participants' needs. Each participant should be treated as an individual with their own specific needs. They will have personal goals they want to achieve from the activity and the leader has a responsibility to help them meet those goals using the available resources.

Know your participants

In order to plan a sports activity to meet the needs of the participants, the leader needs to know some key information about them.

Age

The leader needs to know the age of their participants. They also need to understand any differences in physical and mental maturity, especially in children going through puberty. Long-term athlete development (LTAD) can help with this. Further planning will be required for mixed age groups as many activities will have to be adapted.

See Unit 23 for more information on working with children in sport

Ability

Beginners will require a lot of demonstration, instruction and supervising whereas experienced participants will require activities that are challenging. A mixed-ability group poses the most problems; the leader has to plan activities at several levels of difficulty and still offer progression and differentiation.

Gender

Males and females develop at different rates. Small differences at a young age tend to widen significantly during puberty, so most physical education is taught in single-gender classes. Leaders need to be aware of the differences and plan appropriate activities. Be particularly sensitive in mixed-gender groups to avoid discrimination based on gender.

Numbers

Know the number of participants that are expected to turn up. Large numbers create problems, especially safety problems. The higher the numbers, the higher the chance of collisions in confined spaces and the harder it becomes for the leader to watch everyone and meet their specific needs. Have enough leaders per participant for safety and legal requirements. Plan activities so that all participants are included with minimal waiting time. Make sure there is enough equipment for the groups you have organised. Odd numbers of participants can pose problems. Have contingency plans in case the number of participants goes up or down and in case participants arrive late or leave before the end of the session.

Specific needs

Participants are individuals with their own specific needs. They may have medical requirements to consider when the activities are planned. Disabled participants may have access needs and may require the activities to be adapted. Some participants may have cultural issues and religious beliefs that need to be respected.

Medical consent

Before any activity can begin, the leader must have medical approval for participants with medical conditions. Medical decisions should be taken only by people with the appropriate medical qualifications. The leader's plans must ensure that qualified people are available to take these decisions when they are needed.

Plan early, plan thoroughly

A leader can only deal with situations if they plan their activities early and base their plans on accurate information about the participants. If this information is not available, the leader should be prepared to cancel the session unless they have contingency plans to deal with all eventualities.

Resources

An effective leader makes the best use of the available resources. Here are some examples.

Equipment

There needs to be enough equipment for the number of participants, either individually or in groups. Lack of equipment can lead to waiting time and reduce time on the activity. Equipment needs to be in good working order and appropriate for the age and ability of the participants, such as small tennis racquets and balls for junior players. If the equipment is stored at the venue, the leader will need access to it and the knowledge to assemble and dismantle it safely.

Time

Several factors determine the time spent on an activity. Effective leaders estimate the amount of time each activity will take and add some time to cover any delays. They plan for setting up and dismantling equipment, organising groups, demonstrating and explaining, doing the activity, extra teaching points, etc. They consider how long the participants can concentrate or how much physical activity they can endure. The youngest participants require the shortest participation time.

Environment

The leader is responsible for maintaining a safe environment for participants. During the planning stage, they check that the environment is appropriate for the planned activities. The size of the coaching space influences the activities that are planned. The environment may include natural surroundings such as hills, woodland and waterways. It could be a large space where the leader may lose contact with the participants or a small indoor space that could be unsafe for large groups. The leader needs to plan carefully so they can use the environment safely and effectively, but also allow the maximum number of participants to be involved at the same time.

Staff ratio

There are legal requirements for some sports and organisations to have a specific ratio of leaders to participants. For groups of children, this may include qualified leaders passed by the Criminal Records Bureau (CRB) and with knowledge of first aid. It is up to the leader to find out the legal requirements and plan for the appropriate number with the correct qualifications. Within the legal requirements, the leader should plan to have enough staff to give maximum benefit to the participants. Sports such as gymnastics require close supervision and may need a small ratio, whereas football can be coached with a larger ratio. Participants usually benefit from having more leaders per participant, regardless of the activity.

Transport

Sports leaders can no longer cram six children into their car and take them to sporting activities. Plan to ensure the smooth transportation of participants to sporting activities. If you share the use of a minibus, find out how to book it and make sure it will be available when you want it. Find out where the keys and fuel cards are kept, and know what to do if there is an accident.

> **remember**
>
> Before transporting a child, there is a legal requirement to seek permission from the child's parents. Insurance of persons and vehicles must be up to date, the condition of vehicles must be regularly maintained, seat belts must be worn and car seats must be used where appropriate.

Targets

Plan a target to achieve by the end of the session. Sessions without targets are harder to evaluate and then it becomes more difficult to plan future sessions. Targets can vary from participants completing a new skill to participants having fun and enjoyment. A target needs to be measurable rather than subjective.

Expected outcomes

The leader should have some idea of what they expect to achieve from the session. They should set targets and outcomes they want their participants to achieve and plan practices they want to get through. The key to good planning is to expect the unexpected, as no matter how well a session is planned, there will always be something that causes the plans to be changed. There might be problems with the facility, equipment and participants, or perhaps the expected outcomes are met and further outcomes need to be considered.

Legal requirements

An effective leader needs to be aware of their legal responsibilities and needs to address them during the planning phase. Here are the main areas of responsibility.

Health and safety

The leader is responsible for the health and safety of all the participants and colleagues during their sessions. A comprehensive risk assessment should be done before any activities take place, as the leader will be liable if an investigation determines that normal practices and procedures were not followed.

Child protection

A leader working with children has a responsibility to protect children from abuse and also needs to protect themselves from false accusations. The leader must ensure that they and all other leaders have a CRB check and that activities are suitably planned to avoid situations that could lead to child abuse or accusations of child abuse. All NGBs that receive funds from Sport England must have a child protection policy and a welfare officer to offer support and guidance.

Criminal Records Bureau
www.crb.gov.uk/

Insurance

A leader should have appropriate insurance that covers public liability and personal accidents. Insurance can be obtained privately or through NGB membership.

Sport England's Clubmark resource pack

www.sportengland.org/clubmark-resource-pack-nov04.pdf

Transport

The legal requirements for transporting participants require a large amount of planning. Organisations that transport athletes regularly should have a transport policy that the leader could use. The leader should avoid transporting participants using their own vehicle.

---

case study 12.8

Community centre

A sports activity leader has been asked to provide activities at a local community centre used by several groups. In the morning it has a group where parents and toddlers do physical activities together. During the afternoon a disability group do activities with a cooperative theme. In the early evening a youth group want some recreational activities. Later in the evening an elderly group want to do some fitness activities.

activity
INDIVIDUAL WORK

1. What do you need to consider so the activities will be safe for the different groups?
2. Suggest possible activities that each group could do.
3. What do you need to consider when planning the activities for the different groups?

---

activity
INDIVIDUAL WORK 12.4

P3

P4

1. Produce a risk assessment for one group at a community centre.
2. Plan how to lead a sports activity for one group at a community centre.

Leading sports activities effectively

Lead

Careful planning and preparation help a leader to deliver a safe and effective sports session. To do this, the leader must recognise that each of the participants is an individual with unique characteristics and use a variety of coaching methods and teaching techniques to provide the most beneficial learning experience for them.

Safe and secure environment

Much of the planning will enable the leader to establish an environment that is safe and secure for the participants. Risk management highlights the potential hazards then implements an action plan to eliminate, minimise or accept the risks. The activity, the facility and the equipment are checked and emergency procedures are established. Before beginning the activity, it is also good practice for the leader to check the participants for any special health and medical requirements, to explain the inherent dangers of the activity and to make them fully aware of their responsibilities to themselves and other participants.

Communication

An effective leader has to be an excellent communicator. They have to be able to communicate their thoughts and ideas in a way the participants can understand. This can be done through verbal communication but also through body language and emotional responses. Many leaders forget that communication is a two-way process and do not receive and interpret information from their participants very well. The leader should be aware of three aspects.

Sending and receiving messages

Not only does the leader have to send clear and understandable messages to their participants, they also have to listen to the participants' responses and check their understanding. One participant may interpret the message completely differently to another; this may confuse participants and frustrate the leader.

Non-verbal messages

Leaders have to be consistent with their messages. Verbal messages should be accompanied by a consistent non-verbal message such as a facial expression or a gesture. Do not confuse participants by giving inconsistent messages, such as a hostile gesture that accompanies words of encouragement.

Content and emotion

Make verbal messages relevant, simple and easily understood. Participants tend to hear only two or three key points. A complex explanation will be wasted. Pitch content at the right level for the participant. Use simple language for beginners and more complex language for experienced participants. Be aware of each participant's individual characteristics such as age and gender; do not patronise participants or cause offence.

Sporting activities, particularly competitive activities, can arouse high emotions. The leader has a responsibility to remain in control of their emotions when communicating messages, otherwise the content and purpose of the message may be lost with the emotion. An effective leader will develop their communication skills through experience.

Skills and techniques

Effective leaders use a variety of skills and techniques. Participants learn new skills in a variety of ways, including trial and error, watching others, listening to verbal instructions, mapping movements, or a combination of methods. The leader has a responsibility to recognise how each participant learns most effectively and to teach them in a way that suits their needs.

Group size

Controlling groups is much easier when large groups are split into smaller, more manageable subgroups. Effective leaders cover this in their planning if they know the group or if they want groups with specific characteristics such as age, gender or physical maturity.

There are several fun ways to establish groups of the same size, gender, age, etc. Group size may be determined by the space available or the number of activities planned. Effective group control can help a session go smoothly.

remember

Verbal and content messages are much easier to send and receive than non-verbal emotional messages that require years of experience to interpret and understand.

remember

If the groups are not known, it is not advisable to allow the participants to choose the groups, as this may lead to favouritism, discrimination and arguments.

Stopping the group

Sometimes the leader wants to stop the group and give out a message. A whistle or clear 'stop' command will stop the group, but this may not be enough to hold their full attention. The leader may have to take away the equipment or ask the participants to place it on the ground. They need to be ready with what they are going to say and keep it short and to the point.

Demonstrating to groups

To convey more information, the leader can work with a subgroup while the rest of the group continue to practise, then they can ask the subgroup to demonstrate what they have just been taught so the rest of the group can see. Another way is to stop the whole group and bring them closer to a particular demonstration. Effective leaders position themselves so that all participants can see and hear them. They use eye contact to engage all participants and they use questions to check the participants' understanding. It is a good idea to ask participants to sit down during a demonstration. It is pointless to make comments while participants are doing an activity. Stopping the group unnecessarily can frustrate participants and wastes valuable practice time.

Demonstration of skills and techniques

A technique is a particular movement pattern that can be performed in isolation; it should also be demonstrated in isolation. Examples are kicking a ball and shooting in basketball. The leader should use eye contact to make sure all participants can see and be seen, and where appropriate they should have the participants sitting in a semicircle. The demonstration should be done accurately and from different angles, so the participants can see it from different angles. A good demonstration requires no comment; any teaching points should be kept to a minimum, as too much information can confuse the participants. If the leader cannot demonstrate, they should ask an able participant to give the demonstration. If there is no one available, they can use video footage of an expert or invite an expert to give a live demonstration.

One skill is the ability to put a technique into context by selecting the appropriate technique for the situation. For example, it is a skill to be able to select a short pass or a long pass in football, a jump shot or a lay-up in basketball. Demonstrating a skill follows the same principles as demonstrating a technique but the demonstration should also emphasise the situation or context.

Coaching methods

Leaders will adopt a particular coaching style that reflects their beliefs, values and expectations. Coaching styles usually range from **participant-centred** to **leader-centred**. The style adopted by the leader will depend on several factors, including the group or participants, the leader's personality and philosophy, the activities and the environment.

Participant-centred

Participant-centred leaders offer guidance to the participants and allow the participants to share in decision making. They will usually empower the participants to explore solutions for themselves. This style is appropriate for a highly motivated group with specific goals.

Leader-centred

Leader-centred leaders take most of the decisions on behalf of the participants. They direct activities and keep close control over the participants' actions and behaviour. This style is usually adopted when working with beginners or large groups.

Use several styles

An effective leader rarely uses just one style. They adapt their style to meet the needs of the participants or the situation. Most leaders use a style that falls somewhere between participant-centred and leader-centred. Tannenbaum and Schmidt (1973) provided a model of leadership behaviour that followed this pattern.

Figure 12.16 Tannenbaum and Schmidt's model of leadership behaviour. Adapted from Sports Coach UK (2003)

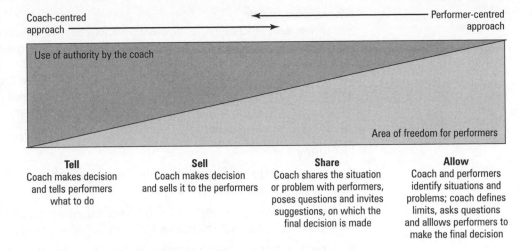

Tell	**Sell**	**Share**	**Allow**
Coach makes decision and tells performers what to do	Coach makes decision and sells it to the performers	Coach shares the situation or problem with performers, poses questions and invites suggestions, on which the final decision is made	Coach and performers identify situations and problems; coach defines limits, asks questions and alllows performers to make the final decision

A combination of telling, selling, sharing and allowing gives the leader a variety of styles to use:

■ Tell – the leader makes all the decisions and does not allow the participant to have any involvement in decision making. Participants are told what to do and how to do it.

■ Sell – the leader makes the decisions and shows the participants what to do, but invites questions and explains why the decisions were made.

■ Share – the leader outlines the problem and invites solutions from the participants. The decision is made based on the participants' suggestions.

■ Allow – the leader outlines the situation, defines the limits to the participants and allows them to explore the solutions themselves. The participants make the decisions and the leader provides a more supervisory role.

Teaching methods

A leader needs to recognise how participants learn. There are three main types of learner: kinaesthetic, visual and auditory. Each participant has a preferred method of learning and it is the responsibility of the leader to match their style and teaching methods to those preferences.

■ **Kinaesthetic learners** – learn best by practising actions and movements associated with the activity.

■ **Visual learners** – learn best by watching others performing skills and using videos of their performance.

■ **Auditory learners** – learn best by talking about the skill and listening to explanations.

An effective leader will provide good explanations and demonstrations, allow practice and provide feedback to enable all participants to learn using their preferred method. Good practice **empowers** participants to be responsible for their own learning. By reflecting on their own performances using feedback and video analysis, the participant can recognise their own errors and begin to understand the leader's instructions. There are several practice methods that can help participants to improve.

Whole practice

Ideally a skill should be taught as a whole so the participant can appreciate the complete movement and execution of a skill. A simple skill is usually practised using this method.

Part practice

When a skill is complex or has an element of danger, it is more appropriate to break it into smaller parts. The parts are taught separately then linked together.

Whole, part, whole

Sometimes part practice on its own is insufficient as it is difficult to see how the parts fit together. Then it makes sense to use the whole, part, whole method. First the participant attempts the whole skill and the leader identifies the parts they are not performing correctly. Leader and participant use part practice to improve the parts that were not performed correctly, then the participant repeats the whole skill and the leader checks for errors. The process is repeated until the participant performs the whole skill without errors.

Delivery

Having decided the type of practice, the leader must choose the method of delivery. There are four main methods:

- Variable – the skill is practised in different situations that the participant may experience during sports activities; it is useful when learning an open skill.

- Fixed – a specific skill is practised repeatedly in the same situation; it is useful when learning a closed skill.

- Massed – the skill is practised without a break until the skill is developed; it is only possible with highly motivated and experienced athletes practising a simple skill.

- Variable – the skill is practised with a series of breaks; it is used with poorly motivated participants or with complex skills that require a high degree of effort. It allows instruction between practices, so it is also useful for beginners.

Review

Effective leaders continually review their performance so they can improve their delivery for future sessions. Leaders receive feedback from participants and other leaders, they watch themselves on video and they use review sheets. Leaders are required to meet the needs of their participants and to help them improve their performances. Consequently, the leader reviews each participant's performance so they can measure the effectiveness of their leadership and plan the content of future sessions.

Figure 12.17 Review your performance by watching it on video

Participant performance

There are several ways to review a participant's performance, but first the leader needs to know the participant's starting point and the participant's goals. An initial assessment will establish the participant's starting point. An effective leader will have a record of each participant; it may cover the technical, tactical and physical attributes of the participant, but it may also include information about their psychological and social attributes.

Leader performance

Effective leaders review their own performance. Perhaps their methods, techniques and styles were inappropriate for the participants or only helped one or two in a group. Find out from participants whether their needs are being met and what aspects of delivery need to be changed. Checklists can be used to review the details of the coaching session and to plan improvements for future sessions.

case study 12.9 — Leader's performance

A leader has just completed a sports activity session and wants to review their own performance so they can plan future sessions.

activity — INDIVIDUAL WORK

1. What aspects of their own performance could the leader review?
2. What techniques could the leader use to review their own performance?
3. How would the leader plan effectively for future sessions?

activity — INDIVIDUAL WORK 12.5

P5 M3

Lead a selected sports activity with support then without support. Video the session so you can review it.

activity — INDIVIDUAL WORK 12.6

P6 M4

1. Using the video footage in Activity 12.4 and a review sheet, identify strengths in the participant's performance and areas that need improvement.
2. Take each area that needs improvement and produce an action plan for the participant's future development.

Formative and summative

A leader uses **formative assessment** to monitor their own performance and the performance of participants. It should be done at regular intervals to assess progress against previously set goals and to decide whether to change the goals or alter the programme. A leader uses **summative assessment** to compare final performances against previously set goals. It indicates whether the sessions have met the needs of the participants.

Feedback

Participants require a variety of feedback to help them improve. Information about a performance can help when reviewing and planning for the future.

Feedback from participants

Feedback from participants tells a leader about the success of their leadership. It might be about how they organised the practices, how effectively they did the teaching or how well they dealt with individual difficulties.

Feedback from a supervisor

Feedback from a supervisor could use comments or grading criteria. It may form the basis of an action plan for future sessions. This feedback is usually very formal and helps develop consistency among sports leaders.

Feedback from observers

Observers such as parents, officials and administrative staff may give verbal feedback after watching a sports session. Their honest opinion of the leader may be as valuable as the criteria on an assessment form.

Strengths and areas for improvement

The leader needs to identify the participants' strengths and areas for improvement. This can be done by comparing performances against previously set goals. Once a participant's strengths have been identified, the leader can plan a programme of activity to maintain the participant's progress. The leader can produce an **action plan** to help the participant develop areas that need improvement. The same goes for reviews of a leader's leadership performance.

Development

After receiving feedback on the sports session, the leader can plan for future development.

See page 114 in Unit 13 for more information on goal setting

See page 265 in Unit 23 for more information on needs

> **remember**
>
> Standing still will only elicit the same or worse results, so it is important the leader moves forward and takes the participants with them. Progress can only be made if strengths continue to advance and areas requiring improvement are developed.

---

case study 12.10   Participants' performance

A leader has just completed a sports activity session and wants to review the performance of their participants to plan future sessions.

activity
INDIVIDUAL WORK

1. What aspects of the participants' performance could the leader review?

2. What techniques could the leader use to review the participants' performance?

3. How would the leader plan effectively for future sessions?

Plan

Development plans are usually called action plans. They are a series of action points to improve areas that need improvement. Action plans, like targets, must be specific and must have a timescale. The phrase 'to do better' is not an action point. A good method is to decide what needs to done, who needs to do it and by when they need to have done it. The leader can then begin to plan resources such as facilities, equipment and transport.

Targets

Setting targets, or goals, helps the leader and participants to improve their performances. It helps them to focus their attention on specific elements of the activity and it helps to improve and prolong their efforts.

Goals can have indirect influence on **psychological states** such as confidence, motivation and anxiety. The leader and participant need to plan carefully so that all goals are agreed and the participant considers them achievable.

See page 151 in Unit 15 for some information on session review

The acronym **SMARTER** is often used to describe **goal setting**. Here is one version:

- **Specific** – use who, what, where, when, why. The phrase 'get fit' is too vague. Be specific: 'I will join a gym tomorrow and work out three times a week.'

- **Measurable** – goals need to measurable so it is clear when they have been reached: 'Run 2000 m in under 2 min.'

- **Achievable** – plan how the goal will be achieved. Most goals require resources such as equipment, finance and time. To run the London Marathon would take a large amount of training time and effort, which may not be possible for some people.

- **Realistic** – a goal that is too easy will demotivate the participant and may cause them to settle for lower standards. A goal that is too difficult may also demotivate the participant into believing they are useless. Reassess goals regularly to make them challenging and motivating.

- **Time-bound** – a goal needs a time limit to focus the participant's attention. Short-, medium- and long-term goals can maintain motivation and help monitor progress.

- **Exciting** – participants are highly motivated by goals that excite them. They can see the benefits of achieving the goal and how it will help them in the future.

- **Recorded** – participants and leaders should record their goals and keep the records so they are easily available. This helps everyone to focus on the goal and monitor progress.

SWOT

SWOT analysis is a powerful tool that can identify and maximise a participant's strengths, exploit opportunities, minimise weaknesses and reduce or eliminate any threats. Here is a summary of **SWOT analysis**:

- **Strengths** – the leader and participant analyse the participant's strengths so they can focus on what has gone well and highlight areas to keep in the programme when planning for the future.

- **Weaknesses** – the leader and participant plan a programme of activities that will improve any weaknesses, now known as areas for improvement.

- **Opportunities** – the leader and participant identify opportunities for development and improvement. They may be new pieces of equipment, a new practice venue or a new way to practise a skill.

■ **Threats** – threats can get in the way of a participant's goals, so the leader needs to minimise or eliminate them. Examples of threats are personal problems, psychological difficulties, financial circumstances and injuries.

case study 12.11 — Motivate a poor performer

One participant has been performing badly for several weeks. They have low self-confidence and lack motivation when training. They do not see any change in their performances in the near future and are contemplating giving up the sport.

activity
INDIVIDUAL WORK

1. How can the leader use goal setting to change the participant's state of mind?
2. How can the leader use SWOT analysis to change the participant's state of mind?

activity
INDIVIDUAL WORK 12.7

D2

P7

1. Justify each point in your action plan produced in Activity 12.6 to improve the participant's performance.
2. Using the video footage and a review sheet, identify strengths and areas that need improvement in your session planning and delivery.

activity
INDIVIDUAL WORK 12.8

M5

D3

1. Take each area of planning and delivery that needs improvement and produce an action plan for your future development.
2. Justify each point in your action plan to improve your own performance.

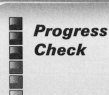

Progress Check

1. Identify four qualities, four characteristics and four roles common to effective sports leaders.

2. Identify four psychological factors that are important for people who lead sports activities.

3. Describe how an effective leader could increase the confidence of their participants.

4. How might extrinsic rewards affect the intrinsic motivation of participants?

5. What should a leader consider when they assess the risk of a hazard?

6. Describe four different leadership styles. Under what conditions are they most effective?

7. What should a leader consider when they plan an effective session?

8. What should a leader consider when they assess the effectiveness of a session?

9. What type of practice methods could be used to improve sports skills?

10. What are SMARTER goals?

Exercise, Health and Lifestyle

Helen Moors

This unit covers:

- The importance of lifestyle factors in health and well-being
- How to assess a person's lifestyle
- Advice on lifestyle improvement
- How to plan a health-related physical activity programme for a person

A healthy lifestyle is important for a good quality of life. People who take part in physical activity, eat a healthy diet, don't smoke, drink in moderation and manage their stress levels are likely to live longer and cope better with the daily demands of life. Lifestyle plays a key role in the prevention of many diseases, including coronary heart disease, cancer and obesity.

To achieve a **Pass** grade the evidence must show that the learner is able to:	To achieve a **Merit** grade the evidence must show that the learner is able to:	To achieve a **Distinction** grade the evidence must show that the learner is able to:
P1 describe lifestyle factors that have an effect on health Pg 77	**M1** explain the effects of identified lifestyle factors on health Pg 82, 98	
P2 design and use a lifestyle questionnaire to describe the strengths and areas for improvement of the lifestyle of a selected individual Pg 96	**M2** explain the strengths and areas for improvement for the lifestyle of a selected individual Pg 96	**D1** evaluate the lifestyle of a selected individual and prioritise areas for change Pg 96
P3 provide lifestyle improvement strategies for a selected individual Pg 96	**M3** explain recommendations made regarding lifestyle improvement strategies Pg 111	**D2** analyse a range of lifestyle improvement strategies Pg 111

grading criteria

To achieve a **Pass** grade the evidence must show that the learner is able to:	To achieve a **Merit** grade the evidence must show that the learner is able to:	To achieve a **Distinction** grade the evidence must show that the learner is able to:
P4 plan a safe and effective six-week health-related physical activity programme for a selected individual Pg 119		

The importance of lifestyle factors in the maintenance of health and well-being

Lifestyle factors

The notion of lifestyle is based on the idea that people generally follow identifiable patterns of behaviour in their day-to-day lives. People keep to a schedule in the hours they work and adopt a pattern in their approaches to diet and exercise. These behaviours are usually habitual and specific to each individual. The concept of a healthy lifestyle emerged when lifestyles began to be evaluated and some were deemed healthier than others.

The World Health Organisation (WHO) defines **health** as 'a state of complete physical, mental and social well-being and not merely the absence of disease or infirmity'. It defines **well-being** as 'a state of being healthy, happy and prosperous'. There is some overlap between the two terms; well-being more clearly adds the emotional concept of happiness and contentment. This unit considers how and why a person should choose to adopt a healthy lifestyle.

Although a person's lifestyle is behavioural, sociologists agree that it is influenced by a combination of choice, chance and resources. The factors that determine whether or not a person's lifestyle is healthy are heavily influenced by the choices they make about how much physical activity they do, how much alcohol they consume, whether or not they smoke, how much stress they are under, what foods they eat, and so on. Other factors, such as where a person lives and under what conditions, also have a serious impact on lifestyle but these socio-cultural factors are not studied in this unit.

activity
GROUP WORK 13.1

P1

Evaluate the mass-media messages related to personal practices and consumer decisions that influence whether a person adopts a healthy or unhealthy lifestyle.

---

i World Health Organisation
www.who.int

'Socioeconomic status, level of education, family and social networks, gender, age and interpersonal influences all affect the choice of lifestyle' (Ochieng 2006).

Physical activity

Liam Donaldson is the UK's chief medical officer. His report 'At least five a week', written in 2004, states:

> The message in this report is clear. The scientific evidence is compelling. Physical activity not only contributes to well-being, but is also essential for good health. ... Being active is no longer simply an option – it is essential if we are to live healthy and fulfilling lives into old age.

Despite this fact, government statistics for 2003 confirmed what many people had already begun to realise – there is a decline in the percentage of adults in England who meet the recommendations for physical activity.

At least five a week

www.dh.gov.uk/en/Publicationsandstatistics/Publications/PublicationsPolicyAnd Guidance/DH_4080994

Government statistics on physical activity levels

www.statistics.gov.uk

Figure 13.1 Percentage of adults in England that met the physical activity recommendations in 2003

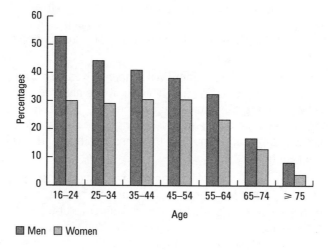

Ever since the beginning of the 1990s, increasing numbers of the population have driven to work or have been dropped off at school in cars rather than walked. From 1992 to 1994 some 61% of primary age children walked to school in contrast to 52% in 2002/3. Now over 70% of adults travel to work by car. According to Sport England, when the Framework for Sport in England was written in 2004, only 30.4% of the population met the government guidelines for physical activity levels. So what exactly are the guidelines to ensure a healthy lifestyle?

Framework for Sport in England

www.sportengland.org

For adults the recommendation is that they participate in at least 30 min of moderate-intensity physical activity (increasing your heart rate, feeling warm and slightly out of breath) at least 5 days a week. In some cases, to prevent weight gain, this guideline could be increased to 45 min. The activity need not be in one block but can be built up in 10 min sessions. For children the recommended guideline increases to a minimum of 60 min per day and twice per week the intensity should be increased so that sufficient stress is put on the skeletal system to ensure healthy bone growth.

Many government agencies are cooperating to implement a plethora of initiatives, all with the main goal of raising activity to within the guidelines, because the health benefits are considerable. According to 'At least five a week', the annual costs of physical inactivity in England are estimated at £10.7 billion in healthcare, and the government would like to cut this spending. There is now overwhelming scientific evidence to prove that people who take part in regular physical activity are less likely to die early and are far more likely to avoid suffering from the following conditions.

Coronary heart disease

Daily physical activity can help reduce the risk of heart disease as it strengthens the myocardium, or heart muscle; this helps to avoid **congestive heart failure**, which is caused by a weak heart muscle. It lowers blood pressure in people who are already hypertensive – have high blood pressure – and reduces the risk of developing high blood pressure. High blood pressure forces the heart to work harder and puts more strain on the heart muscle. Regular exercise lowers the **low-density lipoprotein (LDL)** levels in the blood, improving blood flow and reducing the risk of coronary artery disease and peripheral vascular disease. High cholesterol levels in the blood can cause fatty plaques to stick to the artery walls and narrow the diameter of the lumen. This condition reduces blood flow and is known as atherosclerosis. A total restriction of blood flow through a coronary artery can lead to a heart attack or **myocardial infarction**. A partial blockage, or ischemia, of the coronary artery will cause chest pain called angina. This pain is temporary but is a warning sign that the condition of the cardiovascular system is deteriorating.

Peripheral vascular disease

Peripheral vascular disease occurs in systemic arteries and veins. Atherosclerosis can occur in peripheral arteries and contributes to high blood pressure, or **hypertension**; regular physical activity helps to prevent the build-up of LDL. Regular changes in the volume of blood flow that occur during exercise help to maintain the elasticity of arterial walls and reduce the risk of developing arteriosclerosis. Arteriosclerosis is when the artery walls harden and become less elastic, reducing the size of the lumen and contributing to hypertension and congestive heart failure. Exercise helps to maintain venous return – blood flow back to the heart – so less strain is put on the valves of the veins. One factor that contributes to the development of varicose veins is pressure put on the valves when a person is standing.

Non-insulin-dependent diabetes

Non-insulin-dependent diabetes, or **type 2 diabetes**, develops when there is a problem with the response of the body to insulin. Insulin helps control the level of sugar in the blood. There is no clear evidence that an inactive lifestyle causes diabetes, but being obese does cause diabetes. Physical activity significantly helps to control type 2 diabetes because it helps transport glucose from the plasma into the cell.

remember

Coronary arteries are blood vessels that specifically supply oxygenated blood to the heart. Systemic arteries and veins are the network of blood vessels that transport blood round the body.

Figure 13.2 Atherosclerosis causes fatty plaques to narrow artery walls

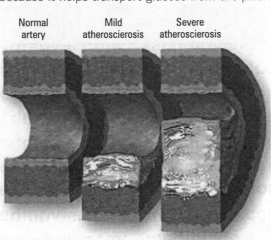

Normal artery   Mild atherosclerosis   Severe atherosclerosis

remember

A body mass index of over 30 kg/m^2 is considered obese. BMI is a person's weight in kilograms divided by the square of their height in metres.

Obesity

Obesity is caused by a prolonged period of consuming far more calories than you actually use. The unused calories are stored as fat in the adipose tissue of the body and essentially a person puts on weight. Physical activity increases the metabolic rate and therefore increases the number of calories used. Obesity is currently rising at an alarming rate and 1 in 6 children were obese in 2002. The incidence of childhood obesity grew from 9.6% in 1995 to 13.7% in 2003. In 2004 the UK government set a public service agreement (PSA) target to 'halt the year-on-year rise in obesity among children under 11 by 2010 in the context of a broader strategy to tackle obesity in the population as a whole'. As the **PSA** target suggests, all age groups show an increase in obesity rates. An active lifestyle makes it far easier to maintain a balance between calorie intake and calorie output and to avoid large fluctuations in body weight.

Government statistics on obesity

www.statistics.gov.uk

The Department of Health 2004 PSA obesity target

www.dh.gov.uk

Figure 13.3 Percentage of adults in England that are obese

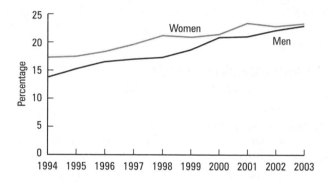

Osteoporosis

Osteoporosis is a skeletal disorder characterised by compromised bone strength that predisposes a person to an increased risk of fracture. Bone is the hardest connective tissue in the body, mainly because it contains deposits of calcium phosphate and calcium carbonate. Bone acts as a store for calcium, and exercise causes more calcium to be deposited, increasing bone density and therefore bone strength. The bone matrix also contains collagen. Collagen gives bone tissue a flexible strength, allowing it to cope with some impact. As people get older, their bone contains less collagen and is less dense; these brittle bones are damaged quite easily. Exercise can partly counteract this process. Growth is a good time to exercise as it will increase bone mineral density and will maximise peak bone mass. Continuing to follow an exercise programme will maintain bone mass and reduce age-related bone loss, reducing the risk of osteoporosis.

See page 100 for more information on physical activity guidelines

Exercise will also preserve muscle strength and postural stability, which can reduce the risk of lower-back problems and can also reduce the risk of falling and possible bone fractures in later life. Bone will become more dense and therefore stronger as more physical demands are placed on the tissue. Two types of exercise are important to bone health: weight-bearing activities and resistance exercises. Weight-bearing activities such as walking and running make your body work against gravity and your legs and feet carry the weight of your body. Resistance activities such as weight training make your muscles work against a weight or resistance to improve their strength.

Figure 13.4 Exercise increases bone mineral density and maximises peak bone mass

Stress

According to Richard S. Lazarus, a professor of psychology at the University of California, stress is a condition or feeling experienced when a person perceives that 'demands exceed the personal and social resources the individual is able to mobilize'. Stress can have a positive impact on a person's life but too much stress can lead to anxiety attacks, depression, a nervous breakdown or even a suicide attempt. In 2000 about 1 in 6 adults in Great Britain had a neurotic disorder.

Regular exercise can help to manage stress. Exercise improves fitness levels, making you stronger, more positive and more able to cope with the daily demands of life. It helps to relax tense muscles, and as you are more physically tired, you are more likely to get to sleep quicker. Exercise improves blood flow to the brain and causes the release of endorphins, which have a positive effect on a person's mood.

Figure 13.5 Weekly prevalence of neurotic disorders by gender GB (2000)

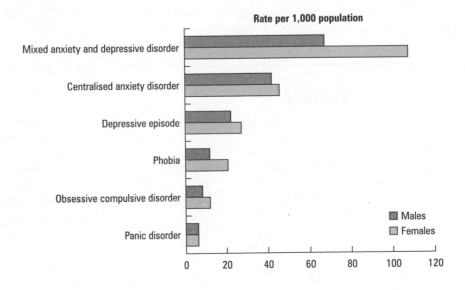

Government statistics on stress
www.statistics.gov.uk
Articles related to stress
www.mindtools.com
National organisation to support people with mental health problems
www.mind.org.uk
Mental health disorders, diagnosis and treatment
www.mentalhealth.com

case study 13.1 — Ben returns from university

Ben, a close friend, has just returned home after his first term at university and has called round to see you. You notice immediately that Ben has put on weight and seems a little down. During your conversation you learn that Ben feels a bit homesick as he lives in a one-bedroom flat away from the university campus and has yet to make friends with anyone in particular. Money is tight, so Ben is buying cheap, ready-cooked meals from a local supermarket. He doesn't really feel like cooking anything. You are surprised to hear that Ben has yet to join a football team, but he says that his course leaves him little free time and there are three important deadlines when he goes back next term. When you ask about his social life, Ben says he unwinds over a couple pints at the local pub three or four nights a week.

activity — INDIVIDUAL WORK

1. Consider Ben's lifestyle and identify all the areas of concern.
2. What health problems might Ben suffer if he doesn't alter his eating or exercise patterns?
3. Do you think that Ben has a drink problem?

activity — INDIVIDUAL WORK 13.2

M1

Interview a friend who has recently returned from university or working away from home. Ask them to describe their lifestyle. Using your knowledge of how lifestyle can affect health, explain to your friend what impact their current lifestyle is having on their health and well-being.

Alcohol

Moderate consumption of alcohol doesn't appear to have a detrimental effect on health and no harm is done if a person stays mostly within the recommended guidelines for responsible drinking. But the recent changes in licensing laws plus the culture of binge drinking are giving the UK a reputation as the most intoxicated country in Europe. Alcohol consumption is rising in the UK, whereas it is falling in other European countries such as France. The Royal College of Physicians has estimated that alcohol-related health problems cost the NHS £3 billion in 2001 and there are other costs for policing and responding to violence by drunken people. Three factors seem to interact to cause a drink-related problem: the consumption frequency and the volume of alcohol consumed; the personality and physiological make-up of the individual; the price, type and availability of the alcohol plus socio-cultural influences of the environment.

Figure 13.6 Drunken violence means a big bill for policing

Figure 13.7 Alcohol consumption per capita in UK adults over age 15

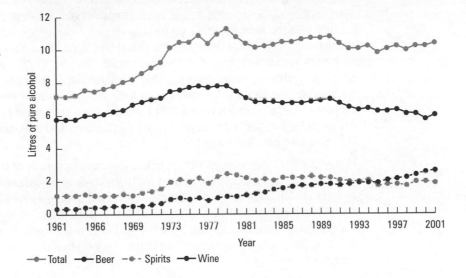

Men can drink up to 3–4 units per day without significant health risks. Women can drink up to 2–3 units per day as women tend to be smaller and have a lower blood volume. Figure 13.8 shows some common drinks and the number of units they contain.

When a person regularly drinks above the guidelines, they put their health at risk and may suffer from memory loss or have minor accidents. People who regularly drink to excess may suffer chronic health problems. Alcohol misuse can affect almost every part of the body.

Alcohol misuse

www.alcoholconcern.org

Alcohol contains calories but has no nutritional benefit, so excessive drinking can lead to malnutrition. Heavy drinkers tend to drink rather than eat; they often feel full and lose their appetite. After a heavy bout of drinking, a person is likely to be sick before they have properly digested their food. Drinkers spend more money on drink than on food, so any food they buy tends to have poor nutritional value. Malnutrition leaves the drinker very susceptible to infection, cirrhosis and some brain disorders.

Figure 13.8 Alcohol units in popular drinks

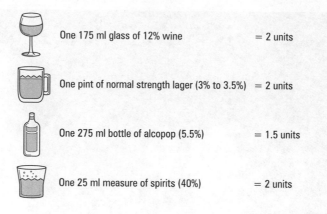

One 175 ml glass of 12% wine	= 2 units
One pint of normal strength lager (3% to 3.5%)	= 2 units
One 275 ml bottle of alcopop (5.5%)	= 1.5 units
One 25 ml measure of spirits (40%)	= 2 units

Alcohol is broken down in the liver. If the liver has to metabolise too much alcohol, its function may be impaired. There are three distinct stages in liver deterioration: fatty liver, alcoholic hepatitis and cirrhosis. Fatty liver is when liver function has started to decline but the drinker will not really suffer any recognisable symptoms. No permanent damage has occurred and if the drinker drastically cuts down their alcohol consumption, the liver function will be restored as liver tissue can regenerate itself.

Alcoholic hepatitis is inflammation of the liver caused by excessive alcohol consumption. Symptoms include sickness and acute abdominal pain. Healing of the liver results in normal liver tissue being replaced by scar tissue. If this process continues, it will lead to cirrhosis, a liver with so much scar tissue that it cannot do its job properly. A person with cirrhosis of the liver will appear jaundiced, lose weight, vomit blood and become anaemic. If they continue drinking, they will die from liver failure. George Best, regarded by many as the greatest footballer in history, suffered from alcohol-related health problems. Despite undergoing a liver transplant, he continued to drink: 'I spent a lot of my money on booze, birds and fast cars … the rest I just squandered.' George Best died on 25 November 2005 aged 59.

Heavy drinkers face a much higher risk of developing cancer of the mouth, pharynx or oesophagus, and it is quite common for them to develop cancer of the liver, stomach and colon. Although some practitioners advocate a small glass of red wine because, they say, it has a positive effect on the circulatory system, most heavy drinkers suffer from hypertension. A person suffering from high blood pressure is far more likely to develop heart disease or suffer a stroke, and binge drinking in particular has been linked to hypertension.

See page 137 in Unit 15 for more information on coronary heart disease

A common side effect of feeling a bit tipsy is to be quite happy and giggly. Yet heavy drinkers can suffer from severe depression and mood swings. Research has found that there is a significant drop in the blood's **serotonin** levels about 45 min after drinking alcohol. Serotonin is sometimes called the 'happiness molecule' and sustained low levels of serotonin can cause clinical depression and anxiety disorders. If all this doesn't make you think twice about keeping within the recommended guidelines for alcohol consumption, it is also possible to suffer from blackouts, insomnia, premature ageing, inflammation of the pancreas, reduced fertility, gout, epilepsy, the list goes on. Cheers.

Serotonin and its effects on the body

www.pubmed.gov

remember

Mild depression can sometimes be managed without prescription drugs. The most effective way of raising serotonin levels is with vigorous exercise. Studies have shown that serotonin levels increase when activity levels increase and the production of serotonin continues to rise for some days after the activity.

Smoking

Here is what the WHO says about tobacco:

> Tobacco is the second major cause of death in the world. It is currently responsible for the death of one in ten adults worldwide. If current smoking patterns continue, it will cause 10 million deaths each year by 2020.

About 25% of UK adults smoked in 2004. The number dropped significantly from the 1970s to the 1990s and has levelled out at about 25%. But despite tough anti-smoking legislation, the number of younger people that smoke is on the increase, which is a concern to health officials. To combat this, the UK government made it illegal to sell tobacco products to people under 18 years old. The legislation took effect on 1 October 2007.

People smoke because of the effects of nicotine, a chemical found in the tobacco plant. Nicotine helps people to relax and has positive psychological effects but it is also extremely addictive. According to the NHS Smoking Helpline, 'The rush you feel when you smoke is not pleasure, but simply the relief of satisfying a craving for nicotine.'

NHS Smoking Helpline
www.gosmokefree.co.uk

Figure 13.9 Tobacco is the world's second major cause of death

Figure 13.10 Percentage of adults in Great Britain who smoked cigarettes in 2004

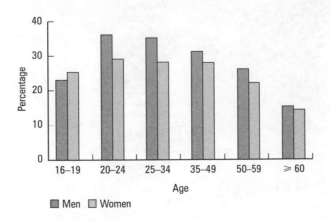

If a person tries to stop smoking, they suffer all the classic withdrawal symptoms. Besides their addictive properties, cigarettes also contain over 400 toxic substances, and the heat in a lit cigarette breaks down the tobacco and produces toxins. Here are the three that cause the most harm:

- Tar is carcinogenic; it causes cancer.

- Nicotine is addictive and increases cholesterol levels in the body.

- Carbon monoxide reduces the oxygen-carrying capacity of red blood cells.

Smoking contributes to several forms of cardiovascular disease. It leads to higher levels of cholesterol, which increases a person's risk of developing atherosclerosis.

See page 137 in Unit 15 for more information on coronary heart disease

Arteriosclerosis is another side effect of smoking; the walls of the arteries harden and become less elastic, which leads to hypertension. Diseased arteries can contribute to other conditions. A coronary thrombosis is a blood clot in one of the arteries supplying the heart. If the clot is large enough, it will produce a heart attack. In a controversial move, some **primary care trusts (PCTs)** are refusing to operate on patients who smoke. They say that a bypass operation is unlikely to be effective if the patient continues to smoke. A cerebral thrombosis is a blood clot in an artery supplying the brain. A severe cerebral thrombosis will cause a stroke. A thrombosis in an artery supplying the legs can cause gangrene. In severe cases the limb may have to be amputated.

As smoke is directly inhaled into the lungs, smokers can suffer from several respiratory diseases. The respiratory airways are lined with tiny hairs called cilia. Cilia help to filter out dust and other particles so the air is clean before it enters the lungs. The chemicals in tobacco smoke damage the cilia so they cannot clean the airways effectively. This leads to a build-up of mucus and can eventually cause damage and disease as the mucus becomes infected. People often refer to smoker's cough, but sometimes the cough deteriorates into chronic bronchitis.

Emphysema is another serious lung disease caused by smoking. It produces a loss of elasticity in the walls of the alveoli. Alveoli are the sites where oxygen diffuses from the lungs into the capillaries and carbon dioxide diffuses from the capillaries into the lungs. As the disease progresses, the walls of the alveoli collapse and this reduces the surface area available for gas diffusion. This means less oxygen enters the bloodstream and carbon dioxide is not removed as effectively. Breathing becomes very laboured as the body struggles to inhale sufficient oxygen to complete simple, everyday tasks. Unfortunately, the damage to the lungs is irreversible.

Cigarette tar is a carcinogen and there is a direct link between smokers and people who develop cancer. The cancer typically develops in the mouth, throat or lungs – it follows the passage of smoke through the body. Lung cancer is a very rare disease among non-

remember

How much damage you do to your body depends on how long you have been smoking, how many cigarettes you have per day, how hard you inhale, and whether your cigarettes are tipped. On average, each cigarette shortens your life by about 11 min.

Figure 13.11 Emphysema produces a loss of elasticity in the walls of the alveoli

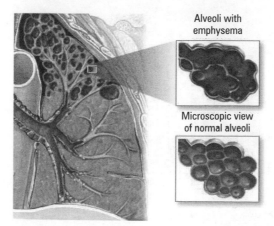

smokers. That is why some people object so strongly when they are subjected to passive smoking – involuntary inhalation of smoke by a non-smoker. Passive smoking increases a person's risk of developing cancer.

In February 2006 representatives of 110 countries met in Geneva for the WHO Framework Convention on Tobacco, where many countries agreed to take measures to reduce tobacco use. The UK government had already set a PSA target in 2004 'to reduce adult smoking rates to 21% or less by 2010, with a reduction in prevalence among routine and manual groups to 26% or less'. Since then it has banned smoking in enclosed public spaces in England from 1 July 2007. The definition of enclosed public space includes offices, factories, pubs and restaurants. Patricia Hewitt, the health secretary at the time, said: 'The scientific and medical evidence is clear – second-hand smoke kills.' Is someone smoking near you?

Government statistics on smoking

www.statistics.gov.uk

World statistics on smoking

www.who.int

The effects of smoking

www.gosmokefree.co.uk

Net Doctor

www.netdoctor.co.uk

A breakdown of the toxins in cigarettes

www.dh.gov.uk

World Health Organisation

www.who.int

case study 13.2

Passive smoking

Action on Smoking and Health (ASH) is a public health charity that campaigns to achieve a sharp reduction and eventual elimination of the health problems caused by tobacco. It has gathered information on how passive smoking affects the health of non-smokers. Here are two examples taken from the ASH website:

- Soprano – When I began to study opera I gave up going out almost completely as smoky atmospheres can result in you being unable to sing for up to a week – so I really didn't have a choice.

- Gaming inspector at a casino – The doctors said I had developed asthma due to exposure to second-hand smoke and the only place I was exposed to this high level of smoke was at work.

Action on Smoking and Health

www.ash.org.uk

activity
INDIVIDUAL WORK

1. How has inhalation of tobacco smoke led to the conditions of the soprano and the casino worker?

2. Which argument would you present to a smoker to help persuade them not to smoke around non-smokers?

3. Do you agree with the UK government's legislation to prohibit smoking in public places, which took effect in England on 1 July 2007? Give reasons to support your answer.

Stress

Every person needs some stress to live a productive and healthy life. But when a person is overstressed they no longer think they can cope with the demands on them at that period in their lives. Most people don't like to admit to feeling stressed as they think it is a sign of weakness and an inability to do things properly. The human body can respond to stress in different ways:

■ **Physiological response** – examples are increased heart rate, higher blood pressure and headaches.

■ **Psychological response** – examples are an inability to concentrate, memory loss and feeling confused.

■ **Behavioural response** – examples are changes to appetite, restlessness and increased smoking or drinking.

■ **Emotional response** – examples are impatience, tearfulness and angry outbursts.

See page 130 in Unit 15 for more information on physical activity as part of a healthy lifestyle

Hans Selye studied how the body responds to stress and he found that the body went through three distinct phases. In 1936 he referred to these stages as the general adaptation syndrome:

■ **Alarm** – known as the fight or flight response, it prepares the body for action against a perceived threat or stressful situation. The hormone adrenaline is released into the bloodstream and increases heart rate and breathing rate. This stage can temporarily lower the body's immune system.

■ **Adaptation** – if the source of stress remains, the body tries to protect itself and cope with the long-term situation. This is demanding and drains the body. If the body does not get opportunities to relax and recuperate, the individual will feel very tired, lethargic and irritable.

■ **Exhaustion** – in chronic situations the person reaches mental and physical exhaustion and can become very ill as their immune system collapses.

The two main mental health problems related to stress are anxiety and depression. Anxiety is a feeling of unease which people experience in stressful situations. Anxiety is not necessarily a problem unless it is very prolonged and interferes with everyday activities. For example, post-traumatic stress disorder may be suffered after a car crash where, among other issues, the person continues to feel extreme anxiety about car travel. Depression is a persistent feeling of unhappiness that leaves a person in a constant low mood. The person feels totally unable to cope with the perceived demands that they face. Symptoms include a loss of self-confidence, not wanting to socialise, feeling irritable, no energy, inability to make decisions and loss of sleep. They can feel worthless to the point that some consider suicide.

Stress can contribute to cardiovascular disease. Frequent stress results in higher levels of LDL in the blood, which can cause atherosclerosis. Increased blood pressure also contributes to the risk of angina, a heart attack or stroke. Stress makes any immune-related conditions worse. During stressful conditions the adrenal glands secrete cortisol. In a fight or flight response, cortisol has positive effects on the body, but increased levels of cortisol during prolonged periods of stress suppress the body's immune response, making a person more susceptible to colds and flu. High levels of cortisol have also been linked with hypertension. Stressful conditions reduce the blood supply to the stomach. This can then interfere with the digestive process. Prolonged stress can contribute to the development of stomach ulcers and will exacerbate existing problems such as irritable bowel syndrome.

Mental health disorders, diagnosis and treatment
www.mentalhealth.org.uk
Stress linked to hypertension
www.bupa.co.uk

Table 13.1 External sources of stress

Work-related stressors	Personal stressors
Chasing promotion	Death of a relative or friend
Conditions such as heat, overcrowding, noise	Divorce
Change of work patterns	Injury or illness
Threat of redundancy, uncertainty	Marriage
Conflict with other employees	Looking after children or relatives
Responsibility	Pregnancy
Overwork	Change in finances
Underwork	Mortgage or loan repayments
Temporary contract	Moving house
Unrealistic targets	Christmas
Change in job	Holidays
	Retirement

Diet

There are several reasons to maintain a healthy diet. A healthy diet provides the body with the nutrients it needs to work efficiently and effectively. It can help to manage some health problems such as diabetes and can reduce the risk of developing conditions such as cardiovascular disease and cancer. The right foods can provide more energy and vitality for life while maintaining a healthy body weight. Food is usually central to entertaining friends and family, it can be very enjoyable and may produce a feel-good factor.

We need to eat to obtain enough energy to complete our daily tasks; we have to keep pace with our body's metabolism – the sum of all the chemical reactions that take place in the body. The basal metabolic rate (BMR) measures the amount of energy we would use if we remained at rest. Our daily intake of food has to cover the BMR plus any additional energy for other activities such as a 20 min walk to work or a 45 min game of squash, as well as the more functional activities of the body such as digestion and excretion.

Men can usually consume 2500–3000 kcal per day and women 2000–2200 kcal per day without putting on weight. If you are particularly active or have a physically demanding job, you will probably need to eat 4000–6000 kcal per day, depending on body size, age and gender. By eating the same amount of energy as you use, you will maintain a constant body weight. Metabolic rates vary from person to person, and your metabolic rate slows down as you get older, so when you're 40, don't expect to eat what you eat now without putting on weight.

Body weight is considered in terms of body fat and fat-free weight or lean body mass. The body fat is the amount of fat stored in the adipose tissue, and the lean body mass is the weight of the rest of the body. Men carry an average of 12–15% of their body weight as fat, whereas women carry about 20%. To lose weight, we need to lose some of our fat stores. We can do that by going on a low-calorie diet and by increasing our physical activity.

A balanced diet contains approximately 15–20% protein, 30% fat and 50–55% carbohydrate. You also need to have enough vitamins and minerals, fibre and water in your diet. Here are some guideline daily amounts:

- Energy ~2000 kcal
- Protein 45 g
- Carbohydrate 230 g
- Total sugars 90 g
- Fat 70 g, of which 20 g saturated fats
- Fibre 24 g
- Salt 6 g.

What should you actually eat to achieve this balance? Think in terms of grams consumed, and most food labelling now provides this information. If you want to work out how much fat, carbohydrate, protein or alcohol contributes to the total calorific value of a food, then use these multipliers:

- 1 g of fat = 9 kcal
- 1 g of carbohydrate = 4 kcal
- 1 g of protein = 4 kcal
- 1 g of alcohol = 7 kcal.

The food groups that you should eat regularly are shown at the bottom of the food pyramid in Figure 13.12. The foods you should eat just occasionally as a treat are at the top of the pyramid. Here is a balanced diet for one day:

- Eat 6–11 portions of bread, rice, pasta, potatoes or cereal, preferably wholegrain. Wholegrain foods are made with the entire seed of the plant such as grains of wheat, corn, rice, oats and barley. Refining the grain means you lose 25% of the protein. Wholegrain food retains all its roughage, its vitamins (B and E) and its minerals (magnesium and iron).
- Eat at least 2–4 portions of fruit and 3–5 portions of vegetables per day. This will ensure that the body receives the essential minerals, vitamins and antioxidants.
- Eat 2–3 servings of dairy products and 2–3 servings of meat or fish. This will provide the protein so the body can synthesise all the amino acids required by the body. Protein provides the structure for all living things; they are responsible for growth and repair.
- Avoid foods high in saturated fat, sugar and salt. So only occasionally eat foods such as chocolate, crisps and cakes.
- Drink 6–8 glasses of water per day to avoid becoming dehydrated.

The British Heart Foundation has lots of advice on what to eat to ensure a healthy heart. A balanced diet can:

- help to keep cholesterol levels low;
- help to reduce the risk of hypertension;
- help to reduce the risk of a stroke;
- help to reduce the risk of vascular disease (atherosclerosis and arteriosclerosis).

Figure 13.12 Food pyramid: eat more foods from the bottom, fewer from the top

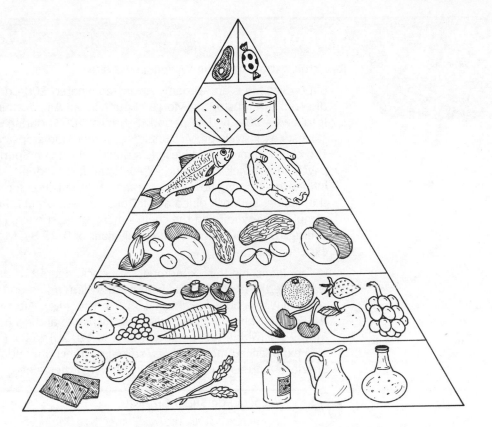

 Benefits of a healthy diet
www.food.gov.uk
Benefits of wholegrain foods in the diet
www.wholegrainscouncil.org
Dietary guidelines to reduce the risk of coronary heart disease
www.bhf.org.uk
Cholesterol and its contribution to coronary heart disease
www.patient.co.uk

If you maintain a healthy body weight, you avoid putting strain on your heart through obesity. Avoid some foods to reduce the risk of heart disease. Eat some fat, but limit saturated fats and foods high in cholesterol as they contribute to atherosclerosis. Saturated fats are found in animal products such as beef, lamb, pork, butter, eggs, cream and cheese. Most processed foods are high in saturated fats and also trans fats, which are used to help prolong the shelf life of products and are known to be linked with coronary heart disease. A high salt intake will increase the risk of high blood pressure. There is a lot of salt in the food we eat without adding salt on the plate. Processed foods contain high levels of salt and one meal can contain more salt than the recommended maximum for a day (6 g). Avoid putting salt on the table and try not to add salt during the cooking process.

Eating lots of fruit and vegetables will help to prevent the build-up of fatty plaque on the walls of coronary arteries. Oily fish such as mackerel, salmon and sardines contains omega-3 fatty acids, which help to prevent the formation of blood clots. Wholegrain foods in the diet will help reduce the risk of heart disease, strokes and type 2 diabetes. More research has recently investigated whether diet affects brain function. Some foods have been identified that provide the ingredients to make various neurotransmitters that generally improve brain function.

case study 13.3

Super Size Me

Read this extract from the Wikipedia website.

Super Size Me is an Academy Award-nominated 2004 documentary film, directed by and starring Morgan Spurlock, an American independent filmmaker. It follows a 30-day time period (February 2003) during which Spurlock subsists exclusively on McDonald's fast food and stops exercising regularly. The film documents this lifestyle's drastic effects on Spurlock's physical and psychological well-being and explores the fast food industry's corporate influence, including how it encourages poor nutrition for its own profit. During the filming, Spurlock dined at McDonald's restaurants three times per day, sampling every item on the chain's menu at least once. He consumed an average of 5,000 calories (the equivalent of 9.26 Big Macs) per day during the experiment. …

Before launching this experiment, Spurlock, age 32 at the time the movie was filmed in 2003, … was healthy and slim, and stood 6 feet 2 inches (188 cm) tall with a body weight of 185.5 lb (84.1 kg). After thirty days, he gained 24.5 lb (11.1 kg), a 13% body mass increase, and his Body Mass Index rose from 23.2 (within the 'healthy' range of 19–25) to 27 ('overweight'). He also experienced mood swings, sexual dysfunction, and liver damage. It took Spurlock fourteen months to lose the weight he gained.

Wikipedia on Super Size Me
http://en.wikipedia.org/wiki/Super_Size_Me

Figure 13.13 'Goes down easy and takes a while to digest,' said A. O. Scott in the *New York Times*

activity
INDIVIDUAL WORK

1. Do you think that fast-food chains have a moral responsibility to limit the amount of salt and saturated fats contained in the food they sell?

2. Do you think that fast-food chains encourage people to adopt unhealthy eating habits?

3. Do fast-food chains provide enough nutritional information about the food they sell so that consumers can make an informed decision about which food to buy?

4. Do you know roughly how many calories are contained in a Big Mac meal?

Treat the brain to the food it likes best:

- **Serotonin** – eat pasta, potatoes, cereals and bread.
- **Omega-3 fatty acids** – eat oily fish like tuna.
- **Choline** – eat egg yolks.

Choline helps to improve your memory. Other foods that improve brain function are liver, meat, fish, milk, cheese and vegetables, especially broccoli, cabbage and cauliflower. If you eat 3–4 oz (85–113 g) of protein, you will feel more alert.

In the western world it isn't lack of food that causes nutritional illnesses, but poor life choices. People are becoming obese by overeating and developing disorders such as diabetes. Even people within weight guidelines digest too much saturated fat, leading to cardiovascular disease and some cancers. Over-reliance on processed foods can lead to a lack of some vitamins, which lowers the body's immune system. It can also make us deficient in some minerals; a lack of calcium can contribute to osteoporosis.

By following basic dietary guidelines, the food that you eat will contribute significantly to a healthy lifestyle. In 2006 the UK government asked PCTs in England to weigh and calculate the BMI of primary age children. The parents of children identified as having a weight-related health problem are contacted by the PCT and supplied with dietary guidelines.

Assessing the lifestyle of a selected individual

A person's daily routine and habits combine to determine their overall lifestyle. Most people in the UK can take some decisions and choices and are largely in control of their lifestyle. Regrettably, the evidence suggests that as a nation we are not making the best judgements about what to do and what not to do. Most people who smoke know that it is not good for their health. A couch potato knows they should do more exercise. Unfortunately, it is only when something finally goes wrong that people try to adopt a healthier lifestyle.

Link See page 130 in Unit 15 for more information on benefits

As the government counts the cost of an increasingly unhealthy population, it has introduced initiatives and strategies to make people adopt healthier lifestyles. Increasing numbers of well-being clinics, help lines and advertisements and increasing amounts of literature put over the benefits of a healthy lifestyle. The first step is to get people to acknowledge that they need to change and to evaluate their current situation.

Lifestyle questionnaire

It is extremely easy to get copies of a lifestyle questionnaire but it is useful to consult your general practitioner (GP) or use a reputable website; the BUPA site offers advice on what you should be doing. When a person joins a gym, they are usually asked to complete a lifestyle questionnaire and have their heart rate and blood pressure measured. The advice they receive will depend on their age, sex, weight, past medical history, etc. Always go to a doctor for medical advice. Most questionnaires will ask questions in the following categories:

- Personal details
- Medical history
- Current health status
- Lifestyle
- Well-being

Lifestyle covers how much a person drinks, smokes, exercises and their eating habits. Well-being covers sleep patterns, emotional state, stress level and self-confidence.

Lifestyle questionnaires
www.bupa.co.uk

case study 13.4

Lifestyle questionnaire

Table 13.2 is an abridged version of a typical lifestyle questionnaire. It has been completed by Dave, a male lorry driver aged 39.

Table 13.2 Dave's lifestyle questionnaire

Personal details

What is your age? 39
What is your sex?   Male ■   Female ☐
What is your height in metres? 1.78   What is your weight in kg? 95
What job do you do? Lorry driver

Medical history

Please tick the relevant box if you have ever suffered from any of the following conditions or illnesses?

High cholesterol	■	Diabetes	☐
High blood pressure	■	Stomach ulcer	☐
Angina	☐	Lower-back pain	■
Heart attack	☐	Joint pain	☐
Bronchitis	☐	Anxiety attacks	☐
Emphysema	☐	Depression	☐
Asthma	☐	Migraine	☐

Have you undergone any operations in the last 12 months? ☐
Have either of your parents suffered from CHD? ■
Have either of your parents suffered from cancer? ☐

Current health status

Please tick the relevant box

	Low	Normal	High	Don't know
Is your blood pressure	☐	☐	■	☐
Is your cholesterol	☐	☐	■	☐

Alcohol

Please tick the relevant box
How many units of alcohol do you drink in an average week?
None   1–5 ☐   6–10 ☐   11–15 ☐   16–20 ☐   21–25 ☐   25–40 ■   41+ ☐
How many units do you drink per night when you go out socially?
None   1–5 ☐   6–10 ☐   11–15 ■   16–20 ☐   21–25 ☐   26+ ☐

Smoking

Please tick the relevant box
Never smoked ☐   Have stopped smoking ☐   Currently smoke ■
If you smoke, how many cigarettes do you have in a day?
1–5 ☐   6–10 ■   11–20 ☐   21–30 ☐   31–40 ☐   41+

Physical activity

Please tick the relevant box
How many times do you exercise per week (minimum of 15 min continuous) e.g. walking, cycling, swimming?
0 ☐   1 ■   2 ☐   3 ☐   4 ☐   5 or more ☐
Are you a member of a gym? ■
Are you a member of a sports club? ☐
What type of exercise do you take part in? Swim

Dietary habits

Please tick the relevant box
How often do you eat the following?

	Every day	2/3 per week	Occasionally
Fried food	☐	■	☐
Processed ready-made food	■	☐	☐
Sweets, chocolate, crisps	■	☐	☐
Three or more portions of fruit	☐	■	☐
Three or more portions of veg	☐	■	☐
Fish	☐	☐	■
Dairy products, milk, cheese, eggs	■	☐	☐
Bread, cereal, rice, potato or pasta	■	☐	☐
Do you add salt to your food while cooking?	☐		
Do you add salt to your food on the table?	■		

Well-being

Please tick the relevant box

Do you feel reasonably happy at the moment?	■
Do you have any family problems?	☐
Do you have a good relationship with your immediate family?	■
Do you see friends regularly?	■
Do you sleep well?	■
Do you have any financial worries?	☐
Do you feel stressed at work?	☐
Do you regularly work overtime?	■
Are you doing any home improvements?	■
Do you feel you can cope with the demands made on you?	■
Do you get time to yourself to relax?	☐

activity
INDIVIDUAL WORK

1. Calculate Dave's BMI.
2. Identify the aspects of Dave's lifestyle that will increase the risk of Dave developing cardiovascular disease.
3. Identify three changes that Dave could make to his lifestyle that would reduce his risk of developing cardiovascular disease.
4. Suggest how Dave's job might have an influence on his lifestyle and health.

remember
Although BMI is used to provide guidelines on a healthy weight, NHS Direct says it is general advice for adults only. It does not apply to children. It does not apply to pregnant women or breastfeeding women. Your BMI may not be accurate if you are a weight trainer or an athlete, if you are over age 60 or if you have a long-term health condition.

NHS Direct
www.nhsdirect.nhs.uk

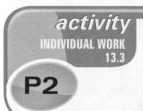

activity
INDIVIDUAL WORK
13.3

P2

Design a lifestyle questionnaire that is suitable for members of your class. Consider the age and likely activities that members of your class may take part in. Ask a friend to complete the questionnaire for you. Go through the results with your friend to identify and describe their lifestyle strengths and their lifestyle aspects that need improvement.

activity
INDIVIDUAL WORK
13.4

M2

Read through the answers your friend gave in Activity 13.3. Note the good and bad points about their lifestyle and calculate their BMI. Write a report for your friend that explains their lifestyle strengths and their lifestyle aspects that give cause for concern.

activity
GROUP WORK
13.5

D1

P3

1. Evaluate your friend's lifestyle, discuss how concerned about it they should be, and discuss what they need to change so they will be able to lead a healthy, active life.

2. Just before they go back to university, what lifestyle advice might you give your friend to help improve their health and well-being?

Consultation

People that complete lifestyle questionnaires are often tempted to put in the desirable answer or to distort the truth slightly. This is usually because they are embarrassed or feel guilty about how much they drink or smoke, or about how little exercise they do. Be sensitive to a person's feelings during a consultation. Hold the consultation in private, observe strict confidentiality and tell the person that all their information is confidential. Explain to the person that they should be as truthful as possible so they can receive the best plan to suit their personal needs.

GPs will quite often question patients, and because they are seen as knowledgeable and trustworthy, people feel more confident to tell them personal information. GPs are also highly skilled in communication and know exactly the right questions to ask. They listen carefully to a patient's responses and can pick up non-verbal cues to get a fuller picture of the patient's lifestyle. Sometimes GPs will put lifestyle information and medical details on an exercise referral form that entitles the patient to do an exercise programme at a local gym assigned to the practice.

case study 13.5

Exercise referral form

Table 13.3 is an example of an exercise referral form for a patient with coronary heart disease. Note that **COAD** is chronic obstructive airways disease, such as bronchitis, and **CVA** is cerebrovascular accident, commonly known as a stroke. Also, **claudication** is pain in the thigh or calf after you have been walking for a while.

Table 13.3 An exercise referral form for someone with coronary heart disease

EXERCISE REFERRAL FORM			
Patient details		Name of GP	
Name		Name of practice	
Address		Address	
Telephone			
DOB			
Cardiac history			
Angioplasty	☐		
Stent	☐		
Angina	☐		
Rest ☐ On exertion ☐			
Arrhythmias	☐		
Current medication			
Aspirin	☐	Warfarin	☐
Anti-arrhythmic	☐	ACE inhibitor	☐
Beta blocker	☐	Diuretic	☐
Other	☐		
Current status: risks associated with CHD			
Resting blood pressure	☐	Physically inactive	☐
Resting heart rate	☐	Smoker	☐
Body mass index	☐	Excess alcohol	☐
Stable type 1 or type 2 diabetes	☐	Stress	☐
Past medical history			
COAD or asthma	☐	Hypertension	☐
CVA or neuro problems	☐	Claudication	☐
Joint or muscular problems	☐	Epilepsy	☐
Other	☐		
The patient is clinically stable ☐			
The patient is waiting for further medical treatment ☐			
The form must be signed by the GP and the patient must give informed consent			

activity
INDIVIDUAL WORK

1. Do you think that NHS money spent on this type of referral is money well spent?
2. Do you think that 12 weeks of exercise is enough to establish physical activity as part of the patient's lifestyle?

activity
INDIVIDUAL WORK
13.7

M1

Explain how the following lifestyle factors increase their risk of coronary heart disese: high BMI, physical inactivity, smoking, drinking to excess, stress.

Providing advice on lifestyle improvement

Once a person's lifestyle has been evaluated, they need some advice on how to improve it. Guidelines are a good start but quite often they need to be backed up with practical suggestions, examples and contact numbers. Leaflets given out with generalised health tips tend to end up in the bin. People need a strategy for change. Modifying lifestyle through behavioural change is not easy and before it can happen, the person must want to change. Unless a person is motivated, any strategy for change will fail. People put up barriers to change as they prefer to stay in their comfort zone, and even if they understand why change would be beneficial, they won't make a long-term commitment to change.

Lifestyle change occurs in several stages. Prochaska and DiClemente (1983) defined five stages that people seem to go through. People move from a polarised view, where they see no point in changing their behaviour, to actively seeking alternative approaches and behaviours. The speed of change differs for each individual but it does help practitioners and counsellors to time their intervention more effectively as the person needs to be in the appropriate stage to be receptive to new strategies and behaviours.

Figure 13.14 Prochaska and DiClemente proposed a model with five stages of change

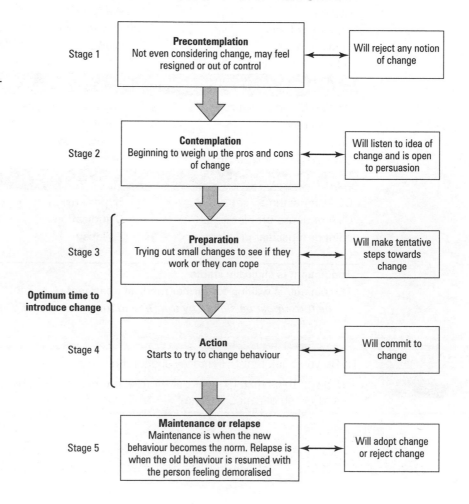

In the pre-contemplation stage, the GP, health professional, family or friend will try to get the person to accept that they have a problem, perhaps by completing a questionnaire. During the contemplation stage they need to prompt the person by asking questions that might prepare the person for change by changing their attitudes and increasing their motivation levels: What is stopping you from changing? What might help you change? And so on. Once the person has reached the preparation stage, the strategies for change can be implemented.

Five stages of change
www.addictioninfo.org

Cognitive behavioural therapy (CBT) is sometimes used once a person reaches the preparation stage. The cognitive aspect deals with thoughts, attitudes and beliefs, and the behavioural aspect considers the action the person takes in response to their thoughts. Put more simply, CBT helps you change how you think and what you do in response to situations, events or problems. There is an identifiable chain that links how you think with how you feel, physically and emotionally, and ultimately with what you do. If you don't think that smoking particularly harms you or anyone else in your family, you feel quite happy smoking and continue to smoke in the family home. But if you are told that your smoking is responsible for your daughter's asthma attacks, you might feel extremely guilty and stop smoking inside the house. By changing one link in the chain, you can create a domino effect where all the other links change as well – create cognitive dissonance. Here is the sequence:

Situation → thoughts → emotions and physical feelings → actions

CBT has been successful in modifying all aspects of lifestyle. It can be used to change exercise patterns, alcohol intake, smoking, stress levels and diet.

Cognitive dissonance
www.en.wikipedia.org

Figure 13.15 Self-help or lip service?

Strategies

See page 130 in Unit 15 for more information on benefits

Physical activity

The guidelines for adults are that they should do a minimum of 30 min of moderate physical activity five times a week. Over the years, different terms have been used to describe different activities, such as sport, physical activity, physical recreation, leisure activities and pastimes. In 2001 the Council of Europe revised the European Charter for Sport and defined sport as 'all forms of physical activity, which through casual or organised participation, aim at expressing or improving physical fitness and well-being, forming social relationships, or obtaining results in competition at all levels'. This definition has been adopted by all the sports councils in the UK. Sport now includes formal and informal activities for leisure, health or social reasons, including recreational activities such as walking and cycling. To this end, Sport England's 2004 Framework for Sport in England identifies four separate markets it will target to increase participation rates.

The guidelines say that children should participate in moderate physical activity for 60 min every day and do vigorous exercise at least twice a week. Through the work of school sport partnerships (SSPs), the government has set targets to increase participation in physical activity. The first target was the PSA of at least 75% of pupils participating in 2 h of high-quality physical education (PE) and school sport inside and outside the curriculum by 2006. This target was achieved but the government provided the infrastructure; a total of over £1.5 billion is being invested in physical education and school sport in the five years to 2008. Sportspeople hope that more money will be promised for a further five-year period.

The government's ambition is to offer all children at least 4 h of sport every week, made up of at least 2 h of high-quality PE and sport at schools within the curriculum. In addition, at least 2 h of sport should be provided after the end of the school day, delivered by school, community and club providers. As lifestyle is all about habit, if children become used to being active, perhaps they will continue to take part in sport through adulthood.

Figure 13.16 Are you a sporty type or on the subs bench?

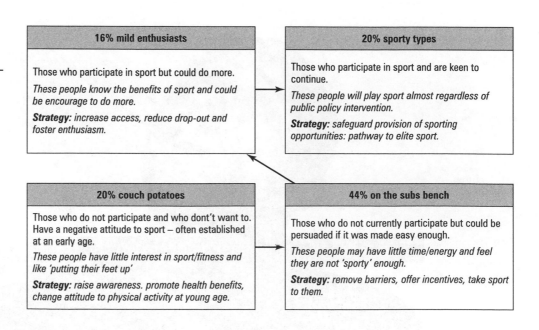

SSPs and the vision for 2010

www.teachernet.gov.uk

www.youthsporttrust.org

www.sportengland.co.uk

The NHS continues to run the exercise referral scheme, where GPs recommend a 12 week exercise programme to patients with low- to moderate-risk conditions such as moderately high blood pressure, high cholesterol, above average BMI, osteoporosis or anxiety. Each exercise programme is run by a specialist trainer in a local gym or leisure centre and consists of a lifestyle assessment and a personal exercise programme. The patient receives help in setting and achieving their lifestyle goals and is given one-to-one support to help motivation. The 12 week programme is subsidised by the NHS.

Figure 13.17 The government has set targets to increase participation in physical activity

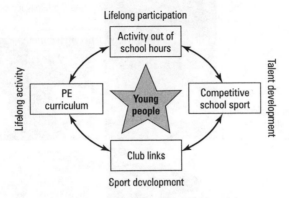

Clinical Answers, an NHS website, said this about the GP referral schemes in 2005:

> Exercise-referral schemes appear to increase physical activity levels in certain populations, namely individuals who are not sedentary but already slightly active, older adults and those who are overweight (but not obese). However, increases in the level of physical activity may not be sustained over time. Further studies are required to assess effectiveness in a range of populations and for different activities, and to find strategies to increase long-term adherence.

Clinical Answers

www.clinicalanswers.nhs.uk

Professional practice

If a GP is worried about the condition of a patient and thinks that exercise intervention will have a positive impact on their health, then they will complete an exercise referral form. The patient is then entitled to a 12 week exercise programme at a local gym assigned to the practice.

Reasons for inactivity

Despite government intervention, people come up with several reasons why they are not active:

- They don't have enough time.
- There are no sports facilities near where they live.
- Equipment or membership is too expensive.
- They don't feel safe or confident enough to take part.
- They don't think they are sporty or have the ability needed.
- They don't have enough energy.

Perhaps one of the main reasons why people are put off being active is that they think that only really strenuous activity benefits health. Explain that 30 min per day of moderate activity is activity where you raise your pulse and get warmer but not necessarily hot and sweaty. You feel slightly out of breath but you can still hold a conversation. Most people can achieve this level of exertion and done regularly it will soon bring health benefits. Any continuous activity is going to improve stamina and will have a positive effect on the cardiovascular system; examples are walking, cycling and swimming. There are a huge range of activities that people can do on their own or with friends, or that families can do together.

Some small lifestyle adjustments can increase a person's physical activity without them having to spend any money at all.

Figure 13.18 People can do many activities on their own, with family or with friends

Take the family ice skating

Sign up for dancing lessons, ballroom, tap or salsa

Go rambling, hillwalking, orienteering or gorge walking

Start kite flying, or power kite sports like kite surfing or kite buggying

Ideas for being more active

■ Don't take the lift, walk up the stairs.

■ For short local journeys, don't take the car, walk.

■ Get off a bus one stop before your destination and walk there.

■ Make gardening a regular activity.

■ Do the housework to music and work faster.

■ Arrange to meet a friend and walk together to the shops, town or park.

■ Start a lunchtime club for walking, cycling or swimming.

■ Do 15 min of yoga, pilates or t'ai chi, at the beginning or end of the day.

If you normally meet friends and socialise in a pub, suggest that you do an activity first, such as a game of badminton, table tennis or pitch and putt. If you know that you easily get bored, take part in a range of activities to keep you motivated. Exercise should be fun, so try activities to music, or exercise in scenic places. Be adventurous and get the adrenaline flowing; try rock climbing, gorge walking, canoeing, mountain biking or skiing.

remember
Thirty minutes of exercise per day will keep you fitter and healthier and boost your sense of well-being.

Alcohol

Increasing numbers of people in the UK depend on alcohol, and most 'social drinkers' are unaware of the dangers or just how much they depend on alcohol. If you have a strong desire to have a drink, if once you have a drink you find it hard to stop, if you need increasingly more units to feel any effect, and if you just can't say no to a drink, you have a drink problem. Alcoholics Anonymous (AA) has a questionnaire of 12 questions and if you answer yes to more than two, it indicates that you have an alcohol-related problem. Here are some of the questions:

■ Do you drink to help you relax?

■ Have you ever been drunk in the morning?

■ Do you lie about how much you drink?

■ Do you drink your drinks quickly?

■ Have you ever forgotten what you have done because you have had too much to drink?

If you are feeling worried, you could telephone the AA helpline on 0845 7697555.

The last person to realise that they have a drink problem is usually the alcoholic and quite often early prevention by family members or friends can help. The person who is drinking to excess needs to have the problems spelled out – starting arguments, straining relationships, violent behaviour, memory loss, accidents, drink driving, etc. – then they need information on where to get help.

The first point of contact is normally the local GP, who may well use the CAGE questionnaire to see if intervention strategies are required. The CAGE questionnaire has four questions; if the patient answers yes to two, there is a high probability that they have a drink problem. The CAGE questionnaire – cut, annoyed, guilty, eye-opener – was developed by J. A. Ewing and it is now used internationally by the medical profession; see Ewing (1984) for more details.

The CAGE questionnaire

■ Have you ever felt you should cut down on your drinking?

■ Have people annoyed you by criticising your drinking?

■ Have you ever felt guilty about your drinking?

■ Have you ever taken a drink first thing in the morning, an eye-opener, to steady your nerves?

Depending on the severity of the problem, there are various levels of help and specialist support. If a person needs detoxification, they may need to enter an NHS clinic or a private clinic; the Priory Group runs private clinics for alcoholics. During detoxification, some alcoholics will need to have medication and medical supervision, others will just need the support of a local group. Detoxification usually takes about 7 days and during that time the person may suffer these withdrawal symptoms:

■ Feeling anxious

■ Sweating or feeling clammy

■ Difficulty sleeping

■ Shaking or tremors

■ Feeling sick.

This is only the first stage of getting the drinking problem under control, as the reasons why a person drinks have then to be resolved. If a person wants counselling, they can visit their GP, contact AA or the NHS, plus they can go to local drug or alcohol advice centres. Specially trained counsellors provide support and mentoring. Other people prefer to attend group therapy sessions at AA or a local group run by the Alcohol Counselling and Prevention Service (ACAPS).

case study
13.6

Framework for Sport in England

Read this extract from the Framework for Sport in England.

What is sport's contribution to physical activity?

The Game Plan analysis was based upon achieving participation in sport and physical activity (including non-sporting related physical activity) at a level of intensity and duration to derive a health benefit – 30 minutes of moderate intensity physical activity at least five times a week (moderate intensity means activity that leaves people feeling warm, sweaty and slightly out of breath).

[Some] 30.4% of people are physically active, meeting the Government's target of five times a week for 30 minutes of moderate intensity – two thirds through the nature of their occupation.

Excluding occupation, 22% achieve the target through sport, 36% through walking, and 42% through housework, DIY and gardening.

Figure 13.19 How people in England met the government exercise target in 1998

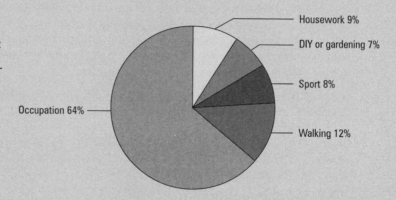

Housework 9%
DIY or gardening 7%
Sport 8%
Walking 12%
Occupation 64%

Framework for Sport in England
www.sportengland.org/national-framework-for-sport.pdf

activity
INDIVIDUAL WORK

1. Suggest strategies that could be implemented by the local authority where you live to try to increase the number of people who participate in sport.

2. Give reasons why so many young people stop participating in sport when they leave school.

3. What local activities might attract people aged 16–20 and increase participation in physical activity?

Help with an alcohol-related problem
www.aa-uk.org.uk
Regional and local advice centres
www.nhsplus.nhs.uk

AA was founded in 1935. Its website carries this statement of purpose:

> Alcoholics Anonymous is a fellowship of men and women who share their experience, strength and hope with each other that they may solve their common problem and help others to recover from alcoholism. The only requirement for membership is a desire to stop drinking.

It is a highly successful organisation probably because it is run by recovering alcoholics who have the experience to help others. They have developed a twelve-step self-help programme that is followed by AA groups worldwide. The fellowship holds two types of meeting. An open meeting that can be attended by alcoholics, family and friends, and a closed meeting that only alcoholics can attend.

CBT is used by some clinics. It tries to change behaviours by modifying everyday thoughts and the emotional responses to those thoughts. An alcoholic is encouraged to keep a diary of events; for every event, the alcoholic makes a note of their thoughts, emotions and behaviours. The person's thoughts, habits and behaviours will be questioned and challenged. If the treatment is successful, the person will develop new ways to think, react and behave in situations and they will no longer need to solve their problems by drinking.

See page 11 in Unit 10 for more information on diet

It is not easy to overcome addiction problems and many recovering alcoholics will relapse. Then they have to start again and go through another rehabilitation programme. The solution is to identify the trigger for their drinking behaviour then to avoid the trigger or change the behavioural response; it is easier said than done.

Smoking

Smoking was banned from public places in England starting on 1 July 2007 and the UK government estimates that over 600 000 people will stop smoking. To accompany the ban, the NHS launched its Get Unhooked campaign with media advertising and a website. Go Smokefree is another NHS website that offers lots of practical help and advice for people who want to quit smoking.

Support for people who want to stop smoking
www.getunhooked.co.uk
www.gosmokefree.co.uk

The first step in tackling any addiction is a desire to change. It is important that a person tries to stop when they are feeling in control of other aspects of their life, so they are confident and positive and can focus their energy on the task in hand – their motivation must be high. Smokers should research products that might wean them off the nicotine then choose the one that works best for them. They may wish to consider hypnosis or group therapy sessions. Hypnosis has been highly successful for some people, and so have self-help books. Acupuncture is used as an aid to stop smoking. Anyone who seeks alternative treatments should check that the treatment will be given by a registered practitioner. There is no clinical evidence to prove that hypnosis or acupuncture helps a person to stop smoking, but if it works for one person it is worth trying.

Table 13.4 Products to help with nicotine withdrawal

Product	Description
Nicotine patches	Available as a 16 h patch or a 24 h patch
Nicotine chewing gum	The nicotine is released slowly and absorbed through the lining of the mouth
Nicotine nasal spray	The nicotine is absorbed quickly through the lining of the nose
Zyban	A prescription drug that alters how your body responds to nicotine. Begin it 2 weeks before you stop smoking and take it for 3–4 weeks
Inhalator	Releases nicotine vapour, which is absorbed through the mouth. It is made from plastic in the shape of a cigarette; it is used like a cigarette

Smokers should get a clear picture of the withdrawal symptoms they could experience before they actually suffer them. It is easier to manage withdrawal symptoms if you have prepared some strategies in advance.

- **Cravings for nicotine** – cravings start out strong and frequent and each one can last 3–5 min. They gradually fade and shouldn't continue beyond 3–4 weeks. Some people keep up their resolve by using **positive affirmations** – I am a non-smoker – keeping busy, taking slow sips from a glass of water, or using an egg timer to watch the seconds elapse as they feel the craving disappear.

- **Headaches, sickness, sore throats** – they will not last long and may only happen in the first few days.

- **Coughing** – this is a good thing. It removes the tar and mucus built up by smoking and is the body's way of reversing damage to the lungs. The persistence of the cough depends on how long a person has been a smoker. While they are coughing, some people tell themselves how much healthier they will be in the long run.

- **Irritability and depression** – exercise takes a person's mind off smoking and can help to counteract changes in mood. It helps people to feel more positive about themselves.

- **Increase in appetite** – one way to avoid putting on weight is to have a handy stash of healthy snacks that combat hunger pangs.

Making lists can help a person to understand the benefits of quitting and make them more motivated to give up smoking. They could list all the diseases and illnesses caused by smoking. They could work out how much money they will save per week, per month and per year then list all the things they could buy or calculate the interest they could earn. Perhaps they could have a regular treat if they stick to their plan. These ideas fall into the contemplation stage of the Prochaska and DiClemente model. A spring clean gets rid of all the smells and stains of nicotine in the new non-smoker's house. Going to the dentist to get the nicotine stains removed from their teeth can boost a person's self-confidence and soon they can look forward to healthier-looking skin and smoke-free hair.

When they reach the action stage, the person should decide on the day and stop smoking. Hopefully, they will get support and encouragement from friends and family. The new non-smoker needs to tell their friends and family, so they can understand the new non-smoker's mood swings. The new non-smoker should try to avoid places where other people will be smoking and where cigarettes will be available; the July 2007 ban will probably make this much easier. New non-smokers should see every day as a small triumph and feel proud of each achievement. In the maintenance stage, the new non-smoker should celebrate short-term goals such as numbers of days without smoking. They must use positive affirmation at all times and they must always think of themselves as a non-smoker.

Stress management techniques

The stress on a person can vary tremendously and different people have different abilities to cope with stress. Perhaps a person can manage two stressful events if they occur one at a time, but if the same two events occur together, then the total stress is too great and the person cannot cope. For example, a person may be able to cope with the stress of moving house on its own and the stress of redundancy on its own, but if they are made redundant in the middle of moving house, then the stress is too great and they cannot cope. Some people have lifestyles that put them under a lot of stress every day. There are strategies to manage stress and avoid exhaustion or burnout.

Stress management strategies

www.mindtools.com

www.everythingandnothing.typepad.com

Time management

You will often hear someone say, 'I haven't got time to do another task,' when an objective person can see that they have. This is because most people do not manage their time effectively, they put themselves under extra pressure and stress, imagine they have no time and protest when given an extra task. Follow these sensible strategies to use time more efficiently and reduce unwanted stress.

Assess your daily or weekly schedule

First, assess your daily or weekly schedule. There may be times when tasks are duplicated unnecessarily. There may be pockets of time that are being wasted, perhaps because you are waiting for someone else. When scrutinised, some tasks might be better carried out by someone else. After evaluation there might be a quicker way to carry out some tasks – there is a tendency to do things the way they have always been done. Some tasks are better carried out one after the other, perhaps because they are similar or need to be done in the same place. The completion deadline of some tasks might need to be changed, which may mean changing other people's deadlines or schedules.

Action planning

Once you have a clear picture of what needs doing, draw up a schedule or to-do list. Depending on the demands of the individual, it may be appropriate to set goals. Goal setting usually involves short-, medium- and long-term goals and they can be applied to almost anything. If a person wanted to lose weight for their wedding in ten months' time, that would be a long-term goal. A medium-term goal might be that they have dropped a dress size before the first fitting in three months' time, and a short-term goal could be to have lost a kilogram by the end of the week. It is very motivating when you cross things off a to-do list or reach a target.

Do not procrastinate

It is human nature to put off the completion of a task, particularly if it is unpleasant or time-consuming. Time is wasted as other less important jobs are finished or nothing is done at all. Stress starts to build up as deadlines loom. It takes self-discipline but the tasks that tend to be put off really need to be done first. Once they are out of the way, a person's mood lifts and they generally feel more motivated and work quicker.

Delegate

People sometimes take on too much because they feel that only they can do the job properly, even though the additional tasks create an unachievable workload. On reflection they may be able to delegate some tasks to other people.

Say no

Being assertive is not the same as being belligerent. At times people have to take control and politely but firmly say no when asked to fulfil an unrealistic request. Perhaps the timescale is too short or perhaps the person does not have the training or resources to do it. If they say yes, it will cause them unnecessary stress.

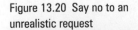

Figure 13.20 Say no to an unrealistic request

Accept that some things are out of your control
Sometimes it is best to walk away from a situation because it is completely out of your control. Why get stressed over something you cannot change? Don't waste energy watering rocks.

Identify 'me' time
Each person needs some time during the day when they can relax, recuperate and do what they like. They can use this 'me' time to practise a range of relaxation and stress management techniques.

Stress management

Positive self-talk
When a person feels that they cannot cope, it may have begun with just a few negative thoughts. People who are naturally anxious may have negative thoughts like this: 'I'm not clever enough to pass my exam.' Someone who thinks they are not clever enough will be anxious before, during and after their exam. This anxiety is not a nice feeling and could cause them to fail, even though they have the knowledge to pass when they are not so anxious. Positive self-talk is a way to reduce anxiety by changing negative thoughts and statements. When a person starts on a negative thought, they stop themselves and rephrase it into a positive thought: 'I'm not clever enough to … No, if I revise thoroughly, I will pass my exam.' This brings a more positive approach to revision and exam preparation. Further positive affirmations will strengthen the positive mood: 'I am good at exams.'

Imagery
Sometimes it helps to clear your mind of all thoughts entirely. Imagery can be very effective for this. Imagine you are in a safe, comfortable place where you feel happy and contented. Some people imagine they are on a beautiful beach with white sand that stretches to clear blue sea. They can hear the waves gently lapping the shore and feel the sun's rays warming their body. There is a small cloud in the sky that is moving slowly away towards the horizon. It is their haven and sanctuary from the outside world. All thoughts are temporarily blocked as they enjoy the peace and tranquillity of their imagined world. The more you use this technique, the quicker you get to the beach.

Meditation
Meditation is another way to relax and when practised frequently lowers breathing rate, heart rate and oxygen consumption. People who meditate sit in a quiet, comfortable and safe place. They focus all their attention on one thing, usually their breathing to begin

Figure 13.21 Meditation is a good way to relax

with, but it could be an object. Breathing should be very slow and controlled and each breath should be mentally counted. The idea is that all other thoughts are blocked as breathing is the sole focus.

Progressive muscular relaxation

Progressive muscular relaxation is better performed lying down in a warm, comfortable place. Tense a group of muscles, e.g. muscles in the lower leg and feet. Hold the contraction for a few seconds then slowly relax the muscles. Move on to another muscle group. Normally this is done systematically by moving through the muscle groups from head to foot or from foot to head. When all the muscles have been relaxed, try to melt into the surface you are lying on. If you do this properly, your limbs will feel very heavy and it will take a little time to get them moving normally when the relaxation period is over.

Physical activity

Physical activity is very good at relieving stress. Exercise helps you to forget the day's negative thoughts and emotions, particularly if you find the activity fun. Exercise causes the body to release mood-lifting chemicals such as endorphins and serotonin. It also lowers high levels of adrenaline built up during a stressful day and leaves you feeling calmer. Stress tends to raise a person's blood pressure. Physical activity counteracts this as it helps to lower hypertension for existing sufferers and lowers the risk of developing high blood pressure.

See page 133 in Unit 15 for more information on physical activity and stress

Life coach

Here's how Elizabeth Scott describes the work of a life coach at http://stress.about.com:

> They deal with stress management as well as time management, goal setting and other key areas of change to help their clients lead more balanced lives that better reflect clients' personal values and priorities. It differs from therapy in that the focus is more on the present and future than the past, more on goals and behaviors than emotions and emotional patterns, and there is a more equal balance of power between the coach and client than between the typical therapist and client.

Definition of a life coach
http://stress.about.com/od/stressmanagementglossary/g/LifeCoach.htm

Diet

A person's diet is very much down to habit. A person may not be aware that they follow predictable patterns of eating, but they may well eat a roast dinner every Sunday, buy fish and chips every Friday, and eat chocolate when they watch a film. If a person develops bad eating habits, they have to change their behaviour to adopt a more healthy approach. This change will only happen if the person is committed to changing their behaviour and if they have reached stage 3, preparation, in the stages of change. It may be easier to begin by changing one thing at a time instead of taking drastic action. Perhaps start by removing the salt from the table or by having porridge for breakfast. Here are some tips to help develop good dietary habits.

Eat at regular times and don't skip meals. Breakfast is the most important meal of the day and gives you the rest of the day to burn off the calories. That is why people should avoid eating their main meal after 6.00 p.m. Keep a food diary to write down what you have eaten, how much and when. This makes it easier to see what you need to change. Choose a variety of foods from all food groups in the food pyramid. This will keep your menu varied and give your body all essential nutrients.

Stick to the recommended amounts of fat, carbohydrate and protein. Food labelling is extensive and many supermarkets are developing easier ways for customers to interpret nutritional guidelines. Some major food manufacturers have introduced labels that show guideline daily amounts (GDAs). Each label lists the percentages of sugar, salt, fat and calories in one serving. The Food Standards Agency (FSA) has approved the use of traffic light labels, where green is good and red should be eaten sparingly – not too much. Some packaging can be very misleading. Many products with labels which say 'only 5% fat' mean that fat is 5% of the product's total weight, but the calories from this fat could be much higher than 5% of the product's total calories.

Try to eat carbohydrate with a low glycaemic index (GI). GI refers to the different effects of different carbohydrates on blood glucose levels. Porridge contains oats; it is a low-GI food and will therefore release energy slowly over a longer period of time, so you will not feel hungry. If you snack on a high-GI food, you will experience a sugar rush, but it will be short-lived. If you have done quite a lot of exercise and quickly need to replenish your carbohydrate stores, then eat a high-GI food.

Limit sugar and sweets. Our palate can get used to the sweetness of some foods high in sugar and become desensitised. Gradually reduce your sugar intake. Following a gradual reduction over a few weeks, even half a spoonful of sugar will taste too sweet in tea or coffee. Don't add salt to your meal – you don't need it. Adding salt is a habit. Some people don't even taste their food before they add salt. Salt can contribute to high blood pressure and most people take in far more salt than the GDA. Your palate will quickly adjust to less salt and over a few weeks you can significantly reduce your salt intake.

Reduce the amount of fat you eat, especially saturated fat. Always trim the fat off meat, take the skin off chicken, drink semi-skimmed milk not full-fat milk; these are simple things but they all make a difference. Include foods high in fibre as fibre helps digestion and excretion and reduces the risk of developing cancer of the bowel. Choose wholegrain foods rather than refined foods. There is far more nutritional value in wholegrain foods and they are a source of fibre. Avoid processed foods as they contain trans fats and food additives. Food additives, identified by E numbers, have a variety of side effects. Many are used in children's sweets to make them more colourful and attractive, but E102, E104, E110 and E122 can make children hyperactive.

Be prepared to cook using fresh ingredients. Cooking can be a social event where everyone helps. It can be very satisfying to produce a meal from scratch and fresh ingredients taste so much better. Drink plenty of water and limit alcohol, caffeine and fizzy drinks. Alcohol contains 7 kcal per gram and very few nutrients. Fizzy drinks attack tooth enamel. Reduce the size of your plate and eat smaller portions; stop eating when you feel full. Your stomach will distend and take in more food if you eat large portions. Cut down what you eat and your stomach will shrink, then you'll feel full after eating less.

Dietary guidelines and food labelling
www.food.gov.uk

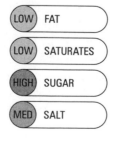

Figure 13.22 Look out for food labels with traffic lights

LOW FAT

LOW SATURATES

HIGH SUGAR

MED SALT

Figure 13.23 Smarties use many colours

---

activity
INDIVIDUAL WORK
13.8

M3

You have been asked by a friend to help them give up smoking but without putting on weight. The fear of putting on weight has always thwarted their attempts to quit smoking. Explain to your friend what lifestyle improvement strategies will help them achieve their goal.

---

activity
GROUP WORK
13.9

D2

Some lifestyle improvement strategies are more effective than others. And some people can find a barrier to every strategy. If you say, 'Eat at regular times and don't skip meals,' they might reply, 'I work shifts and no two days are the same.' Analyse a range of lifestyle strategies. Consider their strengths and their weaknesses. Contemplate potential barriers and try to find a way to make the strategy effective. Put your results in a four-column table with these column headings: lifestyle strategy, strengths, weakenesses or barriers, way to make it effective.

Planning a health-related physical activity programme for a selected individual

People have many reasons for wanting to be more active, but the number one reason is to become fitter and healthier. Many people want to do an activity that requires little equipment or skill, happens at a convenient time and charges an affordable price. Some other reasons that people give are to have fun, to try something new, to have a challenge and to meet people. Some people like to be competitive, whereas others like a relaxing, calm activity. When you plan an activity programme for someone, gather information about them so that what you devise will be suitable and effective.

Collect information

Begin by finding out the person's goals and the reasons why they want to do a physical activity. Here are some examples:

- A young mother wants time to herself to get back in shape and enjoy adult company.
- A recreational runner wants to run a marathon as a personal challenge and to raise money for charity.
- A patient recovering from heart bypass surgery has been advised to do regular aerobic exercise of moderate intensity.

Each person needs a programme of physical activity tailored to their requirements. One programme does not fit all. Having established a person's goals, the next step is to see if they are realistic. Ask the person to complete a lifestyle questionnaire. It also helps to know their medical history, if the person agrees to volunteer it. The physical activity readiness questionnaire (PAR-Q) does not require a person to divulge their medical details but gives a good indication whether that person can safely participate in physical activity. Medical details are confidential and this confidentiality has to be respected. Here is an example of a self-administered questionnaire.

A self-administered PAR-Q

Physical activity should not pose a problem for most people. PAR-Q is designed to identify the small number of people for whom physical activity could be inappropriate or those who should have medical advice about the activity most suitable for them. Common sense is your best guide when answering these few questions. Please read them carefully before taking part in physical activity.

- Has your doctor ever said that you have heart trouble?

- Have you recently experienced any pains in the chest?

- Have you experienced any problems breathing?

- Have you any history of back pain?

- Have you recently been off work due to illness?

- Do you suffer from high blood pressure?

- Have you any bone or joint problem that has been aggravated by exercise or might be made worse with exercise?

- Is there any reason not mentioned here that might affect your ability to take part in physical activity?

If you have answered yes to any of the above questions, you are advised to consult a doctor before you take part in physical activity.

It is also useful to find out about the person's physical activity history. One way to do this is to use the General Practice Physical Activity Questionnaire. Having gathered information about the person's reasons for participation, their lifestyle, medical history

Figure 13.24 A keep-fitter and a marathon runner may have different personal goals

and physical activity history, it should be possible to start considering some goals for their health-related fitness programme.

Table 13.5 General Practice Physical Activity Questionnaire

Date.........................	Name...........................

Question 1

Please tell us the type and amount of physical activity involved in your work.
Please tick one box that best corresponds with your present work from the following possibilities:

Please tick one box only

a. I am not in employment (e.g. retired, retired for health reasons, unemployed, full-time carer, etc). ☐

b. I spend most of my time at work sitting (such as in an office). ☐

c. I spend most of my time at work standing or walking. However, my work does not require much intense physical effort (e.g. shop assistant, hairdresser, security guard, child minder, etc). ☐

d. My work involves definite physical effort including handling of heavy objects and use of tools (e.g. plumber, electrician, carpenter, cleaner, hospital nurse, gardener, postal delivery worker, etc). ☐

e. My work involves vigorous physical activity including handling of very heavy objects (e.g. scaffolder, construction worker, refuse collector, etc). ☐

Question 2

How would you describe your normal walking pace?   Please tick one box only

a. Slow pace (i.e. less than 3 mph) ☐
b. Steady average pace ☐
c. Brisk pace ☐
d. Fast pace (I.e. over 4 mph) ☐

Question 3

During the <u>last week</u>, how many hours did you spend on each of the following activities? Please tick one box only on each row.

	None	Some but less than 1 hour	1 hour but less than 3 hours	3 hours or more
a. Physical exercise such as swimming, jogging, aerobics, football, tennis, gym workout, etc.	☐	☐	☐	☐
b. Cycling, including cycling to work and during leisure time.	☐	☐	☐	☐
c. Walking, including walking to work, shopping, for pleasure, etc.	☐	☐	☐	☐
d. Housework/Childcare.	☐	☐	☐	☐
e. Gardening/DIY.	☐	☐	☐	☐

Key

Inactive	Sedentary job and no recreational physical activity
Moderately inactive	Sedentary job and some but less than 1 hour recreational physical activity per week OR standing job and no recreational physical activity
Moderately active	Sedentary job and 1 to 2.9 hours recreational physical activity per week OR standing job and some but less than 1 hour recreational physical activity per week OR physical job and no recreational physical activity
Active	Sedentary job and 3 hours or more recreational physical activity per week OR standing job and 1 to 2.9 hours recreational physical activity per week OR physical job and some but less than 1 hour recreational physical activity per week OR heavy manual job

When someone attends an aerobics class or fitness class for the first time, the instructor will normally ask them to complete and sign a PAR-Q before they allow them to participate in the class.

General Practice Physical Activity Questionnaire
www.patient.co.uk
PAR-Q
www.clarkson.edu
Practical Physical Activity Questionnaire
www.patient.co.uk

Motivation and goal setting

A personal goal is something that a person wants to accomplish. It gives them something to focus on and plan towards. Motivation is needed to change behaviour, then the person must decide to act, stage 4 of the Prochaska and DiClemente model. Goal setting helps motivation and helps to keep a person on task. Personal goals are more meaningful because they are designed to motivate a specific person. A person can measure their success by achieving the goals they set for themselves and this will give them a sense of accomplishment and pride. To be effective, personal goals need to be goals that the person can achieve. Sometimes it is better to split one large goal into several smaller goals, or chop a meal into bite-sized chunks.

■ Decide on a major long-term goal.

■ Establish the medium-term goals to achieve the long-term goal.

■ Identify short-term goals that will help to achieve the medium-term goals.

See page 151 in Unit 15 for more information on session reviews
See page 72 in Unit 12 for more information on development
See page 265 in Unit 23 for more information on needs

Suppose a person has a long-term goal to run a marathon. They will need to train for a long time and they will need to maintain their motivation during the training. They can help to maintain their motivation if they set short- and medium-term goals as stepping stones. A good medium-term goal may be to run a half-marathon, and a good short-term goal may be to increase their running distance from 5 km to 8 km. Always set SMART goals:

Always choose SMART goals:

■ **Specific** – so you know exactly what you are trying to achieve.

■ **Measurable** – so you can see how well you are progressing.

■ **Achievable** – so you will eventually be successful.

■ **Realistic** – so you have what it takes to achieve them.

■ **Time-bound** – so you reach your goal in a reasonable time.

Goals need to be challenging so they motivate a person to achieve them. If goals are too easy, there is no satisfaction in achieving them. If goals are too difficult, people get discouraged and give up. A person must be fully involved in setting the goals for their health-related physical activity programme. If a person is fully involved in setting their goals, they will be more motivated to achieve them.

Principles of training

Here are some principles to help devise physical activity programmes that are sensible, realistic and safe.

Principle of overload

Training improves fitness by giving your body an overload. In other words, you make your body work harder than normal by increasing the amount of work it has to perform. The body will then gradually adapt to the new level of work and your level of fitness will improve. Overload can be achieved by using the FITT principle and increasing your exercise frequency, intensity and time and varying your type of exercise:

- **Frequency** – train more times per week.
- **Intensity** – run faster or lift a heavier weight.
- **Time** – go for a 40 min run instead of a 30 min run.
- **Type** – go for a swim or bike ride.

Figure 13.25 Weight training uses the FITT principles to achieve overload

Principle of progression

The principle of progression says that the amount of overload should be increased progressively. Wait for some adaptation to occur then increase the overload slightly. Closely monitor your performance so that you don't overload your body too quickly. Show moderation; in other words, be realistic and reasonable about the demands you place on your body. If you are overambitious, you may overtrain and seriously damage your musculoskeletal system and your immune system.

Principle of specificity

Every activity requires a specific mix of fitness components. Your training needs to reflect the contribution of each component, but you must develop good general fitness before you do any specific training. Don't play squash to get fit, get fit to play squash. Here are the three main factors to consider:

- **Person** – training should be specific to a person. Assess your initial state of fitness so that the workload can be accurately estimated. Everyone has limitations, as much of our physical capacity is genetically determined. Being aware of your physiological make-up will help you make the most of your strengths instead of dwelling on your weaknesses.

- Activity – identify the mix of fitness components required then identify the major joints and muscles that are used. Do training that uses these joints and muscle groups and try to reproduce the movement patterns you would use in the activity.

- Energy systems – identify the energy systems used during the activity and their overall contribution to total energy expenditure. Do training that reflects the same balance by manipulating the intensity and duration of your work.

Principle of reversibility

Fitness cannot be stored for future use and your level of fitness is constantly changing. Any adaptations produced by training will be reversed when you stop training; this is sometimes known as detraining.

Principle of variance

The principle of variance says that a training programme should include a variety of training methods. This will help to maintain interest and motivation and it varies the loads you work against. The same thing week after week becomes monotonous and boring. If you do not vary your training, it is very easy to develop overuse injuries. And if you do not give your body sufficient time to recover, you can develop chronic exhaustion.

Appropriate activities

If a person is worried that physical activity might worsen an existing condition, advise them to visit their GP before starting a physical activity programme. Physical activity after prolonged inactivity is a daunting prospect for some people. Check that their initial goals are realistic and manageable. Remind people that it is never too late to start a physical activity programme and that everybody can experience health benefits.

Walking will probably be the chosen activity for most people, and brisk walking is an excellent moderate physical activity. The British Heart Foundation (BHF) says that 'walking two miles [3.2 km] per day can cut the risk of death by half'. BHF promotes the Walking the Way to Health Initiative (WHI) along with Natural England, a new countryside body created from part of the defunct Countryside Agency.

According to government statistics, people are walking the same average distance as they have always walked but they are taking longer walks much more irregularly. Shorter walks do not provide the same health benefits as walking briskly for 30 min every day. The WHI website gives contact details for 350 health walk schemes throughout England plus suitable walking routes for people who want to walk on their own.

Any continuous activity performed at moderate intensity is going to help prevent the risk of developing hypokinetic disease – disease caused by inactivity – such as coronary heart disease. Activities such as cycling, walking and swimming are ideal but so are tennis, badminton and lots of other sports. If a person enjoys an activity, they are more likely to take part and remain physically active.

Training principles and training programmes
www.pponline.co.uk
www.brianmac.co.uk
Walking to health
www.whi.org.uk
Walking for cardiac rehabilitation
www.bhf.org.uk

Figure 13.26 Some people walk their way to health

Exercise intensity

A person will develop their fitness only if they overload the system they want to improve. Sometimes the amount of work is quite obvious; it is easy to see when you add another weight to a weight stack. Heart rate is a good indicator of work in other exercises. Target or training heart rates are commonly used to make sure a person is staying within safe limits but is doing sufficient work to gain health benefits.

Here is a recognised way to determine a target heart rate (HR) training zone. First, obtain your maximum heart rate (MHR) by measuring it in an exercise test or by plugging your age into a formula. There is one formula for men and one for women:

> Women: MHR = 226 – age in years
>
> Men: MHR = 220 – age in years

Now obtain your resting heart rate (RHR) – how many times your heart beats per minute when you are resting. Measure it first thing in the morning. Calculate your heart rate reserve (HRR):

> HRR = MHR – RHR

Finally, choose the percentage of the HRR that you wish to work at, usually 60–80%, and add this figure to your RHR. This will give your training target heart rate (TTHR). Suppose you decided to work at 60%, then here is how to calculate your TTHR:

> TTHR = RHR + 0.6HRR

Here are the calculations for a woman aged 48 with a resting heart rate of 70 bpm (beats per minute) working at 60%:

> MHR = 226 – age in years = 226 – 48 = 178
>
> HRR = 178 – 70 = 108
>
> TTHR = 70 + (0.6 × 108) = 135

The woman would aim to keep her heart rate above 135 bpm during moderate exercise; she would also aim to stay below 156 bpm, which is RHR plus 80% of HRR.

For anyone who finds this a bit too complicated or inconvenient, use a rating of perceived exertion (RPE); it can be just as effective. RPE is based on a person's subjective rating of how hard they are working. The Borg RPE scale goes from 6 to 20 and a person's exercise intensity should be between 13 or 14 (somewhat hard) and 15 or 16 (hard).

Although the Borg RPE is a subjective measure, if you multiply the numbers of the scale by 10, it corresponds very closely to TTHR with a lower level of 130–140 bpm and an

case study 13.7

Walk your way to better health

Read this extract from Saga's six-week programme for walking your way to better health.

Weeks 1–3: get the habit

Research shows that it takes 21 days to establish a habit so the first three weeks are designed to help you do just that.

Week 1: Aim to accumulate 30 minutes' walking three days a week to get used to walking. The easiest way is to take three walks of 10 minutes.

Weeks 2–3: Now you've established a routine, increase the length of time you walk to 15 minutes and aim to do two walks four days a week.

Weeks 4–6: upping the ante

The next three weeks are devoted to increasing the distance you walk, the speed at which you walk and the difficulty of your walks so you are able to cope with longer, more arduous trips.

Week 4: Stick to 15-minute walks but increase the number of days to five days a week.

Week 5: Step up your walking habit by increasing duration to 45 minutes in total five days a week. You can still break it up into 15-minute chunks if that suits you or experiment with doing one longer walk of, say, 30 minutes and a shorter one of 15.

Week 6: Time to increase the effort a bit by adding some more speed and/or endurance to your workout. Continue with five 45-minute walks a week but either try to walk further each time or take a different route and include a few hills and inclines.

Weeks 6 onwards

Aim to increase to an hour of walking every day - remember you can still break it up into smaller chunks if it's hard to find the time.

Walk your way to better health
www.saga.co.uk/health/healthyliving/exerciseandfitness/walking.asp

activity
INDIVIDUAL WORK

1. What information would need to go into a training diary for this six-week programme?

2. How might a pedometer help someone on this programme?

3. After completing the programme, how could a person try to maintain their motivation and increase the intensity of their exercise?

upper limit of 150–160 bpm. With a little practice it can be very accurate. A physical activity rated somewhat hard should leave a person breathless and warm, whereas an activity rated hard should make a person hot and sweaty. Here is the whole scale:

- 6, 7, 8 – very, very light
- 9, 10 – very light
- 11, 12 – fairly light
- 13, 14 – somewhat hard
- 15, 16 – hard
- 17, 18 – very hard
- 19, 20 – extremely hard.

activity
INDIVIDUAL WORK 13.10

P4

1. Plan a safe and effective 6 week health-related physical activity programme for a man aged 40 who is unfit and overweight or for a woman aged 23 who is suffering from work-related stress.

2. Compare your programme with others produced by the group and discuss the strengths and weaknesses of each programme.

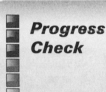

Progress Check

1. List the main lifestyle factors that contribute to the maintenance of health and well-being.

2. Which aspects of an unhealthy lifestyle would contribute to the development of coronary heart disease?

3. What types of question would be asked in a lifestyle questionnaire?

4. Name the five stages of change and identify the stages where it would be best to start intervention for change.

5. Why would you ask a person to complete a PAR-Q?

6. Write your top 10 tips for a healthy lifestyle.

7. A male friend, age 26, has a resting heart rate of 68 bpm. He asks you to give him advice about what his training heart rate should be, working at 75% of his heart rate reserve. Calculate his maximum heart rate and heart rate reserve. What should be his training heart rate?

8. If your friend in Question 7 didn't have a heart rate monitor, where on the Borg RPE should he work to?

9. Give (a) a physiological sign of stress, (b) a psychological sign of stress, and (c) a behavioural sign of stress.

10. Describe three ways of increasing the intensity of a physical activity programme.

Exercise for Specific Groups

Olivia McLaughlin

This unit covers:

- Exercise provision for specific groups
- Exercise benefits for specific groups
- Exercise referral schemes
- How to plan and deliver an exercise session for a specific group

This unit considers the variety of provision available for specific groups in society, especially groups where access to exercise programmes can sometimes be limited. It explores the benefits of exercise for specific groups and the different referral schemes. It identifies the key aspects of planning and delivering an exercise session for specific groups.

grading criteria	To achieve a **Pass** grade the evidence must show that the learner is able to:	To achieve a **Merit** grade the evidence must show that the learner is able to:	To achieve a **Distinction** grade the evidence must show that the learner is able to:
	P1 describe the provision of exercise for three different specific groups Pg 130	**M1** compare and contrast the provision of exercise for three different specific groups, identifying strengths and areas for improvement Pg 130	**D1** analyse the provision of exercise for three different specific groups, providing recommendations relating to identified areas for improvement, and the benefits to specific groups Pg 131
	P2 describe four different benefits of exercise to each of three different specific groups Pg 131	**M2** explain four different benefits of exercise to each of three different specific groups Pg 131	
	P3 describe the exercise referral process Pg 144		
	P4 plan and deliver an exercise session for a selected specific group, with support Pg 148	**M3** plan and deliver an exercise session for a selected specific group, explaining chosen components Pg 148	**D2** plan and deliver an exercise session for a selected specific group, justifying chosen components Pg 148

The provision of exercise for specific groups

Specific groups

 See Unit 23 for more information

Disabled people

Provision for people who live with disabilities has undoubtedly improved over the past few years. The Disability Discrimination Act 1995 (DDA) emphasised the need for equality in society and the need to accept differences in people and to include all in society. The act aimed to make many services more accessible to the **disabled** and to increase their active participation in their communities.

What is provided

There has been massive training to make coaches aware of the needs of disabled people. This enables them to adapt their training sessions to include every member of the group. It provides opportunities to exercise in a fully **inclusive** environment. To support this movement, local councils have introduced specialist disability officers. They provide an expert service to all areas of the country and initiate a customer-centred service. There has also been development in specialist equipment tested by disabled people to ensure a full body workout; the main aim is to provide opportunities to exercise in a fully inclusive environment.

remember
The DDA has kick-started the provision for disabled people in society, including specialist equipment.

Figure 15.1 Sport England works with disabled people

Disability Discrimination Act 1995
www.opsi.gov.uk/acts/acts1995/1995050.htm

Sport England has provided information and access to literature on health and fitness and its impact on lifestyle. In 2005 Sport England launched the Equality Standard for Sport, supported by all four national sports councils and the national governing bodies (NGBs). It is strictly monitored and each sports council must have initiatives that reach disabled people if it wants to receive funding.

Prenatal women

Pregnant women want to optimise their health and fitness. Exercise helps to prepare pregnant women for the physical stress of labour and helps them get back in shape when the baby is born. The government and other agencies have recognised this and have provided facilities where pregnant women can exercise.

What is provided

Pregnant women can consult medical experts and exercise programmes designed for their individual needs. Medical centres provide well-woman clinics where pregnant women can exercise together and discuss fitness and lifestyle. Healthy living classes educate pregnant women about lifestyle and fitness.

Sports centres provide a variety of fitness options for pregnant women. For example, there are gentle exercise classes such as yoga in medical centres. Leisure centres also offer swimming classes for pregnant women. This provides opportunities to exercise in a fully inclusive environment. Communities offer walking groups where pregnant women feel supported and socialise together. The Guild of Pregnancy and Postnatal Exercise Instructors also offers membership and exercise advice.

There are DVDs on sale with specific exercises for pregnant women plus many magazines, books and internet guides on exercise during pregnancy. **Private organisations** sell **prenatal** exercise courses to pregnant women.

Figure 15.2 BabyFit offers fitness programmes for pregnant women

Post-natal women

Post-natal women also require exercise and assistance to achieve optimal fitness. The government has now included exercise in its approach to the care of women post childbirth.

What is provided

Mothers can exercise together and learn about **post-natal** fitness in post-natal exercise classes facilitated by qualified instructors. The NHS also organises post-natal exercise classes. For example, there are specialised aerobics classes for post-natal women. Sure Start organises post-natal classes for young mothers. The National Institute for Health and Clinical Excellence (NICE) runs a government scheme; Active for Life targets new mothers and is run by the Health Development Agency (HDA).

There are also private facilities available for post-natal women. For example, YWCA organises exercise classes for post-natal women. There are also post-natal partnerships working together to provide facilities for new mothers. Private organisations and **public organisations** work sensitively and consider practical issues for new mothers such as crèche facilities, venues and class times.

Equality Standard
www.equalitystandard.org/
BabyFit
www.babyfit.com/
Sure Start
www.surestart.gov.uk/
National Institute for Health and Clinical Excellence
www.nice.org.uk/

Older adults

remember

There are many exercise schemes that give older people longer-lasting health and fitness and that include all members of society.

The Equal Opportunities Act 2004 has lifted the profile of the elderly as a social group. There is also the societal aspect – policy makers now recognise that a healthy elderly population is essential to control healthcare spending and ensure that the country's resources can sustain the increasingly elderly population that will develop over the next decades.

What is provided

Leisure centres put on **OAP** classes that target the elderly. Examples are low-impact aerobics classes, specialised yoga and swimming lessons. Swimming pools offer discounts and elderly-only swimming times. This encourages elderly people who may feel nervous or embarrassed about swimming in front of younger people. It also helps elderly people to interact with each other socially. Personal trainers deliver specialist programmes where the activities are tailored to the needs of one person or one group of people, examples are low-impact activities such as fit balls and walking.

If an elderly person has suffered a stroke or heart attack, their doctor may refer them to an approved personal trainer who will try to rehabilitate them by working on their individual needs. It is crucial to rehabilitate the client back to a healthy state and to prevent any deterioration in their condition. Local colleges now offer classes such as yoga for the over-60s and specialist exercise classes for older people only, so that older people feel more confident and comfortable in their surroundings. Roughly 300 000 **voluntary organisations** offer exercise programmes for the elderly, ranging from Age Concern to the Alzheimer's Society. Without this **provision**, many elderly people and people with **Alzheimer's disease** would not participate in physical activity at all.

Figure 15.3 Many elderly people prefer to exercise with their own age group

If elderly people do not do physical activity, they become less mobile and suffer health problems that could cost the NHS millions of pounds. It is argued that prevention is more effective and cheaper than cure. Age Concern runs local schemes that offer exercise to the elderly. Many elderly people think that exercise is for the young and they don't want to embarrass themselves around young people. Age Concern tells elderly people how they can do exercise with people of a similar age without fear of embarrassment. The aim is to help elderly people feel more comfortable about taking part in activities.

Carers (Equal Opportunities) Act 2004

www.opsi.gov.uk/ACTS/acts2004/20040015.htm

Age Concern

www.ageconcern.org.uk/

Alzheimer's Association

www.alz.org/

Children and young people

Chapter 3 of *Choosing Health: Making Healthy Choices Easier* begins with a quotation jointly attributed to Demos in 2004 and the Children's Play Council in 2002:

> Increasingly, evidence is showing that children and young people do not play out as much as they used to and that their opportunities for free play are restricted.

Choosing Health

www.dh.gov.uk/en/Publicationsandstatistics/Publications/PublicationsPolicyAnd Guidance/DH_4094550

case study 15.1

Don't fall for it!

'Don't fall for it!' is a scheme set up by the London Boroughs of Camden and Islington. It aims to re-educate the elderly about the dangers of falling and how to reduce the threat of falling. One way it does this is to incorporate a variety of exercise options into everyday life for the elderly. The options include exercise to music, walking, trips to parks and gardens, and traditional methods such as swimming and light weights. Elderly people obtain an action pack, complete a form and return it to the health authority. From this, the development officer can assess their needs and place them in a suitable project. There is also practical advice on safety in the home.

Imagine that you receive a referral card for Gladys, aged 78. Gladys has suffered from a broken hip, is slightly overweight and feels isolated. She is nervous around new people but wishes she had more to do with her time. On her referral card, she says she enjoys reading and listening to music. She used to enjoy gardening but she has not been able to do it since she gained weight and had her hip replacement.

activity
INDIVIDUAL WORK

1. Identify some activities that you think Gladys would enjoy.
2. Organise a programme of activity using the FITT principles: frequency, intensity, time and type.
3. Give a specific example of an activity you have included in the programme.

Most of our behaviour that we use in later life is learned in childhood. We are socialised into different behaviours such as eating wisely, learning different hobbies, and exercise. The government recognises this and has included children as one of its target groups to increase exercise and the opportunity to join in. In its Every Child Matters initiative, the government aimed for every child in the UK up to age 19 to feel empowered and supported to stay safe, be healthy, enjoy and achieve, make a positive contribution and achieve economic well-being.

Following this initiative, the government has set a variety of provisions for children. The inspection framework of the **Office for Standards in Education (Ofsted)** now includes how a school contributes to the physical development of a child. There is also growing concern about **obese** children. The celebrity chef Jamie Oliver has highlighted the need for healthy eating in UK schools. But healthy eating is not enough, exercise is crucial too.

What is provided

Schools have had their funding increased to run after-school clubs and to buy sports equipment. The government has changed its thinking on physical education (PE) and wants it to include all areas of society and all groups at risk of not participating, groups such as girls and ethnic minorities. After-school clubs offer children a variety of sports to improve their physical and psychological health and increase their **motivation**. Some schools have set up before-school clubs to offer similar activities. The link between education and sport is now given great importance. For example, children learn about the benefits of healthy eating and exercise. Charities raise funds for sports facilities and educate young people about the importance of exercise; one example is Schoolchildren for Children.

Children's Play Council
www.ncb.org.uk/Page.asp?sve=912
Every Child Matters
www.everychildmatters.gov.uk/
Feed Me Better School Dinners
www.jamieoliver.com/schooldinners
Schoolchildren for Children
www.schoolchildrenforchildren.org/

Schools receive National Lottery funding for children's after-school programmes. Sport England now lets local communities decide how money is spent. It has 49 **community sport networks** that decide and deliver the required local provision. Sport England funds these projects to improve local communities. Its sports development officers coordinate a variety of tournaments and mini Olympics around the country.

Schemes such as Sporting Champions invite famous athletes like Sir Steve Redgrave to visit schools that have achieved **Clubmark** and **Sportsmark** accreditation. These athletes give coaching workshops and other interactive sessions for young people. This is how one advocate described it:

> I am working with Sport England to help show all young people that they can enjoy sport and benefit from improved health, social skills and school results. It is not just about encouraging the sporty kids to become more sporty. Everyone can benefit from and enjoy a Sporting Champions visit.

Leading supermarkets have included children and exercise in their business plans. In two years Sainsbury's Active Kids scheme has bought £34 million of sports equipment and sports experiences for 26 000 schools. Private gyms also target children by offering children's areas with equipment designed for children, such as smaller weights, plus specialised aerobics classes. There has been an increase in holiday activity weeks, where leisure centres and privately owned gyms target children to participate in activities during the school holidays.

Figure 15.4 After-school clubs offer children a variety of sports

Community sport networks
www.sportengland.org/csn.htm
Sporting Champions
www.sportingchampions.org.uk/
Clubmark
www.clubmark.org.uk/
Activemark and Sportsmark
www.sportengland.org/activemark_and_sportsmark.htm
Active Kids
www.sainsburys.co.uk/activekids/active_kids_home_v2.htm

Referred clients

The Department of Health and the **primary care trusts (PCTs)** want to cut the number of people going to the doctor or to hospital. One way to do this is to stop people falling ill.

What is provided

The Department of Health encourages doctors to refer people to clinics for exercise programmes delivered by specialist exercise instructors. Expert trainers tailor fitness programmes to suit the patient's medical condition. New Start is a government scheme where people with similar medical conditions can meet and exercise together. NHS physiologists and trainers are taught how to look after **referred clients**, and all referrals are reviewed by medical experts. There are also reviews that check the well-being of referred clients.

Private training consultancies tailor training schemes to suit a person's lifestyle and fitness requirements. There is specialist funding to improve the facilities of sports centres that take referred clients.

case study
15.2

Partnerships for personal development

Bank Priory School is a specialist school for people with disabilities. Sacred Heart is a mainstream primary school. Students from the two schools formed a partnership to do sports activities. They played adapted tennis, cricket, table tennis and football. Staff from both schools received specialist training. The partnership helped the personal development of all students and staff. The students learned to integrate with their peers and developed social skills. They did frequent exercise which improved their psychology and physiology. Projects like this remove barriers to participation and social stigma, one of the aims of the DDA.

activity
GROUP WORK

1. Assess the importance of projects like this one. Explain why they are crucial to our sporting society and how this came about.

2. Do you think this project is sustainable and should its funding continue? Give reasons for your answers.

Provision

Government provision

Children

The government takes a multi-agency approach that involves schools, local authorities, social services, **Connexions** and the youth offending team (YOT), where everybody works together for the good of the child. By 2008 it hopes to establish a children's trust in every area and wants up to 2500 children's centres. Its ultimate aim is to offer exercise provision to children in every community. The government also wants to develop extended schools that offer after-school activities such as football and netball and it wants to increase the number of specialist schools and academies for sport. It has introduced legislation to limit the sale of school playing fields. One aspect included in the **DDA** is sport and **accessibility**.

Disabled people

The key objective is to give disabled people easier access to sport. It gives every person the opportunity to access sport to improve their standard of living and it improves the quality of service to all able-bodied and disabled people. All sports facilities are inspected to ensure they meet the requirements of the DDA. According to the Department of Health, some of the main requirements of the DDA are to prevent or delay the onset of ill health and disability, to reduce the impact of illness and disability on health and well-being, to identify barriers to healthy living (e.g. cultural appropriateness of services), and to work in partnership with other agencies to develop healthy communities which support older people to live lives that are as fulfilling as possible. This includes working with council services such as leisure and lifelong learning.

Link | See page 77 in Unit 13 for more information on exercise, health and lifestyle

To help older people take part in exercise, the government considers aspects such as cost, transportation and equipment. Exercise is a tool to integrate older people with each other and with different social groups. Exercise can improve the mental health of older people. The government investigates and responds to the specific needs of groups. To deal with the social, political and economic issues that discourage older people from doing sport, the government encourages care homes to hold daily exercise sessions. This builds physical strength and may reduce the number of falls among older people.

Private provision

Thousands of private companies offer hundreds of services for many specific groups. These services include specialist training programmes at private leisure centres for older people and pregnant women. Personal trainers have one-to-one sessions with referred clients and other people. Private swimming pools, dance centres and private gyms offer classes exclusively for pregnant women; this helps to include people who may otherwise feel uncomfortable or embarrassed to participate.

Voluntary provision

remember

Charities cover all specific groups; they offer free services and improve lives.

Many services are provided by voluntary organisations. Schoolchildren for Children is described in Case Study 15.3. Ageing Well is a national project endorsed by Age Concern. It aims to maintain physical, mental and social activity throughout life in the over-50s. The main objectives are to encourage healthy lifestyles and help the elderly get the most out of the health services. Age Concern Gateshead has developed a range of physical initiatives as part of this project.

Schoolchildren for Children
www.schoolchildrenforchildren.org/

Partnerships

Government legislation increasingly requires public services and sporting organisations to work in partnerships. For example, a school may work with a supermarket to achieve a common aim, such as to get young people back into sport.

The government hopes to develop greater community links with disabled people and include their input and ideas. They consult with sports departments to ensure that sporting delivery services satisfy sports policy. Girls in Sport was a project where Nike worked with local schools to include young girls in physical education. Nike provided training and resources to over 2300 schools, bringing benefits to staff and students.

The Department for Culture, Media and Sport (DCMS) aimed to increase the percentage of children that spend a minimum of 2 h per week in and out of curriculum-based subjects to 100% by September 2006. Integrated Training for London consists of the London Active Partnership, London Sports Forum for Disabled People, Sports Coach UK, Sport England (London), Sports Leaders UK, the Youth Sport Trust and some local authority sports development officers. It aims to provide services and opportunities for disabled people to recognise their potential as sportsmen, sportswomen and sports coaches.

case study 15.3 — Schoolchildren for Children

Schoolchildren for Children is a charity that encourages children to raise money through exercise. The money is then used to buy extracurricular sports equipment for their own schools and for schools in the world's poorest countries. Its simplicity is part of its appeal. The children raise a pound each by walking, running or jogging a minimum of 1 mile (1.6 km) as an organised school activity – 50 pence for their own school and 50 pence for schools in developing countries. At the time of writing, 292 schools are registered and 76 644 pupils participate, up from 210 schools and 60 015 pupils in 2005.

activity — GROUP WORK

1. In groups, create a short presentation about a Schoolchildren for Children project or a similar project in your area.

2. Describe the health benefits of the product you have chosen.

Figure 15.5 Games and equipment have been designed for disabled participants

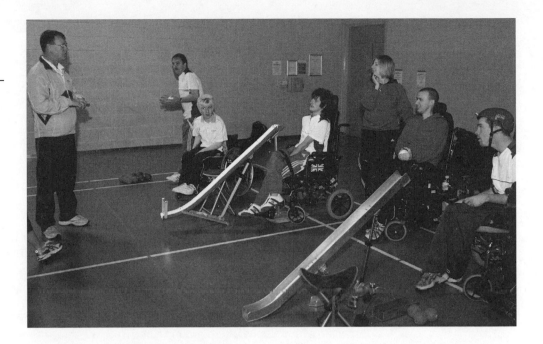

Policies for specific groups

Facilities

The UK has hundreds of facilities to meet the needs of specific groups. For example, there are leisure centres that offer a variety of specialist classes for different groups. National parks offer guided walks for all groups, especially older people. Sport England employs development officers that go to leisure centres and set up weekly activities for people with disabilities, such as bowling for the blind and swimming for people who cannot move their legs.

See page 269 in Unit 23 for more information on sport in society and inclusiveness

The variety of public provision includes community centres that offer classes for prenatal and post-natal women, swimming pools that deliver specialist classes tailored to individual needs and hospital outpatient centres with specialist programmes. The government has offered academy status to schools that offer a specific set of provision to children.

Classes

A range of classes are available to specific sports groups. For example, leisure centres offer swimming for the over-60s, pregnant women, post-natal women, children and the disabled. Leisure centres offer tailored aerobics classes such as low-impact aerobics and hi-lo aerobics. There are a variety of football clubs and associations. Yoga and **pilates** classes have been designed to increase abdominal strength in pregnant women. Specialist **spinning** classes slowly build cardiovascular endurance in the elderly. There are organised walks on nature trails for older people plus special classes for patients with injuries, stroke victims and people who have coronary heart disease.

Equipment

There is a huge variety of equipment, so here are just a few examples. There are specially designed footballs for disabled people such as footballs with bells for the partially sighted or visually impaired and gym balls for pregnant women. Children in schools have access to state-of-the-art gym equipment such as horseboxes and to specially adapted swimming seats for the disabled. Schools also have aerobics mats plus equipment for table tennis, netball, football, cricket and lacrosse.

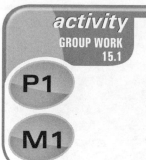

1. In groups of four, research and present the specialist equipment available for three specific groups.
2. Highlight the positives and negatives about the equipment.
3. Identify how this could be improved and the benefits.

Range of activities

There is short tennis for wheelchair users or a bell in a ball for blind cricket. Bowling competitions have been set up by local colleges for children. There are also leisure opportunities for bowling, cricket, football, netball, gymnastics, hockey, aerobics, yoga, pilates and spinning. Referral programmes are available such as group-specific activities for all groups, especially disabled people and the elderly. Local communities have set up initiatives such as active walks for referred clients with coronary heart disease. There are specific gym sessions where groups can participate in activities together.

Choose three groups mentioned in the unit. Design a newspaper article to discuss the provision on offer. Consider whether the available provision is adequate. Identify any areas for improvement and any benefits to the groups. Look at what is on offer and find out about public opinion in the media and through opinion polls.

The benefits of exercise for different specific groups

Exercise brings many benefits. It stimulates the brain, reduces heart disease and increases muscle tissue. Whatever your age, weight or medical condition, there are always exercise opportunities to improve your fitness.

Benefits
Physiological

Prenatal women

Regular cardiovascular training can improve circulation; this helps to reduce **varicose veins** plus swelling and soreness of the feet and ankles, especially uncomfortable during the later stages of pregnancy. Regular exercise can prevent tiredness and lower-back pain; back pain is a common complaint during pregnancy. Regular exercise can also improve muscle tone, strength and endurance. It can make it easier to carry the weight gained during labour and helps a woman prepare for the physical act of labour. Specific exercise can strengthen the **pelvic floor**, and a strong pelvic floor is crucial during labour. Exercise can help to prevent medical conditions such as gestational diabetes mellitus and hypertension; gestational diabetes mellitus is diabetes that develops during pregnancy and hypertension is high blood pressure. Some people argue that women who exercise regularly during pregnancy have a shorter labour with fewer complications. Exercise can also fend off the baby blues as it increases self-esteem. Exercise helps pregnant women to sleep.

Post-natal women

Exercise can be crucial after childbirth. A woman's posture can be improved by strengthening their muscles and their spine. Weight is a big issue for post-natal women. Regular exercise can reduce weight and increase self-esteem. A person who exercises will feel more energetic, and this is just as true for post-natal women. More energy, regular weight loss and higher self-esteem help to improve the lives of new mothers and their babies. Regular exercise can help post-natal women get back into shape and regain their figure.

Children and young people

Obesity is the biggest threat to UK children, but this threat can be tackled as children are eager to learn. Exercise teaches them about their bodies and helps them develop motor skills such as running, catching, coordination and balance. They learn through a variety of activities such as ball games, races and swimming. By participating in games and other physical activities, children learn how to socialise and interact with others. They learn about discipline and compromise, camaraderie and team spirit. They improve their social skills and become better at forming and maintaining relationships with other people.

At crucial stages in psychological development, sport can raise a child's self-esteem and develop their personality. Sport develops a child's skeletal system and improves their motor skills, especially sports that require hand–eye coordination such as tennis and badminton. The ability to juggle is a motor skill. Growing children need exercise to develop their basic fitness skills such as flexibility, endurance and strength.

Sports Xtra sells courses to schools that put on extracurricular sport. Suitable for children at Key Stage 1 and Key Stage 2, they help children develop new skills in a supportive, structured environment and encourage them to form positive relationships with their **peers** and their coach. The courses can be structured to complement what the children learn in class.

> **Link**
>
> See page 282 in Unit 23 for more information

> ⓘ
>
> Sports Xtra
>
> www.sports-courses.com/sports-provision.asp

activity
GROUP WORK 15.3

P2

M2

1. In groups of two, list and describe four benefits of exercise for children, prenatal women and post-natal women.

2. Highlight any examples of exercise provision and their impact on these specific groups.

Referred clients

Referred clients can benefit from sport in several ways:

■ **Increased fitness** – research suggests that regular exercise three times per week can increase fitness and stamina, flexibility and strength. It can also give you a healthier heart and other vital organs.

- Rehabilitation – regular exercise improves the rehabilitation of patients suffering from conditions such as strokes, coronary heart disease, **non-insulin-dependent diabetes**, cancer and osteoporosis. It builds up bone density, heart strength and confidence. This improves the patient's physical and psychological well-being, which makes rehabilitation easier.

- Increased bone density – a **sedentary** lifestyle lowers a person's bone density. Bone mass and bone strength can be increased by aerobic exercises such as walking, running and dancing plus strengthening exercises such as free weights, machine weights and abdominal training. For example, dancing increases bone strength in the legs, hips and feet.

Because it is so diverse, sport can give everyone the opportunity to participate in physical activity. There are some sports that people do all through their life, such as cycling, swimming, aerobics, walking, tennis and badminton.

case study 15.4 — Exercise referrals in Glasgow

Read this extract from 'The Social Benefits of Sport', a report by Greater Glasgow NHS Board in 2002. Note that **systolic blood pressure** is the highest blood pressure in the arteries and occurs at the end of the cardiac cycle, whereas **diastolic blood pressure** is the lowest blood pressure and occurs during the resting phase of the cardiac cycle.

An example of good practice, and demonstrating positive partnerships between sport and health professionals, is the Glasgow GP Exercise Referral Scheme. This is coordinated by a team of Health and Fitness Development Officers (HFDOs) within Glasgow City's Cultural and Leisure Services and largely funded by NHS Greater Glasgow. GPs refer appropriate patients to an HFDO who identifies a local exercise programme. An evaluation of 5,173 who were referred to the scheme found that:

- 31% of those referred continued on the programme, 12% of referrals attended until the three-month assessment, 5% of referrals attended until the six-month stage, 5% until the nine-month stage and 9% per cent returned at the final 12-month assessment.

- Some participants decided to leave, for reasons such as deciding to buy equipment and exercise at home, or finding alternative forms of exercise. Some stopped because they felt that they had been 'cured', and their health returned.

- The duration of physical activity per week increased with participation on the programme (especially between baseline and the three-month stage).

- There were reductions in systolic blood pressure for those participating beyond baseline stage, and reductions in diastolic blood pressure for those participating for at least three weeks.

- There was a reduction in depression and anxiety for those who moved beyond the baseline stage.

- Over 60% saw improvements in their general health and general fitness, and in how they felt about themselves.

- The most frequently-mentioned additional benefit was the social aspects of the programme.

- Over two-thirds felt that participation had given them the confidence to exercise independently (this increased with length of time of programme).

1. Comment on the successes of the Glasgow referral scheme and any improvements that could be made.

2. Contact referred clients and GPs to find out how an increase in exercise has helped them.

---

i The Social Benefits of Sport

www.sportscotland.org.uk/pages/download.aspx?id=%7B4C627DBE-C848-4FBC-9E65-929241A8AFA4%7D

Figure 15.6 Greater Glasgow NHS Board understands the social benefits of sport

Psychological

Regular exercise releases **endorphins** into the brain, which immediately make you feel happier. The more exercise you do, the more endorphins you produce and the happier you become. That is why some people become addicted to exercise.

Link See Unit 13 for more information on exercise, health and lifestyle

Exercise also helps to ease nervous energy and tension built up during a stressful day. Regular exercise will release tension and pent-up aggression, which ultimately reduces anxiety. Some people argue that regular exercise can alleviate depression. Here are some other things that exercise can do. Collectively they help to boost confidence and banish depression.

- Increase your sense of mastery, which can help people who don't feel in control of their lives and moods.

- Increase self-esteem.

- Provide a distraction from your worries.

- Improve your health and body, which can help lift your mood.

- Help you get rid of built-up stress and frustration.

- Help you sleep better, which can often be a problem when you're depressed.

remember
Exercise can overcome depression by making a person feel more confident and empowered. GPs think this is very valuable, often more valuable than **antidepressants**.

Specific groups

Older adults

Evidence suggests that even temperate exercise can cut the risk of developing heart complications in later life. Exercise is crucial in later life and can provide real benefits. Here is what Shephard (1997) has to say:

> A regular programme of moderate exercise is a very appropriate recommendation for almost all older adults. Moreover, there is no known pharmacological remedy that can so safely and effectively reduce a person's biological age and enhance his or her quality-adjusted life expectancy.

Exercise has many physiological benefits for older people. For example, regular physical activity can improve core conditions such as endurance, flexibility and strength, all crucial for mobility and independence in later life. Exercise can also increase a person's chances of living longer and reduces heart attacks, strokes and potential falls.

Exercise can improve confidence and self-esteem in older people as they will feel stronger in body and in mind. Regular exercise can make older people feel stronger as it increases muscle mass and strength. Stronger people feel more able to protect themselves and this increases their self-confidence.

NHS documents highlight several health benefits of exercise for older people:

- **Disease prevention and management** – reduced risk of coronary heart disease and stroke, reduction in high blood pressure, enhancements to the **immune system**, reduced impairment and improved strength in people with a variety of neurological disorders, improved quality of sleep, a reduction in accident falls, prevention of post-menopausal **osteoporosis** and improvements in stair climbing and walking ability.

- **Psychological benefits** – improved perception of health and a reduction in stress and anxiety, depression, isolation and loneliness.

- **Social benefits** – wider social networks, new friendships and more intergenerational activity.

- **Fewer complications of immobility** – fewer complications such as **deep vein thrombosis**, gravitational **oedema**, contractures, pressure sores and severe constipation. Gravitational oedema is a swelling of the legs caused by accumulation of fluid; a contracture is a thickening of joint tissue that leads to deformity.

Services for older people

www.dh.gov.uk/en/Policyandguidance/Healthandsocialcaretopics/Olderpeoplesservices/index.htm

National Health Service

www.nhs.uk

Disabled people

Exercise is crucial for disabled people. Here are some of the benefits:

- It provides an opportunity to socialise.
- It increases and stabilises mobility.
- It controls weight gain.
- It increases muscle mass.
- It improves overall health such as endurance, flexibility and strength.
- It maintains a healthy heart.
- It strengthens the main systems of the body such as the respiratory, cardiovascular and muscular systems.

case study 15.5

GATE analysis

Manchester primary care trust (PCT) has set up Getting Active through Exercise (GATE) to provide a variety of exercise classes for all people over 65. The classes offer walking, swimming, aerobics and yoga to enhance mental and physical well-being. They also educate people about their bodies and how to look after themselves. One of GATE's main aims is to reduce the amount of falls suffered by older people in their homes.

GATE teams work closely with other local partnerships such as health agencies and NHS bodies. It is the only one of its kind in Manchester. No other provision for older people focuses only on the link between health improvement and exercise. GATE's ultimate goal is for different public, private and voluntary agencies to work together to promote health and exercise among the elderly.

Falls Prevention in Manchester
www.manchesterpublichealthdevelopment.org/mphds/falls-prevention.html

activity
INDIVIDUAL WORK

1. Design a presentation of about 15 min that describes and explains the benefits of exercise for three specific groups.

2. Give detailed descriptions of the available provision and name some real-life examples.

Exercise also has psychological benefits:

- It releases stress.
- It helps with sleep.
- It increases vitality.
- It increases self-esteem and confidence.

Figure 15.7 Exercise is crucial for disabled people

case study 15.6 — Inclusive Fitness Initiative

Read this extract from the Barrow Sports Council website.

What is the Inclusive Fitness Initiative?

Research conducted by the Gary Jelen Sports Foundation in 1998 investigated the barriers that prevented disabled people participating in gym based physical activity. The research found that fitness suites were inaccessible for a number of reasons:

- A lack of accessible fitness equipment for disabled people.
- A lack of disability awareness among facility staff providing a barrier to participation.
- A lack of awareness amongst disabled people of the benefits of exercise and healthy lifestyle activities.
- A lack of accessible leisure environments.

Inclusive Fitness Initiative – is a Sport England Lottery Funded project working with a number of fitness facilities across the country to support them to become accessible to disabled and non-disabled people. Currently there are a number of fitness facilities applying for IFI status within Cumbria including:

- Hoops Basketball Centre (Barrow-in-Furness)
- Sheepmount (Carlisle)
- Kendal Leisure Centre (Kendal)
- ActiveZone Lakes College (Workington)

These fitness facilities are seeking funding through the IFI to purchase adaptive fitness equipment and to deliver staff training and hope to be launched in Summer 2005.

What the IFI offers disabled people

IFI facilities offer a wide range of benefits to disabled customers, including:

- Facilities that have undertaken both physical and communication access improvements.
- Equipment that has been accredited through testing by disabled people, and will enable the vast majority of disabled people to access a full body workout.
- Staff that have a high level of training and an understanding of the needs of disabled people both inside and outside the fitness suite.
- The opportunity to exercise in a truly inclusive environment.
- Access to healthy lifestyle choices.

Barrow Sports Council
www.barrowsportscouncil.org.uk/subpages-disability/sports_innit.htm
Inclusive Fitness Initiative
www.inclusivefitness.org

activity
INDIVIDUAL WORK

1. As a sports therapist, write an article for a female referred client who is disabled.
2. Use your article to explain how sport and exercise can benefit her.
3. Describe the types of exercise she can do to improve her general fitness.

Referred clients

This section considers the types of client that are referred and the benefits it brings.

Obesity

A person can be classed as obese if they are at least 20% heavier than the correct weight for their height. Research suggests over half the adults in England are obese. The UK government has established the Association for the Study of Obesity to raise awareness and has set up schemes to combat obesity. Here are some of the widely accepted benefits of exercise for obese people:

- Weight loss – may be gradual but it's worth it.
- A stronger heart – reduces blood pressure.
- Delayed onset of type 2 diabetes.
- Increased metabolism – helps people burn off food more quickly.
- Assistance in lifting depression.
- More confidence and better body image.
- A sense of control over weight loss and weight gain.
- Improved body perception.

Sedentary lifestyle

Computer games, the internet and digital television have brought many benefits but they have also encouraged a couch potato lifestyle that has led to an overweight and unfit population who prefer to watch sports than take part. Exercise can improve overall health and fitness but it can also bring families together, build friendships and strengthen relationships. Some families go on bike rides together and some play football.

Coronary heart disease

Coronary heart disease (CHD) is seen as the biggest threat to people in the western world. It reduces the blood supply to the heart muscle by thickening the inside walls of the **coronary arteries** so they become narrower or completely blocked. This thickening is called **atherosclerosis**. The thickening usually happens when a person has a high level of low-density lipoprotein (LDL), or bad cholesterol, in their blood.

CHD patients experience all the usual benefits of exercise, covered earlier in this unit, but one benefit is particularly important for CHD patients. Exercise increases levels of high-density lipoprotein (HDL), or good cholesterol, which reduces atherosclerosis and improves blood flow through the arteries. Exercise also decreases the amount of triglycerides in the bloodstream; high levels of triglycerides can also lead to CHD.

Pulmonary or metabolic disease

Two related pulmonary diseases are **chronic bronchitis** and **emphysema**. In both diseases there is chronic obstruction of the airways so it is more difficult to inhale air into the lungs. The obstruction is generally permanent and worsens with time. Here are some of the benefits that exercise can bring:

- Fewer negative effects of short-term exercise
- A stronger heart and improved circulation
- Increased endurance and better lung adaptation
- A better blood supply to the brain, hence better cognitive function
- Enhanced self-esteem and a sense of empowerment.

Injuries

Athletes experience a wide range of injuries and they use exercise during and after recovery. Exercise plays a crucial role in rehabilitation and prevention of future injury. Here are the benefits it brings:

- Increased endurance and lung capacity
- A gradual rebuilding of strength

- Increased circulation and muscular strength
- Wellness facilitation of the injury
- A greater sense of belongingness and team identity
- Increased self-esteem and empowerment.

Arthritis

The umbrella term 'arthritis' is used to cover most rheumatic diseases that produce inflammation of the joints leading to severe pain, stiffness and soreness. Here are some of the benefits that exercise can bring:

- Increased joint movement
- Stiffness relief
- Increased flexibility
- Increased muscle strength, which helps to support the joints

---

case study 15.7 — YWCA's obesity briefing

The YWCA has noticed that young women are at severe risk of becoming obese and has produced an obesity briefing that calls for several things to happen.

The YWCA is calling for:

- A reform of PE in schools to include a wide range of physical activities which are more attractive to today's girls and young women; PE kits that are deemed comfortable by young women; showers to be made optional

- Leisure centres to offer targeted and low cost activities which appeal to young women

- Parents, teachers and youth workers alike to promote healthy eating and exercise

- The Government to sponsor a targeted media campaign promoting healthy eating and a wide range of physical activity

- The Government to encourage the media and fashion industry to present realistic images of women, following on the success of 'Listen Up' – the Government-sponsored campaign in 2000

- Sustained funding for innovative projects set up and developed by women's organisations.

The same briefing document contains this paragraph on outdoor activities:

Young women working towards the Duke of Edinburgh award at the YWCA's GK centre in Plymouth take part in a variety of outdoor activities. These include hiking, sailing and orienteering. Additionally, they have successfully participated in the Ten Tors Challenge consisting of two days walking and a night camping on the moors.

YWCA obesity briefing
www.ywca-gb.org.uk/docs/Obesitybriefing.pdf

---

activity
INDIVIDUAL WORK

1. Identify the reasons why females may not participate in sport and physical activity.

2. Provide practical solutions that could encourage females to participate more.

3. Research initiatives in your area that target females to participate more in sport and physical activity.

- Improved cardiovascular fitness
- Increased stamina.

Exercise also helps to control a person's weight so they are not as heavy and put less strain on their joints. There are many schemes for **arthritis** sufferers. South Norfolk Council offers a referral programme where patients socialise together, exercise and improve their condition and gain access to new workouts and treatments.

case study 15.8 — Healthier Hull

East Riding of Yorkshire Council has developed an exercise referral scheme:

'Exercise Referral' is a physical activity scheme which enables GP's and other health professionals to recommend a course of exercise for patients with a variety of medical problems. Participants are referred to a 20 session programme which includes activities such as gym training, swimming and toning sessions to name but a few.

Exercise Referral is aimed at inactive people, with a variety of medical problems who wish to become more active. Suitable medical problems may include people who are overweight, have high blood pressure, have low risk coronary heart disease factors, are depressed, have joint problems/osteoporosis and have low self esteem or social problems.

Over 30 leisure centres work alongside GPs in the area to provide specialist facilities to injured clients. All referred clients are monitored and their progress is checked. All instructors are suitably qualified and are able to handle clients in group or one-to-one settings. A press release from the council in 2006 sets out some of the results:

Between January and December 2005, 258 people were referred onto the scheme, with 167 completing their 20-session programme. Nearly 60 per cent of those completing their programme went on to join the gym membership scheme at their local leisure centre.

Other results include:

- 70 per cent of participants lost weight.
- 66 per cent reduced their body mass index.
- 59 per cent reduced their blood pressure.
- 46 per cent reduced their resting heart rate.
- 81 per cent reported an improvement in their health.

And here is some feedback from a client:

The scheme is an excellent initiative and without it I wouldn't have taken the plunge!

Exercise referral in East Riding
www.eastriding.gov.uk/az/FACE_CATEGORY_page_PROC?pParentCat=
1048&pType=1#link1935
www.eastriding.gov.uk/newsflash/archive/06041806699.html

activity
GROUP WORK

1. In pairs, create a factsheet about the East Riding scheme. Your factsheet should be designed for a person who has had injury problems and should explain how the scheme can help them.
2. Discuss why the scheme is there and the benefits people receive when they attend.

Osteoporosis

Osteoporosis is a loss of normal bone density, mass and strength, leading to increased porosity and vulnerability to fracture. Here are some of the benefits that exercise can bring:

- Increased muscle strength for greater protection
- Increased bone density
- More bone formation
- Lower bone loss due to ageing
- A greater sense of well-being.

The Body

www.thebody.com

Mobility problems

Lack of mobility makes it very difficult for people to take part in society. They have difficulty getting around due to stiff joints, arthritis and soreness. Here are some of the benefits that exercise can bring:

- Stronger muscles that build and repair more easily
- A greater sense of power and confidence
- Loss of weight, hence lower stress on the muscles
- A more active part in society.

Exercise referral schemes

Exercise referral process

The UK government has heavily promoted exercise referral schemes. Without rehabilitation or support, a patient who has already had one heart attack has a much higher chance of having a second. Exercise referral schemes can help patients improve and maintain their fitness on the road to recovery. Exercise on Prescription is a government scheme run by the British Association of Sport and Exercise Sciences (BASES) and monitored using a national quality assurance framework.

British Association of Sport and Exercise Sciences

www.bases.org.uk/

Referral professionals

Doctors refer patients to fitness experts. The doctor makes a medical diagnosis and if the patient satisfies criteria for a fitness programme, the doctor makes the referral. For example, if you are obese and your health is at risk, a doctor can refer you to a specialist fitness training instructor. The instructor can then devise a fitness programme to meet your needs. If you have arthritis, the doctor may refer you to a physiotherapist who can help. Medical examinations required for insurance policies such as life insurance policies could flag up problems for referral. Doctors can identify possible problems when patients come for routine consultations and check-ups.

Sports clubs and referrals

Sports clubs can refer their players to specialist organisations and people. A good example of this is if a player suffers from a torn ligament, they will be referred to physiotherapists and sports therapists who will consult with the client and devise a programme to match their needs.

remember

All the referrals must be on paper. A phone call is not sufficient. Doctors and sports therapists have their own banks of professionals. Physiotherapists and doctors need to complete a consultation form.

Figure 15.8 A fitness
specialist asks patients to
complete the PAR-Q

PAR-Q Medical Status Questionnaire

Being more active is very safe for most people. However, some people should check with their doctor before they start becoming much more active. If you are planning to become much more physically active, start by answering the seven questions below. If you are between the ages of 15 and 69, the PAR-Q will tell you if you should check with your doctor before you start. If you are over 69 and you are not used to being very active, check with your doctor.

Common sense is your best guide when you answer these questions. Please read the questions carefully and answer each one honestly: place a tick in the space to the left of the question to answer yes. Leave blank if your answer is no. Please ask if you have any questions. Your responses will be treated in a confidential manner.

[ ] Has your doctor ever said that you have a heart condition and that you should only do physical activity recommended by a doctor?
[ ] Do you feel pain in your chest when you do physical activity?
[ ] In the past month, have you had chest pain when you were not doing physical activity?
[ ] Do you lose your balance because of dizziness or do you ever lose consciousness?
[ ] Do you have a bone or joint problem that could be made worse by a change in your physical activity?
[ ] Is your doctor currently prescribing drugs (e.g. water pills) for your blood pressure or heart condition?
[ ] Do you know of any other reason why you should not do physical activity?

If you answered YES to one or more questions
Talk with your doctor by phone or in person BEFORE you start becoming much more physically active or BEFORE you have a fitness assessment. Tell your doctor about the PAR-Q and which questions you answered YES to. You may be able to do any activity you want, as long as you star slowly and build up gradually. Or you may need to restrict your activities to those that are safe for you. Talk with your doctor about the kinds of activities you wish to participate in and follow his/her advice.

If you answered NO honestly to all questions
You can be reasonably sure that you can:

* Start becoming much more physically active. Begin slowly and build up gradually. This is the safest and easiest way to go.
* Take part in a fitness assessment. This is an excellent way to determine your basic fitness so that you can plan the best way for you to live actively.

Even if you answered NO to all questions, you should delay becoming much more active:

* If you are not feeling well because of a tempporary illness such as a cold or a fever. Wait until you feel better.
* If you may be pregnant. Talk to our doctor before you start becoming more active.

Sports therapists

Sports therapists provide programmes, give advice and oversee the rehabilitation of particular injuries and conditions. They can review cases and refer clients to beneficial schemes. For example, a client suffering from diabetes can be referred to schemes that will make them feel more comfortable.

Physiotherapists

Doctors refer many patients to physiotherapists. A physiotherapist can make further diagnoses and identify the main areas of concern. Then they may refer the patient to a fitness scheme. For example, a patient who suffers from arthritic pain might receive initial treatment by a physiotherapist and then be referred to a tailor-made exercise programme once the inflammation and acute pain have subsided.

Referral process

The process begins with a diagnosis from a doctor or physiotherapist. The patient is then referred to a fitness specialist who asks them to complete the PAR-Q. This questionnaire reveals a clearer picture of the patient's needs so the fitness specialist can devise a training programme. Figure 15.10 is an example of an exercise referral form.

PACE Exercise Referral Scheme

www.warwickdc.gov.uk

Figure 15.9 After the PAR-Q there is an activity referral form

ACTIVITY REFERRAL FORM

Referral details

Surname ....
First name ....

Address ....
....
....

Postcode ....
Telephone ....

Health check

Please tick and complete relevant sections
( ) No medical problems   ( ) Male
( ) Medical condition   ( ) Female

Details of any medical condition
....
....

Any other relevant information
....
....
....
....

Current medication
....
....

Figure 15.10 Warwick the PACE maker

PACE Exercise Referral Scheme

The Warwickshire Exercise Referral Scheme (PACE) is designed to increase the number of people who take part in moderate activity on a regular basis and who have medical conditions which will benefit from this increased activity.

Who can join the PACE scheme?

- Patients with existing selected medical conditions (see below) who do not currently take part in physical activity
- Over 16 years of age
- Motivated to start an active lifestyle
- Patients of any of the local doctors practices listed below

What medical conditions are included in the scheme?

To be referred a patient must have been diagnosed with one or more of the follwoing conditions:

- Hypertension
- Diabetes
- High risk of coronary heart disease
- Lower back pain
- Osteoporosis
- Coronary Rehabilitation
- Obesity

Press Release New Obesity Criteria for PACE

Which practices are part of the scheme in the Warwick District ?

- Priory Medical Centre, Warwick
- Cubbington Road Surgery, Leamington Spa
- Croft Medical Centre, Leamington Spa
- Radford Road Surgey, Leamington Spa
- Warwick Gates Family Health Centre, Warwick Gates
- Lapworth Surgery, Lapworth

What does the scheme include?

The scheme is designed around 24 exercise sessions over a 12 week period (2 sessions per week) which take place in the local Leisure Centre and include gym activities, swimming, aerobics and water aerobics. Patients purchase vouchers at the leisure centre and use a voucher each time they attend an exercise session. Before starting the programme patients will meet with trained gym staff who will help them chose which activities are best for them and give them advice on how to train and achieve the best from the activities. Trained staff are always on hand to offer advice during the 12 week programme.

Vouchers cost £10.80 for a book of 8 off peak vouchers (day time and weekends) and £15.95 for a book of 8 peak voucers (all other times)

The scheme is currently in operation at:

Newbold Comyn Leisure Centre

St Nicholas Park Leisure Centre

If you feel you could benefit from the scheme and are a patient at one of the above doctors surgeries please speak to your Practice Nurse or doctor on your next visit.

case study 15.9

Fitness for Life

Read this extract from the website of Ribble Valley Borough Council.

As many of you will know, there are numerous benefits to be gained from regular exercise or physical activity including weight control, reduced blood pressure, strengthened muscles and bones and an improved sense of well being. However, many people feel nervous about starting exercise either because they do not know what to expect or because they are concerned about going too far and hurting themselves. However, the 'Fitness for Life' exercise referral scheme is an ideal start.

Fitness for Life is available throughout the Ribble Valley. Your GP or Practice Nurse can refer you onto the scheme if they think you will benefit from regular exercise or physical activity. Suitable people include those who are currently inactive or have specific medical conditions such as high blood pressure, diabetes or joint problems. People referred onto the scheme will benefit from:

- Free initial consultation including health check
- Discounted rates at participating centres
- Access to specific Fitness for Life exercise sessions
- Free re-assessment health check

You will meet with your Health and Fitness Consultant and together you will discuss the best type of exercise for you. Exercise sessions are held in the following venues:

- Roefield Leisure Centre
- West Bradford Village Hall
- Newton Village Hall
- Trinity Youth and Community Centre
- Longridge Sports Centre
- Ribblesdale Pool
- Gisburn Festival Hall

You will be able to start your exercise programme in a safe environment with other like-minded participants. Regular Re-assessments will help keep you motivated and make sure you are still benefitting from your exercise programme.

If you are interested in Fitness for Life you can pop in to see your GP or Practice Nurse who will assess whether the scheme is appropriate for you.

Fitness for Life in Ribble Valley

www.ribblevalley.gov.uk/site/scripts/documents_info.
php?categoryID=1039& documentID=532

activity
GROUP WORK

1. Create a factsheet that describes Fitness for Life in Ribble Valley. Your factsheet should say who can take part, how they take part and what are the benefits. Make your factsheet user-friendly and include images.

2. Research exercise referral schemes in your area and compare them with Fitness for Life in Ribble Valley.

Types of scheme

Exercise for the elderly

Elderly people suffer from conditions such as arthritic pain and coronary heart disease. They need low-impact exercises that are not too strenuous. The London Borough of Lambeth has set up Healthy Active Heart Club, where elderly people do activities such as healthy walks to help their hearts. It is free, relaxing, boosts confidence and helps people make new friends.

Age Concern Lambeth

www.ageconcernlambeth.org.uk/index.cfm?id=3147

---

case study 15.10

Mrs Rogers gets energised

When Mrs Rogers started an exercise referral scheme, she could not exercise for more than 10 min at a time. But she threw herself into the sessions and the walks programme. As a regular walker, she was given a pedometer and log to document her progress every week for a month.

This month she logged an average of over 10 000 steps per day. This is more than the recommended number of steps per day. She said, 'I've not felt this energised for years.'

---

activity

INDIVIDUAL WORK

1. You have to find the funds for a scheme such as Healthy Active Heart Club in your area. Devise a presentation for your local council that stresses the needs of this programme and its benefits.

2. You receive funding. Write a proposal for the committee to help them decide how to use it and what resources to buy.

---

activity

INDIVIDUAL WORK 15.4

P3

Find out about an exercise referral scheme and write a review of it for a local newspaper.

Planning and delivering an exercise session for a specific group

Effective practitioners follow three stages for all sessions: planning, delivery and review.

Plan the session

Aims

The aims of the session must be something that everyone can achieve. Do not plan a football session for children aged 7 where you aim for every child to get a cross in the box. This is too much to ask of a 7 year old. Here are some realistic aims for youngsters:

- To introduce participants to passing and moving

- To demonstrate the concept of creating space

- To teach participants to pass the ball using the inside of their foot.

It is equally unrealistic to expect a group of elderly people to run non-stop for 20 min, but they could probably walk for 20 min at a leisurely pace. Here are some other unrealistic aims for elderly people:

■ To achieve a working heart rate of 150 bpm (beats per minute)

■ To play a game of Kwik Cricket.

Here are some realistic aims for elderly people:

■ To raise their heart rate in a comfortable manner

■ To play a game of crown green bowls at a group pace.

Outcomes

Outcomes are more specific and they need to be measurable. They must include the main focus of the session and provide stepping stones to improvement. The number of outcomes should reflect the available time in the session. A 1 h session generally requires about three or four outcomes, but it all depends on what you are doing.

Validity

Do my outcomes reflect the aims of the session? Are they going to get the result I want? Ask yourself these questions when you are formulating your outcomes. If the aim of a netball session is to introduce participants to throwing and catching, an outcome on shooting does not fit the aims of the session.

Reliability

Can each outcome be achieved by all participants in a group and by all similar groups? Can it be repeated? Suppose you are delivering a session to a group of prenatal women where the outcome is 'to be able to swim 50 m', ask yourself whether this is achievable for all the women in the group and for other groups of prenatal women.

Example outcomes

■ Demonstrate the ability to swim 50 m

■ Walk about 5 km

■ Hold the down-faced dog pose in yoga for 30 s

■ Throw, catch and move in a netball session

■ Shoot a football at the net five times.

Resources

Consider resources in your session plan. For example, it is not valid to plan a session in a swimming pool for 60 min when you only have the pool for 45 min. There are three main types of resources: human resources, facilities and equipment.

Human resources

Without the correct staff/participant ratio under the NGB guidelines, it is not safe to run a session. For example, if you are taking a football session for 12 people it is not realistic to have only one coach. It will not be productive and the coaching will be poor; it could even be dangerous if some participants have disabilities. Plan the session around the participants, not the other way round. If you don't have enough people for a session, do not do the session; it is highly unsafe and may threaten your quality of coaching.

Facilities

Incorrect facilities could jeopardise the safety of participants. Always stick to the NGB guidelines on facilities. Ask around to find out about the quality of facilities and the owner's attitude to safety. Try to use a leisure centre that has an excellent reputation and that has been recommended by a trusted source. Location is an important aspect of a session. Elderly people are unlikely to attend a gym session held 48 km from where they live. Always plan the session to suit the participants.

Equipment

Examine all the equipment before you arrange any sessions. Find out about any equipment that has been adapted or specially developed for specific groups such as the disabled. Make sure all the equipment is safe and if you have any doubts, do not use it. For example, in a football session, if the goalposts are not properly weighted down, do not use them; set up some cones instead. Unsafe equipment is not just dangerous, it produces poor sessions that waste everyone's time.

See Unit 2 in *BTEC National Sports Book 1* for more information on health and safety in sport

Medical history

When you plan a session, you must know the medical conditions and screening results of all the participants. Suppose some participants have coronary heart disease, then you must tailor the session to suit these participants and use a variety of innovative ideas. Obtain informed consent from all parents or guardians of children that take part in a session. Tell parents and guardians that if they want to take photographs of children, they need to obtain permission before the session begins. One way to do this is to give a permission form to the parents or guardians of all children in the session and have everyone sign it before you allow any photography in that session.

See Unit 23 for more information on working with children in sport

Other considerations

Health and safety

Follow the NGB guidelines on health and safety. If in doubt, do not run the session. Always check that your insurance covers the activities you are delivering. If you work for a leisure centre, read and understand its policies. If you work privately, get private insurance – this is really important.

See Unit 2 in *BTEC National Sports Book 1* for more information on health and safety

Participants

Many participants might not have done sport for many years and will probably be nervous, not fully fit and a little bit scared. Your planning and delivery must take this into consideration. Offer something for participants at all levels of ability; this is called differentiation. For example, a yoga session for pregnant women can offer something to the inexperienced yogi and the experienced yogi.

Timing and sequencing

Timing and sequencing should reflect three things: the participants, the session's aims and outcomes, and the available time. Always include a warm-up and a cooldown. Allow for skill progression. It is great to have session plans with timings, but don't be too rigid when you deliver them. If things don't work or take longer than you planned, revise your timings. Don't rush participants, especially newcomers or people who are anxious. A patient and flexible approach usually goes down much better.

Ability level

Plan your sessions to suit the ability of your participants. Remember that your session outcomes need to be valid, reliable and achievable. For example, do not produce outcomes on **tumble turns** or race starts for a group of novice swimmers.

Marketing

Market sessions in the best places. An obese person may not attend leisure centres very often, but if their doctor knew about your sessions, they might refer the obese person to you. Therefore it makes more sense to market your specialist services to doctors. Before new facilities are built or before existing facilities introduce new services, they do market research to estimate the demand.

> **remember**
> Always plan the session around the participants, not the coach, equipment or location.

Deliver the session

Safe and effective

Follow health and safety principles at all times so you protect yourself and the participants from harm.

Warm-up

A warm-up prepares the body for sport both physiologically and psychologically. Begin with a comfortable pulse raiser that includes every participant and reflects the needs of each participant. A jog may not be an appropriate warm-up for prenatal women, but walking is probably okay. Get the participants to stretch their muscles after a pulse raiser so they will avoid pulling, tearing or ripping their muscles during the main part of the session. Reflect the needs of the group and show awareness and respect. Adolescent

---

case study 15.11

IFI hotspot

Read this extract from the website of Bolton University.

Marketing fitness facilities to disabled people (Bury)

The Inclusive Fitness Initiative was established following research undertaken by the Gary Jelen Sports Foundation, which found that usage of fitness facilities by disabled people was low. An application to Sport England resulted in the English Federation of Disability Sport receiving £1m to establish a pilot initiative with local authorities to find ways of increasing the usage of fitness facilities by disabled people. Bury Sports Development were successful in being one of the national pilots and one of the requirements of receiving funding from the Initiative was to produce a marketing plan, which would outline how the facilities in question would attract disabled users. Guidelines were given by the Inclusive Fitness Initiative programme staff as to what elements needed to be in the marketing plan. Bury sports Development produced their marketing plan by initially setting up a focus group comprising duty officer, gym manager, Sports Development officer, sports Development officer (disabled people) and the leisure center manager. The result was that a marketing plan was produced, which was implemented by having a launch and organizing a series of workshops. At the workshops, people who had influence over provision for disabled people or people from disability groups were shown the adapted fitness facilities and how disabled people could use the equipment. The people attending then went and informed others about the facility. Other methods to promote the facility including adverts, article in a sports directory, posters and leaflets. A link was also made with other schemes eg exercise referral programme, who sent people to the fitness facilities. The results of the marketing showed an increase in the number of disabled groups using the facilities. There was also an increase in usage of the fitness facilities by disabled people who came to the leisure center, but did other activities.

 Bolton University on IFI in Bury
http://data.bolton.ac.uk/cslm/marketingbury.html

---

activity
INDIVIDUAL WORK

1. Devise a checklist to help someone plan a session. Include all the points in the extract. Cover all the relevant issues, such as health and safety, the reliability and validity of outcomes and activities, and the marketing involved.

2. Discuss the benefits of the Inclusive Fitness Initiative for people with disabilities.

girls may be embarrassed to do some types of stretching around boys and a good coach will cater for this. Some coaches use a second pulse raiser before they begin the main activities. This gets everyone ready and prevents last-minute injuries.

- Warm-ups should start slowly and build up gradually.
- Focus on the movements and muscles used in the main activities.
- Use them to increase body temperature, heart rate and breathing.
- Warm blood in joints and muscles frees up movement.
- Warm-ups usually have three parts:
  - Gentle aerobic exercise such as jogging or skipping
  - Gentle stretching
  - Exercise at three-quarters pace, such as running or cycling.

BBC Sport Academy

http://news.bbc.co.uk/sport1/hi/academy/default.stm

Maintenance component

The nature of the session depends on the skill and fitness of the participants and the experience of the coach. Try to feel comfortable with the session and allow it to flow.

Session

Skills

Aim to develop skills within a game scenario. For example, develop throwing and catching skills during a netball session then finish with a game that emphasises those skills. Come fully equipped with different techniques to enhance participants' skills. For example, a yoga practitioner knows the principles behind different yoga poses and will plan their session plan to illuminate those principles. A football coach might plan a sequence of sessions to develop players' skill at crossing the ball.

---

activity
GROUP WORK 15.5

P4

M3

1. Design and deliver warm-up activities for the disabled with support.
2. Explain your choice of components.

---

activity
GROUP WORK 15.6

D2

Justify each of the components in your warm-up activities in Activity 15.5.

Games and activities

A good session helps the participants acquire new knowledge and skills then gives them a chance to apply it, perhaps on their own but usually in a game. Suppose children have worked on shooting skills in basketball, they could then move on to a game where the player with the ball inside the circle must shoot three times. Or suppose children with visual impairments have worked on kicking skills, they could move on to a game where each player must pass the ball before they shoot. A group of swimmers could work on breathing skills then use them as they swim 100 m. Post-natal women could work on breathing skills for yoga then use them in some yoga poses. The activities should reflect the overall aims of the session, so a walking session for the elderly should have walking as its main activity, not running or jogging.

Cooldown

Remember to have a cooldown; it's just as important as the warm-up. Tailor the cooldown to suit the participants, so don't make elderly people run for 5 min. Choose activities such as walking, stretching and sculling – moving slowly up and down a swimming pool using minimal movement. Always include a pulse lowerer and keep things entertaining. For children playing football, make the stretches entertaining and perhaps do them in time to music.

See Unit 4 in *BTEC National Sports Book 1* for more information on sports coaching

Delivery

Rapport with participants

Rapport is being able to reach the participants on their level. Do not use difficult words with children and rush them to understand something. To build **rapport**, you need to be consistent in your decisions. If you challenge one participant for doing something that's incorrect, you cannot let another participant go unchallenged if they do they same thing. Chat to the participants and reach them on their level. For example, if you are delivering a session to prenatal women, feel free to ask them about their pregnancy; allow them to discuss issues or seek advice from you and from the group. They will thank you for this.

Bernstein's code

> **remember**
> Timid people who have not exercised for a while may not be as confident as others.

The sociologist Basil Bernstein proposed that professional people such as doctors, lawyers and teachers use words and language to exclude people without similar education or professional status. A set of complicated words that exclude people is known as an elaborated code, and the term 'elaborated code' is a very good example. Many people frown on language that is used to exclude people. Sport is full of jargon; a nutmeg, for example, is when a footballer plays the ball through the legs of an opponent. Some people can be intimidated by jargon and they may not want to come back for another session. Bernstein recommended that people use simple words which are easy to understand and help people to feel included. A set of simple words is called a restricted code. Remember to use simple words when you try to build a rapport with participants; be approachable and people will respond.

See Unit 11 in *BTEC National Sports Book 1* for more information on sport and society
See Unit 16 in *BTEC National Sports Book 1* for more information on psychology for sports performance

Motivation

Become aware of what motivates each participant; you will recognise it fairly quickly. Intrinsic motivation comes from within a person and includes elements such as beating personal targets or reaching individual milestones. Extrinsic motivation comes from outside a person and could be winning trophies or beating an opponent. Include both types of motivation in your sessions. For example, have games where people compete against each other (extrinsic motivation) and activities where participants work on personal goals (intrinsic motivation).

See page 289 in Unit 16 in *BTEC National Sports Book 1* for more information on motivation

Communication

Use all types of communication in your sessions, verbal and non-verbal, although you will probably rely heavily on verbal communication. Non-verbal communication – gestures, facial expressions, body stance, demonstration, etc. – often expresses your thoughts more effectively than the words you say. A swimmer in the pool may not be able to hear their coach on the poolside, but they can get a lot of information from gestures and body language. Folded arms may mean the coach is unhappy; arms waving like a victory salute probably suggest the coach is very pleased. A good coach should always demonstrate an activity or ask somebody to give the demonstration. A good demonstration helps all participants but especially helps the visual learners.

Learning styles

There are many ways of looking at learning styles. The four main styles that are often considered today arise from work on neurolinguistic programming by Richard Bandler and John Grinder: visual (seeing), auditory (hearing), kinaesthetic (moving) and tactile (touching).

How visual learners prefer to learn

- Look at the teacher's face intently.
- Look at wall displays, books, etc.
- Often recognise words by sight.
- Use lists to organise their thoughts.
- Recall information by remembering how it was set out on a page.

How auditory learners prefer to learn

- Listen to verbal instructions from the teacher.
- Use dialogues, discussions and plays.
- Solve problems by talking about them.
- Use rhythm and sound as memory aids.

How kinaesthetic learners prefer to learn

- Learn best when they are involved or active.
- Find it difficult to sit still for long periods.
- Use movement as a memory aid.

How tactile learners prefer to learn

- Use writing and drawing as memory aids.
- Learn well in hands-on activities such as projects and demonstrations.

Teaching English
www.teachingenglish.org.uk

Observation skills

Make observations during all activities. Be in position and ready to make observations right from the start of the activity. Feel free to jot things down in a notebook, unless a participant asks you to refrain. Give the participants time and space to correct their mistakes. Do not rush in too quickly.

Correction of technique

If you notice that a participant is not grasping a technique, help them in a supportive and non-judgemental way. This will build a rapport between you and all the participants, not just the person you help. The other participants will notice the way you behaved, and your supportive, non-judgemental approach will reassure them.

Modifications to exercises

Modify exercises to suit the needs of the participants. There are a variety of modified ball sports for disabled participants. Ensure that your session plan accommodates these adaptations and justifies them too.

Feedback

Give feedback to each participant and use the medal–mission–medal method. First tell them how they did things well (medal), then tell them how they can improve things (mission) and finally say how well they did (medal). Here is an example for a child swimmer: 'That was very good, your breathing technique was well timed. All the stroke needs now is more of a pull in the arm; it may help if you try to go a bit slower. Well done, you are really coming along.' Always give constructive feedback and avoid feedback that could make a person feel insecure and undermined.

Review the session

See page 114 in Unit 13 for more information on goal setting

Methods

Coaches who review their sessions and welcome constructive feedback often grow from strength to strength. Evaluation helps a coach to develop their sport-specific, interpersonal and communication skills. This improves their coaching sessions and helps them progress. There are several ways to evaluate your performance. Here are a few examples.

Questionnaires

Questionnaires are quick, easy, cheap and informal. You can hand them out at the end of a session for completion by participants, observers and even you. Table 15.1 is an example of a questionnaire for a football coaching session. Notice that the information is sometimes limited to yes/no answers. A follow-up chat gives a participant the chance to expand on their answers.

Table 15.1 A questionnaire for a football coaching session

	Yes	No	Don't know	Maybe
1. Did you enjoy the session?				
2. Do you think skills have been learned and developed?				
3. Was the pace of the session comfortable?				
4. Were the activities useful to enhance the skills?				
5. Did you learn from the session?				
6. Was there enough time for each activity?				
7. Would you prefer more group work?				
8. Did you enjoy working individually?				
9. Did you feel physically able to complete all the activities?				
10. Would you come back to this coach for more sessions?				
Please use the space below to add any extra comments that you think may be useful				

Many thanks for your time spent completing this questionnaire

Peer feedback

Peer feedback is feedback from other coaches – expert comment from people you work with. It is widely used and often contains really good suggestions. Good peer feedback is patient and supportive. It can range from a formal write-up to an informal chat, and most peer feedback is relatively quick to obtain.

Checklists

Checklists are quick, cheap and reliable. Design checklists that record the things you really want know. Here are some suggestions: Was the warm-up appropriately timed? Did I communicate effectively with the group?

Self-evaluation and SWOT analysis

Be honest and constructive when you evaluate yourself, otherwise it's a waste of time. SWOT analysis looks at strengths, weaknesses, opportunities and threats. You can apply SWOT analysis to all sessions. Table 15.2 is a SWOT analysis of a swimming session for disabled children.

 See page 72 in Unit 12 for more information on development

Table 15.2 A coach's SWOT analysis for a swimming session with disabled children

STRENGTHS	WEAKNESSES
What went well	**What could be improved**
Timing of session	I did not communicate effectively
Good warm-up	I could not get on the right level with the children
Activities were appropriately paced	The cooldown was a bit boring for the children
OPPORTUNITIES	**THREATS**
How I can change things	**What could stop me changing things**
Speak to other coaches about how to get on better with children	Not much time before the next session
Research other cooldowns	No easy access to the resources
Spend more time with children and learn how to communicate with them	

Take the knowledge you gain from self-evaluation and use it in your next session to help your professional development (Figure 15.11).

Figure 15.11 Follow this reflective cycle for every session

The session is completed

Self-evaluation via questionnaires, checklists peer observation and journals

A personal target is made for the next session

The information and personal targets from evaluation are taken in and used in the next coaching session

Development plan

After the evaluation, formulate some SMART personal targets:

■ **Specific** – set yourself specific targets like this: to improve my non-verbal communication over a month by observing more experienced coaches. This target is too vague: to improve my communication skills.

■ **Measurable** – make your targets easy to measure like this one: to improve my demonstration skills by performing at least five demonstrations in each session. It is hard to measure this target: to improve my demonstration skills.

■ **Achievable** – coaching skills take a lifetime to develop; set small, achievable targets and build your expertise gradually.

■ **Realistic** – set yourself challenges that require just a bit more effort; each success brings a little more progress and will give you more confidence for the next challenge.

■ **Time-based** – set deadlines for your targets, but no longer than 2 months, otherwise you could lose interest and give up.

1. In pairs, using the examples cited above as a guide, review the planning and delivery of a chosen exercise session for a group of children.
2. Devise some SMART targets and some non-SMART targets.

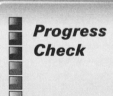

The ER in SMARTER is for evaluated and reviewed. These two aspects should be incorporated to complete the full coaching circle.

Progress Check

1. What are the benefits of exercise for (a) pre- and post-natal women, (b) older adults and (c) children and young people?
2. Give examples of schemes that help the specific groups in Question 1.
3. Explain how organisational partnerships can benefit the health of specific groups.
4. Identify exercises that would suit each of the specific groups in Question 1.
5. Explain what happens when a GP refers a person to a fitness expert.
6. People with illnesses can get benefits from exercise. List some of the benefits.
7. What checks should be done before a person starts a fitness programme?
8. What are the main components of an exercise session?
9. What methods are used to review an exercise session?

Sports Injuries

Helen Moors

This unit covers:

- How to identify risk factors and how to prevent common sports injuries
- A range of sports injuries and their symptoms
- Methods for treating sports injuries
- How to plan and construct treatment and rehabilitation programmes

Sport has many health benefits but there is always the risk of injury. Prevention is better than treatment, so a large part of this unit looks at the main factors that can lead to injuries or that predispose performers to injuries. Then it considers different ways to minimise those risks. It also explains what to do once an injury has occurred.

grading criteria	To achieve a **Pass** grade the evidence must show that the learner is able to:	To achieve a **Merit** grade the evidence must show that the learner is able to:	To achieve a **Distinction** grade the evidence must show that the learner is able to:
	P1 describe extrinsic and intrinsic risk factors in relation to sports injuries Pg 169	**M1** explain how risk factors can be minimised by utilisation of preventative measures Pg 176	
	P2 describe preventative measures that can be taken in order to prevent sports injuries occurring Pg 178		
	P3 describe the physiological responses common to most sports injuries Pg 178	**M2** explain the physiological and psychological responses common to most sports injuries Pg 180	**D1** analyse the physiological and psychological responses common to most sports injuries Pg 180
	P4 describe the psychological responses common to sports injuries Pg 178		

<table>
<tr><td rowspan="2" style="writing-mode: vertical-lr">grading criteria</td><td>To achieve a **Pass** grade the evidence must show that the learner is able to:</td><td>To achieve a **Merit** grade the evidence must show that the learner is able to:</td><td>To achieve a **Distinction** grade the evidence must show that the learner is able to:</td></tr>
</table>

	To achieve a **Pass** grade the evidence must show that the learner is able to:	To achieve a **Merit** grade the evidence must show that the learner is able to:	To achieve a **Distinction** grade the evidence must show that the learner is able to:
	P5 describe first aid and common treatments used for four different types of sports injuries Pg 188		
	P6 design a safe and appropriate treatment and rehabilitation programme for two common sports injuries, with support Pg 192	**M3** design a safe appropriate treatment and rehabilitation programme for two common sports injuries Pg 192	**D2** evaluate the treatment and rehabilitation programme designed, justifying the choices and suggesting alternatives where appropriate Pg 192

How common sports injuries can be prevented by the correct identification of risk factors

More and more people are being encouraged to take up sport, but people who play sport run the risk of injury. A **sports injury** is commonly defined as an injury resulting from acute trauma or repetitive stress associated with athletic activities. Sports injuries can affect bones or soft tissues such as ligaments, muscles and tendons. But the range is much wider than that; we need to consider physiological, psychological and environmental factors, and this makes it much harder to reach a precise definition. Sports injuries are so prevalent that there is a recognised branch of medicine called sports medicine which deals with injuries or illnesses brought about from doing sport. The term 'sports medicine' was officially coined at the International Congress of Sports Medicine in 1928. Sports medicine covers many disciplines such as cardiology, pulmonology, orthopaedic surgery, exercise physiology, biomechanics and traumatology.

Some risk factors of doing sport are hardly thought about, perhaps because they are just assumed to be there. In law the term **volenti non fit injuria** is often used when a plaintiff is trying to claim damages as a result of an injury which they think was caused by negligence. Volenti non fit injuria is used as a defence in tort – a civil wrong, whether intentional or accidental, from which injury occurs to another – where there is a voluntary assumption of risk. In other words, when a person takes part in an activity accepting and fully aware of the risks, then they cannot later complain or ask for compensation for an injury suffered. Most national governing bodies (NGBs) of sport make clear that a person has to take responsibility for their actions and accept the level of risk involved. You can see an example in this mission statement from the British Mountaineering Council (BMC):

> The BMC recognises that climbing and mountaineering are activities with a danger of personal injury or death. Participants in these activities should be aware of and accept these risks and be responsible for their own actions and involvement.

Perhaps this comes as no surprise. Climbing a mountain on the end of a rope is quite a risky activity. However, in 2005 four men who took part in the Great North Run died of sudden arrhythmic death syndrome (SADS), a condition that can occur at any time but is far more likely to occur during physical exertion. Even people who take up walking run the risk of developing an overuse injury that could prevent them taking part for a period of time. So it is important to identify the risks of an activity then take all reasonable steps to minimise them. Risks are usually categorised as being extrinsic or intrinsic.

History of sports medicine
http://en.wikipedia.org/wiki/Sports_medicine#History
SADS and cardiac risk in the young
www.sads.org.uk

Extrinsic risk factors

Extrinsic risk factors are factors, other than physical factors related to the performer, that can increase the incidence of injury. Some examples are the coach, the environment and the equipment used.

Coaching

Most sports sessions are led by a coach. Do not underestimate the coach's role in risk management. Under the law of negligence, the coach has a duty of care to ensure the safety of the people they are working with. Whether the coach is employed or working as a volunteer, the level of care must be appropriate to the activity and the participants. Here are some situations that could lead to problems:

- Activities are not planned in a logical way to give progression and development.
- The coach ignores a child's height, weight, age, skill level, experience and maturity.
- Potential risks are not communicated to participants, officials and spectators.
- No records are kept on relevant medical information, previous injuries and previous accidents.
- There is no clear code of conduct and behaviour for the participants.
- Participants are not clear about the rules of the activity and do not adhere to the rules, including NGB guidelines.
- There are no clear sanctions when a person breaks the rules.
- The coach is not qualified or experienced enough for the activity they are coaching.
- Injured players are selected for the team or injured players are allowed to remain on the field of play.

Figure 17.1 Every coach has a duty of care to keep people safe

■ Treatment given to an injured participant is given by an untrained individual.

■ There is no clear leadership in high-risk situations.

Incorrect technique

If the performer does not replicate the desired technical and biomechanical movement pattern for a particular skill, this can place undue stress on joints and associated soft tissue, leading to injury. This is particularly true of activities where a lot of force is applied. Incorrect technique during the lift is the most common cause of injury in weight training. Many people do not know the technique required for each exercise so they can avoid stresses and strains on their body that may cause injury. Always seek advice so the lift is performed at the right angle and through the correct range of motion. The weight should be under control, with no bouncing movements; do not use your back to compensate for lack of muscle strength. Demonstrate the correct technique before any increase in resistance. Even a skill like running can be made more efficient by maintaining linear momentum and reducing joint impact, hence reducing the likelihood of injury.

Running at speed combined with fast overarm bowling creates huge potential for injuries. Fast bowlers use three techniques: front on, side on and mixed. The mixed technique seems to contribute to lower-back injuries as the cricketer has to absorb excessive ground reaction forces and these forces can affect the lumbar region of the spine. This can cause degeneration of the discs between the vertebrae and soft tissue damage. Many injuries can be related to poor technique, so do a full skill analysis to identify where techniques can be improved. Performance analysis software, such as Dartfish, Kandle and Quintic, is widely used for this. The English Institute of Sport began using Dartfish in 2006.

Kandle
www.kandle.co.uk
Quintic
www.quintic.com
Dartfish
www.ambra-solutions.co.uk
English Institute of Sport
www.eis2win.co.uk

Figure 17.2 Analyse performance with a software package

Environmental factors

Performers have to cope with a wide variety of environmental conditions such as very hot or very cold weather, high pollution levels, or training and competing at high altitude. Prolonged intensive exercise in a hot environment is a big challenge to the body's homeostatic mechanism that maintains a constant internal environment. Higher heat production combined with a lower capacity for heat loss leads to hyperthermia, or high body temperature; prolonged hyperthermia will cause the performer to collapse from heat stress.

During the build-up to the Seoul Olympics in 1988 and the Athens Olympics in 2004, national organisers were concerned about the hot climate, but they were also concerned about air pollution. Air pollution can affect performers that need effective oxygen transport and oxygen uptake in their bodies. Some performers acclimatise themselves to heat in special chambers that allow them to adjust the temperature, humidity and oxygen partial pressure, but exercising in polluted air is not a good idea and can trigger a nasty asthma attack in some people.

Ski resorts have recently experienced a lack of snow and evidence suggests this is due to man-made climate change. The lack of snow has meant that more people are packed on to higher slopes, creating congestion and increasing injuries caused by collisions. Off-piste snow is more unstable and this has led to more accidents. In 2006 there were 57 skiing-related deaths recorded in the French Alps, twice the yearly average.

Surface conditions can also contribute to sports injuries. Prolonged running on hard surfaces can lead to overuse injuries, usually knee and ankle injuries. Sports such as football and rugby are not supposed to be played on frosty ground. If the ground is still frozen, studs cannot grip effectively and performers who land heavily after a tackle or fall can suffer severe bruising, breaks and concussion. Large amounts of surface water after rain can lower traction; performers can lose control then collide with another player or overstretch, injuring soft tissue.

> **remember**
> Sports officials usually decide whether or not a surface is fit for purpose.

> **Link**
> See page 21 in Unit 10 for more information on energy balance and climate

Figure 17.3 Lack of snow means bigger crowds on the higher slopes

Clothing and footwear

Most NGB rules stipulate the safety clothing and equipment that must be worn. Here are some examples:

- The Football Association stipulates that shin pads must be worn.
- The English Hockey Association says that goalkeepers must wear their helmet throughout the match unless they are taking a penalty stroke.
- MCC rules say that all batsmen must wear a helmet and face guard.
- Mouth guards are strongly recommended for hockey and rugby players.

Players involved in contact sports, such as American football, usually wear full body armour and a helmet with face guard. Rugby is another contact sport but the players wear very little padding, especially when compared with American football. Perhaps that's one reason why rugby is the number one sport for injuries. Serious injuries can easily happen in sports that use hard balls, such as cricket and hockey.

Myocardial contusion – bruising of the heart muscle – can be caused by a blunt trauma to the chest, such as the impact of a hockey ball struck from close range. That is why a hockey goalkeeper wears protective padding to cover their chest. Bruising of the heart can disrupt its conduction system and keep a player out of the game for several months. Ski slopes are becoming more crowded, so skiers are advised to wear a helmet.

Essentially, performers should wear protective clothing that is recommended by the guidelines of their sport. It should be well fitted and it should satisfy appropriate safety standards. For example, a mouth guard is more effective when moulded to the shape of the performer's mouth and should be suitable for the impacts that occur in their sport.

How mouth guards work

www.opro.com

Figure 17.4 A mouth guard is more effective when moulded to fit your mouth

Figure 17.5 People with flat feet should wear shoes that give stability

Over recent years the footwear industry has developed a specialist market for sports footwear. It has used scientific methods to analyse the weight distribution through the foot, the ground reaction forces, the angle of impact and other factors. Then it has designed the most appropriate footwear for each sport. Performers no longer pick up a pair of Green Flash trainers at a sports shop, instead they go to a sports shoe specialist that analyses their movement patterns, their weight, the shape of their foot and how their foot makes contact with the ground. They will also be asked about the types of surface they play on. This extract from *Runner's World* offers advice on footwear to runners with flat feet:

The flat foot

This has a low arch and leaves a print which looks like the whole sole of the foot. It usually indicates an over-pronated foot – one that strikes on the outside of the heel and rolls inwards (pronates) excessively. Over time, this can cause many different types of overuse injuries.

Best shoes: Motion control shoes, or high stability shoes with firm midsoles and control features that reduce the degree of pronation. Stay away from highly cushioned, highly curved shoes, which lack stability features.

Footwear for running

www.runnersworld.co.uk

Safety hazards

Risk management tries to control the level of risk associated with a particular activity. Most sports have risk management procedures.

- **Hazard or risk factor** – a condition, object or situation that may be a potential source of harm.

- **Risk** – the likelihood that a hazard will have an impact on people or the environment.

Identify the safety hazards then do safety checks to reduce the risk to performers. Do not start an activity until you have done these safety checks.

Environment safety checks

Officials are usually responsible for checking the condition of the playing surface. For example, before a football or rugby match, the pitch should be checked for any animal faeces and foreign objects, such as glass, cans and litter; all should be removed. The surface should be checked for any holes or patches of surface water, and the match should be abandoned if the ground is too hard; perhaps it is frozen solid in the cold or baked solid in the heat. Surfaces in a sports hall should be checked for any liquid spills or excessive dust. Check for sufficient run-off space behind basketball backboards, etc. Check there is no equipment stored round the edge of the playing area.

Equipment safety checks

Check the equipment to be used during the activity and the equipment worn by the performer. A lot of equipment is now transported to a site then erected, so check that items such as football goals have been properly assembled and secured to the playing surface. Rugby posts should be covered with protective pads and properly secured. There are very strict guidelines on the use of climbing ropes; always check ropes before use. Gym equipment must be secured and must have a maintenance check every year. Always use appropriate equipment for an activity and follow NGB guidelines on its use.

First-aid provision

Adequate first aid no longer means a bucket of cold water and a sponge. Clubmark accreditation demands a fully qualified first-aider to assess and treat injuries. A first-aid kit is a minimum requirement at local events and the St John Ambulance usually attends local festivals and tournaments where more people take part. The higher the likelihood of serious injury, the greater the level of first aid. Any major stadium hosting an international

Figure 17.6 First-aiders no longer rely on a bucket and sponge

rugby event will have a fully equipped treatment room with a doctor, anaesthetist and physiotherapist on hand; a good example is the Millennium Stadium in Cardiff. It is routine for players to return to the field after having a cut stitched. Serious injuries require prompt and professional treatment, and event organisers have a responsibility to ensure that's what happens.

Risk assessments

A risk assessment usually covers three main issues: what things can happen, what is the likelihood they will happen, and what will be the consequences if they do happen. By managing risk, you provide a safer environment for everyone and reduce the likelihood of being sued for negligence. The nature of the sport and the degree of organisation will dictate the scope of the risk assessment, but all risk assessments follow the same steps. Figure 17.7 is a framework for a risk assessment.

Figure 17.7 Follow this framework for risk assessment

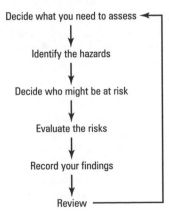

An audit is normally used to identify the **hazards**. Here are some questions it might include:

- Are coaches aware of any medical conditions of the participants?
- Does the club keep records of previous injuries?
- Are the performers advised to warm up and cool down?
- Are training sessions carried out safely with the correct techniques?
- Are your coaches qualified?
- Do you have a club member who is qualified in first aid?
- Do you modify games – rules and equipment – for junior players?
- Do you provide water during matches and practice sessions?
- Do you have a mobile telephone on hand for emergencies?
- Do you complete a safety checklist before you start an activity?
- Do you have a first-aid kit? Is it regularly checked?
- Do you have a maintenance plan for equipment?
- Do you check that all participants are wearing the correct safety equipment?
- Are the playing surfaces checked before play starts?
- Are changing facilities cleaned and kept tidy?

The overall objective is to avoid risk entirely or to reduce the level of risk. Each hazard is given a rating for three separate categories:

- Hazard rating, e.g. will it result in minor injury
- Likelihood rating, e.g. is it unlikely or possible
- An overall risk rating, e.g. low, medium or high.

The overall risk rating is the product of the hazard rating and the likelihood rating. Now consider how each hazard will be controlled or eliminated.

Intrinsic risk factors

Intrinsic risk factors are **risk factors** that are due to the structural and physiological make-up of the individual as well as their level of preparation and skill.

Training effects

Training should be well planned. Proper training should significantly reduce the risk of injury, but things can still go wrong and sometimes, unfortunately, they do.

Muscle imbalance

The muscles that surround a joint can be divided into mobilisers and stabilisers. Stabilisers tend to give postural and joint stability, whereas mobilisers produce the force and movement required. When they work effectively, they complement each other and produce efficient joint movement. Repeated use can cause the mobilisers to shorten and the stabilisers to lengthen and weaken. The mobilisers then inhibit the stabilisers and produce an imbalance between the two muscle groups. This imbalance can lead to injury.

Weak rotator cuff muscles can lead to problems with any sport relying on vigorous overarm actions such as tennis and bowling in cricket. This condition can be resolved by using the correct flexibility and strengthening exercises. More recent work focuses on identifying muscle imbalance in pre-participation screening plus extra assessments during training and competition. Many young performers are now advised to work on core stability muscles such as the transverse abdominus and multifidus, and the rotator cuff muscles that stabilise the shoulder joint (supraspinatus, infraspinatus, teres minor and subscapularis).

Figure 17.8 Rotator cuff muscles

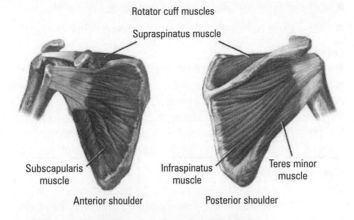

Rotator cuff muscles

Supraspinatus muscle

Subscapularis muscle

Anterior shoulder

Infraspinatus muscle

Posterior shoulder

Teres minor muscle

Figure 17.9 Vigorous overarm actions can injure weak rotator cuff muscles

Rotator cuff

www.physicaltherapy.about.com

Core stability

www.sportsinjurybulletin.com

Detecting muscle imbalance

www.pponline.co.uk

Good preparation

Good preparation helps to reduce injuries. If you travel in a cramped car, arrive with no time for a warm-up, or forget things so you have to borrow equipment, you will suffer the consequences. Here are some guidelines for good preparation:

- Collate all appropriate clothing and equipment for the activity.

- Eat an appropriate meal at the right time before the activity.

- Be fully hydrated and bring fluids to drink.

- Allow enough time to warm up and cool down.

- Choose the right footwear for the surface.

- Do not take part if you are injured or feel ill.
- After exercise, have a shower and change your clothes.

Level of fitness

The body can cope with considerable amounts of stress and forces but only when it is accustomed and has adapted to dealing with the increased demands. Ensure that participants are physically prepared before they do a new activity. Movements that require a sudden burst of strength, speed or controlled force can easily produce injury if the performer is not fully conditioned. Prepare properly for prolonged periods of activity. Training for a marathon requires several months not several weeks.

Overuse injuries

Overuse injuries are usually caused by putting excessive loads on the body, using an incorrect technique, using inadequate equipment, using inappropriate clothing or not allowing sufficient recovery time.

- Excessive loads can arise from inadequate conditioning or inappropriate overload.
- A poor backhand can cause tennis elbow.
- Inappropriate tennis equipment could be the wrong racquet size, the wrong racquet grip or the wrong racquet tension.
- Inappropriate clothing could be wearing shoes without the correct support or cushioning.

Many coaches say that training plus recovery equals adaptation. After exercise, especially resistance exercise that involves eccentric contraction, a performer can experience delayed onset of muscle soreness; the muscles usually start to feel sore 12–48 h after the event. One explanation for this soreness is structural damage to muscle fibre and connective tissue. This damage can also cause an inflammatory reaction that causes histamine to accumulate outside the muscle cells. It is advisable to alternate a heavy, intensive training session with a lighter, more moderate session to allow recovery.

Delayed onset of muscle soreness
www.sportsmedicine.about.com

Individual variables

Age

Most people reach their physical prime in their twenties or early thirties. Ageing lowers a person's performance in strength and endurance activities by 1–2% per year. A person's maximum heart rate drops along with stroke volume, body weight tends to drop but the percentage of fat tends to rise. There is a deterioration in the proteins elastin and collagen, which give stretchiness and flexibility to the soft tissues of the body. An older muscle, with poorer elastin, will not have the contractile speed or strength of a younger muscle and will be more prone to strains and tears. An older person's body synthesises less protein, so there is an overall reduction in muscle mass. Less calcium is deposited in bone and the bones of an older person are less dense and more susceptible to fracture.

Fitness level

It is not possible to store fitness. A person's fitness may be very good after training, but if they stop training, perhaps because of an injury, their fitness will drop. Fitness has several components, so a person may have good flexibility but relatively poor cardiovascular endurance. A person's cardiovascular endurance is influenced by their percentage of slow-twitch muscle fibres and this percentage is inherited, so a person's genes can influence their fitness. A person who has inherited more fast-twitch muscle fibres, which make them better suited to anaerobic activities, will not achieve the aerobic capacity of a person who has inherited a high percentage of slow-twitch muscle fibres, however hard they train.

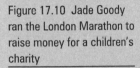

Reality check

Read this extract from the BBC News website.

Jade slated over race 'training'

Reality television star Jade Goody has been criticised by London Marathon organisers for failing to train properly for the 26.2-mile (42 km) race.

The Big Brother celebrity, running for children's NSPCC charity, is thought to have dropped out after 18.5 miles.

Ms Goody has said she 'got bored' with training and had instead been 'eating curry and Chinese, and drinking'.

Marathon director David Bedford said it was 'almost at times suicidal' to start the race without adequate preparation.

'We, of course, recommend that everyone that takes part in the marathon trains, and to start by thinking I'm just going to walk round and not even be able to walk a marathon clearly shows she's done nothing and is not in good shape,' he told LBC News.

i   Jade story on the BBC News website
http://news.bbc.co.uk/1/hi/uk/4939384.stm

Figure 17.10 Jade Goody ran the London Marathon to raise money for a children's charity

activity
INDIVIDUAL WORK

1. Do you think that people should be required to do rigorous training before they are allowed to race in a marathon?

2. Do you think runners should be screened before running a marathon to try to reduce the incidence of sudden arrhythmic death syndrome?

Growth development

The skeletal frame starts out as cartilage then is gradually replaced by bone in a process called ossification. Ossification begins in the diaphysis – the primary ossification site in the main shaft of the bone – then occurs in the epiphyses. An **epiphysis** is a secondary ossification site at the end of a bone. A plate of cartilage is left between the diaphysis and each epiphysis; this is where bones lengthen until they reach maturity. The plate is known as the epiphyseal plate or **growth plate**, and when growth stops, it fuses and becomes bone.

As bones do not fully mature until ossification is complete, young performers can run the risk of damaging the epiphyses or the epiphyseal plate. Injuries to the epiphyseal plate can bring a partial or complete stop to bone growth or sometimes they can accelerate it. Injuries can occur from impact or repetitive overuse. Growth plate overuse injuries have been recorded in performers such as throwers, runners, badminton players and gymnasts.

> **remember**
>
> Training programmes, especially rates of progression, should be tailored to the athlete. Do not apply rigid rules based on an athlete's age or time spent training.

Figure 17.11 Young performers can damage their growth plates

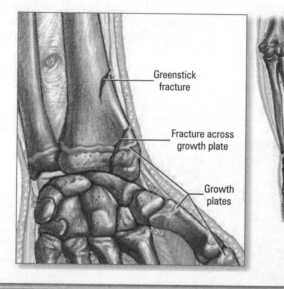

Greenstick fracture

Fracture across growth plate

Growth plates

Adolescent arm bones

case study 17.2 — Gymnast wrist

Most young gymnasts will have the pain for a minimum of 3–4 months before they seek any treatment.

- Symptom – a painful wrist with mild swelling and tenderness.
- Cause – excessive loading of force with hyperextension of the wrist, e.g. vaulting, floor exercises, bar work.
- Assessment – there are 29 sites of ossification in the wrist, so it is difficult to pinpoint any growth plate damage but magnetic resonance imaging (MRI) will help to determine whether it's bone or ligament damage.
- Treatment – there are different treatments for bone and ligament damage.
  - Ligament – immobilisation or surgery.
  - Bone – splint or cast to immobilise.

activity
INDIVIDUAL WORK

1. What can a gymnastics coach do to minimise the risk of the young gymnast developing gymnast wrist?

2. What can be done to make sure that a young gymnast seeks medical advice as soon as the symptoms appear?

Other issues during growth arise when there is a rapid change in the relative lengths of the long bones and their associated muscle groups. An imbalance between the two can damage bone and muscle tissue. Each athlete has their own growth pattern, so take care when coaching young performers.

Previous injury history

The body repairs damaged soft tissue, such as muscle tissue, with scar tissue. Scar tissue is made of collagen fibres, which means it is not the same as the original muscle tissue and it is not as strong. It is important to stretch the collagen fibres during rehabilitation to retain the flexibility of the tissue. Otherwise the muscle could be painful and stiff and could have a weakness that leaves it susceptible to further injury.

Sometimes you need to find the root of the problem that caused the injury. Address any muscle imbalance after rehabilitation by doing further work on strength and flexibility. Sometimes it is a performer's technique that is causing an injury to recur. Encourage the performer to change their movement patterns. Following an injury, a performer may sometimes compensate by putting more strain on other joints, or they can alter their posture. This causes further injuries that may not immediately be associated with the earlier injury.

Flexibility

Flexibility is the range of movement possible around a joint and depends on the amount of stretch allowed by the ligaments, joints, tendons and muscles. Different joints have different structures, hence different degrees of flexibility. The shoulder is a ball and socket joint that allows a lot of movement, whereas the knee is a hinge joint that allows more limited movement. Here are some other factors that influence flexibility:

- The bony features of the joint
- The elasticity of the muscle tissue
- The length of tendons and ligaments
- The elasticity of the skin and the amount of adipose tissue
- The amount of stretch allowed by the antagonistic muscle
- The temperature of the muscle and connective tissue
- Age – you become less flexible as you get older
- Females are generally more flexible than males.

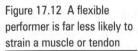

remember
Ask performers to keep a record of previous injuries so they can give a complete injury history to the people that treat them.

remember
Sports physiotherapists give their patients a schedule of flexibility exercises that will rehabilitate their injury.

Figure 17.12 A flexible performer is far less likely to strain a muscle or tendon

The olecranon process is a bony feature that prevents the elbow joint from hyperextending. In general, being flexible means that a performer is far less likely to strain a muscle or tendon and is far less likely to sprain a joint by stretching or tearing a ligament. Most performers incorporate flexibility work into their warm-ups and cooldowns. Too much flexibility, or hypermobility, can lead to a joint being lax; for example, if the ligaments surrounding a joint are stretched, it can lead to lack of stability and joint integrity. If a joint becomes unstable, the muscles cannot control the limbs and joints through the full range of movement and there is a much higher risk of injury.

The Beignton and Horan index is used to assess whether or not a person has hypermobility. A score of 4 or more indicates hypermobility. Here are some other scores and what they indicate:

- 2 – bending the little finger backwards beyond 90°
- 2 – passive apposition of thumbs to forearm
- 2 – hyperextension of elbows beyond 10°
- 2 – hyperextension of knees beyond 10°
- 1 – forward flexion of the trunk with knees extended so that the palms rest flat on the floor in front of the toes.

Nutrition

Diet aids performance and has long been accepted as an important feature of a healthy lifestyle. More recently, research has investigated whether nutrition can help to prevent sports injuries. It is known that when glycogen stores are low, then muscle protein is used as an energy source – protein provides roughly the same number of kilocalories per gram as carbohydrate. If the body does not receive sufficient carbohydrate, then glycogen levels will fall, more protein will be used and this could decrease muscle strength. After a bout of exercise there is an increase in muscle protein synthesis, so a performer's diet should include more protein to help increase muscle mass.

Bone is the hardest connective tissue in the body, mainly because it contains deposits of calcium phosphate and calcium carbonate. Bone stores calcium and exercise causes more calcium to be deposited, increasing bone density and therefore bone strength. Calcium in the diet maintains bone strength and reduces the risk of stress fractures.

Free radicals are created as by-products of aerobic respiration. Any performer who relies heavily on the aerobic energy system will produce significant amounts of **free radicals** in the muscle cells. Free radicals can damage muscle cells, they can cause muscle inflammation and they contribute to delayed-onset muscle soreness (DOMS). The good news is that free radicals can be neutralised by **antioxidants**. Free radicals are very unstable and react quickly with other compounds. Antioxidants combine with free radicals and prevent them from doing any further damage. Two extremely effective antioxidants are vitamins E and C. Any performer doing aerobic activity will benefit from taking vitamin supplements.

Good nutrition also helps to rehabilitate an injury. The body increases its demand for protein when it is wounded or under stress. B vitamins help increase the rate of metabolic functions linked to wound healing and vitamin C aids collagen synthesis to form scar tissue. Vitamin K is needed to make thrombin, which is needed for blood clotting.

Nutrition and wound healing
www.dietetics.co.uk

Sleep

Lack of sleep is often linked with a drop in performance. That is why motorway signs urge motorists to take a break when they feel tired. Sleep happens in several stages that last different lengths of time. As you begin to fall asleep, your muscles start to relax and your breathing becomes shallower; your sleep is quite light at this stage. Then it becomes deeper and you no longer respond to external stimuli. During the stage of deepest sleep, the body's recovery processes are most active and they prepare it for the next day. A consistent pattern of disturbed sleep will mean that your body does not get enough recovery time. If a performer does not get enough recovery time, they can be more prone to receiving an injury or find it harder to recover from an existing injury.

Postural defects

Most people's joints are correctly aligned to cope with the forces they experience during everyday activities. But when joints are out of alignment, known as structural deviation, then the muscles may have to work much harder; this can cause muscle imbalance and some tendons can become lengthened or twisted. Problems can also be caused by a difference in leg length. As one side is higher than the other, the pelvis tilts sideways and can cause the spine to move laterally, called scoliosis. Poor posture, known as functional deviation, can also cause muscle imbalance that leads to a variety of conditions. Try to improve a performer's posture as it can be the reason behind many overuse injuries. For example, a distance runner that has a pelvis with an exaggerated forward tilt may develop an overuse injury of the knee. Here are some examples of postural defects:

- **Lordosis** – an exaggerated hyperextension of the spine which can be caused by a shortened erector spinae and iliopsoas and weak abdominal muscles.

- **Kyphosis** – hyperflexion of the thoracic vertebrae. This can be caused by a weak trapezius muscle and rhomboids and shortened pectoral muscles.

- **Scoliosis** – a lateral curvature of the spine that resembles the shape of an S or a C. It is usually caused when one leg is shorter than the other, or when a person stands with one leg straight and one leg bent. Carrying a weight predominantly on one side can also contribute to the condition, such as a mother supporting a baby on one hip.

Figure 17.13 Lordosis can be caused by a shortened erector spinae and iliopsoas and weak abdominal muscles

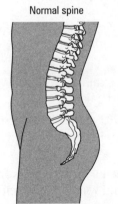
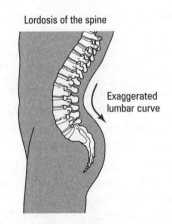

Normal spine Lordosis of the spine

Exaggerated lumbar curve

activity
GROUP WORK
17.1

P1

Have a group discussion about the sports you play and the risk factors in those sports. Make a list of the hazards. Agree definitions for 'extrinsic risk factor' and 'intrinsic risk factor'. Use your list of risk factors to draw two posters – one that shows extrinsic risk factors and one that shows intrinsic risk factors.

Preventative measures

Prevention is always better than cure. It is impossible to prevent sports injuries but it is possible to minimise the chance that they happen and the damage caused if they do. As sport becomes more and more professional, it places greater and greater demands on the performers. Injuries to players went up when rugby union became a professional sport in 1995. Players now train at higher intensity and play higher-intensity matches. Fitter and faster, today's rugby players experience collisions and tackles that can damage their bodies severely.

The Rugby Football Union (RFU) has been under pressure to follow rugby league and ban contested scrums because there is a risk of spinal injury. The International Rugby Board acted quickly to prevent spear tackling after Brian O'Driscoll, the British and Irish Lions captain, suffered a dislocated shoulder in a test match against New Zealand. O'Driscoll was out of the game for five months. Now any player found guilty of a spear tackle will be banned from the game for six months.

In 1996 damages were awarded to a young player who was injured when a scrum collapsed (*Smolden* v. *Nolan and Whitworth*). The court ruled that the referee had failed to discharge his duty of care and had not supervised the game to the standard expected. Changing the rules, banning players who flout the rules and having games officiated correctly are just three ways to minimise sports injuries.

Judgement in *R. V. Vowles*
www.hmcourts-service.gov.uk
Judgement in *Smolden* v. *Nolan and Whitworth*
http://www.timkevan.com/articles/sports%20injury%20article%2015-10-03.html

case study 17.3

Paralysis payout

Read this December 2002 story from the BBC News website.

Rugby player wins paralysis payout

A former amateur rugby player paralysed when a scrum collapsed has won the right to a massive compensation payout from the Welsh Rugby Union (WRU) in a landmark ruling.

Front-row Richard Vowles, 29, from Llanharan, south Wales, broke his back in a match playing for the village side in January 1998.

At the High Court in London, the WRU admitted responsibility for the match referee's failure to opt for uncontested scrums, which caused the collapse while Mr Vowles was playing hooker.

It is the first time an amateur referee in any sport has been held liable for injuries in an adult amateur game and will have 'horrendous consequences' for all sport, according to the WRU.

The ruling appears to make governing bodies responsible for duty of care on the field.

Richard Vowles story on the BBC News website
http://news.bbc.co.uk/1/hi/wales/2571993.stm

activity
INDIVIDUAL WORK

1. What 'horrendous consequences' do you think the WRU expected after this ruling?

2. The WRU accepted vicarious liability and paid the damages awarded to Mr Vowles. What is vicarious liability?

3. If you have suffered a sports injury, what are the benefits of being affiliated to an NGB?

Figure 17.14 Damages were awarded to a young player who was injured when a scrum collapsed

Role of the coach

A well-informed, well-prepared coach can significantly decrease the likelihood of an injury occurring. Here are some points to consider.

Knowledge of the performer

It is becoming more and more common to ask serious performers to complete a pre-participation physical evaluation. This enables the coach to have specific information about the performer that will help them make more informed decisions about the performer's preparation and conditioning.

Before a footballer signs for a new club, they have to undergo a thorough medical examination. They have to disclose their previous injury history and they usually have to be injury-free before any contract is signed. Table 17.1 is an example of a pre-participation physical evaluation.

A performer should also be asked about their medical history. This will often provide a much better insight into potential problems. Here are some specific points to find out:

- Previous illnesses, hospitalisation, etc.
- Family history of coronary heart disease, cancer, etc.
- Allergies to wheat, dairy products or nuts
- Incidence of concussion
- Eating disorders such as bulimia
- Exercise-induced asthma.

Qualifications

Keep your knowledge up to date and regularly renew your qualifications. The Royal Life Saving Society (RLSS) National Pool Lifeguard qualification is only valid for two years. Sports Coach UK, formerly the National Coaching Foundation, provides many courses and resources for coaches. It administers the UK Coaching Certificate to provide quality assurance for qualifications run by individual NGBs. Here is an extract from the Sports Coach UK website:

Table 17.1 Pre-participation physical evaluation

Name		
Height		Heart rate
Weight		Blood pressure
Percentage body fat		Vision R 20/ L 20/
Medical	**Normal**	**Abnormal findings**
Appearance		
Eyes, ears, nose, throat		
Heart		
Lungs		
Abdomen		
Lymph nodes		
Skin		
Musculoskeletal system	**Normal**	**Abnormal findings**
Foot		
Ankle		
Knee		
Hip		
Spine		
Shoulder		
Elbow		
Wrist		
Clear to take part		
Clear after completion of rehabilitation for		
Not cleared for participation		
Reason		
Signed		
Date		

The UK Coaching Certificate is an initiative to endorse coach education programmes, across sports within the UK, against agreed criteria including:

- the endorsement of the coaching qualification a coach will take
- the development of appropriate resources to deliver effective and high quality coach education programmes
- quality assured administration and management structure of coach education provision provided by sports
- quality assured training provision of coach education programmes.

Coaches can now follow a nationally recognised pathway of qualifications and can take extra courses such as child protection and first aid.

Sports Coach UK

www.sportscoachuk.org

Coaching participants

Coaching children is entirely different from coaching adults. Children are still growing, so consider their physiological, social and emotional maturity. Do not put too much stress on immature bones. Find out the most appropriate times to develop strength, speed, etc.

See page 166 for more information on growth plate injuries

Many NGBs are now following the **long-term athlete development (LTAD)** model (Balyi 2001). It was presented as a six-stage model in Sport England's 2004 Framework for Sport in England. Stage 1 introduces the fundamentals to 6 year olds. Stage 3, training to train, is seen as the 'window of optimal trainability', where large gains in strength can be made in males aged 12–16 and females aged 11–15. The gains continue into stage 6.

Children vary in height, weight, fitness and skill, so be careful when selecting children to work together or to compete against each other. Coaches have a greater duty of care when coaching children; they are considered to be in *loco parentis* 'in place of the parent'. Remind children to do warm-ups and cooldowns, to rehydrate themselves and to wear extra layers on cold days.

Figure 17.15 Many NGBs follow the LTAD model

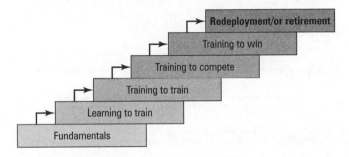

Communication

Effective communication effectively helps to minimise the risk of injury. Communication is a two-way process. Check whether each participant has heard and understood what you have said. Here are some points to remember:

- Have you got everyone's attention and are they listening? This is particularly difficult to gauge when dealing with young children.

- Have you given a clear explanation? Do not use too many technical terms. Give a demonstration if necessary.

- Has everyone understood what has been said? If in doubt, ask a person to explain what you have said in their own words.

- Has the person acted on what you have said?

Make your verbal guidance CRISP:

- Clear

- Relevant

- Interpretable

- Short

- Positive.

Long-term athlete development
www.sportsdevelopment.org
Framework for Sport in England
www.sportengland.org

case study 17.4

Mountford v. Newlands School

This is the first case where a club or school was found liable for injury caused by the selection of an ineligible player. The Court of Appeal, presided over by Lord Justice Waller, upheld that a school was vicariously liable due to the fact that a member of staff had selected a boy that was over the age group for a junior team rugby match and that the boy's size, weight and maturity had contributed to a player from the opposition being injured. The boy was in the same year group but was one year older than the other boys.

The judge found that the cause of the injury was as follows. It is reported in paragraph 48 on the BAILII website (24 January 2007).

> I see no difficulty here. It is obvious that the presence of RK on the field materially increased the risk to the C [the claimant] (among others), by virtue of the far superior height and weight of RK, that a tackle (lawful or otherwise) would lead to injury. Rule 5 was intended to protect players such as the C from that risk and that is exactly the risk which eventuated. I do not think that the C has to exclude the possibility that he could have been similarly injured by a lighter tackler. That seems to me to be tantamount to saying that a participant in a risk sport can never prove that the negligence of an official or organiser caused him damage.

(i) British and Irish Legal Information Institute
www.bailii.org/ew/cases/EWCA/Civ/2007/21.html

activity
INDIVIDUAL WORK

1. In your opinion what effect, if any, will this ruling have on school sport?
2. Quite often a talented younger player is selected to play for an older age group. For example, a 14 year old may play in an under-16 side. Do you think this should be allowed?

Equipment and environment

Before the start of any sports event, there are things that need to be done in order to show an adequate duty of care to all participants, officials and spectators. People are easily distracted, so use a safety checklist and delegate someone to carry out the checks. Draw up the checklist after you have done a safety audit.

 See page 56 in Unit 12 for more information on extrinsic risk factors

Here is a safety checklist for a junior football match on a Sunday morning:

- Are all participants wearing shin pads?
- Are all participants wearing football boots?
- Have the studs been checked?
- Has all jewellery been removed?
- Are all the children free of injury?
- Are separate water bottles available for the players?
- Is a first-aid kit available?

- Has someone got a mobile phone?
- Has someone got all the contact numbers for the parents?
- Is there an inhaler available for player 10, who has asthma?
- Is there warm, waterproof clothing available for the substitutes?
- Is the referee qualified?
- Is the pitch clear of all litter and debris?
- Is the pitch soft enough to play on?
- Are there any holes or very uneven surfaces on the pitch?
- Are the goalposts secure?
- Is the netting secure?
- Are the sidelines free of all obstructions?
- Are the corner flags in place and will they give way if a player collides with them?
- Are spectators standing back from the sidelines?

Some parents may want to join in the children's game. Try to persuade them not to do this, as it is extremely easy for children to get injured by adults. More organised clubs do safety checks but they also do all the relevant risk assessments and put them in an appendix to their health and safety policy. Do a risk assessment on all the facilities that are used, all the different sessions that take place, all the activities that are played, all the equipment that is used and all away travel. Table 17.2 is an example of a risk assessment form.

Figure 17.16 Have a safety checklist and tick off every item before anyone kicks a ball

Table 17.2 A risk assessment form

Risk assessment									
Club									
Assessment date									
Names of assessors									
Activity, facility, equipment									
Potential hazard	Who it affects	Existing control measures	Hazard rating (A)	Likelihood (B)	Risk (C = A × B)	Further action required	Initials	Target date	Finish date

Notes
(A) Hazard rating: use 1 for minor injury, 3 for major injury, 5 for serious injury
(B) Likelihood: use 2 for unlikely, 4 for occasional, 6 for probable
(C) Risk: 2–4 is low, 6–12 is medium, 18–20 is high; review control measures for risks above 6

activity
INDIVIDUAL WORK
17.2

M1

Produce a risk assessment form for a sport of your choice. Identify and evaluate all potential risk factors. Describe some measures to minimise the risk from each risk factor.

A range of sports injuries and their symptoms

A sports injury causes physiological damage but it can also have a big psychological impact. An athlete who has dedicated several years of training to achieve their goal will suffer a huge psychological blow if they receive an injury just before their big event.

Physiological responses
Injury response cycle for any tissue

Primary and secondary damage
An injury causes tissue destruction; this is **primary damage**. The dead or damaged cells release their contents into the area surrounding the injury and this initiates an **inflammatory response**. The blood vessels at the injury site are damaged and become blocked. The blocked blood vessels cannot deliver oxygen, so other cells die from lack of oxygen, or hypoxia; this is secondary damage. Effective first aid can minimise secondary damage.

Inflammatory response
The inflammatory response is the beginning of the healing process; it starts immediately after the injury. Oedema – accumulation of fluid and swelling – helps to transport a high concentration of proteins and fibrinogen to the area. Chemicals irritate the neuroreceptors, which produces pain, and the swelling restricts the movement of the body part. There is also haemorrhaging as blood is lost from damaged blood vessels. Leucocytes and phagocytes are delivered to the injured area so they can dispose of the injury products such as damaged cells.

> **remember**
> Pay attention to the performer's mind and body during any rehabilitation.

Blood clotting

The body patches damaged blood vessels with a clot; the clot is removed once the tissue is repaired. This process is called haemostasis. Platelets in the blood are activated by thrombin and converge on the injury site. Fibrinogen causes the platelets to clump together and bind to collagen so they form a plug over the damaged wall of the blood vessel. This plug is made more stable by a fibrin mesh and the final result is a clot. Once the tissue has been repaired, the clot is dissolved by plasmin.

Fibroblastic repair

Fibroblastic repair is the formation of scar tissue to repair injured tissue. It begins within the first few hours of injury but it can take weeks or months to complete, depending on the type of tissue. The capillary network needs to be renewed so there is a good supply of oxygen and vital nutrients. Granulation tissue begins to form, which contains type III collagen, among other things. Type III collagen is randomly deposited to give strength to the wounded area.

Maturation remodelling

Maturation remodelling involves the realignment, or remodelling, of the collagen fibres in relation to the original tissue fibres and the lines of stress it will experience, making it more efficient. The type III collagen is replaced with type I collagen to increase strength. Early use of range of motion (ROM) exercises will help the remodelling process. Note that bone is a unique tissue because it heals by formation of new bone, as opposed to scar tissue. The length of time that a tissue takes to mend varies and will depend on the extent of the trauma. Here are some times to use as a guide:

- Skin 2–3 weeks
- Muscle 4–6 weeks
- Tendon 6–8 weeks
- Ligament 6–8 weeks
- Bone 12–16 weeks
- Nerve 12–18 months.

Muscle strain

A **muscle strain** is damage caused by overstretching the muscle rather than by external impact. It usually happens during dynamic actions produced at speed and can be made worse by a lack of control. Muscle strains are graded by their severity:

- Grade 1 – a mild strain that requires 2–3 weeks' rest with limited damage to a small number of fibres.
- Grade 2 – a more severe strain that requires 3–6 weeks' rest. A large proportion of the fibres are damaged.
- Grade 3 – a complete rupture of the muscle that will normally require surgery. Rehabilitation will take about 3 months.

A **ligament sprain** is a joint injury that stretches or tears a ligament. A ligament is strong connective tissue that joins one bone to another and provides joint stability. Sprains too are graded by their severity:

- Grade 1 – a sprain with mild pain and minimal damage to the ligament; there is some limited swelling.
- Grade 2 – a sprain with more ligament damage and the joint appears loose, it is painful with more swelling.
- Grade 3 – a sprain with complete tearing of the ligament and the joint is very loose and unstable; it is extremely painful and swollen.

A haematoma is localised swelling filled with blood from a damaged blood vessel. A muscle haematoma is caused by external impact on the muscle and is usually diagnosed as an intramuscular haematoma or an intermuscular haematoma. An intermuscular haematoma is usually not as severe as an intramuscular haematoma.

- **Intramuscular haematoma** – bleeding occurs within the muscle. The muscle sheath retains the blood in the muscle and increases the pressure in the muscle. Swelling lasts more than 48 h as blood can't escape.

- **Intermuscular haematoma** – bleeding occurs between muscles. Swelling and bruising remain for 24–48 h after injury but, due to gravity, they often appear further down the limb from the injury site.

Myositis ossificans – bone growth within the muscle – is a complication that can occur with a muscle contusion, or bruising. It happens when blood from an intramuscular haematoma calcifies and turns into bone tissue in the muscle.

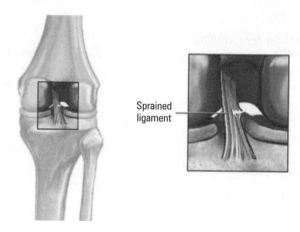

Figure 17.17 A ligament sprain is a joint injury that stretches or tears a ligament

Sprained ligament

Link See page 208 in Unit 20 for more information on assessment

---

activity
GROUP WORK
17.3

P2

As a group, produce a list of injuries that group members have experienced. For each injury, write down some preventative measures that might have stopped it from occurring.

---

activity
GROUP WORK
17.4

P3

P4

In pairs, interview someone who has recently experienced a serious sports injury. Have one person from the pair ask the questions and have the other person write down the responses. Prepare some appropriate questions before doing the interview. Here are some suggestions:

1. When you first realised you had an injury, how serious did you think it was?
2. How did you feel when you were told the severity of your injury?
3. Did you worry about losing your place on the team?
4. What physiological responses did you experience as a result of your injury?
5. Can you identify any specific stages during your rehabilitation process?

Go through the transcript of the interview. Identify and describe the interviewee's physiological responses and their psychological responses.

Psychological responses

Readjustment pattern

Research suggests that all performers follow similar patterns of psychological readjustment. The degree of psychological trauma depends on the severity of the injury but it also depends on the consequences for the performer. It could mean missing a few Sunday football matches or it could cost them a place in a Premiership side; it could even mean missing a World Cup.

Denial

Sustaining an injury puts the body into shock. First the injured performer tends to underplay the injury. They deny that they have a problem: 'I'll be okay in a minute.' Soon afterwards, they're carried off the field on a stretcher.

Anger

As reality dawns and they see just how injured they are, denial is replaced by anger. The anger can be directed at themselves or at other people. A performer may get angry with themselves for not preparing thoroughly or because they might have avoided the injury if they had taken a different decision. They may feel anger towards the person who caused the injury. They may feel anger towards the coach, especially if they think the coach gave them bad advice.

Frustration

A performer may feel frustration at having their goal blocked or snatched away from them. Jonny Wilkinson is said to have cried tears of pure frustration when he came back from injury and was injured again in his very first match.

Isolation from teammates

Depression doesn't always occur but an injured performer can feel very isolated as they become detached from the team and their teammates. The impact of this separation will depend on how much they have relied on the emotional support and comradeship of their teammates. The problem can be alleviated by involving the injured player in the running of the team, such as giving team talks and advising on team selection.

Anxiety

Anxiety is often experienced by a performer who thinks that their replacement may become a permanent member of the team. The performer's level of anxiety will depend on the importance they give to their place in the team. Losing a place in a Sunday league may not seem as important as losing a place in a Premiership side and the wages that go with it. Uncertainty about when the performer will regain full fitness and anxiety from fears of recurrence can produce a downward spiral into depression.

Acceptance

Acceptance is when the performer fully acknowledges the extent of the injury and begins to focus on rehabilitation.

Response to treatment and rehabilitation

Motivation and goal setting

A goal gives a performer something to aim for, something they want to accomplish. They can focus on their goal and make plans to achieve it. Personal goals are more meaningful to performers. Goal setting helps motivation and keeps the performer on task. They can measure their success by achieving the goals they have set and gaining a sense of accomplishment and pride. Effective goals need to be manageable and sometimes it is better to split one large goal into smaller, bite-sized chunks. Goal setting is far more appropriate for a performer trying to recover from a long-term injury as they need to maintain their motivation and have a positive approach to rehabilitation. The prospect of a long period of recovery can be overwhelming, but setting goals makes everything seem much more manageable:

- Decide on a major long-term goal. After a sports injury, it will usually be to return to pre-injury fitness levels.

- Establish the medium-term goals to achieve it. Depending on the severity of the injury, a medium-term goal might be to get back a full range of mobility around a particular joint.

- Identify short-term goals that will help to achieve the medium-term goals, perhaps to perform a series of mobility exercises every day.

Long-term goals are achieved over a long period of time. To maintain enthusiasm and motivation, set short- and medium-term goals as stepping stones towards the long-term goal. Always set SMART goals:

- **Specific** – so you know exactly what you are trying to achieve.

- **Measurable** – so you can see how well you are progressing.

- **Achievable** – so you will eventually be successful.

- **Realistic** – so you have what it takes to achieve them.

- **Time-bound** – so you reach your goal in a reasonable time.

A performer on a rehabilitation programme needs to be fully involved in setting their goals so that they feel ownership and control over what they are trying to achieve.

---

activity
GROUP WORK 17.5

M2

Produce a written report for the interviewee in Activity 17.4 that explains the interviewee's psychological and physiological responses to their injury.

---

activity
GROUP WORK 17.6

D1

Analyse the psychological and physiological responses you reported in Activity 17.5. Present your analysis to the rest of the group.

How to apply methods of treating sports injuries

Types of sports injury

Hard tissue damage

> **remember**
>
> The human skeleton has 206 bones and four main functions: to provide support for the body, to provide protection for vital organs, to produce blood cells and to provide attachment for muscles.

Bone is the hardest connective tissue in the body, mainly because it contains deposits of calcium phosphate and calcium carbonate. Bones and joints often get damaged during sport.

A bone may be completely fractured or partially fractured. Fractures have three main causes:

- Trauma to the bone caused by impact.

- Osteoporosis can contribute to bone fractures as the bones become less dense and therefore weaker.

- Overuse injury produces a stress fracture.

remember
Fractured means broken.

Fractures may be divided into two categories:

- **Closed or simple fracture** – the bone is broken but has not come through the skin.

- **Open or compound fracture** – the bone and the skin are broken. Either the trauma breaks the bone and the skin, or the trauma breaks the bone and the force of the fracture breaks the skin. The bone does not necessarily protrude from the wound.

Here are some different types of fracture:

- **Transverse fracture** – a break across the bone.

- **Greenstick fracture** – a fracture on one side of the bone, causing the bone to bend.

- **Comminuted fracture** – a fracture that results in three or more bone fragments.

- **Spiral fracture** – a fracture where a bone has been twisted apart.

- **Vertebral compression fracture** – a fracture specific to the vertebrae that occurs when force pushes together the anterior, or front, parts of the vertebrae.

Figure 17.18 Some typical bone fractures

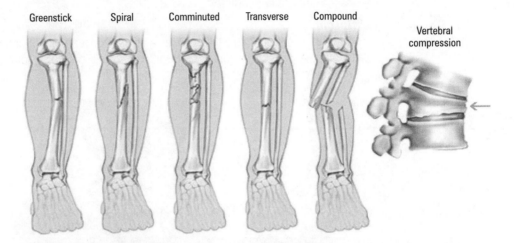

Greenstick   Spiral   Comminuted   Transverse   Compound   Vertebral compression

A stress fracture is an incomplete fracture. It appears as a very thin crack in the bone and is sometimes called a hairline fracture. Stress fractures usually occur in weight-bearing bones, such as the tibia; they are common overuse sports injuries. A dislocation occurs when two bones that come together to form a joint become separated. Most dislocations are caused by contact sports such as rugby and high-impact sports that involve extreme stretching or falling. Rugby players commonly dislocate their shoulder joints. A medical expert can manipulate the bones back into place. Dislocations of the knees, hips and elbows are less common as the joints are quite stable and need extreme trauma to cause a dislocation.

Figure 17.19 Dislocated shoulders are common in rugby players

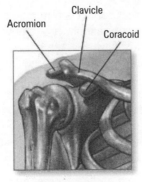

Acromion   Clavicle   Coracoid

Normal anatomy

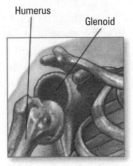

Humerus   Glenoid

Dislocated shoulder

The term 'shin splints' refers to pain at the front of the lower leg. It doesn't describe a specific problem, just the symptoms of pain. The most common cause of shin splints is inflammation of the periosteum of the tibia – the periosteum is connective tissue surrounding the bone – but do not assume this is the cause. There are other causes of shin splints, such as a stress fracture.

Soft tissue damage

Soft tissue includes muscle, tendons, ligaments, synovial tissue, fascia, nerves, blood vessels and fat. In other words, tissue that connects, supports or surrounds other tissues and organs. Here are some common injuries to soft tissue.

Haematoma

Haematoma is localised swelling filled with blood from a damaged blood vessel.

Abrasion

Abrasion is superficial damage to the skin but it also causes damage to superficial blood vessels and nerve endings.

Sprain

A sprain is a joint injury that causes a stretch or tear to a ligament. A ligament is strong connective tissue that joins one bone to another, providing joint stability. Sprains are graded from 1 to 3 by severity.

Figure 17.20 Ligaments are completely torn in a type 3 sprain

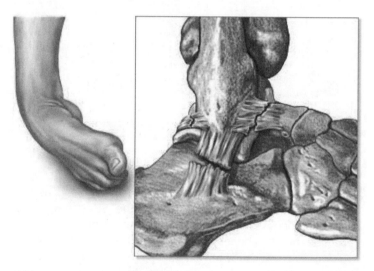

Strain

Strain is damage caused by overstretching the muscle rather than by external impact. This usually happens during dynamic actions produced at speed and can be made worse by a lack of control. Muscle strains are graded from 1 to 3 by severity.

Tendonitis

A tendon is a band of fibrous tissue that connects a muscle to a bone. When a muscle contracts it transmits the force of the contraction through the tendon, which pulls on the bone to produce movement. Tendonitis is when a tendon becomes inflamed and painful through overuse. It can also be caused by the tendon moving over a roughened surface or slightly out of alignment. Achilles tendonitis causes pain and swelling in the back of the heel and is a common problem among runners. It should be treated, as prolonged problems with the Achilles tendon could lead to a complete rupture of the tendon. Rotator cuff tendonitis, or shoulder tendonitis, is usually experienced by performers who regularly perform vigorous overarm actions such as racquet strokes.

Tendon rupture

A tendon experiences considerable force and can sometimes snap or rupture. A ruptured tendon is a serious injury that prevents the associated muscle from producing any movement. A complete rupture of a tendon takes months to rehabilitate.

Tennis elbow

Tennis elbow, or lateral epicondylitis, is thought to be due to small tears of the tendons that attach the extensor muscles of the forearm at the elbow joint. It can be caused by any repeated twisting movements of the hand, wrist or forearm. It is called tennis elbow, but it is not exclusive to tennis.

Cartilage damage

The human body contains three types of cartilage. Two are most commonly associated with sports injuries: articular cartilage and fibrocartilage. Articular cartilage covers the articulating surfaces of bone and can be damaged by trauma or overuse. If the cartilage breaks down, it can lead to osteoarthritis. Osteoarthritis is a type of arthritis caused by the breakdown and eventual loss of articular cartilage in one or more joints. Articular cartilage acts as a cushion between the bones of the joints and protects the bones from wear and tear.

Fibrocartilage forms the menisci in the knee joint and the vertebral discs between the vertebrae of the spine. Damage to a meniscus usually involves a tear; it causes swelling and sometimes the knee can give way. When the vertebral discs become worn or slip in the vertebral column it can damage nerves and this may lead to back pain.

Figure 17.21 Tennis elbow affects tennis players and other sports performers

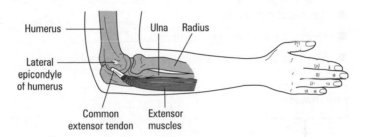

Humerus   Ulna   Radius

Lateral epicondyle of humerus

Common extensor tendon   Extensor muscles

Other sports injuries

Blister

A blister is a pool of body fluid that sits beneath the upper layers of the skin. It is usually formed in response to a burn or friction where the surface layer of the skin has separated from the second layer of skin. Common sites for blisters are the soles of the feet (e.g. friction between the skin, sock and shoe), the heel and the hand (e.g. friction between the skin and a racquet handle).

Cramp

Cramp is an involuntary contraction of a muscle that does not relax, a muscle spasm. Cramps can affect any skeletal muscle but commonly affect the quadriceps, hamstrings and gastrocnemius, as muscles that work across two joints are more susceptible to cramp. There are several reasons why a muscle cramps:

- Inadequate stretching
- Muscle fatigue
- Dehydration
- Depletion of electrolytes.

The muscle should be stretched and gently massaged and the performer should rehydrate with water and additional electrolytes.

Concussion

Concussion describes an injury to the brain as a result of an impact to the head. Concussion happens quite a lot in contact sports such as rugby and in other sports involving hard balls such as hockey and cricket. Hockey and cricket performers wear protective helmets. Concussion is graded by severity:

- **Grade 1, mild** – the performer is dazed but does not lose consciousness, or pass out.
- **Grade 2, more severe** – the performer does not lose consciousness but has a period of disorientation and does not remember the event.
- **Grade 3, most severe** – the performer loses consciousness for a brief period and has no memory of the event.

Detailed descriptions of sports injuries with diagnosis and treatment

www.medicinenet.com

www.sportsinjuryclinic.net

First aid

Basic first aid can save lives in an emergency. It may sound dramatic but it's true.

- Stay calm and assess the situation.
- Do not put yourself in danger.
- Only help if it is safe for you to help.
- Assess the casualties.
- Deal with anyone who is unconscious first.
- Send for medical assistance as soon as possible.

Figure 17.22 If a casualty is not responding, check their airway to see if they are breathing

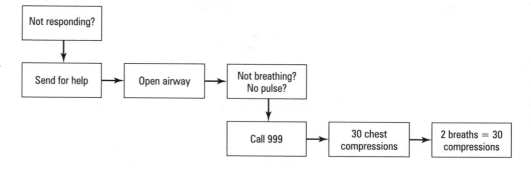

```
Not responding?
    ↓
Send for help → Open airway → Not breathing?
                              No pulse?
                                  ↓
                              Call 999 → 30 chest      → 2 breaths = 30
                                         compressions     compressions
```

Unconscious casualty

If a casualty is not responding, check their airway to see if they are breathing and check to see if they have any circulation. If there are problems, start cardiopulmonary resuscitation (CPR). If the casualty is unconscious but is breathing and has a pulse, put them into the recovery position and keep them warm.

Figure 17.23 Use the recovery position when a casualty is unconscious but breathing

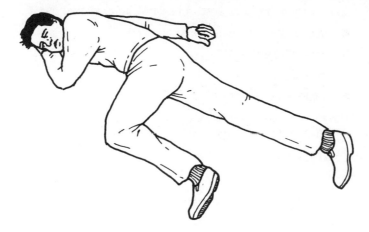

Bleeding

Depending on the extent of blood loss, it may be necessary to apply direct pressure on the injury. It is preferable to raise the body part to minimise blood flow, but this should only be done if the body part is not broken and can be supported. Cover the wound with a dressing and bandage firmly.

Suspected fractures

Do not move a casualty, especially if you suspect a back injury. A casualty should only be moved if they are in danger of further injury. Send for medical help and keep the casualty warm and reassured.

Shock

Trauma of any kind can leave a person in shock. Assess the casualty for these signs of shock:

- Trembling or shaking
- Feeling sick
- Pale skin or blue lips
- Slight confusion
- Shallow breathing
- Weak, raised pulse.

Lie the casualty down and slightly raise their legs, with support if possible. Keep the casualty warm and tell them they are safe. Do not give them anything to drink or eat. If they are sick, roll them on to their side.

Prevention of infection

If possible, anyone providing first aid should wash their hands first or put on disposable gloves before treating the casualty. Try to clean the wound with water and remove any dirt and grit. Apply a cover to the wound, but only if a clean dressing is available. Keep casualties separate and clean your hands before treating the next person.

Accident report forms

remember

Always summon qualified assistance.

Keep a record of all injuries as this can help to establish any patterns or trends that might help control the risk of injury in the future. Records are also needed to prove that the appropriate duty of care was shown to the casualty. Accident report forms should include the following information:

- Date, time and location of the accident
- Name and status of the injured person, e.g. player, official, coach, spectator
- Details of the injury
- Details of any first aid provided
- What happened to the casualty afterwards, e.g. went to doctor, went to A&E
- Name, contact details and signature of the person who dealt with the accident.

Common treatments

Most sports injuries occur on the field of play and the coach or manager is often called on to make an immediate assessment of an injury. With experience it is possible to recognise some injuries and treat them appropriately but it is always sensible to follow some basic guidelines that help identify the extent of the injury. Remember SALTAPS and follow its advice:

- **See the injury occur** – this helps to give a sense about the force of impact, the angle of impact, whether the limb or joint was twisted, etc.

- **Ask the player questions** – use straightforward questions like these: Where does it hurt? How painful is the injury? Has this happened before?

- **Look at the injury** – look for any visible signs of swelling, damage to the skin or changes in alignment of the joint or limb. If possible, compare the injured limb with the non-injured limb.

- **Touch** – if necessary, gently touch the injured area, perhaps to feel any change in alignment.

- **Active movements by the player** – can the player move the injured part? Can they put their weight on the injured part?

- **Passive movements by the first-aider** – gentle mobilisation can detect any restrictions in the range of movement, for example.

- **Strength** – ask the player to move the injured body part while you resist the movement. This will reveal how strong it is and how well it is functioning.

Some injuries are minor and the player can continue the activity. If there is any doubt about the extent of the injury, the player must be removed from the activity and examined by a medical expert.

There is a recognised protocol for treating minor sports injuries. It goes by the acronym PRICED:

1. **Protection** – protect the body from further injury by immobilising the injured area. If necessary, use a splint or sling, a walking stick or crutches.

2. **Rest** – try to rest and avoid doing anything that causes pain or discomfort. Doing some mobilisation exercises can help as long as they are not weight-bearing. To maintain conditioning, it is advisable to exercise muscle groups unaffected by the injury.

3. **Ice** – apply ice to the area immediately. To avoid ice burns, make sure the skin is not in direct contact with the ice; the area should not turn white. Apply for 15–20 min then reapply every 2–3 h. The ice will help to reduce the pain and swelling and will help to reduce secondary damage to the area.

4. **Compression** – to help control the swelling, apply compression such as a bandage or Tubigrip. Make sure that blood circulation is not restricted and loosen the bandage if the area feels numb.

5. **Elevation** – to help reduce swelling, elevate the injured area above the level of the heart. Gravity helps to reduce swelling by draining the excess fluid.

6. **Diagnosis** – seek advice on the injury from someone in the medical profession and get an accurate diagnosis and treatment plan.

Treatment of injuries
www.worldclasscoaching.com

Typical treatments for minor injuries

Taping, bandaging and strapping

Taping, bandaging and strapping can help to prevent, treat and rehabilitate an injury. Tape and bandage provides support and protection but need not limit function unless a body part has to be immobilised or movement restricted; for example, non-stretch tape is used to keep ligaments in a shortened position to help repair. Stretch tape or Tubigrip is used in the early stages of treatment, usually with a dressing to aid compression that controls swelling. During the healing process, the tape or bandage should be replaced when the structures are in a relaxed position that helps the support given by connective tissue. Have the strapping applied by medical staff as they will know the most effective type to use.

Figure 17.24 Tape supports and protects an injury but need not limit function

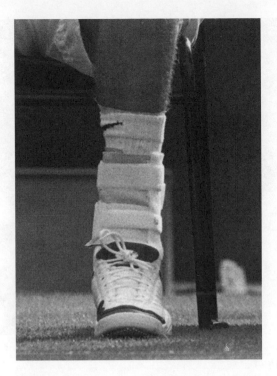

Splints

Splints are used to protect and support bones and soft tissue. They are sometimes used as an intermediate treatment until a cast can be applied. Splints can be custom-made or bought as part of a first-aid kit. They have Velcro straps so they can be adjusted easily but they don't offer as much support and protection as a cast. They are often used to immobilise an injured joint or limb so an injured player can be stretchered off the field or taken to hospital. A brace is sometimes used to help support a joint during rehabilitation; this offers a degree of protection and allows some function in the joint.

Heat treatment

Heat treatment is usually applied to increase blood flow to the injured area, to relax the muscle and to reduce pain. Products such as gel pads, wheat bags and electrically heated pads will provide the required heat. Heat treatment is particularly good at relieving stiff muscles and joints, but it should only be applied for about 30 min and should not make the skin go red or burn. Do not use heat treatment if the area is still swollen. Do not apply a heat pad to an open wound or stitches.

Cold treatment

Cold treatment reduces the blood flow to an area, which helps to control swelling and reduce pain. It is usually applied immediately after the injury has happened. Cold treatment causes blood vessels to constrict, so it is also used to stop a nosebleed. A cold gel pack or ice should not be placed directly on the skin and it should be removed after 20 min, but the skin should be checked regularly to make sure it is not white.

Pain-relief sprays

Pain-relief sprays are available as hot or cold treatments and are a much more convenient way of applying treatment. They can be kept in a kit bag or first-aid kit and can be an immediate source of relief. Heat sprays are quite often used before an activity to help prevent muscle strain.

Electrotherapy

Electrotherapy includes ultrasound, laser treatment and neuromuscular electrical stimulation. Ultrasound is a form of heat treatment for soft tissue injuries. Ultrasound uses sound waves to vibrate deep into the injured tissue; this creates heat that helps to increase blood flow and speed up the healing process.

Figure 17.25 Ultrasound increases blood flow and speeds up healing

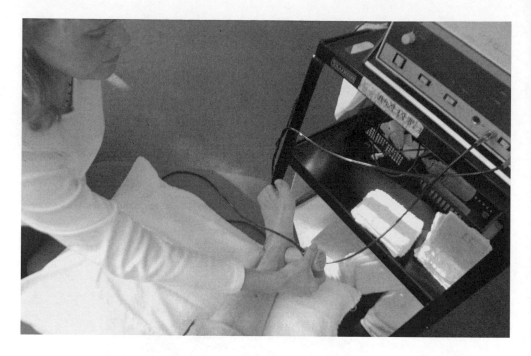

remember

Always seek appropriate specialist help.

Laser treatment

Laser treatment has the same effect as ultrasound and is used for the same reasons. A very low power laser light penetrates deep into the injured tissue. After an injury, a muscle or group of muscles may lose their ability to perform voluntary contraction. This can quickly cause the muscle tissue to atrophy, or waste away, lowering the strength of the muscle. Neuromuscular electrical stimulation is used to make the muscle contract and limit the atrophy.

(i) Sports injuries and treatment

www.sportsinjurybulletin.com

www.sportsinjuryclinic.net

activity

GROUP WORK 17.7

P5

Organise the class into small groups. Each group receives a card that details a common scenario for a sports injury. The group has to role-play the injury scenario. The role play should clearly show a common cause of the injury and how to treat the injury. At the end of each role play, the class should discuss whether the treatment was appropriate.

Planning and constructing treatment and rehabilitation programmes for two common sports injuries

Treatment

Once an injury has been properly diagnosed, the required treatment can be outlined. Depending on the extent of the injury and the type of tissue, rehabilitation can take anything from a week to several years. Performers with an injury often continue to train and play matches; this is counterproductive as it lengthens recovery time and increases the risk of further injury. Self-diagnosis should be avoided as a little knowledge is usually dangerous. Always go to a medical expert for diagnosis and treatment.

Immediate treatment

Immediate treatment is the initial treatment given to any sports injury. Generally speaking, the more immediate the treatment, the better the outcome and the shorter the overall recovery time. A small cut may just need to be cleaned and given a dressing. For a more serious injury, you may need to give pain relief and reduce any swelling. Unfortunately, many performers delay seeking medical advice and continue to train with an injury. This exacerbates the situation and lengthens recovery time.

Long-term treatment

Long-term treatment manages rehabilitation so the performer returns to their pre-injury fitness. It can take weeks to heal a bone fracture or months to reconstruct an anterior cruciate ligament.

Rehabilitation

A rehabilitation programme will usually consist of five distinct phases to restore full function after an injury. It tries not to be overambitious and uses a progressive approach to avoid setbacks. A positive mental attitude helps healing and a performer needs a lot of patience.

Figure 17.26 RICE sprains: rest, ice, elevation and compression

- **Phase 1** – this is immediate medical management needed during the acute phase of an injury. Focus on pain relief, swelling reduction and protected mobilisation.

- **Phase 2** – now focus on restoring the range of motion by extending the soft tissue. It is usual to begin with non-weight-bearing exercises to help regain mobility.

- **Phase 3** – flexibility work continues, but now the main aim is to restore muscle strength progressively. If the muscle is very weak, begin by holding a gentle isometric stretch. As strength improves, perform isotonic exercises but without any extra load. Lead on to resistance exercises then proprioceptive exercises such as standing on one leg.

- **Phase 4** – the main aims are to retrain sport-specific movement patterns and to improve coordination with agility drills; gradually increase the speed of the agility drills.

- **Phase 5** – return to sport-specific training and perform at pre-injury levels.

---

remember
- An isometric contraction is when the muscle increases in tension but there is no change in its length, so no movement occurs.
- A concentric muscle contraction is the most common form of muscular contraction. It occurs when a muscle acts as a prime mover and shortens under tension, creating movement around a joint.
- In eccentric contraction the muscle acting as the antagonist lengthens under tension, usually returning to its normal resting length. A muscle contracting eccentrically is acting as a brake to help control the movement of a body part during negative work.
- Negative work describes a resistance that is greater than the contractile strength of the muscle, such as gravity.

Methods to improve the lost range of motion

Injury and inactivity can produce a loss in range of movement and most rehabilitation programmes will involve some flexibility work. Flexibility is improved by stretching, moving a joint to just beyond its point of resistance. To see improvement, hold a stretch for a minimum of 10 s and make each mobility session last for at least 10 min. For best results, the body should be warm, so the exercises should be performed after a warm-up, during a cooldown, or after a warm bath, warm shower or heat treatment. To be effective, flexibility training needs to be done at least three times per week.

The muscles and joints have their own safety mechanisms to maintain joint integrity and avoid overstretching the muscle. They contain proprioceptors that respond to changes in muscle length and exertion force. A muscle contains muscle spindles that are sensitive to the change in muscle length and the rate of change in muscle length. When a muscle is stretched, the muscle spindle becomes stretched and sends sensory information that triggers the stretch reflex. The stretch reflex prevents muscle damage caused by excessive stretch; it makes the stretched muscle contract. When a muscle contracts, it produces tension in the muscle and this is registered by the Golgi tendon organs. If the tension exceeds a threshold, it stimulates a lengthening reaction that relaxes the muscle; this is known as autogenic inhibition.

Proprioceptive neuromuscular facilitation

Proprioceptive neuromuscular facilitation (PNF) is a very effective type of flexibility training. First it forcefully contracts the muscle to be stretched; this stimulates the lengthening reaction, so the body can momentarily override the stretch reflex and the muscle will stretch further than usual.

Static stretching

A performer can achieve static stretching by moving into a position that takes the joint beyond its point of resistance, lengthening the soft tissue around the joint. The performer holds the position for a minimum of 10 s then relaxes. In a passive stretch, another person moves the performer's joint beyond its resistance point then holds it there.

Figure 17.27 Muscle-strengthening exercises: resistance band exercises (left), proprioceptive exercises (right)

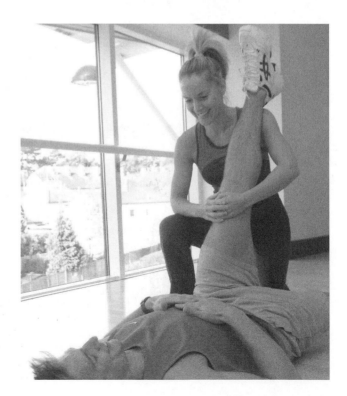

Muscle-strengthening exercises

Muscle-strengthening exercises should use progressively increasing resistance. When a muscle is very weak, work it isometrically or against gravity; do not use any extra resistance. As muscle strength increases, gradually increase the resistance by using resistance bands or weight training. Introduce proprioceptive exercises such as standing on one leg. Strength training normally starts after the range of joint motion has been restored; it is made more and more sport-specific as the rehabilitation draws to its end.

Coordination exercises

Coordination exercises are task-oriented exercises and will be used to improve agility (speed and coordination) in the final phase of rehabilitation. Check that the performer has a big enough range of motion and enough strength to do agility drills safely and effectively.

Strength training programmes and agility drills

www.pponline.co.uk

An ankle sprain rehabilitation programme

Phase 1

Here are some initial treatments to limit secondary damage and promote healing:

1. Rest.

2. Fill a plastic bag with ice then wrap it in a cloth. Place it on the ankle for 15–20 min. Do this 3–5 times per day for the first 24–72 h. Leave a minimum of 90 m between each ice pack.

3. Wrap a stretch bandage from the toes up to the midcalf. Wear the bandage until the swelling goes down. Loosen the bandage if the toes start to turn blue or feel cold.

4. Support the lower leg and foot during elevation.

5. Use a walking stick or crutches to keep body weight off the ankle.

Phase 2

Perform gentle non-weight-bearing mobility exercises to improve the range of motion at the ankle joint; for example, try to form the letters of the alphabet using the ankle. Repeat this 3–4 times per day for the first 3–10 days. Perform stretches to improve the flexibility of the lower leg muscles, such as the gastrocnemius stretch. Place the hands on a wall with the right foot behind the body. Keep the right knee straight and the heel in touch with the ground. Lean forward until you feel a stretch along the gastrocnemius. To feel the stretch, you may have to move your foot closer to the wall or further back.

Phase 3

Perform exercises such as toe raises to improve the strength of the lower leg muscles. Stand with one hand on the back of a chair for support, then rise up on your toes, hold it for 2 s and lower. Do not bounce. Do two sets of 10 repetitions. When the exercise becomes easy, perform it with one foot at a time.

Phase 4

Perform agility drills such as box jumps to improve strength and coordination. Make a cross on the ground using two strips of tape and mark four boxes 1 to 4. Place both feet in box 1 and jump into box 2. Now go from 2 to 3, from 3 to 4 and from 4 back to 1. Face forward the entire time. Take off and land on the balls of the feet. Repeat the exercise but do the jumps in this order: 1 to 4, 4 to 3, 3 to 2, 2 to 1. Do the jump sequences five times in each direction, 1234 and 4321. Begin slowly then gradually increase speed. Eventually perform the jumps on one foot at a time. You can also introduce more sport-specific movement patterns.

Phase 5
Return to normal patterns of training; monitor for any signs of weakness, pain or swelling.

Ankle sprain rehabilitation
www.thefootandankleclinic.com

Figure 17.28 To feel the stretch, you may have to move your foot closer to the wall

activity
GROUP WORK 17.8

P6

Arrange for a sports physiotherapist to give you a talk on the design of rehabilitation programmes. Alternatively, present some case studies that outline a variety of rehabilitation programmes. As a group, identify two common sports injuries, such as muscle strain and joint sprain. Design a treatment and rehabilitation programme for each of the two injuries.

activity
INDIVIDUAL WORK 17.9

M3

Take the two sports injuries chosen by the group in Activity 17.8. Now apply them to a different joint and muscle group and consider a different degree of severity. Design a safe and appropriate treatment and rehabilitation programme for these two new cases.

activity
GROUP WORK 17.10

D2

Work as a pair. One person presents their treatment and rehabilitation programme to the other person. They explain their choice of treatment and exercise regime. After the presentation, the other person evaluates the programme and suggests any appropriate alternative strategies or exercises. Swap roles and repeat the activity.

Psychology

Uncertainty can lead to anxiety that may hamper the recovery process, so try to reduce the amount of uncertainty for the performer. Fully explain the injury to the performer and the treatment stages during the healing process. Advise them to be realistic about how long it will take to return to their sport and encourage them to be patient. Prepare the performer to face any specific difficulties. Identifiable treatment stages with clear goals will help to motivate the performer. As the performer reaches each stage, they will feel one step closer to full fitness.

Table 17.3 Short-, medium- and long-term goals

Short-term goal	Medium-term goal	Long-term goal
Perform a full set of flexibility exercises	Achieve a full range of movement at the joint	Return to sport

case study 17.5   Jonny Wilkinson

Jonny Wilkinson scored the points from a drop goal to secure an England victory in the 2003 World Cup. Then 1167 days later, he ran out wearing another England shirt and scored 27 points against Scotland at Twickenham.

Stats
Age: 28
Height: 5 ft 10 in (1.78 m)
Date of birth: 25 May 1979
Position: fly half (no. 10)
Plays for Newcastle Falcons in the Premiership
Country debut: 4 February 1998
International Player of the Year 2002
Rugby World Cup winner's medal 2003
Sports Personality of the Year 2003
Honours: OBE 2004 in the New Year Honours List
Major setbacks
Fractured vertebra (Dec 2003)
Neck operation (Feb 2004)
Left knee ligament damage (Jan 2005)
Appendicitis (Sept 2005)
Groin operation (Nov 2005)
Right knee ligament damage (Sept 2006)
Lacerated kidney (Nov 2006)

Figure 17.29 Jonny Wilkinson overcame many setbacks

activity
INDIVIDUAL WORK

1. What do you think motivated Jonny Wilkinson to return to top-class rugby despite his numerous setbacks?

2. Despite his long lay-off from international rugby, why do you think that Wilkinson still holds lucrative deals with sponsors such as Adidas and Lucozade?

Encourage the performer to think positively and to use positive self-talk. Even though they cannot take part in matches, it often helps team players to recover if they can be included in team talks and do their rehabilitation exercises while their teammates train. It can be incredibly demoralising and very counterproductive when an injured player is dropped from a squad and denied access to support networks they had when they were fit and which they now need more than ever.

Jonny Wilkinson's book *My World* is published by Headline, ISBN 0-7472-4276-3
Psychological rehabilitation techniques
www.sportsinjurybulletin.com

Record

Rehabilitation is more effective when there are accurate records from the moment of injury to the end of the rehabilitation programme. An injured performer will often see several different people during their rehabilitation process, so out-of-date or inaccurate records can lead to mistakes in their treatment. Coaches and researchers can look at sets of records. Sometimes they find patterns or trends that help to develop better treatments.

After an injury, a performer may be in shock and perhaps unsure about what happened. Use the accident form to clarify the details, especially the nature of the injury and any treatment given. The next stage is to document the consultation that is normally carried out by a doctor or a physiotherapist. Table 17.4 shows the type of information recorded.

Table 17.4 Consultation record made by a doctor or physiotherapist

Personal details of the patient
Brief medical history or injury history From patient
Details of the injury From patient
Details of what caused the injury From patient and accident report form
Objective assessment of the injury By medical professional
Diagnosis
Treatment or rehabilitation programme
Time and date of next appointment

Working with a physiotherapist, the performer should keep a rehabilitation diary that logs all the exercises they have completed and the progress they have made in the healing process. To help motivate the performer, split the rehabilitation programme into stages and set short- and medium-term goals along the path to full recovery. Agree specific targets such as what exercises should be completed, how many repetitions and how many times per week; the performer will get a sense of achievement when they reach these targets.

Table 17.5 How to achieve a medium-term goal using several short-term goals

| | Medium-term goal: restore full range of motion to ankle joint by end of March | | |
	Short-term goal for week 1	Short-term goal for week 2	Short-term goal for week 3
Target	Mobilise joint	Increase flexibility of gastrocnemius	Week 3 target
Exercises	Alphabet exercises, 4 reps per day	Calf stretch, hold for 10–15 s, 4 reps per day	Week 3 exercises
No. completed			
Day 1			
Day 2			
Day 3			
Day 4			
Day 5			
Day 6			
Day 7			
Comments			

A performer is usually quite motivated when they perform the exercises with a physiotherapist during a treatment session, but they are often less motivated when they do the exercises at home. A diary can help to keep them focused. Occasionally a performer can suffer lack of motivation during sessions with the physiotherapist. This needs to be monitored as it could be a sign of depression caused by a negative attitude to the rehabilitation programme. Listen for comments like these: 'What's the point? It's never going to be strong enough to play again.' A rehabilitation adherence scale can be useful in these situations (Table 17.6).

Table 17.6 SIRAS: sport injury rehabilitation adherence scale

To be completed by the physiotherapist at the end of each of the patient's treatment sessions						
For each of the following, circle the number that best indicates the patient's behaviour						
1. The intensity with which the patient completed the rehabilitation exercises during today's appointment						
Minimum effort	1	2	3	4	5	Maximum effort
2. During today's appointment, how frequently did the patient follow your instructions and advice?						
Never	1	2	3	4	5	Always
3. How receptive was this patient to changes in the rehabilitation programme during today's appointment?						
Very unreceptive	1	2	3	4	5	Very receptive

Adapted from Brewer *et al*. (1995)

Research by primary care trusts (PCTs) supports the view that realistic, agreed goals between patient and physiotherapist help to motivate the patient. Therefore a rehabilitation process is more likely to succeed if it records treatment and exercise regimes and if it has set timescales and measurable objectives.

See page 212 in Unit 20 for more information on documentation

Figure 17.30 Will it ever be strong enough to play again?

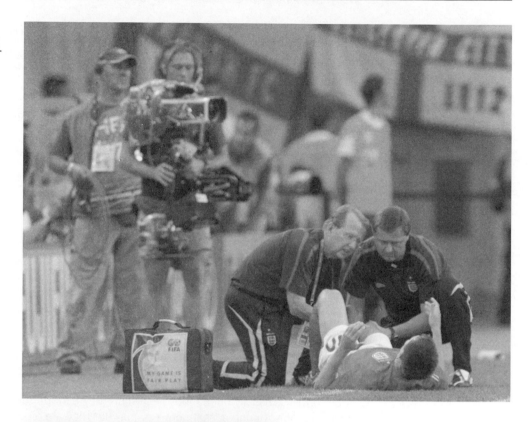

Figure 17.31 Rehabilitation succeeds through measurable objectives

Progress Check

1. What is an extrinsic risk factor? Give an example.
2. What is an intrinsic risk factor? Give an example.
3. An incorrect technique can lead to the development of a sports injury. Give three examples of this.
4. Choose an activity. Give an example of an environment safety check for this activity.
5. What is muscle imbalance? What problems can it cause?
6. What is a growth plate? Name three activities where young participants might be susceptible to growth plate injuries.
7. What is scar tissue?
8. How can diet (a) help to prevent injury and (b) help the rehabilitation process?
9. What does SALTAPS stand for?
10. Describe the stages of the injury response cycle.

Sport and Exercise Massage

Kate Randerson

This unit covers:

- Effects and benefits of sport and exercise massage
- Sport and exercise professionals
- Massage requirements of sports performers
- Techniques for sport and exercise massage

This unit considers the theory and practice of massage for exercise and sport. It considers how massage techniques affect the physiological and psychological well-being of a sports performer and the different techniques to use before competition, after competition and between events at a competition. It explains how to do regular planning and produce treatment plans.

grading criteria

To achieve a **Pass** grade the evidence must show that the learner is able to:	To achieve a **Merit** grade the evidence must show that the learner is able to:	To achieve a **Distinction** grade the evidence must show that the learner is able to:
P1 describe the effects and benefits of sport and exercise massage Pg 203	**M1** explain the effects and benefits of sport and exercise massage Pg 203	
P2 describe the role of sport and exercise professionals Pg 204		
P3 conduct an assessment on two different athletes, identifying areas that require sport and exercise massage Pg 208	**M2** explain the sport and exercise massage requirements of two different athletes Pg 208	**D1** compare and contrast the sport and exercise massage requirements of two athletes Pg 208
P4 describe six contraindications to massage treatment Pg 218		

To achieve a **Pass** grade the evidence must show that the learner is able to:	To achieve a **Merit** grade the evidence must show that the learner is able to:	To achieve a **Distinction** grade the evidence must show that the learner is able to:
P5 demonstrate an appropriate sport and exercise massage treatment, for a selected athlete, with support Pg 224	**M3** demonstrate appropriate sport and exercise massage treatment, for a selected athlete Pg 224	**D2** analyse the appropriate sport and exercise massage treatment, for a selected athlete Pg 234
P6 review their performance in demonstrating sport and exercise massage treatment, identifying strengths and areas for improvement Pg 237		

grading criteria

The effects and benefits of sport and exercise massage

The word 'massage' is derived from the Arabic *mass'h* 'to press gently', but the practical use of massage is evident not only in ancient Chinese books but also in Egyptian scriptures. Similarly, the Japanese developed massage techniques that are now recognised as shiatsu treatments. The Romans used massage in their bathhouses and spas, treatments that remain popular today.

Modern massage techniques were developed by Henrik Ling (1776–1839), a Swedish professor who developed techniques for effleurage, **petrissage**, vibration and friction. Massage is a therapeutic, sensory treatment used to manipulate the soft tissue of the body such as skin, muscles, fat, ligaments and tendons. The outcome of a massage depends on the choice of technique and other factors such as the depth of the massage, the massage medium, the underlying tissue, and the athlete's medical conditions. The outcome can vary from athlete to athlete, and from session to session for the same athlete.

Physical and mechanical effects

Blood and lymph

Massage movements usually follow venous return, which is towards the heart. Massage pressure creates a pumping action that helps the circulatory system. This improves the supply of oxygen and nutrients to the tissues and the removal of waste products such as lactic acid and carbon dioxide. Valves in the venous system prevent a backflow of blood, but the pressure of massage manipulations such as deep **effleurage**, kneading and squeezing causes the vessels to refill rapidly with oxygenated blood from an arterial vessel.

Lymphatic vessels are blind-ended structures that have a system of valves and are situated close to the venous system. Lymphatic fluid is moved by muscular contraction, so there is a greater chance of the lymphatic vessels becoming sluggish and congested. This is particularly true during injury when interstitial fluid that is not 'collected' by the blood capillaries builds up and produces swelling.

Massage movements will help to eliminate these waste products and speed up the interchange of fluids within the **lymphatic system** and at cellular level, stimulating the flow of **lymph** towards the lymph nodes.

Lymph nodes are found in groups throughout the body. They are present in the neck, groin, knees and elbows. Two large ducts in the chest, the right lymphatic duct and the thoracic duct, drain lymph from the body and deposit it in the venous system.

Skin

The combination of massage and a medium over the surface of the skin has beneficial effects in nourishing and stimulating the epidermis. Application of pressure removes dead skin cells in a process called **desquamation**; this aids cell regeneration, improves skin texture and gives it a healthy glow. The heat produced from massage techniques also stimulates the sebaceous glands and the sudoriferous glands, or sweat glands, to create a more supple and soft skin tone. The increased activity of sweat glands helps to remove waste products.

Sebaceous glands are the skin's natural protectors. They produce sebum, a waxy substance that has fungicidal and bacterial properties. Sebum also prevents moisture loss from the skin. Sebaceous glands are found all over the body except on the palms of the hands and the soles of the feet.

Muscles

Different massage techniques produce different responses to muscle tissue. The more stimulating **percussion** techniques will stimulate the blood supply and help maintain the elasticity of the muscles. The slower, deeper movements such as effleurage will help to relax and remove waste products from the muscles. Frictions will help to break down recent scar tissue, while specific localised pressure can reduce tension nodules in the muscles. Techniques applied around joints can have a warming effect that stimulates the production of synovial fluid and increases range of movement (ROM).

Stretching

The effects of massage and the increased circulation help the soft tissues to become more pliable, especially ligaments and tendons as they do not have the same elasticity and extensibility as muscles. The overall effect is to separate the fibres according to their direction, which helps to improve flexibility and prevent injury.

See page 92 in Unit 3 in *BTEC National Sports Book 1* for more information on how stretching can be included in a fitness programme
See page 203 in Unit 6 in *BTEC National Sports Book 1* for more information on how stretching can be included in a fitness programme.

Figure 20.1 Lymph nodes (left) and blood vessels in the human body

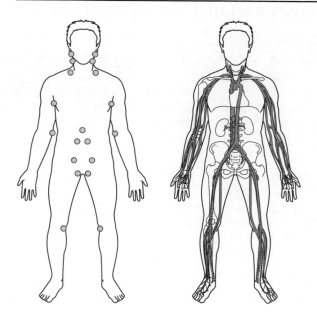

Ligaments

Ligaments are strong, soft tissues with little flexibility that attach bone to bone. When an uninjured ligament is palpated, the fibres should have a smooth, silky feel. A recently injured ligament may feel like a tiny knot or it may feel gritty to the touch. In such cases, massage therapy may be appropriate to remodel the injured tissue.

Remodelling and scar tissue

Recent scar tissue can feel firm and compact but will give a little when pressure is applied. Older scar tissue can feel as solid as bone. Friction massage is also called cross-fibre massage in the post-acute stage, when the tissue has plastic properties. It can help to prevent excessive scar tissue formation. The friction movements break the tissue into smaller particles that can be digested by phagocytes and reabsorbed into the lymphatic system. After a cross-fibre technique, the tissue is immediately remodelled by applying movements in the fibre direction of the soft tissue.

Opening microcirculation

Normal circulatory function requires vessel walls that are flexible, pliable and that allow filtration and absorption of essential substances for normal cellular functions. Massage movements stretch these walls to varying degrees, which improves their function and capacity.

Physiological effects

Nervous system

The autonomic nervous system controls the sympathetic and parasympathetic nervous systems, which are responsible for controlling involuntary movements and body functions. Some manipulations have a sedative effect on sensory nerve endings, whereas other movements will stimulate and revive. Any tension present in the soft tissues is detected by mechanoreceptors; this adds further stress to the sympathetic nervous system, causing it to work harder than necessary. Advanced therapy techniques such as **trigger point** work help to return nerve pathways to normal function and reduce pain.

Table 20.1 The autonomic nervous system

Sympathetic	Parasympathetic
Increases heart rate	Decreases heart rate
Increases blood pressure	Decreases blood pressure
Dilates blood vessels in skeletal muscles	No effect on most blood vessels
Increases production of sweat	No effects
Constricts blood vessels to the skin blood	No effect on most blood vessels
Dilates bronchioles	Constricts bronchioles
Increases metabolic rate	No effect
Decreases digestive system activity	Restores digestive system activity

Benefits

Reduced stress

Coupled with the physiological effects, the psychological effects of massage can play a major part in stress relief. Do not underestimate the psychological benefits of the treatment and the masseur's listening. The idea of being cared for, along with a treatment plan designed specifically for the person and including one-to-one time, can promote feelings of relaxation, satisfaction and contentment. The results can be quite dramatic, particularly if used with specific relaxation techniques and positive visualisation that promotes feelings of vigour and increased energy.

Visualisation is when the athlete creates or recreates a positive image in their mind; they could visualise scoring a goal or winning a race.

See page 309 in Unit 16 in *BTEC National Sports Book 1* for more information on visualisation and imagery

Improved body awareness

A full initial consultation before any sports massage plus posture and gait analysis can identify why athletes experience a restricted range of movement or discomfort. Where possible, the masseur may also want to discuss and observe training regimes and techniques before treatment. Many athletes may feel the benefits of massage treatment when it is combined with postural adjustments and movement modifications, particularly if they improve performance. Simple techniques such as correct sitting and standing can heighten an athlete's awareness of their own body position during everyday and sporting activities.

Pain reduction

Sport and exercise massage can give relief from pain and tension in the muscles; the analgesic effect blocks the pain signals from the skin and mechanoreceptors. But techniques such as **frictions** used when mobilising scar tissue can feel very uncomfortable during application, and some athletes may find that their improvement is 48 h after treatment.

- Advise athletes on the likely effects and subsequent outcomes of their treatment.

- Never continue with a technique if it distresses the athlete.

- If a treatment has to be stopped, record the treatment duration and the reason why on the record card.

Figure 20.2 Oh, I look taller

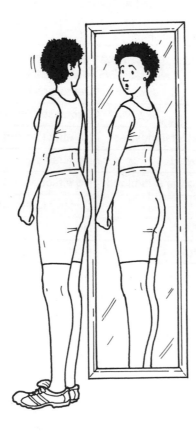

- Whenever possible, look at the athlete's body language and facial responses to treatment.
- Provide clear, concise aftercare information.
- Where possible, use simple written information sheets for the athlete to take away.

activity
INDIVIDUAL WORK 20.1

P1

M1

1. Describe the physiological and therapeutic benefits of sport and exercise massage.
2. Explain how massage could benefit a particular sportsperson.

The role of sport and exercise massage professionals

Role

Knowledge

The sport and exercise masseur must have a clear understanding of their roles and responsibilities and must not stray outside them. Besides the practical skills of massage, there are other important considerations for safe working. A masseur's role will depend on where they work, but here are some general aims:

- Promote healing
- Prevent injury
- Identify potential areas of injury
- Prepare for competition or training
- Aid recovery after sporting activity
- Liaise with other healthcare professionals, coaches and trainers
- Enhance overall sporting performance.

See page 46 in Unit 2 in *BTEC National Sports Book 1* for more information on legislation and regulations

Additional treatments

With further training, a sport and exercise masseur can improve their theoretical and practical skills. Check your professional indemnity insurance to see that it covers any new skills you have acquired. Before taking any courses, check that they award a certificate of competence. Here are some workshops, seminars and courses to consider:

- First-aid courses
- Prophylactic taping and strapping
- Heat treatments – paraffin wax, infrared, spa baths, sauna and steam treatments
- Electrical percussion treatments – audiosonic, percussion vibration, gyratory vibration
- Specific exercise and training regimes.

case study 20.1   Badminton briefing

A local group of badminton players have asked you to present a 10 min briefing to 20 members on the role of a sport and exercise masseur.

activity
INDIVIDUAL WORK

1. Prepare a presentation that explains the work of a sport and exercise masseur and that clearly defines its scope.
2. Include details of other relevant healthcare professionals that may be used by sports clubs.

Figure 20.3 Prepare properly to give your presentation

Continuing professional development

Membership of a professional body can help a sport and exercise masseur to refresh their existing skills and acquire new skills. Most professional organisations require their members to record the practical skills they learn each year plus any relevant courses they attend or activities that help their personal development. This is usually logged as hours per year, or maybe as points. Each masseur has a responsibility to keep adequate records of their professional development. Some professional organisations require the masseur to have a personal development plan (PDP) that indicates any future interests or potential avenues of development. Professional bodies can ask for a summary of the hours or points achieved before they renew membership.

activity
GROUP WORK 20.2

P2

Research the professional bodies that sports masseurs may join. Keep details of their membership fees and their requirements for continuing professional development.

Career opportunities

A sport and exercise masseur can be self-employed or they can work as an employee. Here are some places that offer work:

- Fitness and health clubs
- Gymnasiums
- Clinical practice
- Sports clubs, amateur and professional.

Some masseurs prefer to be self-employed and to practise a wide range of skills in a variety of work environments. Certificates of attendance are often given to delegates at conferences and even supervised practical workshops. An attendance certificate does not mean the holder can safely practise these skills on athletes.

Sports Massage Association

www.sportsmassageassociation.org

International Council of Health, Fitness and Sports Therapists

www.fht.org

Record cards

Masseurs need to keep detailed record cards and update them each time the athlete visits for treatment and advice. A competent masseur will liaise with the athlete to devise treatments that meet their needs and enhance their performance. Record cards hold very personal and specific details about each athlete, so they should be stored safely in a lockable, fireproof cabinet that is only accessible to relevant staff.

Some clinics hold records on computer. Check that these records are protected from viruses and check that your personal indemnity insurance will cover you if you hold records on computer.

Figure 20.4 Sports masseurs work in sports clubs and gyms

Too much information takes a long time to read and obscures the important details, so just record the key points. Here are some symbols that help to keep entries concise.

Symbol	Meaning
Rx	treatment
PC	present condition
HPC	history of present condition; how, when, why, causes
S	signs, such as swelling, bruising, loss of function; symptoms
I	irritability; mild, moderate, severe
N	nature of pain; chemical, mechanical, joint, muscular
>	improving
=	no change
<	getting worse

Some record cards have anterior and posterior views of the body. They can be marked and dated to give the masseur and athlete a visual picture of any problem areas. They are sometimes linked to a visual analogue scale (VAS) of pain, where 0 is the least pain and 10 is the most pain:

0 · · · · 5 · · · · 10

Some masseurs show athletes a VAS and ask them to indicate their level of pain from 0 to 10. Some sport and exercise masseurs may also use a body atlas attached to the record card and treatment sheets. They mark it with a pen or highlighter to indicate an athlete's injuries, pain or discomfort.

The effects of treatment

An athlete may feel tenderness in their soft tissues during treatment; its severity will depend on many factors, such as training intensity, any previous injury, earlier interventions and choice of massage technique. Always work in the best interests of the athlete. Careful thought and planning help to deliver the most appropriate method.

Table 20.2 Four main purposes for massage

Purpose	Explanation
Recovery	After exercise to facilitate complete recovery
Maintenance	To prevent injury and maintain optimum health
Remediation	When a condition that may be debilitating needs improving
Rehabilitation	To promote healing as a restorative application

See page 186 in Unit 17 for more information on recovery after a sporting activity

Relaxation techniques

Relaxation techniques can be used by the athlete and the masseur to aid in the preparation and recovery from sporting events. Each athlete may have developed their own relaxation strategy; this can include having a specific post-event massage, listening to music, watching a film or even reading a book. However, there are other advanced massage strategies that may be used by the therapist to promote recovery and aid relaxation. Muscle energy techniques (METs) relieve muscular tension and promote relaxation; neuromuscular techniques may be used to relieve pain and reduce tension.

For maximum benefit, most relaxation techniques require controlled breathing and clear communication between the therapist and the athlete. Special training is required before a masseur can practise relaxation techniques.

Strapping and taping techniques

Strapping and taping techniques are generally used as a prophylactic support to help prevent further injury and protect a previously injured area such as a ligament. There are many types of tapes and bandages that produce different effects; some prevent movement as much as possible (zinc oxide tape), whereas others limit the range of movement or prevent swelling (elastic adhesive bandages, cohesive bandages). For each athlete, the masseur needs to be trained to know the most appropriate tape to apply and the safe way to apply it.

Manipulation

Massage gently manipulates the soft tissues, but other professional therapists such as physiotherapists, osteopaths and chiropractors may use a combination of manipulation and mobilisation to help an athlete recover from injury. Safe treatment requires a very thorough knowledge of human anatomy and physiology. A therapist with inadequate knowledge could cause further injury. Most healthcare professionals have done at least three years of training at degree level, and the training usually combines academic study with clinical placements.

Chartered Society of Physiotherapists

www.csp.org.uk

General Chiropractic Council

www.chiropractic-uk.co.uk

General Osteopathic Council

www.osteopathy.org

Health Professions Council

www.hpc-uk.org

See page 55 in Unit 2 for more information on legislation that affects premises

Reason for requesting massage

- To relax the athlete and reduce stress levels
- To alleviate aches and pains
- To stimulate the superficial tissues
- To improve lymphatic drainage and reduce swelling
- To limit the formation of scar tissue and promote healing
- To maintain current status for exercise and activity.

Electrotherapy

Electrotherapies are usually applied by qualified sports therapists or chartered physiotherapists, which means they must have done a specified number of hours of recognised training and clinical experience. They need to have detailed knowledge of the human body and its response to injury.

Different treatments have different effects on the body. Here are some electrotherapies: ultrasound, interferential therapy (IFT), transcutaneous electrical stimulation (TENS) and electrical muscle stimulation (EMS). Some relieve pain – they are analgesic – some stimulate muscle fibres during rehabilitation and some speed up healing.

activity
INDIVIDUAL WORK 20.3

P3

M2

Choose any two of these sports performers: marathon runner, footballer, hockey player, cricketer.

1. Which areas of the body would massage treatment focus on?
2. What massage manipulations or techniques would be included?

activity
INDIVIDUAL WORK 20.4

D1

1. For the two sports performers in Activity 20.3, compare the treatments for the two performers and state any similarities and differences in the depth and speed of the messages.
2. What factors need to be considered when assessing the performers' needs?

Identifying the sport and exercise massage requirements of athletes

Assessment

Initial consultation

Always allow sufficient time for the initial consultation. Use it to find out relevant information from the athlete and discuss any matters that arise. Keep detailed and up-to-date records of all treatments. Always establish the reasons why the athlete requires a massage treatment. After the initial consultation, you may need to refer the athlete to another healthcare professional.

Record the details of the initial consultation on a consultation or treatment form, then file it in a safe place, ideally a lockable filing cabinet. Update the information each time the athlete attends for treatment. Only relevant staff should have access to these records. Therapists have a responsibility to maintain accurate records. This is required by their personal indemnity insurance and by the Data Protection Act 1998. Complete all records in black ink and update them every time you give a treatment.

Hold all consultations in private, so the masseur and the athlete cannot be overheard or disturbed, and so that all information about the athlete remains confidential.

Referral to practitioners

Whenever a treatment requires medical consent, always obtain the consent in writing before you proceed with the treatment. Usually, the athlete obtains the written consent from their doctor and gives it to the masseur. You can help the process by giving the athlete a standard letter for their doctor to sign and return. Some doctors may want to see the athlete.

A standard letter should include the address of the massage clinic or sports club, the athlete's full name, address and date of birth, and a space for the athlete to sign and date that they agree to have this information sought on their behalf. It also include the masseur's name. Finally, it has a statement that the doctor can modify to grant or withhold consent for massage treatment, plus spaces for the doctor's signature and the date of their reply.

Attach the doctor's response to the athlete's consultation sheet and keep it for future reference. Never proceed with any treatment while you are waiting for consent. Do not allow any athlete to persuade you into giving them treatment before you have received the required consent. Explain to the athlete that you are acting in their best interests and protecting their health and safety. If you treat an athlete without the proper consent, you will invalidate your personal indemnity insurance and you will not be covered if you are sued for malpractice.

Why a detailed consultation is required

A detailed consultation provides all the relevant details to plan the first massage and to assess the athlete's future treatments and goals.

- Reassure the athlete and gain their confidence.
- Establish a rapport with the athlete.
- Collect relevant information on the athlete's physical health, including:
  - their past medical history (PMH)
  - any contraindications
  - their present condition (PC)
  - the history of their present condition (HPC).
- Gain an insight into the athlete's lifestyle, training schedules and work commitments.
- Identify the treatment needs and expectations of the athlete.
- Explain in full the proposed treatment, its frequency and the short- and long-term goals.
- Establish an agreed treatment plan with estimated costs.
- Answer the athlete's questions on the agreed treatment plan.

Simple injuries

Haematoma

Haematoma is bruising in the muscle tissue usually caused by direct impact. The extent of the bruise will depend on the amount of blood flowing to the muscles at the time of injury. The debilitating effects of a haematoma depend more on their location than on their cause. Some general signs and symptoms include pain and tenderness at the area of impact, a feeling of deadness in the muscle, muscle weakness with pain on contraction and stretching. There are two types of haematoma, intramuscular and intermuscular. Use their specific symptoms to help decide on the best course of treatment.

Intramuscular haematoma

Intramuscular haematoma is bleeding within a muscle caused by a contusion or muscle strain. The haematoma is limited to the intact muscle fascia, or sheath; blood flow is retained and this increases the intramuscular pressure, which limits bleeding but compresses the blood vessels. The signs and symptoms include heat and swelling, and sometimes evidence of bruising. Muscle power and joint ROM come back quickly; there may be a loss of power but no loss of stretch.

Intermuscular haematoma

Bleeding occurs between the muscles. The muscle sheath, fascia and adjacent blood vessels are damaged but blood can escape to the interstitial spaces, so there is no increase in pressure. There is no noticeable swelling but there is evidence of bruising away from the injury site up to 24–48 h after impact. Muscle power returns slowly and there is limited joint ROM plus loss of power and loss of stretch.

Figure 20.5 Intramuscular haematoma is bleeding within a muscle

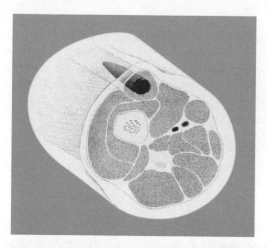

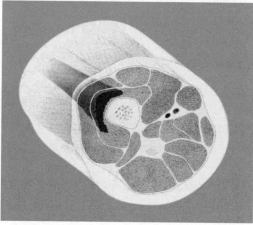

Muscle tears

Muscle tears such as strains and ruptures are some of the most common sports injuries. Most are minor and may not need a medical practitioner, but even the most minor strain can cause future problems if they are not treated properly from the outset.

Tendon injuries

Tendons are connective tissues that attach bones to muscles. They have high tensile strength but very limited flexibility (approximately 5%) so they cannot accommodate sudden forces during everyday activities and sport. After age 35, tendons gradually degenerate and lose their elasticity, so there is an increased likelihood of tendon injury, often to the Achilles tendon, during sport and exercise. Intrinsic and extrinsic factors contribute to inflammation in tendon injuries.

Figure 20.6 Intermuscular haematoma is bleeding between muscles

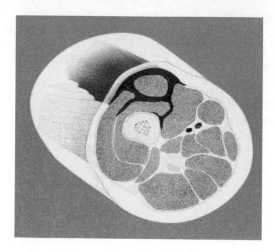

Table 20.3 Tendon injuries: intrinsic and extrinsic factors

Intrinsic factors	Extrinsic factors
Repetitive movements	Heel tabs from shoes or boots
Poor technique	Tight shoelaces
Rubbing against other soft tissue or bone	Faulty equipment
Repetitive loading	Free or static weights too heavy

Inflammation

Any soft tissues, such as muscles, tendons, ligaments and bursae, may develop inflammation. Some of the signs and symptoms are easy to detect but palpation may be the only way to discover inflammation in deeper tissues. Discomfort and pain may be caused by a chronic or non-acute condition, or it may be due to an acute problem that requires the athlete to be referred to other healthcare professionals. Some common symptoms of inflammation are pain, heat, swelling and loss of function. Always consider these symptoms in relation to the athlete, their past medical history, their present condition, the sporting activity and the training schedules.

Figure 20.7 Any soft tissues may develop inflammation

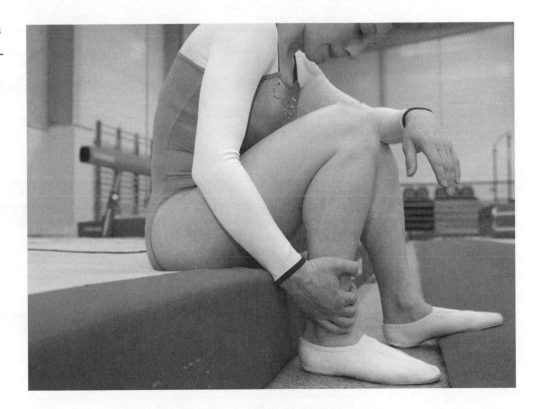

Ligament injuries

Ligament injuries can be caused when a joint is moved beyond its normal range of movement, often under load or by a force that is too great. Ligaments attach bone tissue to bone tissue and are joint stabilisers, so ligament damage can sometimes be accompanied by bone damage. An avulsion fracture is when a tendon or ligament breaks off a small piece of bone. The danger with ligament injuries is a build-up of scar tissue that causes the ligament to become thick and inflexible. Laxity, or lengthening of the ligament, may contribute to joint instability; tethering, or shortening of the ligament, restricts normal movement.

Documentation

Records

Table 20.4 shows the information that should be recorded on a treatment form. For subsequent treatments, a brief consultation is usually sufficient to establish the effects and outcomes of the previous treatments, their effectiveness and whether to adapt individual treatments or the whole treatment plan. Map them on to the short- and long-term goals. These notes are often called SOAP notes – subjective, objective, assessment, planning   (Table 20.5).

Table 20.4 Record card

Personal details	
Name	
Address	
Date of birth	
Home telephone	
Work telephone	
Occupation	
Doctors details	
Name	
Address	
Telephone	
Past medical history (PMH)	
Surgical operations, investigations, MRI, X-rays	
Serious illness or infection	
Injuries, when they occurred, how, treatment received	
Involvement of other healthcare professionals	
History of present condition (HPC)	
When was the injury sustained?	
How does it feel now?	
What treatment has been applied, if any?	
How would you describe the pain or ache?	
When is it least painful and most painful?	
How has it affected daily life and training schedules?	

Short-term goals

Short-term goals are used to help plan each treatment and meet longer-term goals; they can also motivate the athlete, especially if massage is used as part of a rehabilitation programme. Always discuss short-term goals with the athlete, and if you have the athlete's consent, discuss them with the athlete's coach or trainer. Short-term goals help a masseur to:

- establish a priority of treatment
- measure the effectiveness of a treatment
- monitor healing and recovery.

Goals should always be realistic, measurable and observable and are usually seen as stepping stones on a path to full function.

Table 20.5 SOAP notes

Subjective: what the athlete tells the therapist
Update of previous information or relevant new information
Response to the previous treatment, improved or not
Level of function
Compliance to homecare recommendations
Objective: what the masseur sees, feels or measures
Measurable information
Observable information
Repeatable procedures
Treatment
Area treated, skin condition, colour, musculature, palpation, massage
Technique, range of movement (ROM), homecare advice
Assessment: summary of the major problems from the subjective and objective assessments
Review of the treatment: depth, rate, techniques
Response of athlete during treatment
Reaction of treatment area during treatment
Priorities for the next treatment or homecare
Planning: a plan for the athlete's subsequent treatments
Treatment techniques the athlete will receive
Area to be treated
Frequency, timing, depth of treatment
Location of treatment room: clinic, training area, pitch side
Position of the athlete: lying, sitting, standing
Treatment progressions: linked to exercises, training schedule
Referral to other healthcare professionals: doctor, podiatrist, osteopath

Long-term goals

Long-term goals may be a return to full ability or full sporting activity in an agreed timescale, or the reduction of aches and pains after exercise activity. Discuss all long-term goals with the athlete and amend them together when you see how the athlete has responded to massage treatment.

Having written up the SOAP notes, record the treatment provided then sign, date and initial in black ink. Add a page number; it helps you keep the records in sequence.

See page 94 in Unit 3 for more information on the aims of exercise for particular groups.

See page 144 in Unit 15 for more information on the aims of exercise for particular groups

Table 20.6 Treatment sheet

Confidential		
Title	DOB / /	
Name		
Address		
Telephone	Mobile	
Medical history, medication, allergies		
Occupation, sporting activities, hobbies		
Date of first consultation		
Present conditions		
History of present condition (HPC)		

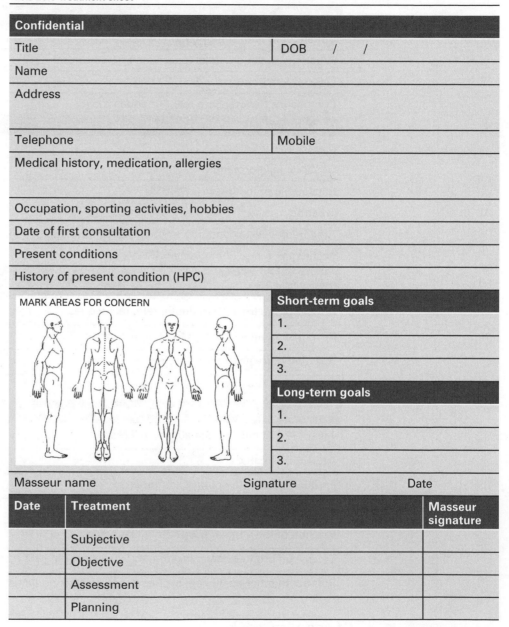

MARK AREAS FOR CONCERN

Short-term goals
1.
2.
3.

Long-term goals
1.
2.
3.

Masseur name	Signature	Date

Date	Treatment		Masseur signature
	Subjective		
	Objective		
	Assessment		
	Planning		

Effects of treatments

A sport and exercise masseur needs a thorough knowledge of common sports injuries. This helps them to devise treatment plans and to recognise the nature and mechanisms of typical injuries. Table 20.7 is one way to classify injuries.

Table 20.7 How to classify muscle and ligament injuries

	Muscle injury	Ligament Injury
First degree, mild	Little disruption to a few fibres; gradual onset, some soreness or tightness; difficult to locate on palpation	Minor fibre disruption; no instability at the joint; some discomfort that eases; minimal signs and symptoms of inflammation
Second degree, moderate	Moderate fibre disruption (up to 50%); sharp pulling sensation; bruising possible; aches after training and exercise; pain and spasm	Moderate fibre disruption (up to 50%); some joint instability; noticeable signs and symptoms of inflammation
Third degree, severe	Severe to total disruption (100%); severe pain, snapping sensation; bruising; gap may be palpable	Almost all fibres torn (100%); joint instability severe signs and symptoms of inflammation

Consider how the injury occurred as this will influence the healing process and the choice of massage treatment; it may even mean that massage is inappropriate. Each athlete has their own rate of healing and this will depend on other important factors.

Table 20.8 Stages following an injury

	Acute	Sub-acute	Subsequent
Time after injury	1–3 days	2–21 days	> 21 days
Principal process	Inflammation	Repair	Remodelling
What happens	Pain, swelling, redness, heat, loss of function	Development of repair, removal of debris, growth of new capillaries, absorption of oedema	Promote healing, maintain joint mobility, static muscle work, ice or heat

See page 155 in Unit 17 for more information on the possible causes of injury

Care at home

When the massage has been completed in a clinical setting, the athlete should be permitted to remain sitting or lying for a few minutes before they start to move slowly. Athletes who have been lying down may feel a little dizzy when they start to move. Allow the athlete to get dressed then ask for their feedback about the treatment. This feedback will help you to plan their future sessions and the work they should do at home.

Many athletes like to drink a small amount of water after a massage. Some athletes feel an immediate improvement after treatment, whereas others feel it the next day. Explain this to the athlete during or after the treatment. Where necessary, give clear guidelines on any aftercare procedures that include gentle mobility or stretching exercises.

Health and safety

Any sport and exercise masseur has a responsibility to work in the best interests of their athletes and to protect them as far as possible from danger during treatment. This includes treatment in a clinical environment, in changing rooms and on the field of play. Do a simple risk assessment to minimise injury and maintain the welfare and safety of athletes. Detailed guidelines are available from the Health and Safety Executive (HSE). Risk assessments generally have five stages (Table 20.9).

remember

Tissue healing will differ from athlete to athlete. Here are some of the factors that influence the healing process: age, previous injuries, adherence to rehabilitation programmes, medication.

Health and Safety Executive
www.hse.gov.uk

Table 20.9 Five-stage risk assessment

1. Identify any potential hazards	2. Decide who could be harmed and how	3. Evaluate the risks and decide on precautions	4. Record the findings and implement changes	5. Review the assessment and update
Training kits blocking exit doors	All personnel and visitors	Tripping, falling	Notes made and clear signs placed to state clearly exits to be kept clear	Checked against accident book records; regular daily inspection to ensure clear exit paths
Allergy to oil	Individual athletes	Anaphylactic shock	Consultation document clearly indicates allergies checked for	Check at each visit that there are no changes to medical history; have alternative massage media; do not use nut oils

Fire exits

Masseur and athlete must know the main fire exits, safe evacuation routes and assembly points in a clinic, gym or fitness centre. There should be adequate numbers of fire extinguishers and fire blankets plus other fire safety equipment.

Proposed treatment

Pre-, inter- and post-event massage

Use pre-event massage to prepare an athlete for a specific event, use inter-event massage to aid recovery between events, and use post-event massage to support recovery after competition or activity:

- Massage on the day of an event should not be deep or relaxing.
- Pre-event massage usually lasts about 10 min and includes more superficial techniques.
- Post-event massage can last up to 45 min and includes deeper manipulations.
- Do not use massage to substitute for a warm-up.

The timing of massage techniques will vary according to the needs of the athlete or the team.

Suggested treatment duration

There are general timings available for Swedish body massage routines. Each treatment and its timing will differ to meet the needs of the athlete. Sport and exercise massage is similar to Swedish massage except that it rarely includes treatment to the abdomen.

A general full body massage can take up 60 min, excluding consultation time, but a sport and exercise masseur is more likely to treat only specific areas of the athlete. Always allocate enough time to the initial consultation and the SOAP notes. Here are some timings to use as a guideline:

- Back and neck: 15–20 min
- Anterior leg: 10 min each leg
- Posterior leg: 10 min each leg
- Arms: 10 min each arm.

Contraindications

Check the athlete for contraindications before you begin any treatment. A contraindication is a condition that means the treatment should not be carried out. Deal with contraindications discreetly and professionally. Any athlete under age 18 should be accompanied by an adult. Contraindications can be considered in three categories.

case study 20.2 — Treatment plan for a marathon runner

Alison Smith, age 38, is a runner preparing for the London Marathon. She has 7 months to prepare her training schedule. One of Alison's friends has found sports massage very therapeutic and has suggested that she seek advice about the effects and benefits of the treatments from a qualified sports masseur.

activity
INDIVIDUAL WORK

1. Describe how Alison could benefit from sports massage.
2. Explain how a treatment plan could be devised for Alison.
3. Discuss the treatment plan, its short-term goals and its long-term goals.

Total contraindication to treatment

- Rheumatoid arthritis
- Multiple sclerosis
- Any contagious disease
- Severe psoriasis, eczema, dermatitis
- Myositis ossificans
- Melanoma.

Localised contraindications

- Bruises
- Fractures
- Varicose veins
- Superficial irritation to the skin
- Cuts, grazes, open skin, rashes, bites, stings, wounds, burns
- Sunburn
- Localised inflammation, redness, lumps or bumps of unknown origin
- Warts and skin tags plus moles that are large, lumpy or inflamed
- Metal pins or plates
- Scar tissue, usually under 6 months old.

Contraindications that require medical consent

- Diabetes
- Heart conditions such as coronary heart disease
- Extremely high or low blood pressure
- Epilepsy
- Cancer or a history of cancer
- Post-operative scar from a recent operation
- Phlebitis.

 Link

See page 46 in Unit 2 in *BTEC National Sports Book 1* for more information on responsibilities when working with children or vulnerable adults in sport
See page 245 in Unit 21 for more information on responsibilities when working with children or vulnerable adults in sport
See page 289 in Unit 23 for more information on responsibilities when working with children or vulnerable adults in sport

1. Describe six contraindications to massage.
2. State the type of contraindication for each condition.

case study

20.3

Lumbar pain in a weekend cricketer

Tom, age 18, is a wicketkeeper who plays amateur cricket on Saturdays and Sundays through the competition season. He has played a variety of sport since he was a small boy. Recently Tom has complained of discomfort and pain in the lumbar area of his back, and occasionally suffers from pins and needles down the back of his leg. Tom books his first appointment with you for a sport and exercise massage treatment.

1. Explain the details you would need to record about Tom's condition.
2. You decide to refer Tom to his doctor. Draft a letter that you could send.
3. Discuss the details you should explain to Tom about his requested massage treatment.

remember

- Keep spare black pens close by to write up treatment notes. Never use corrector pen on errors. Strike a line through the incorrect information then initial and date it.
- Have a blank treatment record card ready before the athlete arrives for treatment.
- After treatment, update the SOAP notes. Whenever possible, do this while the athlete is present, then store them safely in a lockable, fireproof cabinet.
- Read the SOAP notes carefully before the athlete arrives for their next appointment; monitor the athlete's progress.
- Check that there are no new contraindications since the previous treatment.
- Always ask the athlete how they responded to their previous treatment.

Demonstrating different sport and exercise massage techniques

Client preparation

A sports masseur may be required to work in different environments. Massage may be performed with little or no equipment or in a treatment room dedicated to massage and related treatments. Other possibilities are a first-aid room or a designated area in a changing room.

A treatment room should have enough space for a plinth so the masseur can walk all the way round it without feeling cramped. There should also be space for a small table or trolley that holds the preparations and clean laundry. The treatment room should be clean, tidy and welcoming. The flooring should be easy to clean but not noisy, slippery or too cold. Provide a secure space to store the athlete's personal belongings during the treatment.

Figure 20.8 A treatment room should be clean, tidy and welcoming

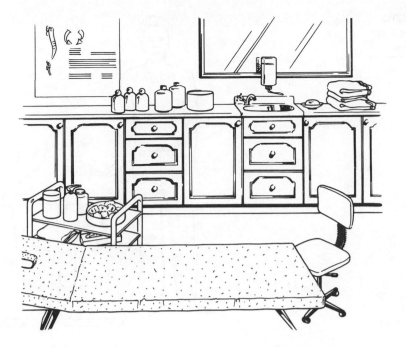

The room or cubicle should be fully enclosed. If curtains are used, check that they give full privacy to the athlete. Check that all doors can be fully closed but not locked from inside or outside.

Temperature and ventilation

The room should be warm enough so the athlete is not too cold and the masseur is not too warm. It should be well ventilated but not draughty.

Basins and bins

Within the treatment area there should be a washbasin with a supply of soap and disposable towels. Provide a wastebin with a lid and a liner; empty it at the end of every working day. Have a supply of clean laundered towels for the athlete plus a roll of tissue, extra pillows and blankets.

Equipment

Massage plinths come in several types – portable, static, hydraulic – and prices vary considerably for the different types. Whichever type you select, choose a plinth that is secure and robust so it will be safe as well as long enough and wide enough for clients of many sizes.

If the plinth is too low or too high, you will have to stoop or stretch to work on the athletes. This will cause you to develop back problems and then you will not be able to use your body weight correctly during treatments. Portable plinths allow easy height adjustments, even between treatments; this is a big advantage, so consider it carefully before you buy a plinth. When the plinth is adjusted to the correct height, your fist should be just touching the edge of the plinth when you stand beside it with your arms hanging down and your hand in a gentle fist.

Plinths may also be available with a face hole to ensure that the athlete's neck and upper back is not twisted when lying prone on the plinth. If this is not available, you can buy a U-shaped face cushion.

Some other accessories are D-rolls that go under the athlete's elbows, knees or ankles to support their joints during massage treatment, washable plinth covers to protect the upholstery and limit wear and tear with daily use, tissue roll holders at the base of each plinth, and small trolleys to store massage products.

Figure 20.9 If the plinth is too low or too high, you will have to stoop or stretch

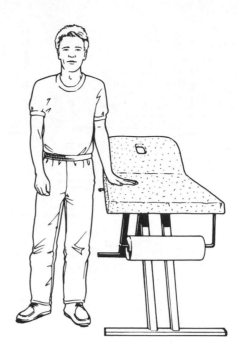

Towels and tissues

The masseur has a professional responsibility to maintain the highest standards of hygiene and to prevent cross-infection during massage treatments. Provide fresh towels for each athlete, replace the tissue roll on the plinth for the next treatment, and wash your hands before and after each treatment. Where possible, use disposable items such as spatulas and tissues; put all waste in a covered bin. Used towels should be put in a covered laundry bin and emptied at the end of the working day or when full.

Trolleys, sinks, taps, the plinth and any other work surfaces should be wiped down daily with a chlorine preparation diluted to the manufacturer's instructions. Some companies sell hand cleansers intended for use after hand washing. Do not use them instead of hand washing.

Personal hygiene

Have a daily bath or shower to keep your skin, hair and nails clean and to remove odours of stale sweat. Use antiperspirant or deodorant to prevent excessive sweating and mask the odour of stale sweat. Keep your hair clean and neat. Tie back long hair; never let it fall forwards so it touches your face or touches the athlete.

Take good care of your hands. They must be smooth and warm for massage. Have short nails that do not extend beyond the fleshy part of the fingertip. Long nails make it impossible to perform massage movements correctly and they can harbour dirt and bacteria. Do not use nail enamel as some athletes may have an allergic reaction to it.

If you have a large cut or abrasion on your hand, do not do any massages. If you have a small cut on you hand, you can still do massages but put a waterproof dressing over the cut to make it hygienic. Always wash your hands immediately before and after giving a treatment. Dry them using a disposable paper towel.

Keep jewellery to a minimum. Wear no more than a wedding ring and small earrings. Rings, bracelets and watches can harbour micro-organisms and can injure the athlete if they are dragged on the skin. The ideal option is to wear no jewellery at all.

Wear clothes that allow you to move around freely, especially clothes that do not restrict your arm movements. A polo shirt and tracksuit trousers are ideal for a sports masseur. They give you free movement and they look professional in all the work environments you are likely to encounter. Wear a full shoe that helps your posture and supports and protects your feet while you are giving massage treatments.

remember

Having a dress code signals professionalism and makes it easier for players, coaches, referees and visitors to identify the masseur. This saves valuable time during busy days and improves everyone's safety.

remember

Pay attention to hygiene and cleanliness. They are important responsibilities and it is very easy to spread infections through poor hygiene.

Figure 20.10 Portable plinths allow easy height adjustments – (a) general purpose plinth; (b) face cushion; (c) steps; (d) portable plinth; (e) head rest; (f) back massage; (g) electric height-adjustable plinth

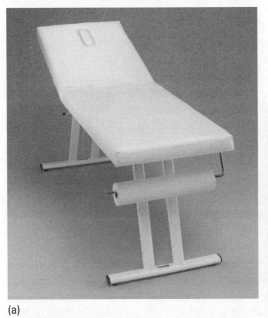

(a)

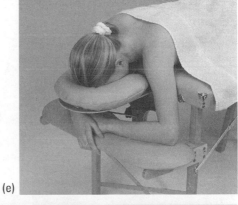

(b)

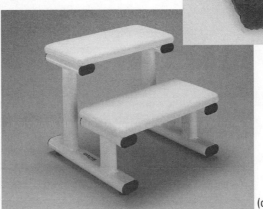

(c)

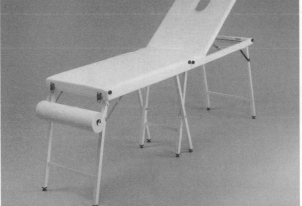

(d)

(e)

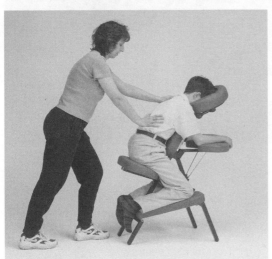

(f)

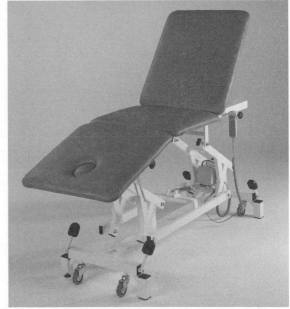

(g)

Before the athlete arrives

Before the athlete arrives, prepare the treatment area and get ready all the equipment and products for the massage treatments. This is a professional approach and it shows the athlete that you are organised and have planned carefully for their treatment.

Prepare the massage plinth

1. Where possible, place a washable, fitted towelling cover over the plinth then disposable tissue on top of the cover. Some masseurs use a clean bath sheet instead of a plinth cover. A bare plinth is too cold and unwelcoming when the athlete first lies down.

2. Have a second bath sheet available to cover the athlete and keep them warm during the treatment. You may also need a blanket if the athlete feels cold.

3. Have easy access to extra pillows, blankets and D-rolls to support the athlete's joints during treatment. The D-roll can be placed underneath the athlete's knees when they sit or lie supine on the plinth, the D-roll can be placed under the athlete's ankles when they lie prone on the plinth. If you roll up a clean hand towel, it can substitute as a D-roll.

Prepare the treatment table or trolley

Before you buy a table or trolley, choose one that is fit for purpose: Is it big enough? Is it stable and smooth? Are its surfaces easy to clean? Does it have small storage drawers for pens and small disposable items? Does it move easily on castors? How many shelves does it have?

Figure 20.11 Choose a trolley that is fit for purpose

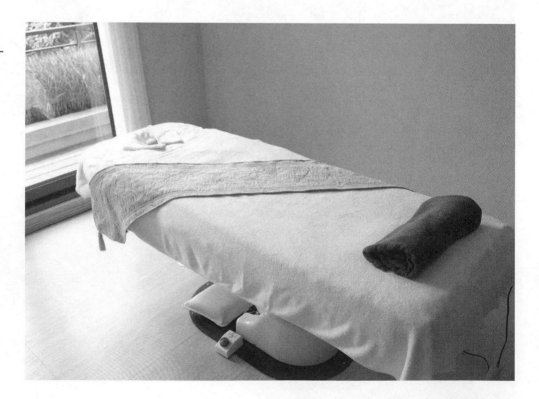

Cleaning routine

The treatment table or trolley should be wiped down between every treatment to prevent cross-infection.

1. Clean the shelves then cover each shelf with a sheet of disposable tissue.

2. Stock the shelves with the following items:

- A bottle of surgical spirit or skin wipes
- A bottle of eau de cologne
- Clean wooden or plastic spatulas
- Massage oil, cream, lotion, gel and powder
- A small plastic bowl containing cotton wool
- A small plastic bowl for the athlete's jewellery
- A small plastic measuring beaker.

Prepare the athlete for treatment

Greet the athlete in a welcoming and professional way so they receive a good first impression. Many athletes may be nervous about receiving a treatment. The masseur's clear communication and positive body language can help to relieve an athlete's anxiety about the treatment.

The following steps are fairly straightforward but there is always room to improve your consultation technique:

1. When the athlete first arrives, offer to take their outdoor clothes and store them securely.
2. During the initial consultation, it can help the rapport between masseur and athlete if they sit at the same level while the masseur records the athlete's details.
3. When necessary, explain to the athlete which garments need to be removed, ask them to sit or lie on the plinth, provide a robe or bath sheet for them, and if possible, screen the area while they undress.
4. After conducting objective tests and measures, discuss the treatment plan and costs with the athlete.

See page 53 in Unit 12 for more information on stress and anxiety in sport
See page 294 in Unit 16 in *BTEC National Sports Book 1* for more information on stress and anxiety in sport

Demonstrate safe and effective massage

Massage treatment lying down

Some athletes may be less mobile than others, so always help the athlete on to the plinth if they need assistance. Some clinics provide a small footstool for stepping up to the plinth, and hydraulic plinths can be lowered electronically so it is easier for athletes to get on.

The athlete is usually asked to lie centrally on the plinth and, where possible, their joints are supported by towels, D-rolls or pillows. Warmth and comfort are essential ingredients of therapeutic massage; a relaxed and calm athlete will derive far more benefit from the treatment.

Cover the athlete with a large, clean towel. Uncover the area you are going to treat then re-cover it when you have finished the treatment. An athlete should never remove their underwear.

Massage treatment in a sitting position

Sometimes it is necessary to complete a massage with the athlete in a sitting position; it may also be more comfortable for some upper-back and neck treatments. Then the plinth should have sufficient pillows for support, ideally placed at the end or the middle of the plinth, and the plinth should be covered with a clean towel. The athlete can then remove their outer clothes and lean forward with their arms and head resting on the towel. Provide a towel to cover the athlete's back until the massage begins.

remember

Prepare the working area and plinth for each treatment before the scheduled appointment. Ensure there is adequate clean laundry. Wash your hands immediately before the massage treatment. Remove used laundry and put it in a laundry basket. Dispose of soiled tissue roll and used consumable products. Wipe over the trolley or table and put new tissue on the shelves. Put a new roll of tissue and clean laundry on the plinth.

Figure 20.12 Cover the athlete with a large, clean towel

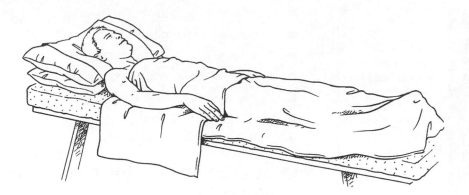

1. Practise preparing the different working areas before treatment.
2. Complete a sport and exercise massage on an athlete from a named activity with support and without support.

remember

Always maintain the athlete's privacy. Reassure the athlete throughout the consultation and procedure. Invite them to ask any questions. Observe their body language during the consultation and treatment. Never assume that you know what areas need treating; discuss it with the athlete. Explain clearly which items of clothing need to be removed before treatment. Agree all treatment plans with the athlete, unless there is a danger of causing harm or injury. When you give a back massage on female athletes, *always* ask their permission to undo their bra straps before commencing treatment.

Therapist's posture

Masseurs adopt the correct posture and stance to avoid getting back injuries. A good masseur adapts their posture for each treatment so they can work safely without hurting themselves. Two standing positions can be used in massage:

■ Walk standing – one foot in front of the other; used when massaging up and down the athlete's body.

■ Stride standing – the feet are placed a small stride apart; usually used when working across the athlete's body.

Massage techniques

Massage techniques or movements can be group into five categories (Table 20.10).

Table 20.10 Five main techniques

Technique	Movement
Effleurage	Stroking
Petrissage	Kneading, wringing, picking up, skin rolling
Frictions	Circular, transverse, linear
Tapotement or percussion	Hacking, cupping, beating, pounding
Vibrations	Vibration, shaking

Figure 20.13 A good masseur adapts their posture for each treatment

remember

When you give a massage, keep your lower back straight, relax your shoulders, and have soft or bent knees. Apply depth and pressure through your body weight, not through your arms. Position your body close enough to the plinth so that you do not overreach when you give the treatment.

Effleurage

Effleurage takes its name from the French *effleuer* 'to skim over'. It is a superficial movement used at the start of a massage to apply the massage medium and helps the masseur to become aware of the athlete's underlying tissue. It also accustoms the athlete to the masseur's touch. Pressure is applied on the upward movement and always follows venous return; a lighter movement is used when returning back down to the starting point. For treating larger areas, the whole surface of both hands should be in full contact with the athlete's body, and the hand surfaces should be moulded to the treatment area. The pads of the fingers or thumbs may be used for treating smaller areas. Effleurage is used to link different massage manipulations and all massage treatments should start and finish with effleurage.

Therapeutic benefits

- Gently warms the skin and produces an erythema
- Improves lymphatic and venous return
- Can help to reduce non-medical oedema
- Removes dead skin cells, aids desquamation
- Its warming action stimulates sweat and sebaceous glands
- Reduces muscle tension
- It has a sedative effect on sensory nerve endings.

Petrissage

Petrissage takes its name from the French *petrir* 'to knead'. Petrissage movements include kneading, wringing, picking up, and skin rolling. Petrissage movements include a systematic controlled pressure applied to the soft tissue by controlled compression or by lifting the tissue away from underlying structures. The depth and intensity of the pressure will depend on the type of massage and the area being massaged. Less depth is required when treating the upper arm, or brachium, but more pressure is needed for the gluteal muscles.

Figure 20.14 Effleurage has several therapeutic benefits

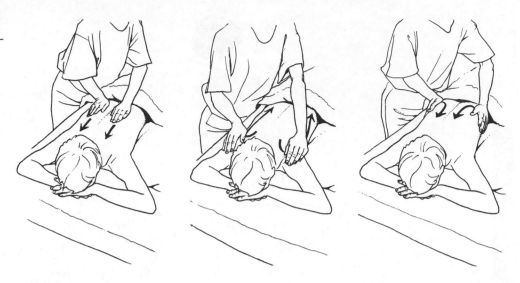

Kneading

- **Flat-handed or palmar kneading** – the palmar surfaces of the two hands work simultaneously to compress then release the underlying tissue. The hands work in a circular motion, applying pressure on the upward part of the circle.

- **Alternate kneading** – pressure is created by working one hand slightly before the other. The hands are placed on either side of the limb or body part.

- **Single-handed kneading** – one hand performs the kneading manipulation while the other supports the tissues on the opposite side.

Figure 20.15 Single-handed kneading

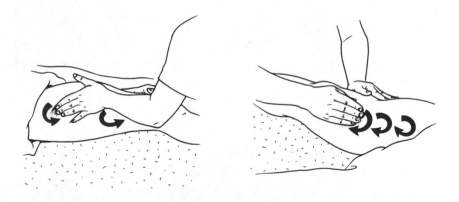

- **Double-handed kneading** – the hands work side by side to move the tissues in large circles.

Figure 20.16 Double-handed kneading

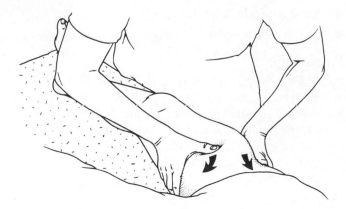

■ **Reinforced kneading** – one hand lies directly on top of the other to produce a very deep pressure. Also known as ironing, it can be useful on large or dense muscle groups.

Figure 20.17 Reinforced kneading

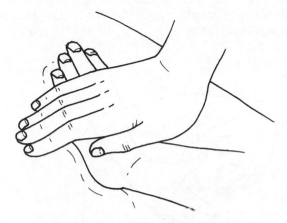

■ **Squeezing kneading** – each hand alternately grasps and squeezes soft tissue; as one hand releases an area of tissue, the opposite hand squeezes adjacent tissue. It is a rhythmical technique and the hands maintain contact with the treatment area until the treatment is finished. Take care to avoid pinching the athlete.

Figure 20.18 Squeezing kneading

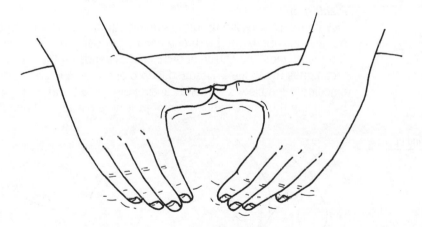

■ **Finger and thumb kneading** – the fingers or thumb apply pressure in small circular movements; try to achieve depth on the upward part of the circle, but use less pressure on the downward part of the circle. The fingers or thumb stay in contact with the tissue throughout.

Figure 20.19 (a) Finger and (b) thumb kneading

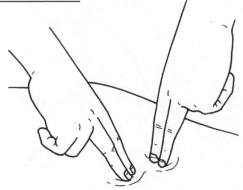 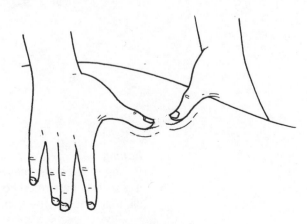

Wringing

Wringing lifts tissues away from the underlying bone. Both hands work simultaneously so the fingers are on one side of the tissue and the thumb is directly opposite. The tissue is drawn forward with one hand and pushed away with the other, and the manipulation is repeated along the length of a muscle. Smaller areas may be too small for hand wringing and may require digital wringing.

Figure 20.20 Wringing

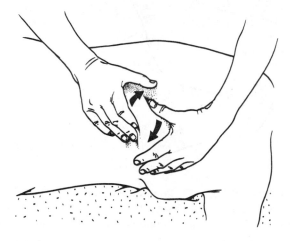

Picking up

Picking up involves lifting soft tissue away from the underlying structures. Single-handed picking up is performed with one hand and double-handed picking up is performed with two hands; the choice of technique depends on the area being treated. In both techniques the tissue is lifted, squeezed and then released. Great care is needed to avoid pinching the athlete's skin and causing discomfort and bruising. Pinching can be avoided by placing the whole hand in contact with the tissue throughout the manipulation.

Figure 20.21 Picking up

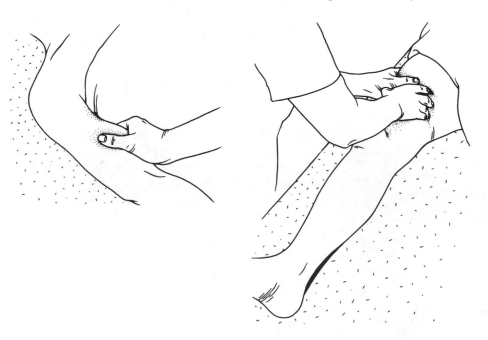

Rolling

Rolling is where the masseur oils the skin and muscle between their fingers and thumb; it is usually performed horizontally across the tissues in a smooth, gliding manner without pinching the skin.

Figure 20.22 Rolling – skin rolling: (a) hand position; (b) pulling the tissue into a roll with the fingers; (c) squeeze and lift; (d) pushing the roll back with the thumbs; (e) (f) muscle rolling

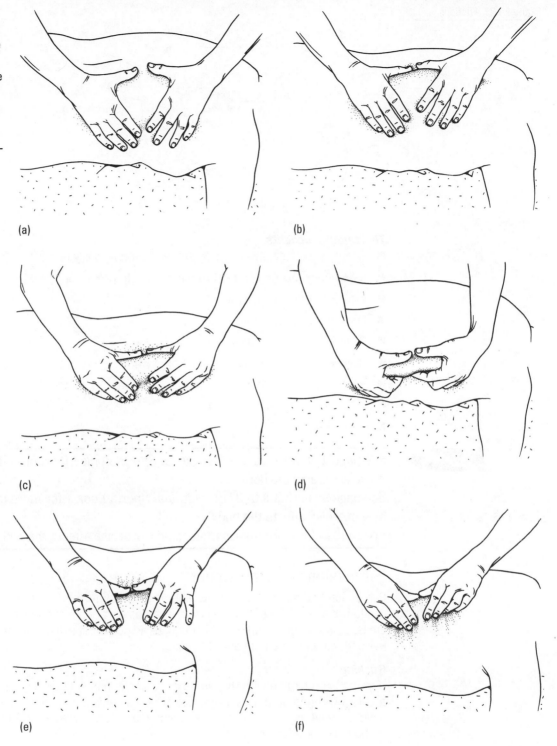

(a)

(b)

(c)

(d)

(e)

(f)

Frictions

Frictions are deep pressure movements applied using the fingertips or the thumbs in a circular or transverse manner, with pressure on the subcutaneous tissue. They can be used to loosen scar tissue during rehabilitation, particularly in tendons and ligaments, and to help remodel tissue to prevent further injury. In transverse frictions the thumb or fingers are placed at 90° to the tissues, followed by a deep forward and backward transverse movement. Circular frictions produce movements in very small circles so the depth of pressure increases to a maximum and is then released.

Figure 20.23 Frictions

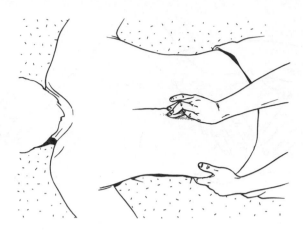

Therapeutic benefits

- Dilates subcutaneous blood vessels and produces erythema
- Its pumping action can help to remove waste products
- Increases the flow of lymph
- Loosens local adhesions
- Relieves tension nodules
- Relieves pain and increases range of movement
- Promotes relaxation when performed slowly and rhythmically
- Improves scar tissue
- Aids relaxation.

See page 2 in Unit 1 in *BTEC National Sports Book 1* for more information on how exercise affects the body

See page 80 in Unit 3 in *BTEC National Sports Book 1* for more information on how exercise affects the body
See Unit 13 for more information on how exercise affects the body

Percussion and tapotement

Percussion and tapotement involve light rhythmical movements to stimulate and invigorate an area. They should not be used as part of a relaxing treatment. Avoid bony areas; restrict them to areas with adequate adipose tissue. The movements include hacking, cupping, beating and pounding.

Hacking

Hacking is performed with the ulnar border of the hands (little finger) at right angles to the area being treated. It is a light but brisk manipulation applied alternately with each hand, moving up and down the area being massaged. Always perform it by movement of the wrist, not the elbow.

Cupping

Sometimes known as clapping, cupping is when the hands are cupped with the palmar surface face down. Like hacking, it is a light, brisk movement generated from the wrists and covering the whole area to be treated. It produce a hollow sound on the skin. Cupping is less invigorating than hacking, but is not advised for a relaxing massage.

Beating

Beating is a deep movement made by rapid or slow contact of a hand shaped into a loose fist. The contact with the treatment area is by the dorsal (back) surface of the distal phalanges and is generally used to treat areas adequately covered with adipose tissue, such as gluteals and thighs.

Pounding

Pounding is very similar to beating. It is applied alternately by the ulnar border of the loosely clenched fist. Use it only on areas with sufficient underlying tissue.

Figure 20.24 Percussion techniques: (a) hacking, (b) cupping, (c) beating, (d) pounding

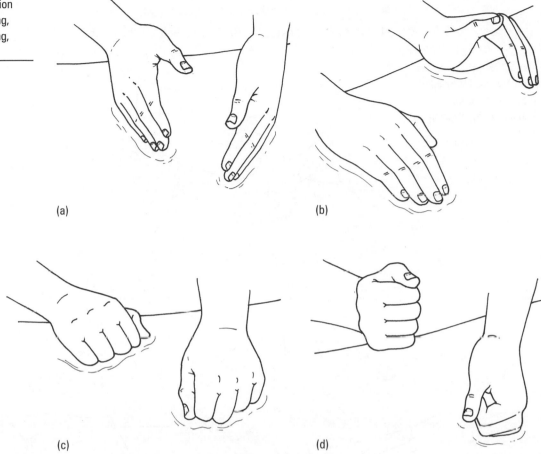

(a)

(b)

(c)

(d)

case study 20.4

Aching legs after Sunday matches

Jack plays football once a week in the local Sunday League team; he plays in midfield. He trains for 1 h every Tuesday evening and sometimes plays five-a-side football on a Thursday after work. He has a stressful job as an electrician but he has noticed that his legs are aching, especially after the Sunday game. He contacts you and would like to have sport and exercise massage treatment on a Monday evening. He has no contraindications and is keen to maintain his current exercise and training regime.

activity
INDIVIDUAL WORK

1. What type of massage would you focus on for Jack?
2. Explain why you have chosen this particular type of massage. Include details of the techniques you could use plus the depth, speed and frequency of the treatment.
3. Describe the benefits of the massage and the time spent completing the massage each session.
4. Plan the long-term and short-term goals of Jack's treatment plan.

Therapeutic benefits

- Localised erythema created by the increased stimulation of circulation
- Warmth and heat produced by localised tissue stimulation
- Stimulation of sensory nerve endings
- Invigorating and may increase local metabolic rate
- Increased removal of waste products from the area.

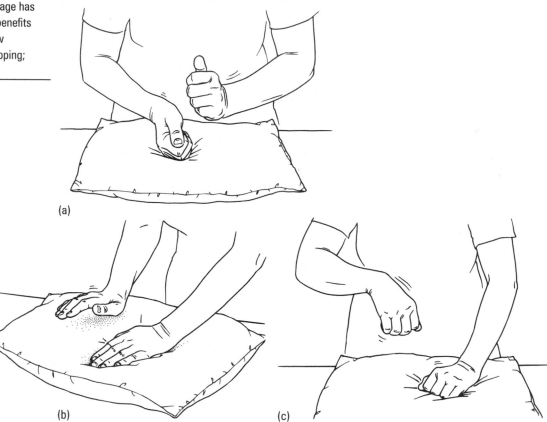

Figure 20.25 Petrissage has several therapeutic benefits – practice on a pillow (a) pounding; (b) clapping; (c) beating

(a)

(b)

(c)

Vibrations

Vibration manipulations also include shaking manipulations and are primarily used for their sedative effects on tissues.

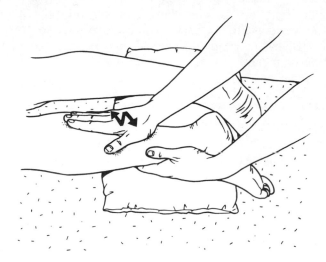

Figure 20.26 Vibrations

Vibrations

To create vibrations, the masseur produces a slight trembling with their hands or fingers on the treatment area, either up and down or from side to side. It takes considerable practice. An alternative method is the static procedure, where the **vibrations** are held in one place on the tissue. Both techniques can be performed with the whole of the hand or with the fingertips and/or thumb.

Shaking

Shaking is where the masseur uses one hand to shake a muscle group and their other hand to support the adjacent tissue. It is used to relax or invigorate the muscles and joints and may also be used with slight traction when applied in the horizontal plane.

Figure 20.27 Shaking

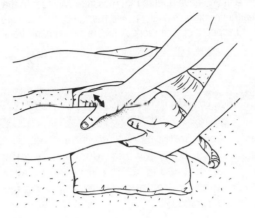

Therapeutic benefits

■ Relieves tension and can relax the athlete

■ Soothing to sensory nerve endings

■ Mild analgesic effect.

Application of techniques

Rapport between masseur and athlete

Try to develop a rapport with the athlete based on trust and confidence. Begin developing a rapport during the initial consultation and build on it every time the athlete requires a massage. Remember that a body massage is a very personal treatment. All athletes need to be aware that any massage they receive is in their best interest and supports their needs.

See page 127 in Unit 4 in *BTEC National Sports Book 1* for more information on establishing trust

See Unit 12 for more information on establishing trust

See page 302 in Unit 16 in *BTEC National Sports Book 1* for more information on establishing trust

See Unit 21 for more information on establishing trust

Treatment evaluation

Sport and exercise masseurs should record verbal feedback from the athlete after treatment, but they may also ask the athlete to complete a simple questionnaire that gives a general evaluation of their treatment. The athlete can complete the questionnaire while the masseur is tidying up or they can do it anonymously, after the session. Questionnaire feedback can be very useful to the masseur and can also help the athlete if it leads to better treatment strategies. Do not give athletes too many questionnaires; use them at carefully chosen points during a course of treatment.

activity
GROUP WORK
20.7

D2

Design a simple athlete feedback questionnaire that will help you analyse the sport and exercise massage treatments for a variety of athletes.

> **remember**
> Never discuss an athlete's treatment without their written consent. Only work within your scope of practice. If you have doubts that massage will benefit the althlete, refer them to an appropriate healthcare professional. Provide treatment that you are qualified to practise. Be professional in all aspects of your work. Athletes are primarily your clients, not your friends.

case study 20.5

Shoulder aches from tennis training

Andrea is a tennis player who trains two afternoons per week and plays in local amateur tournaments each Saturday and Sunday during the tennis season. After training sessions she has noticed aches in her shoulder, although she has no pain. She has an allergy to nuts. Andrea approaches you for a full body treatment on Thursdays, which is her rest day.

activity
INDIVIDUAL WORK

1. Decide on the best overall massage treatment for Andrea. Include named techniques in your answer.

2. Describe at least three massage media you could choose for the treatment. Give clear reasons for your choice.

3. State clearly the timing of the treatment and where the massage treatment would be focused.

Procedure for full body massage

During full body treatments some masseurs prefer to commence work on the athlete's back before working on the limbs as this can give a clear indication of postural aches and pains through palpation and massage. Others start treatment on the limbs then finish by treating the back; this may be a more relaxing technique and permits the masseur to establish the problem areas before working on the athlete's back.

Link | See page 12 in Unit 1 in *BTEC National Sports Book 1* for more information on muscles

Step 1
Start with the athlete in a supine position supported with a pillow behind the head and a D-roll beneath the knees. Cover them with a large bath sheet, and a blanket if required.

1. Right arm
2. Right leg, anterior
3. Left leg, anterior
4. Left arm.

case study 20.6 — Pre-event massage

Sam is a sport and exercise masseur for a local amateur football team that plays a full game every Saturday afternoon. When Sam arrives one Saturday he has five players waiting to see him for a pre-event massage. It is 45 min before the game kicks off and the coach is now becoming impatient as he wants the players to warm up. Sam is also aware that 10 min before the game starts the coach has a team-building session in the changing room.

activity
INDIVIDUAL WORK

1. What are the factors that Sam will need to consider?
2. Plan a treatment schedule for Sam so that all the players can be massaged.
3. Explain how Sam could liaise with the coach about pre-event massage.

Step 2

Move the athlete into a prone position, take away the pillow and place the D-roll beneath the ankles.

1. Left leg, posterior
2. Right leg, posterior
3. Back and neck.

Suggested routines

Back massage

Apply the massage medium to the whole back and neck. Ensure the athlete's hair is protected with a towel or tied up so you can massage their neck.

1. Effleurage to the whole back, including the lateral aspects (superficial and deep)
2. Double-handed kneading to the back
3. Reinforced kneading (ironing)
4. Finger or thumb kneading up the erector spinae muscles
5. Finger or thumb kneading around the margins of the scapula
6. Thumb frictions up the erector spinae muscles
7. Thumb frictions around the margins of the scapula
8. Wringing to the lateral aspects of the back and upper margins of the shoulders
9. Picking up to the lateral aspects of the back and upper margins of the shoulders
10. Skin rolling across the back and shoulders
11. Hacking to the whole of the back
12. Cupping to the whole of the back
13. Vibrations to the back
14. Effleurage.

Anterior leg and foot

Apply the massage medium to the whole of the anterior and lateral aspects of the foot and leg. If it is more comfortable for them, the athlete may lie in a semi-inclined position with a D-roll placed underneath their knees.

1. Commencing at the foot, effleurage to the whole leg and foot
2. Effleurage to the anterior and lateral thigh

> **remember**
> Listen to your athlete as you give the massage treatment. Keep checking with them so that you know you are applying the correct pressure.

3. Kneading (squeezing to the quadriceps)

4. Alternate kneading to the abductors and adductors

5. Reinforced kneading (ironing) to the quadriceps

6. Finger or thumb kneading to tensor fascia lata

7. Thumb frictions to the tensor fascia lata

8. Wringing to the anterior, medial and lateral thigh

9. Picking up to the anterior, medial and lateral thigh

10. Skin rolling to the anterior, medial and lateral thigh

11. Hacking to the anterior, medial and lateral thigh

12. Cupping to the anterior, medial and lateral thigh

13. Vibrations to the anterior, medial and lateral thigh

14. Effleurage to the anterior, medial and lateral thigh

15. Effleurage over the patella

16. Finger kneading around the patella

17. Thumb frictions around the patella

18. Effleurage over the patella.

remember

Cover the thigh with a towel to keep the athlete warm.

Lower leg and foot

1. Effleurage to the lower leg

2. Finger kneading to the lateral aspect (peroneus muscles)

3. Finger kneading around the posterior aspects of the ankle (lateral and medial malleolus)

4. Effleurage to the foot (dorsal and plantar surfaces)

5. Circular thumb kneading with both thumbs to the plantar surface

6. Circular thumb kneading with both thumbs to the dorsal surface

7. Effleurage to the foot (dorsal and plantar surfaces)

Posterior leg and foot

1. Effleurage to the full leg

2. Kneading to the hamstrings

3. Reinforced kneading (ironing) to the hamstrings

4. Finger or thumb kneading to the hamstrings

5. Thumb frictions to the hamstrings

6. Wringing to the hamstrings

7. Picking up to the hamstrings

8. Skin rolling to the hamstrings

9. Hacking to the hamstrings

10. Cupping to the hamstrings

11. Beating and pounding to the upper thigh and gluteals

12. Vibrations to the hamstrings

13. Effleurage to the posterior thigh.

Lower leg

1. Effleurage to the lower leg

2. Alternate kneading to the lower leg

3. Reinforced kneading to the lower leg

4. Finger kneading around the Achilles tendon

5. Thumb frictions around the Achilles tendon

6. Wringing to the lower leg

7. Picking up to the lower leg

8. Skin rolling to the lower leg

9. Hacking to the lower leg

10. Cupping to the lower leg

11. Vibrations to the lower leg

12. Effleurage to the lower leg.

Arm and hand

The athlete may be placed in an inclined position with a towel covering the opposite arm and shoulder to ensure they are warm. When the medium is being applied and during the first effleurage strokes, the arm should be by the athlete's side. When treating a relatively small area like the arm, tissues and joints should always be supported by the masseur's free hand, supported by a small pillow, or placed across the athlete's abdomen. Apply the massage medium to the whole arm starting at the hand.

Arm

1. Effleurage to the upper arm (brachium)

2. Alternate kneading to the anterior and posterior aspects of the deltoid

3. Single-handed kneading to the lateral aspect of the deltoid

4. Single-handed kneading to the biceps and triceps brachii

5. Single-handed picking up to the biceps and triceps brachii

6. Wringing to the biceps and triceps brachii

7. Light hacking across the upper arm (brachium)

8. Effleurage to the lower arm

9. Thumb kneading to the lateral aspect of the arm (upper margins)

10. Alternate thumb kneading to the centre of the forearm from the carpals

11. Picking up to the lateral aspect of the arm (upper margins)

12. Effleurage to the lower arm.

Hand

1. Effleurage to the thenar and hypothenar muscles

2. Thumb kneading to the thenar and hypothenar muscles

3. Thumb kneading down each digit

4. Effleurage to the hand.

activity
INDIVIDUAL WORK 20.8

P6

Keep a simple log or diary that you can complete after every massage treatment. Record the techniques you were good at and the techniques that you need to practise. From this log or diary, produce two action points that you can work towards for subsequent treatments.

- The treatment area and massage timings will depend on the needs of the athlete.
- Massage treatments need to be properly balanced; consider bilateral treatments.
- Referred pain may be the result of injury, poor technique or bad posture. An objective assessment may reveal that the treatment area is not the area where the athlete feels discomfort.
- Avoid moving the athlete unless it is part of the massage treatment.
- After a full body treatment, allow the athlete to rest for a few minutes before getting up from the plinth, especially after a relaxing massage.
- Once you have placed your hands in contact with the athlete, try not to remove them until you have completed the procedure for that area.
- Take great care when massaging on or near the popliteal fossa, the femoral triangle and the cubital fossa.

Massage media and essential products

Massage media are used to provide a slight slip so that you do not drag your hands over the athlete's skin. The required amount will depend on the condition of the athlete's skin, the size of the area being treated and the effects of the massage. Apply enough medium to obtain controlled massage movements but not too much so your hands slip and slide without giving much benefit to the athlete.

Massage media are usually chosen using these factors:

- The masseur's available products
- The athlete's preferences
- Any contraindications, including allergies to nut oils
- The area to be treated
- The massage techniques to be applied
- The condition, if any, being treated.

Nut oils include almond, peach nut and macadamia oils. Some alternatives to nut oils are grapeseed oil, borage oil, olive oil and sunflower oil. There are many varieties of oil and each has different effects on the skin. Oils vary in colour, viscosity and quality.

Essential products

Essential products may be placed near the plinth or on a trolley. For economy and hygiene, some masseurs prefer products that have pump dispensers that deliver a measured quantity, but this is a personal choice and may depend on the working environment.

Spatulas

Spatulas are made of wood or plastic; wooden ones are cheap and disposable. Spatulas are used to scoop a roughly measured amount of cream from a container. They prevent the masseur's fingers from contaminating the cream that remains in the container.

Small plastic bowls

Small plastic bowls have many uses. It is often a good idea to put out at least three or four. They can be used to hold a measured amount of powder for the massage medium, fresh cotton wool or the athlete's jewellery.

Surgical spirit

Have a plastic bottle of surgical spirit, label it properly and keep it handy. Surgical spirit is used to degrease the less sensitive areas of the skin. Applied to the feet with cotton wool pads, it removes any odours and allows the masseur to check for contraindications such as athlete's foot or verrucas. There are also impregnated wipes specifically for these treatments.

Table 20.11 Massage media

Medium	Advantages	Disadvantages
Oil Most commonly used medium	Usually cheap to purchase (sweet almond, soya bean, grapeseed) Nourishes the skin, ideal for all skin types Provides good slip without dragging the skin	Athletes can be allergic to nut oils Some oils are expensive to purchase, such as borage and evening primrose May leave the skin feeling greasy
Cream	Absorbed easily into the skin, good for dry skin Can be used on hairy areas Feels less greasy on the skin	Hands can drag on the skin if they have little oil base Can be more expensive Greater quantities are often needed
Lotions and emulsions A mixture of oils and water	Easily absorbed by the skin, suitable for most skin types Ideal for smaller areas such as hands and feet May have added ingredients such as peppermint and lavender	Not usually used for a full body treatment or larger areas May be difficult to purchase Larger quantities needed, hence less cost-effective
Gels	Can have a cooling effect on the skin Used on specific areas of treatment May be used in rehabilitation techniques and frictions	Not suitable for large areas Not readily available for purchase
Powder Cornflour, talcum powder	Prevents excessive slip Non-greasy, absorbs surface oils and water, so it is suitable for greasy skin Used for very deep applications Generally applied to small areas for specific treatment Cheap to purchase and readily available	Inhalation of powder, especially talcum powder Can clog the pores of the skin when applied directly to an area Athlete can have allergies to powder Always choose unperfumed powder
Pre-blended oils Usually a blend of aromatherapy oils in a base oil	Blends can be ordered for specific conditions, such as muscle aches and pains Athletes may feel more benefit up to 48 h after treatment Do skin sensitivity tests at least 24 h before the first application	Can be expensive to purchase Athlete may not like the smell or aroma Can only be used to treat one body area Should be left on the skin after treatment for maximum effect Some blends can cause a skin reaction for athletes with sensitive skin, so a patch test is required before treatment

Eau de cologne

Eau de cologne may be used at the end the treatment to remove any excess oils or products from the skin. Different colognes have different smells or aromas and some athletes prefer the masseur not to use cologne. Always ask the athlete if they would prefer the medium to remain on the skin or to have it removed with eau de cologne. Warn them that cologne can feel quite cold on first application, especially after a massage. Store eau de cologne in a clearly labelled container inside a flammables cupboard. Some masseurs store it in a bottle, whereas others prefer to use an atomiser spray that gives a fine mist.

Plastic measures

Plastic measures are cheap and easy to replace. They are ideal for measuring out a small quantity of the athlete's preferred massage medium.

remember

To reduce the risk of contamination, never try to pour oil or any other product back into a stock container from a small bowl or any other receptacle. Keep all bottles clean and label them clearly. Always have a sufficient stock of products for the massage treatments. Wash your hands before and after every treatment, preferably so the athlete can see that you have washed them.

Progress Check

1. State three therapeutic effects of massage.

2. Describe the effects of massage on blood and lymph.

3. What are visualisation techniques? Give some examples from sport.

4. Discuss how massage can benefit the nervous system.

5. Describe the stages of risk assessment. Use an example from sport and exercise massage.

6. Explain what SOAP means.

7. State the reasons why athletes may seek sport and exercise massage treatment.

8. Define contraindication. Give specific examples of contraindications.

9. Distinguish between the symptoms of an intramuscular haematoma and an intermuscular haematoma.

10. Explain how muscle injuries are classified. Give examples of the signs and symptoms.

11. What are the important factors for a good treatment environment?

12. List the items needed to prepare the massage plinth and trolley.

13. Why is good posture important when providing massage treatment?

14. List the five main massage groups and name the movements in each group.

15. What factors should a masseur consider when they plan a massage treatment for an athlete?

16. Describe the different massage media that can be selected for a treatment.

17. Using a chinagraph pencil, mark the margins of the popliteal fossa and the cubital fossa.

Rules, Regulations and Officiating in Sport

Mike Hill

This unit covers:

- Rules, laws and regulations in sport
- Roles and responsibilities of officials
- Performance analysis of officials
- How to officiate effectively

Officials are often undervalued. They need fitness of body to shadow the fittest performers and follow the game. They need quickness of mind for rapid decisions and clarity of thought for sound judgements on subtle rules. They may get help from sensors and replays, but they have to know the latest laws like the back of their hand. On the vast majority of decisions, officials get it right. In this unit, you research and present the rules and regulations for a sport of your choice. You develop an understanding of all the officials involved in your sport. You analyse their performance and then you try it for yourself.

<table>
<thead>
<tr>
<th>To achieve a Pass grade the evidence must show that the learner is able to:</th>
<th>To achieve a Merit grade the evidence must show that the learner is able to:</th>
<th>To achieve a Distinction grade the evidence must show that the learner is able to:</th>
</tr>
</thead>
<tbody>
<tr>
<td>P1
describe the rules, laws and regulations of a selected sport   Pg 245</td>
<td></td>
<td></td>
</tr>
<tr>
<td>P2
apply the rules, laws and regulations of a selected sport in three different situations   Pg 246</td>
<td>M1
explain the application of the rules, laws and regulation of a selected sport in three different situations   Pg 246</td>
<td></td>
</tr>
<tr>
<td>P3
describe the roles and responsibilities of officials in a selected sport   Pg 247</td>
<td></td>
<td></td>
</tr>
</tbody>
</table>

grading criteria

grading criteria

To achieve a **Pass** grade the evidence must show that the learner is able to:	To achieve a **Merit** grade the evidence must show that the learner is able to:	To achieve a **Distinction** grade the evidence must show that the learner is able to:
P4 devise suitable criteria to analyse the performance of officials in a selected sport Pg 251		
P5 analyse the performance of two officials in a selected sport, identifying strengths and areas for improvement Pg 257	**M2** explain the identified strengths and areas for improvement of two officials and make suggestions relating to improvement Pg 257	**D1** justify suggestions made in relation to improving performance for two officials from a selected sport Pg 257
P6 officiate, with support, in a selected sport Pg 258	**M3** officiate in a selected sport Pg 258	
P7 review own performance in officiating in a selected sport, identifying strengths and areas for improvement Pg 260	**M4** explain the identified strengths and areas for improvement, and make suggestions relating to improvement Pg 260	**D2** analyse own performance and justify suggestions made in relation to improving own performance Pg 263

The rules and regulations of a selected sport

Rules and regulations

All sports activities require rules to ensure fair competition and protect participants from injury and accident. All performers should have a good grasp of the rules before beginning an activity. Many governing bodies produce a simple overview of their rules and also offer basic courses where people can learn about the key rules in the sport.

The rules of a sport cover the following items:

- **Playing area** – dimensions, size of targets and goals, playing surface.
- **Time** – how long the whole game lasts, periods of the game, any extra time.
- **Equipment** – what types of equipment the performers may use.
- **Teams** – sizes and substitutions.
- **Safety** – safety of the game, any equipment and how the game is played.
- **Scoring** – this is perhaps the most important aspect.

All sports require a scoring system so there is a result at the end of the game. The rules and officials work to make the scoring system clear and easy to follow. In some sports the winner is the team or individual that scores the most points and goals; in these sports the referee keeps a record of the score. In more complex games such as cricket and baseball, the winner is determined by other factors such as how many players are out and scores in several innings; the officials are assisted by scorers who record and

Figure 21.1 Gymnasts are awarded marks for technical ability and artistic ability

display the scores as they happen. The scoring is more subjective in aesthetic sports such as gymnastics, trampolining and diving; a team of judges will watch and then award marks for each performance. Marks may be given for the technical ability and control shown in the performance and how pleasing it was to the eye.

Usually an official such as a referee or umpire will administer the rules. Referees have a difficult job and should always be respected and listened to. The official's task is to ensure all the players have the opportunity to play to the best of their ability and potential in a skilled and safe contest.

Each sport is organised and overseen by a national governing body (NGB). It is the NGB's role to publish and maintain the rules of its sport. All governing bodies issue a handbook setting out the rules of the sport. These rules can change from year to year, so always read the latest edition. Many NGBs post updated versions on their websites, so this is a good place to start your research. At the start of each season, check to see if there are any new rules and ask coaches or referees to explain them to you.

Figure 21.2 Referees have the power to warn players or send them off

Software that teaches the laws of individual sports
www.rslmedia.com

Situations

Ignoring the rules can lead to injury and foul play. When a player breaks a rule, it is called an illegal act. The problem for the officials is to interpret whether this illegal act was intentional or merely an accident. Intentional illegal acts need to be penalised, a foul is awarded and the player who was offended against or their team is usually given a free kick, pass or hit. Referees and umpires have the power to warn players or send them off for breaking the rules. In extreme circumstances, governing bodies have the power to ban a person from the sport altogether.

Application of the rules is not an exact science. Good officials should be concerned with the effect of an illegal act rather than the act itself. In football, if a defender pushes an attacker in the act of shooting at goal and it affects the shot, this is an infringement and should be pulled up. If the attacker scores the goal, then the official can allow advantage to be played.

Sports have many written rules but they also have **unwritten rules**. The idea of **fair play** means that players are expected to treat their opponent as an equal and although they will want to beat them, they will try to beat them by adhering to the rules and a code of conduct that has grown up through tradition; this idea is called **sportsmanship**. Examples are shaking hands and cheering the other team off the pitch at the end of a game.

If any rule in sport is broken, it is called **cheating**. To cheat not only destroys the game but detracts from a player's personal achievement. A victory through cheating is a hollow victory – you get the extrinsic rewards but not the intrinsic fulfilment, and that's what makes it hollow. Sport relies on some form of mutual respect between opponents as it often involves high-speed contact with lethal weapons, where disregard for the rules could mean serious injury.

The opposite of sportsmanship is **gamesmanship**, where players use whatever means they can to beat their opponents. The only aim is to win, and although they will not actually break the rules, a player will bend them to their advantage. The best example is probably footballers who dive in the penalty area to persuade the referee to award them a penalty kick.

Figure 21.3 A victory through cheating is a hollow victory

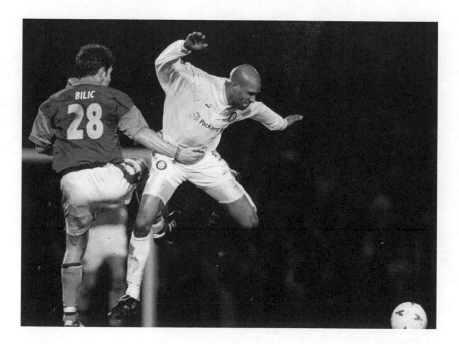

Here are some sports NGBs in the UK:

Sport England
www.sportengland.org

Sport Scotland
www.sportscotland.org.uk

Sports Council Wales
www.sports-council-wales.co.uk

Sports Council Northern Ireland
www.lotteryfunding.org.uk/nireland/sports-council-ni

Sports Officials UK
www.sportsofficialsuk.com/

---

activity

INDIVIDUAL WORK 21.1

P1

1. Choose a sport then create a booklet that gives a basic overview of its rules and regulations. Aim it at a group of Year 7 pupils who are about to do a block of this sport in their PE lessons. Cover the key rules and try to keep the wording as simple as possible.

2. Use a copy of the rules on the NGB website for your chosen sport, or see if your local library has a copy. Don't just copy out the rules. Try to explain how and why they are used.

The roles and responsibilities of officials involved in a selected sport

Officials

> **remember**
>
> A sports official administers the rules and regulations according to the official interpretations in the NGB handbook.

Officials may be umpires, line judges, timekeepers, scorers, linesmen, referees, fourth officials, video referees and judges. Your sport may have other examples, so check with your tutor or teacher to see if you can use these roles when you work on this unit.

An official in sport is defined as any person who controls the actual play of a sports competition by applying the rules and laws of the specific sport. They will need to make judgements on rule infringement, performance, scores and time allocations. Officials have a big role in seeing that everyone participates in the correct spirit, including the coaches.

Official roles

Officials have been involved in sport for thousands of years. At the ancient Olympics in Greece, special officials called hellanodikai were appointed to oversee the running of the games and settle any disputes between performers. They were considered so important that they were required to live for 10 months in seclusion before the games to help them prepare and also to be away from coaches and spectators who might try to influence their decisions during the games. Hellanodikai decisions were final and athletes and their coaches faced harsh punishments if they broke any rules at the ancient Olympics.

The official's role in sport came of age at the end of the nineteenth century, when the majority of modern sports went through a period of rationalisation, where a governing body was formed and a standardised set of rules were created and distributed. It was now the role of the officials to ensure that performers adhered to these rules.

Figure 21.4 Officials see that everyone participates in the correct spirit

All sports officials have a demanding role. They must have a thorough understanding of the game and communicate effectively with players, coaches and spectators. They need to keep a calm head in very tense moments, especially in finals where one decision could mean the difference between a trophy and no trophy. They have a duty to interpret and apply the rules and they have the right to ignore protests.

Key roles

Select an appropriate role to use in your assignment. Each role applies to some sports but not others.

- **Arbiter** – takes the final decision.
- **Judge** – takes a decision after weighing and considering a range of factors.
- **Communicator** – uses verbal and non-verbal communication so that everyone understands them.
- **Timekeeper** – ensures the game is played within the official time limits.
- **Scorekeeper** – keeps a formal record of the score as the game progresses.
- **Safety officer** – ensures that everyone participates in a safe and secure way.

When working with younger players, the official's role does change slightly. As well as applying the rules, officials also need to act as role models and educators, showing the principles of fair and unbiased decision making as well as explaining their decisions and the rules of the game.

activity
INDIVIDUAL WORK 21.2

P2

M1

1. Officiate on three different occasions. You can choose the same role on each occasion or a different role on each occasion.
2. Ask someone involved in the game to complete a witness statement commenting on your performance. Templates for this can be downloaded from the BTEC section of the Edexcel website. After each experience, write a short summary of how you applied the rules, laws and regulations.

case study 21.1

Football officials

Four officials oversee professional football matches: a referee, two assistant referees and a fourth official.

The referee enforces the laws of the game, they award free kicks for foul play, and they keep a check on the time and the score. The referee can also postpone, stop, suspend or call off a match if there are weather or crowd problems.

The assistant referees help out with decisions such as throw-ins and offsides and sometimes their view of an incident is better than the referee's.

The fourth official, based on the touchline, keeps a record of substitutions, ensures that coaching staff stay in the technical areas marked around the dugouts, and signals how much time is added on at the end of each half.

activity
INDIVIDUAL WORK

1. How do the officials at a football match work as a team'?
2. What do you think would be the best ways for them to communicate?

activity
INDIVIDUAL WORK 21.3

P3

A large team of officials are required to run an athletics meeting. Choose a role from the following list: chief referee, meeting manager, field judge, track judge, starter or marksman, timekeeper, photofinish judge, technical manager or clerk of the course.

Produce a presentation which describes the roles and responsibilities of officials in a sport of your choice.

Assistant referee

remember

The referee makes the final call on everything.

An assistant referee helps the referee to make decisions and acts as an extra pair of eyes. In sports such as football and rugby, it is usual for each assistant to be responsible for a specific part or half of the pitch. Assistant referees are mainly involved with decisions on the boundaries of play, they are closer to the boundary or on the boundary, they also rule on offside. Assistant referees assist with substitutions; they signal to the referee that a team wishes to make a substitution and may also check the new player's kit and appearance before they enter the pitch.

The assistant usually signals to the referee and rarely takes decisions. Here are some key points to remember:

- The referee makes the final decision.
- Make your signals clear and decisive.
- Keep up with play and stay in the line of sight.
- Assistant referees stay silent during the game.

In most sports there is a line of sight across the pitch, and that's where you need to be. Assistant referees may not coach or direct the players in any way.

The referee is the final judge and only they blow the whistle. Never shout at the referee to get their attention. Make eye contact with the referee so they can give you subtle signals. Talk to the referee before the game to make sure you both know your responsibilities.

Responsibilities

What makes a good official?

Being a good official is a delicate balance. The best officials can blend into the background until they are needed, then they command authority and respect. Here are the basic requirements for good officiating:

- Be firm and fair without being officious and arrogant.
- Be impartial.
- Apply the rules and/or score without pressure from players, coaches or fans.
- Command respect from players, coaches and spectators.
- Be confident.

This section investigates these requirements in more detail and considers how good officials can be developed.

After a narrow defeat, losing managers or coaches often blame it on one mistake by an official when, more likely, it was due to many mistakes by the losing team. The higher the level of competition, the greater the stakes for coaches and players, and the greater the pressure on officials. This is often linked to financial rewards for the winning team. People become so desperate to win at any cost, they may disregard the rules and disrespect the officials.

Does the official need to have played the game?

Does the official need to have played the game? This question sparks heated debate, especially among elite performers. Some argue that you have to understand a sport inside out before you can officiate it and, they say, the only way to get that understanding is to play. Officials that have played a sport can also draw on their playing experience when they make a tough call. Others argue that an official who thinks like a player may not always apply the rules stringently. They say that good officials can develop from dedicated students who develop insight and knowledge of the rules without ever competing. The key point is that the officials must have the respect and confidence of the performers. In some sports this respect is more easily granted to ex-players, whereas in other sports it makes no difference whether the official has played.

Figure 21.5 Rugby union: a path for referees in England

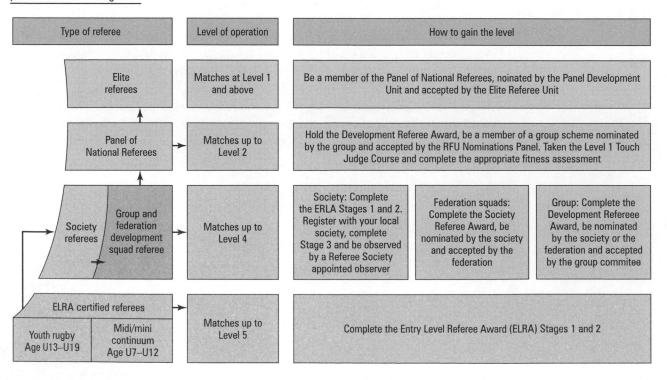

Communicating information

Sports officials must thoroughly understand the current version of the rules. They must practise standing in the correct positions until this becomes second nature. They must use the correct signals to tell everyone their decisions. This helps officials to stamp their authority on the game. Timing is another important skill. Good officials let play continue to see if there is any advantage.

Sports officials need to be as fit as possible. They need to keep up with players and make decisions at the same time. Most officials now undergo pre-season fitness training to help them prepare for the physical demands of the job. They also plan and perform training sessions throughout the season.

Training programmes for all levels of referees and assistant referees can be found on these websites:

FA in England

www.thefa.com

FA in Scotland

www.scottishfa.co.uk

FA in Wales

www.faw.org.uk

FA in Northern Ireland

www.irishfa.com

Referee fitness

www.thefa.com/GrassrootsNew/Referee/NewsAndFeatures/Postings/2004/07/RefereeFitness.htm

Football Referee

www.footballreferee.org

BBC Sport Academy

http://news.bbc.co.uk/sportacademy

Figure 21.6 Football: signals for assistant referees

Establishing and maintaining relationships

Effective officials are neither too friendly nor totally aloof. Players prefer officials to act like someone who has an important job to do. When working with younger players or players that are less experienced, officials can adopt a more helpful approach and will often spend time teaching and explaining the rules and regulations. Players get upset when officials are dictatorial, so be humane and approachable. Show respect for the players and coaches you work with, in order to gain their respect.

Why do they do it?

Purdy and Snyder (1985) found that officials gave these reasons for doing their job:

- Interest and enthusiasm for their sport
- Challenge and excitement offered by officiating
- The extra money provided by officiating
- The feeling of power and being in control
- Health and safety.

Officials also help to maintain a safe environment where sport can be played; for example, they control unruly players and help to avoid pitch invasions. This work often starts before play, when officials inspect the playing surface. If there is severe weather, the officials may have to decide whether the game can be played.

> **remember**
> Reading the game is about vision, timing and position – you need all three.

Figure 21.7 Officials may abandon a game due to bad weather

Analysing the performance of officials in a selected sport

Officials

When it comes to performance analysis, treat the official as if they were a player. There is much more information on analysing a player's performance and the same methods can be used for an official.

activity
INDIVIDUAL WORK 21.4

P4

Produce an observation checklist that can be used to analyse the performance of officials in your chosen sport. Your checklist should include the responsibilities from Activity 21.3.

Choose the most appropriate methods for watching and recording the official's performance. Here are some things you will need to identify:

■ Their strengths and weaknesses

■ Their relationships with players, coaches and the other officials

■ How effectively they used signals and other communication

■ How they made decisions and applied the rules

■ Their control of the game and any situations that arose.

Many sports websites have assessment checklists. Download them and create a version you can use. You may need to adapt them to suit the official you are analysing.

Athletics

www.ukathletics.net

Badminton

www.badmintonengland.co.uk

Basketball

www.englandbasketball.co.uk/

Cricket

www.ecb.co.uk

Football

http://thefa.com

Hockey

www.englandhockey.co.uk/

Netball

www.england-netball.co.uk

Rugby union

www.rfu.com

Ruby league

www.therfl.co.uk

Swimming

www.britishswimming.org

Tennis

www.lta.org.uk

Volleyball

www.volleyballengland.org

Table 21.1 Assessment criteria for UK football referees

Assessment criteria
Appearance
Signals
Stoppages
Advantage
Cooperation with assistant referees
Application of the laws
Positioning and movement
Overall control and authority

When you analyse an official's communication skills, look at their verbal and non-verbal communication. Judge the official on how well they make verbal calls and how well they make any signals. Consider the emphasis they give to their calls. Good officials are not as forceful on obvious calls as on close calls; they use more force on close calls to reinforce their authority. If there are close calls, see whether the official uses a strong, clear voice and whether they give clear signals. See how well they communicate with the other officials, verbally and non-verbally. Blowing the whistle looks simple, but well-prepared officials practise the different tones.

Officiating in tennis

A large team of officials cover each top-level tennis match. The umpire's decision is final unless a match referee has been appointed. Then the umpire's decisions can be appealed on points of law by going to the match referee; the referee's decision is final.

Some tennis matches have linesmen, net cord judges and foot fault judges. Their decisions are final on questions of fact, but if the umpire thinks that a clear mistake has been made, then the umpire has the right to change the decision of an assistant or order a let to be played.

Figure 21.8 Tennis: a team of officials cover top-level matches

Training to be a tennis official

- **Level 1** – a basic introduction to tennis officiating; it concentrates on the rules of tennis and the basic techniques and procedures of chair and line umpiring.

- **Level 2** – intermediate schools for officials who have demonstrated sufficient commitment and experience in officiating. People who pass the written examination and practical exercise become white badge officials of the International Tennis Federation (ITF).

- **Level 3** – an advanced school that turns white badge officials into international officials through a combination of written, oral and on-court exams.

Officiating in athletics

The first qualification in athletics officiating is the Level 1 Assistant Officials Award. Here are the things it teaches:

- How to measure distances and times

- How to make and share judgements

- How to record observations, judgements and data

- How to ensure safety and report concerns

- How to liaise and communicate with other officials and athletes

- How to report rule infringements, follow procedures and apply rules.

Successful candidates are fully qualified and insured to assist at athletics events. The course costs about £10.

Officiating in basketball

England Basketball's Level 1 (Apprenticeship) Referee and Table Official Course will teach you how to officiate lower-level basketball games; it lasts one day and costs about £20.

England Basketball
www.englandbasketball.com

Figure 21.9 Basketball: England Basketball runs courses for officials

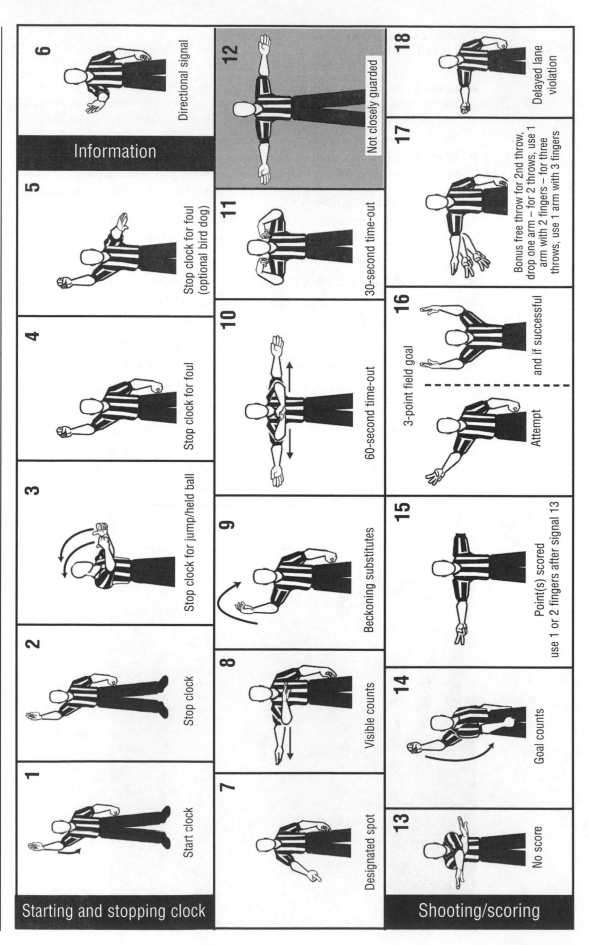

Figure 21.10 Basketball: official signals used by the National Federation of State High School Associations

Starting and stopping clock

1 — Start clock

2 — Stop clock

3 — Stop clock for jump/held ball

4 — Stop clock for foul

5 — Stop clock for foul (optional bird dog)

6 — Directional signal

Information

7 — Designated spot

8 — Visible counts

9 — Beckoning substitutes

10 — 60-second time-out

11 — 30-second time-out

12 — Not closely guarded

Shooting/scoring

13 — No score

14 — Goal counts

15 — Point(s) scored use 1 or 2 fingers after signal 13

16 — Attempt — and if successful — 3-point field goal

17 — Bonus free throw for 2nd throw, drop one arm – for 2 throws, use 1 arm with 2 fingers – for three throws, use 1 arm with 3 fingers

18 — Delayed lane violation

case study 21.2

Playing advantage

Watch a game of your chosen sport.

activity
INDIVIDUAL WORK

1. Review the performance of a sports official. Consider how many times the official intervened in the game. Were these interventions necessary or were they for trivial issues?

2. Could more advantage have been played?

3. If the official played advantage, did they indicate that they had seen the incident but felt advantage should be given? Did they indicate it to all players involved in the incident?

Analysis

Method

remember

Situations could include a player in an illegal position, an injured player, illegal challenges, disallowing a score, cautioning or sending off a player for foul play.

When you analyse an official's performance, look for their strengths as well as areas that may need improvement. Table 21.2 shows a variety of methods you could use to do the analysis. Try to choose an appropriate method; **notational analysis** generates a lot of data and **performance profiling** can take a long time.

Table 21.2 Methods for performance analysis

Method	Points to consider
Live observation	Allows you to track the official's every move; especially useful for looking at positioning, but you may not always be able to work out exactly what the official is saying or doing; it is also difficult to make accurate notes
Video analysis	You can stop and rewind; the cameras are more likely to follow the players and it may be difficult to track the official
Notational analysis	Gives you a lot of data to study, but you may lose a sense of how the game is flowing and how the officials are helping this flow; it is best suited to team sports
Performance profiling	Allows very specific training and development for the official; you need to have a lot of contact with the official you are watching; it takes a lot of time
Player and coach questionnaires	Simple to devise; they require contact with teams and coaches; you may need to weigh up the thoughts of the winning team and the losing team

Areas for improvement

Most sports governing bodies now have well-structured development pathways for referees and officials. Before you do the analysis, find out the current level of the official and perhaps speak to them about what is required for them to progress to the next level. Most officials need to do training and assessment to move up a level. In your case studies, identify exactly what is required and try to suggest a location.

The fitness of officials is related to the level of the sport – the higher the level, the greater the fitness. Include an assessment of the official's current fitness and suggest a target and training plans to give them the fitness they need for the next level.

Figure 21.11 Include an assessment of the official's current fitness

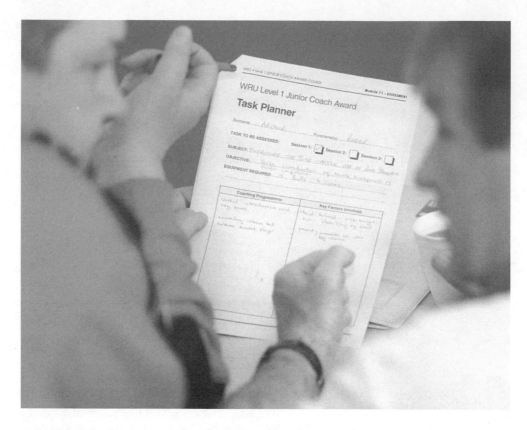

Development

Consider a range of ideas when you plan a development programme for a sports official you have worked with. The value of each idea will depend on the official and the sport.

Courses and retraining

Most governing bodies offer a pathway of qualifications; see Case Study 21.3. The higher the qualification, the longer and more demanding the course.

Websites

Websites dedicated to officials offer ideas and techniques that you could apply.

Special clinics

Local and regional associations often put on clinics and workshops where officials can share ideas and discuss rules and regulations. Top-level officials will often be invited to lead the sessions. Try to find out if your sport has local forums for sports officials.

Publications

Most governing bodies produce handbooks and guidelines for officials, often available as PDF downloads on websites. For more popular sports, such as football and tennis, there are independent texts and handbooks. Give your officials up-to-date copies of the rules and regulations.

Local tournaments

Offer to officiate at local tournaments. It may be hard work to officiate many games in a short time, but it will be valuable experience and you can watch and meet other officials.

Games

Referees watch as many games as they can. This is the best way to develop their knowledge and technique. Step up to officiate adult or more senior games.

remember

To improve an official's performance, some key areas to plan are practice, training, further qualifications, self-analysis and buddy systems.

Assessors

If an official is working on the governing body pathway, then they will have regular formal assessments that give valuable feedback and often contain specific areas for improvement. Assessors can also be sounding boards. Bounce ideas off an experienced assessor.

Talk with friends

Talk with friends, colleagues, associates, players, coaches, mentors and administrators. Listen to what they say. Ask them to identify your strengths and weaknesses.

SEAA says

The South of England Athletic Association (SEAA) gives the following advice to athletics officials:

- Be ready for the first event well in advance of its start time.
- Take to the meeting a book of rules for competition.
- Take equipment and clothing for all weathers.
- Courtesy and cooperation at all times.
- Be aware of and respond to the needs of other officials.
- Process results as quickly as possible.
- If you need to cross the centre, do it quickly and safely, especially when throwing events are under way.
- When crossing the track, take care not to impede athletes.
- Refer any complaints to the meeting referee.

Fitness for umpires

www.englandhockey.co.uk/

activity
INDIVIDUAL WORK 21.5

P5

M2

1. Select two games where you can analyse the officials on duty.
2. Produce a report for each official that identifies strengths and areas for improvement, explains why you have chosen these strengths and weaknesses and suggests how they could improve their performance.

activity
INDIVIDUAL WORK 21.6

D1

For each of the officials discussed in Activity 21.5, justify your suggestions.

Rugby officials

Course	Referee grade	Level of game
Entry Level Referee Award	14–15	Probationer. Lowest leagues, 2nd XV or lower junior sides
Society Referee Award	11–13	1st XV, lower league
	9–10	Any junior game Division 1 county leagues
	8	Any junior game Selected senior matches Division League 4
Development Referee Award	7	Any senior game to which society appoints Division League 3
	6	Any senior game anywhere Division League 2
Touch Judge Examination Fitness Examination Foul Play Examination	5	Any divisional game anywhere Selected National League 3
	Panel national referees	Any game in national leagues

activity
INDIVIDUAL WORK

1. How many levels of officiating are there in your sport?
2. How do you progress from one level to another?
3. How do the skills and knowledge required differ from level to level?

Officiating effectively in a selected sport

Apply the rules and laws

Your key aim is to allow the game to progress smoothly and within the rules. You can achieve it by being in the correct position to see the play, to react immediately to rule infractions and to make all players aware of your decisions using verbal and non-verbal communication.

activity
INDIVIDUAL WORK
21.7

P6

M3

Officiate a selected sport with support. Now officiate a selected sport without support. Produce a record sheet that describes your role in each game. Highlight how you applied rules, laws and regulations. Get somebody to complete an observation record of your performance; templates are available on the BTEC pages of the Edexcel website.

Edexcel
www.edexcel.org.uk

Perhaps work out a plan of action for the games you have to officiate:

Before the game

- Get there at least 30 min before play starts.
- Warm up correctly.
- Introduce yourself to players and coaches. Talk through any key rules, regulations and recent updates. Agree communication channels, usually through the captains.
- Be polite and friendly but remember that coaches and players will expect you to maintain a distance.
- Look over the playing area and identify any potential problems.
- Check any equipment.
- Ensure the health and safety of all participants.

During the game

- Don't overanticipate; it's better to be a second late than to blow early and rule incorrectly.
- Don't rush your signals by being overanxious; rushed signals are often missed by players.
- Enforce all rules, especially early in the game. If you overlook minor infringements to help the game flow, it can frustrate players, who then take the law into their hands.
- Communicate with players and the other officials.
- Check your position regularly and keep up with the flow of the game. Use any breaks in play to move into a better position.
- Don't overreact to complaints, be calm and firm, and penalise any dissent.

After the game

- If you can discuss your performance and the game with any other officials, ask for advice or suggestions on your performance.
- Have a small notebook to record key points from the game. This will help you to write up your assignment.
- Record your strengths and areas for improvement. Record any new rules or techniques that you learned.
- Do you have any questions or queries about the rules and regulations? Will you need to look up the answers or ask someone?

Figure 21.12 Look over the playing area to check for potential problems

Review the game

- Formative assessment, perhaps in a diary, tends to be ongoing and gives instant feedback. Note the good and bad points from your performance.
- Summative assessment usually occurs at the end of a training period. It could be an external assessment or a formal examination.
- Perhaps design an officiating record that combines both types of assessment.
- You could use formative assessment to identify key areas that you want to work on.
- You could set yourself a target of, say, 4 weeks to achieve these improvements then use summative assessment to check whether you have achieved your goals.

activity
INDIVIDUAL WORK 21.8

P7

M4

1. Complete one of the self-question templates in Table 21.3 to review your own performance at officiating a selected sport.
2. Produce a table that identifies the strengths and areas for improvement of your officiating performance.
3. Explain why you have chosen the strengths and weaknesses you have identified and suggest how you could improve your performance.

Table 21.3 Self-evaluation questionnaire

	Mostly	Sometimes	Never
Control of the competition and approach			
Did I ensure a safe environment was established for the participants?			
Did I provide support and encouragement for my fellow officials?			
Did I contribute to a 'sense of team' among the officials?			
Did I show enthusiasm while participating?			
Did I and participants have fun during the competition?			
Did I remain composed during the competition?			
Did I intervene at appropriate times?			
Was I approachable during the competition?			
Communication			
Did I use verbal communication with the participants in a positive manner?			
Was my non-verbal communication executed in a decisive and authoritative manner?			
Did I give compliments sincerely and honestly?			
Did I use sarcasm to get my message across?			
Did I explain my decisions to participants?			
Did I communicate to coaches and other officials in a positive manner?			
Decision making			
Were my decisions appropriate?			
Were my decisions in accord with the spirit of the competition?			
Was I positive and decisive in my approach to decision making?			
Was I consistent with my decision making?			

Reprinted with permission from the Australian Sports Commission

case study 21.4

Swimming officials

Have a look at these qualifications offered by British Swimming:

■ **Club timekeeper** – this qualification covers the practical aspects of timekeeping. It is a short theory session followed by practical assessment. There is no minimum age but you need to be a registered member of a British Swimming club or a member of the Institute of Swimming.

■ **Level 1 judge** – this qualification covers the roles of chief timekeeper, timekeeper and inspector of turns. The minimum age is 15 years and you have to complete a course workbook. There is no formal examination but you will be required to answer oral questions. On completing this course you could become a licensed official.

■ **Level 2 judge** – this qualification includes the duties and roles of all judges and the theoretical roles and duties of a starter. The minimum age is 15 years. There is a course workbook and you receive a practical assessment.

■ **Starter** – you have to be a level 2 judge before you can take this qualification. You train by doing a prescribed number of practical experiences as a starter then you take a formal practical assessment. Successful candidates are known as level 2S judges.

British Swimming
www.britishswimming.org

activity
INDIVIDUAL WORK

1. List all the officials required in your sport.

2. For two of the officials in your sport, produce a checklist of their duties before, during and after competition.

3. For the same two officials you chose in Question 2, list the equipment they need to do their duties.

Feedback

Feedback helps you develop your skills, This can be done by you or by someone else who has seen you officiate. Feedback can help you identify key areas to work on. Table 21.4 can be used to review your performance; you could adapt it so it can be used by a person who watches you officiate.

case study 21.5

Hockey officials

Young umpire ⟶ Foundation umpire ⟶ Level 1 ⟶

National badge ⟵ Level 3 ⟵ Level 2 ⟵

activity
INDIVIDUAL WORK

1. Produce a similar flow chart for the progression of officials in your sport.

2. How does each level relate to the age and ability of the performers they officiate?

Table 21.4 Self-evaluation checklist for officials

Appearance
Did I look smart and confident before, during and after the game I officiated?
Was I distracted by anything or anyone during the game?
Signals
Did I use the whistle effectively and with confidence?
Did I always use signals to back up the decisions I gave?
Stopping play
Were there any incidents of time wasting? Did I deal with them effectively?
Was I effective at getting the game restarted after stoppages?
Advantage
Did I make it clear to the players I was allowing advantage?
Did I speak to offenders after advantage had been played?
If no advantage accrued, did I stop the game and penalise the original offence?
Cooperation with other officials
Did I seek advice from the other officials?
How well did I communicate with the other officials?
Offences
Did I identify and take control of dangerous play?
Positioning
Did I anticipate play well and feel that I was always in the best position to make a decision?
Did my positioning at set plays allow me a clear view of all concerned players?
Did I keep a distance from the immediate location of play so I got an overall view of the pitch and players?
Did I use stoppages to move into the best position for the next phase of play?
Control and authority
Did I feel that I had the respect of the players and that they responded well to my actions?
Did I deal calmly but firmly with any dissent?
Did I hesitate over any of my decisions?

Areas for improvement

Competent sports officials strive to improve their performance and their understanding of the rules. One way is to watch as many games as you can, live or on TV, and analyse the performance of the officials. Perhaps focus on the areas you need to work on. How do the officials handle situations better than you? Pay particular attention to their position during specific plays.

INDIVIDUAL WORK 21.9

D2

Produce a written report on your performance as a match official in Activity 21.7. Your report should analyse the roles and responsibilities you had in the game. It should contain an in-depth review of your strengths and weaknesses. Include a plan that explains how you could improve your performance in the future.

Progress Check

1. What is the name for sports organisations that have control over rules?
2. Choose a sport and list five areas that are covered by its rules.
3. Explain the term 'illegal' in the context of sports officiating.
4. During a game, a sports official needs to give information to players. What information?
5. What kind of sports official is an arbiter?
6. How do sports officials help to keep players safe during a game?
7. What is the role of the fourth official, or off-pitch official, in your sport?
8. What is a performance pathway in the context of sports officiating?
9. How do assessors develop the performance of sports officials?
10. Sports officials should always give the correct signals. Why and what are the benefits?

Working with Children in Sport

Andrew Procter

This unit covers:

- Children's needs and rights
- Effects of sport on child development
- Good practice in child protection
- What to do if you see signs of abuse

Working with children can be very rewarding and satisfying, but it also carries big responsibilities. The influence of the sports leader is crucial to a child's social, physical and psychological development. Fun, enjoyable experiences can give a child a healthy, lifelong attachment to sport, whereas poor experiences can discourage a child forever. This unit investigates the needs and rights of children enshrined in legislation. It has a big section on child development followed by sections on the leader's role and good practice when working with children. It explains how to recognise the signs of abuse and how to act correctly if you notice these signs in a child or if a child tells you they are being abused.

grading criteria

grading criteria

To achieve a **Pass** grade the evidence must show that the learner is able to:	To achieve a **Merit** grade the evidence must show that the learner is able to:	To achieve a **Distinction** grade the evidence must show that the learner is able to:
P5 describe the five kinds of abuse and potential consequences of abuse Pg 298		
P6 describe four different signs of potential child abuse, in sporting contexts, and the courses of action in suspected cases of child abuse Pg 304	**M5** explain four different signs of potential child abuse, in sporting contexts, and the courses of action in suspected cases of child abuse Pg 304	**D2** analyse the courses of action in suspected cases of child abuse Pg 304

The needs and rights of children

Link See page 121 in Unit 15 for more information on specific groups

Educational needs

Skill development

One of the most rewarding aspects of coaching children is to see the improvement and development of their skills. Young children can experience large improvements as they develop and an effective coach will be able to guide the young performer through a series of well-constructed practices that help with this progression.

Children begin to develop their movement patterns from birth. Some are reflex actions where the child might move quickly to a sudden noise or light, but by age 2 they are able to perform more complex and refined movements such as reaching and grasping. The style of learning at this stage is through trial and error; a child may attempt to grab or reach for something, succeed after several trials and make a link between the length of their limbs and the distance to an object.

Figure 23.1 Basic movement patterns are evident in children

The effective coach provides appropriate stimuli to encourage children to move. Children are attracted by bright colours and objects that have different textures when touched. Most toys use this theme in their design. Basic movement patterns include static balance (standing on one leg), dynamic balance (landing on one leg), locomotion (crawling and walking) and manipulation (reaching and grasping).

Once children reach the age of 6 or 7 they should begin to develop more complex movements that use basic movement patterns but with some form of order (Table 23.1). These more complex movements must be developed fully or a child will find it difficult to coordinate movements in the changing environment of sports.

Table 23.1 Specific movement in the fundamental movement skill category

Movement	Example	Description
Static balance	Single-foot balance	Child learns to balance unaided for 3–5 s
Dynamic balance	Running	Child learns to balance while moving at speed
Dynamic balance	Beam balance	Child learns to balance on a narrow beam while moving forwards
Locomotion	Standing long jump	Child learns to coordinate upper and lower body muscles in ordered fashion to get maximum distance from a standing start
Manipulation	Striking tennis ball with racquet	Child learns to find appropriate ball position, body position and racquet position to make contact and hit the ball

Adapted from Gallahue and Ozmun (2001)

Motor programming

A child stores the **motor programme** for a specific movement in its long-term memory. Without experiences, the child will not have a motor programme for specific movements in sport. Seeing a movement through demonstration will not have the same effect as trying it for themselves so they can feel the movement and recognise the cues that make the movement unique. A coach should provide children with opportunities to practise movements that are common to several sports so they can create motor programmes for a variety of situations.

Spatial awareness

It can be frustrating to watch children play sport, especially in teams, as their use of space is usually quite poor. Children chasing a ball look like bees round a honeypot and are almost oblivious to the space around them. In racquet sports, children have difficulty hitting an object or they return the object with little regard to their opponent's position and the space on the court. In sports such as diving, trampolining and gymnastics, children have to learn very quickly where their body parts are as they produce more complicated moves.

Core skills for all sports require spatial awareness. Catching, throwing, striking, etc., are fundamental to many sports, so an effective coach will encourage children to practise these skills and help children use them in a variety of situations.

Psychological needs

Motivation

Young performers participate in sport because they have **intrinsic motivation** or **extrinsic motivation**. Intrinsically motivated children participate in sport for the fun and enjoyment of it. They feel happy when they complete tasks and are rewarded by the pleasant feelings of achievement and mastery. They do not expect external rewards and tend to remain in sport for a long time.

Figure 23.2 Children's use of space is usually quite poor

Extrinsically motivated children participate in sport to be rewarded for their efforts. The reward may be something tangible such as a certificate or a medal, or something intangible such as praise or acknowledgement from others.

The problem with most sporting activity for children is that **tangible rewards** are the norm. Too many extrinsic rewards can diminish or even eliminate a child's intrinsic motivation. Children tend to drop out of sport when they get older as the tangible rewards disappear.

Extrinsic rewards can have a positive effect if the coach uses them sparingly and when they are well deserved. The image of a gold medal around an Olympic champion can motivate a child for a long time.

Communication

Communicating with children is different to communicating with adults. A coach must never assume that a child understands everything they say. They need to explain things in very simple terms and usually they need to give a visual example.

Figure 23.3 Intrinsically motivated children do sport for fun and enjoyment

An effective coach will remain patient in the early stages of learning as they may have to repeat themselves several times or rephrase instructions for people with special needs or different needs.

Children tend to follow the most influential members of the group, so a good coaching strategy is to make sure the influential children understand and allow the rest to follow.

Demonstrations can be very effective as children are excellent at copying and mimicking actions. Once they have tried a movement themselves, children can use their own experiences to help them understand the coach's comments.

Figure 23.4 Do not assume that a child understands everything you say

> **remember**
>
> Children have a very limited attention span, so give concise explanations. Lengthy explanations or lengthy practice sessions can hinder a child's development.

Confidence building

Children's confidence is very fragile, especially when they perform in front of others. Build confidence by providing a positive coaching environment. Bandura (1997) demonstrated that self-confidence had four main factors:

- Performance accomplishments
- Vicarious experiences
- Verbal persuasion
- Emotional arousal.

Performance accomplishment is by far the most influential factor over anything that is said or seen by the child. Being successful at something will increase a child's self-confidence, so the coach needs to set **SMART** goals, as the more success the child experiences the more self-confidence they will develop.

See page 72 in Unit 12 for more information on development
See page 114 in Unit 13 for more information on goal setting
See page 70 in Unit 12 for more information on session reviews

SMART goals

- **Specific** – use who, what, where, when, why. The phrase 'get better' is too vague. Be specific: 'I will improve my shooting this week.'

- **Measurable** – goals need to measurable so it is clear when they have been reached: 'Have ten shots at goal.'

- **Achievable** – plan how the goal will be achieved. Most goals require resources such as equipment, finance and time. A child may not be able to achieve ten shots at goal if they are not in a position to shoot.

- **Realistic** – a goal that is too easy will demotivate the participant and may cause them to settle for lower standards. A goal that is too difficult may also demotivate the participant into believing they are useless. Reassess goals regularly to make them challenging and motivating.

- **Time-bound** – a goal needs a time limit to focus the participant's attention. Short-, medium- and long-term goals can maintain motivation and help monitor progress.

Cultural

Communities and Local Government was launched in 2006 and developed out of *Sustainable Communities: Building for the Future*, published by the UK government in 2003. Here are its aims:

- To help people and local agencies create cohesive, attractive and economically vibrant communities.

- To ensure that communities can fulfil their own potential and overcome their own difficulties, including community conflict, extremism, deprivation and disadvantage.

- To empower communities to respond to challenging economic, social and cultural trends.

Community, opportunity, prosperity

www.communities.gov.uk/

In 2006 the Department for Culture Media and Sport (DCMS) collaborated with Sport England and other agencies to launch Where We Live, a programme to develop sport, arts, heritage, the built environment, museums, libraries and archives. It says that culture is valuable for creating sustainable communities and here are some of the reasons it gives:

- **Bringing people together** – it provides opportunities for people to come together and get to know each other through shared and complementary interests.

- **Developing identity and sense of place** – it provides enduring and active symbols of a community's history and interests.

- **Making places more attractive** – culture helps create attractive, well-designed environments that incorporate accessible green space and a distinctive public realm.

- **Making us healthy and happy** – cultural opportunity encourages people to be active and do the things they enjoy. This increases people's physical and mental well-being and helps build healthy communities.

- **Enhancing people's skills and helping prosperity** – creative and cultural businesses, and access to knowledge through libraries and other facilities, unlock potential and stimulate learning and enterprise.

- **Providing positive activities for young people** – it offers a focus for social interaction and harnesses the energy of young people constructively.

Social inclusion

Children enjoy being part of groups that have similar interests, such as fashion, music and computer games. Sport provides children with a way of being included in something that improves their communication skills, interaction and cooperation with others. Being good at sports gives children a social standing and respect among their peers, which can be used as a tool to influence social groups. In contrast, sport can also provide a barrier to some children who are less physically able. They are unable to gain social recognition among their peers and are excluded from groups. If they do not have other interests that can provide the same social needs, then they can become isolated and introverted.

Gender awareness

Boys and girls have similar body compositions up to puberty. Both genders can enjoy many sports and physical activity on an equal footing, despite attempts by adults to stereotype gender through activities, such as boisterous contact games for boys, skipping and clapping games for girls. Differences become much more apparent at puberty. Girls develop physically and mentally before boys. When boys reach puberty they become much stronger and more physically active than girls. Sports become gender-oriented, although more girls are participating in boys' sports such as rugby and football. In fact, football has now become the biggest and fastest-growing female sport.

Community identity

Throughout their lives, many people have little contact with their local community. Many do not communicate with their neighbours and commute large distances to work. Sport allows children to gain some sense of community. Being a member of the local sports club can provide a large network of friends and social contacts where children can be involved. Most sports have a uniform that children can wear as a badge of identity that gives them pride and a sense of belonging.

Figure 23.5 More girls are participating in boys' sports such as rugby and football

Social needs

Anti-crime initiatives

A common complaint, especially from school-aged children, is the lack of things to do after school and during school holidays. That is when most crime occurs, so the government and local agencies have provided state-of-the-art facilities and qualified coaches to help cut crime and meet children's needs. Positive Futures and Edutain are two schemes where children can take part in sport instead of crime. Sport is also used as a way of dealing with crime among NEETs aged 16–18; a NEET is a person that is not in education, employment or training. The Community Sports Leaders Award (CSLA) has educational and employment outcomes.

Dealing with antisocial behaviour

Giving children facilities, equipment and qualified coaches has helped channel their antisocial behaviour into something more productive.

Positive Futures Research Project

www.positivefuturesresearch.org.uk/

Health promotion

Research shows that physical activity can help in the prevention and treatment of health-related illnesses such as heart disease, stroke, hypertension, colon cancer, obesity and type 2 diabetes. Although children do not suffer from these diseases, physical activity can help to control weight and prevent obesity in childhood, which may lead to problems later in life.

According to the 2004 chief medical officer's report, children and young people should achieve a total of at least 60 min of at least moderate-intensity physical activity each day. At least twice a week this should include activities to improve bone health – activities that produce high physical stresses on the bones – plus muscle strength and flexibility.

One aim of the national strategy for PE, School Sport and Club Links (PESSCL) is that by 2008 some 85% of schoolchildren will receive at least 2 h of high-quality PE within and beyond the school curriculum.

Rights

UN Convention on the Rights of the Child

The UN Convention on the Rights of the Child is an international human rights treaty that applies to all children and young people aged 17 and under. It gives children and young people the right to express their views and have their views considered on all matters that affect them, plus the right to play, rest and leisure and the right to be free from all forms of violence. It is separated into 54 articles; some articles give children social, economic, cultural, civil or political rights and other articles say how governments must publicise or implement the convention.

All children and young people up to age 18 have all the rights in the convention. Some groups of children and young people – children living away from home, young disabled people, etc. – have additional rights to make sure they are treated fairly and their needs are met.

Convention on the Rights of the Child

www.unhchr.ch/html/menu3/b/k2crc.htm

Every Child Matters

In 2003 the UK government published *Every Child Matters*, a Green Paper in response to the death of Victoria Climbié. Victoria Climbié was a young girl who was horrifically abused, tortured and eventually killed by her great aunt and the man with whom they lived.

Every Child Matters: Next Steps followed after wide consultation with parents, children and professionals. Finally, the government passed the Children Act 2004 to bring about more effective and accessible services to meet the needs of children, young people and families.

The government's aim is that every child should receive the support they need to:

- be healthy,
- stay safe,
- enjoy and achieve,
- make a positive contribution, and
- achieve economic well-being.

This means that the organisations involved with providing services to children – hospitals, schools, police, voluntary groups, etc.– will have to share information and cooperate to protect children and young people from harm and to help them achieve what they want in life. The idea is to give children and young people far more say about issues that affect them individually and collectively.

Every Child Matters

www.everychildmatters.gov.uk/

Right to education

Every child should have the right to education and be able to reach their potential, regardless of their background or circumstances.

How schools contribute to well-being

- They help each pupil achieve the highest possible standards of education.
- They deal with bullying and discrimination and keeping children safe.
- They become healthy schools and promote healthy lifestyles through personal, social and health education lessons, drugs education, breakfast clubs and sporting activities.
- They ensure attendance, encourage pupils to behave responsibly, give them a strong voice in the life of the school and encourage them to help others.
- They help communities to value education and to see it as a way out of the poverty trap.
- They help parents to support their children's learning and development.

The Office for Standards in Education (Ofsted) has included Every Child Matters in its inspection framework for schools and colleges.

Ofsted

www.ofsted.gov.uk/

Responsibilities and duties of parents

Parents and guardians have the biggest influence during the early years of their child's development. It is their responsibility to meet the rights of every child to have a safe, secure and stable home life from which to thrive. But many factors can affect the

> **remember**
> Doing well in education is a young person's most effective route out of poverty and disaffection.

quality of parenting, so the government plus other agencies and local authorities have introduced support mechanisms that can help parents and carers fulfil their role.

Accountability of coaches, officials and administrators

Once a child has been handed over to a coach, the coach is **in loco parentis**. Any actions, remarks, thoughts and ideas from the coach will be closely monitored by the child and may be imitated by the child. The coach has to be accountable for their actions as they can affect the needs and rights of the child and their development. In some sports such as gymnastics and swimming and during summer camps, the coach can see more of the child than the parent, so they may have a bigger influence on the child's physical, psychological and social development. Officials and administrators also have to be accountable when they deal with children. All staff in a club or organisation should know the club's policies and act accordingly.

Issues

Minimum ages for mixed-sex competition

Most national governing bodies (NGBs) of sport have rules about mixed-sex competition. Sports where physical contact and physical ability are the overriding attributes do not allow mixed-sex competition after age 11. Puberty begins in girls at about age 11 and that is why mixed-sex competition has to cease.

Some sports promote mixed-sex competition, including tennis and badminton. People think that mixed-sex competition is a good idea in target sports and sports which do not have a large physical element.

When many girls reach age 11, they feel as though their rights are being ignored. They feel able to participate and they want to participate, but some sports' rules on mixed-sex competition forbid them to participate.

Figure 23.6 Once a child has been handed over, the coach is in loco parentis

Cost of winning

Children first, winning second. There is too much emphasis on winning at junior levels – defeat is regarded as failure. Unfortunately, there can only be one winner, so most children are classed as failures, but an effective coach should not be promoting these ideas.

There is too much emphasis on outcomes not processes. Young participants should not be worrying about the outcome but looking forward to the thrill of participation. Fear of failure is a major reason why children drop out of sport.

Sport should be fun and can still be competitive, but to emphasise winning and losing can diminish a child's **self-esteem**. Many sports have tried to address this problem by curbing the creation of superteams, so the competition is fairer and more competitive. Winning by a big margin is less enjoyable than winning a close game, and losing a close game is less humiliating than being trounced.

Economic exploitation

Globalisation and sport's huge popularity have contributed to the economic exploitation of child athletes. Talented young athletes are identified at a young age then trained to become professionals. Their social, psychological or physical development may be overridden for financial gain. It takes 10 000 h of training to reach elite status and residential training centres for young sports performers are now commonplace. Children's rights are being disregarded in pursuit of success. Many children burn out by the end of their teens and suffer injuries that affect them for life. Within this climate, it can be difficult for coaches, parents and guardians to uphold children's rights, empower children so they choose their own training regimes, and help children reflect realistically on their chance of success.

Figure 23.7 Fear of failure is a major reason why children drop out of sport

activity
GROUP WORK 23.1

P1

M1

1. Obtain copies of the UN Convention on the Rights of the Child and *Every Child Matters*.

2. In small groups, choose one of the documents and summarise the main points.

3. Describe and explain how sport can meet the needs and rights of children outlined in the two documents.

4. Present your findings to the other small groups.

The effects of sport on the development of children

 See page 124 in Unit 15 for more information

Sport is a very powerful influence on performers, especially children. A positive influence can develop valuable qualities such as leadership, confidence and self-esteem. A successful and effective coach will provide a safe and secure environment where children feel protected and, given the right opportunities, will experience enjoyment and achievement. Alternatively, the pursuit of excellence in sport could have an adverse effect on child development through exploitation and overtraining that causes psychological, social and physical damage.

Social effects

Learning respect for others

> **remember**
>
> Poor behaviour and lack of respect for others on the sports field can also transfer to everyday situations.

A good coach will help children learn to respect others, particularly officials and opposing players and coaches. They can do this by providing examples of good practice. Congratulating the opposition in defeat and not ridiculing them in victory will teach the child to handle success and failure in the same way. Thanking the officials and all coaches and administrators for their efforts will show respect for others and earn respect in return. These examples of good practice in sport may stay with a child and influence other aspects of their lives.

Development of coping ability

Coping with difficulty

Sports are inherently difficult and few children can do things correctly first time, so the coach and child must be patient when they acquire new skills. A child who consistently finds tasks difficult can soon develop a feeling of **learned helplessness** – if they are unable to do one skill, they lose confidence and convince themselves they are unable to do any skills required for the sport. This can lead to early dropout from the sport. Provide lots of positive feedback during learning; don't put too much emphasis on outcomes, focus more on the process of acquiring skills. A series of short-term goals can increase confidence and provide a pathway to success.

Figure 23.8 Teach children how to be dignified in victory and defeat

Coping with failure

If the correct goals are set, then failures should be rare. But if there are setbacks, help the child to cope with failure. Constant failure can be very demotivating, so provide situations where the child is successful. Perhaps alter the difficulty of the task or focus on rewarding the process and effort rather than the outcome. It is inevitable that children will fail in sport, but the coach must put these failures into perspective and not emphasise winning as the only goal. If the child is improving, then the child is successful.

Development of self-concept

Children develop a self-concept through their physical characteristics, what they can do and what people say about them. Young children tend to describe themselves based on what they look like, but their achievements become more important to them as they mature, especially when they can show them in front of others.

Comparing their own abilities against others' abilities forms a significant part of their social status and self-image. Being good at games is highly valued and enables children to gain status and have good social relations. Comments from significant others have a major impact on self-concept. Significant others are usually the people the child listens to and takes notice of, such as family, teachers, friends and coaches. A few well-placed words from the coach can increase a child's self-concept, whereas a few derogatory words can destroy it.

A problem for many coaches is that children have idols or people they would like to be. They compare themselves against the preferred model and this can have a major impact on their self-concept if they don't meet the criteria.

Improved emotional well-being

There is evidence that physical activity is important for children's psychological well-being. Children with lower physical activity levels have more symptoms of psychological distress than more active children. Sport and exercise can provide an important arena for youngsters to be successful and this is experienced through positive effects on self-esteem and self-perceptions of competence and body image, with a stronger effect for those already low in self-esteem. Physical activity helps to reduce stress, **anxiety** and depression in adolescents. However, physical activity can also create distress if children are poor at sport but are required to perform in front of more able children. Pressure on talented children to perform can also lead to negative emotions. Be aware of sport's impact on emotions and carefully control its effects on children's feelings.

Improved communication and interpersonal skills

Participating in sports is very difficult without communication and building relationships with others. Most children's sports involve interaction with other people, such as the coach, teammates, officials and opponents. Sport is invaluable for this aspect of children's development and research shows that children who participate in physical activity develop confidence, are able to communicate effectively and have excellent social skills.

Improved cooperation skills

From early childhood to age 5, children are very self-centred and do not find sharing and playing with others very easy, especially if they do not have siblings. They do not play cooperatively; they tend to play alongside other children but not with other children. They do not want to share a ball, they want one ball to themselves.

From 6 to 9 years, children will form small friendship groups and play in a world of make-believe where they take on different roles. They compete regularly to see who's best and who can get the upper hand. During late childhood, from 10 to 13 years, children play sport because their friends do. They are able to understand the concept of teamwork and help one another to achieve a goal. During adolescence, peer groups have a strong influence on children's effort and motivation towards sport, but those who play become

> **remember**
>
> An effective coach encourages children to reach realistic goals and aspirations they have set for themselves. An effective coach encourages children to accept themselves for who they are, not what they want to be.

fully aware of how effective it can be to work together. They help one another and can fill in for others if they are missing.

Many sports require children to work in teams, which poses problems for the coach. The coach has to keep the children working towards the same goal, using the abilities and personalities of the team members to enhance the team, and must maintain the welfare and development of each child. One child's personal goals may conflict with another's; for example, one child may play to win whereas another child may play for friendship. The competitive child may have to accommodate others or play on their own. Playing out of position or being substituted to allow others to play can be very frustrating for a child and often its parents too.

Increased social competence

Sport is very important in children's social development, especially when it develops peer status and acceptance. Games and sports are domains where young boys compare themselves with others and establish peer acceptance. Because sport is highly valued by children, being good at sport helps children to become socially mobile.

When children play freely at games, it is clear that the most able become the team leaders and captains and they pick their teams based on ability. Less able children are usually left until last or left out of games. This can have a major effect on their opportunity to interact with other children and to develop social skills.

Children with poor physical skills find it difficult to be accepted by their peers and suffer from low self-esteem and self-worth, causing stress and anxiety in sporting situations. Be aware of this and ensure all participants are involved fully and experience some form of success in front of others. Pick teams to give a fair contest and make sure the less able do not always get minor roles.

Psychological effects

Increased self-esteem

Sport can have positive and negative effects on self-esteem as it can alter a child's perception of themselves through accomplishment or failure. A successful child will have a healthy self-esteem, particularly if their successes are reinforced through praise and recognition from significant others. Even if they fail sometimes, a child will persist with a task while their self-esteem is high. A child who is unable to succeed in sports will

case study 23.1   **Coach and four**

A new coach arrived at a well-established under-11s team that had won the league the previous year. The team was dominated by a group of four boys. They were the best players and their skills made them the most popular among their peers. After watching the first game, the coach soon realised that although they were successful, the contribution from other team members was limited and many played minor roles while the four boys dominated possession and the field. During the game, the coach heard many derogatory comments from the boys about other team members. Everybody seemed happy at the end of the game, including the parents and most of the other team members. The coach was not so happy.

activity
INDIVIDUAL WORK

1. Why might the coach have been unhappy, even though the team won?
2. What effects might the four boys have had on other team members?
3. What can the coach do to change the dynamics of the team?
4. What problems might the coach come across if they change things?

Figure 23.9 Sport helps to develop peer status and acceptance

quickly develop low self-esteem, particularly if their failure is witnessed by others and they receive no support from significant others.

Here are some simple methods to develop and maintain healthy self-esteem in a child:

- **Avoid unrealistic promises** – be honest with the child without being derogatory. Positive comments about effort and completion rather than winning will improve self-esteem.

- **Be a positive role model** – be positive about yourself and demonstrate an optimistic attitude to the child.

- **Identify and redirect inaccurate beliefs** – children often compare themselves with other children. Try to help the child focus on their own successes, not what others do.

- **Positive and accurate feedback** – reward effort as well as outcomes with positive comments about the child's performances.

- **Safe environment** – protect children from bullies and other situations that may cause physical or psychological harm.

- **Constructive experiences** – use activities that require cooperation rather than competition and activities where an older child can help a younger child.

Increased range of motor skills

As a child develops, they acquire an increased range of motor skills, but only if they are exposed to them. Fine motor skills such as writing and manipulating small objects can be enhanced in the early years by exposing the child to activities that require manual dexterity. Painting, jigsaws, cutting, and playing with play dough and blocks help children develop fine motor skills. Begin with large objects and make them progressively smaller so the child has to become more accurate, using a pincer grip.

Sport has a bigger role in the development of gross motor skills, where whole body movements are needed in running, jumping and hopping. Playground games such as

Figure 23.10 Playground games can develop gross motor skills used in some sports

hopscotch, tig, skipping and going to the park or play area to work on apparatus can develop gross motor skills used in some sports. Kicking and striking balls can be made progressively more difficult by reducing the size of the ball, the striking area and the target.

Development in perception of success or failure

At about 5–7 years, children find it difficult to distinguish between effort, ability and outcome, so it is very difficult for them to make **attributions** about success and failure. In the early years, effort is associated with success and lack of effort with failure. As children get older, they realise that some children can do things that are hard and others can't. This is the beginning of their notion of ability. From about 9–10 years, a child's ability becomes the principal factor for success, and effort is perceived as having little influence.

Table 23.2 A model of sports-related attributions

	Internal attribution	**External attribution**
Stable	Ability	Coaching
Unstable	Ability (form)	Luck
	Practice	Task ease
	Effort	

Adapted from Lee (1993: 125)

The attributions made by children can influence how they feel about sport. An effective coach ensures that attributions about success and failure do not have a negative effect on a child's feelings. Children who attribute their success to internal factors, such as the ability they have and the effort they put in, tend to feel pride in their performance and are more likely to continue with the sport and grow in self-confidence. Children who attribute their failure to the same internal factors will not experience the same positive feelings.

Another factor that could contribute to self-confidence is the prediction of future success. If a child is competing against someone they have previously beaten and they attributed the success to stable factors such as their ability and the excellent coaching they received, then they are more likely to feel confident about the forthcoming contest. But if they thought the success was due to unstable factors, such as a stroke of luck or a bad day for their opponent, then future success may seem less likely.

Reduced anxiety in children

Sport exposes children to situations that cause anxiety, so coaches use techniques to try to reduce anxiety and improve performance. If children are exposed to sporting situations that cause them anxiety, it may have more serious effects on their emotional development and well-being. It has been suggested that children should not participate in sport which causes anxiety, such as competition, but lack of exposure to stressful situations will only delay the effects and make it harder for children to learn how to cope.

There are five main forms of anxiety in childhood:

- **Generalised anxiety** – worries and fears about a wide range of future events.
- **Separation anxiety** – worries about real or imaginary separation from a parent because of illness, injury or death.
- **Social anxiety** – worries about the loss of friends, attractiveness or meeting new people.
- **Performance anxiety** – worries about performing in front of others, taking a test or competing in sport.
- **Fears and phobias** – of a person, a situation or an object.

Younger children tend to have separation anxieties, older children have social anxieties and adolescents usually suffer from performance anxieties due to the number of times they are assessed.

Help a child to reduce their anxiety by explaining that feelings of anxiety are experienced by all athletes to some degree. It helps if you can identify the cause and effects of the child's anxiety. Provide feedback that gives a variety of reasons for failure as this helps to avoid a negative self-fulfilling prophecy. Do not attribute failure to lack of ability; this will avoid a feeling of helplessness in the child. It will not help to take the child away from the cause of their anxiety; it just delays the anxiety. It is better to expose the child to situations that cause anxiety in a gradual way so they are able to cope with the threat as it increases through their childhood. Carefully selected competition with realistic expectations can enhance the child's enjoyment, whatever the outcome.

Effect of the family and parental involvement

Whenever a child participates in sport, their family usually provides considerable support. Alongside the coach, family have the greatest influence on the child, through their attitudes, beliefs and behaviours. From the coach's perspective, some parental influences on the child should be encouraged and integrated into the coaching process, some have to be tolerated and some should be eliminated from the coaching process. Coaches have many stories about parents who put enormous pressure on children and show inappropriate behaviour towards coaches, children, officials and other parents. But parents are a vital cog in the wheel of child development.

According to Lee (1993: 43), in 1987 Hellstad proposed that parental involvement lies on a continuum (Table 23.4).

> **remember**
>
> Do not eliminate parents from the coaching process. Educate them to work alongside you for the mutual benefit of the child.

Figure 23.11 Some parental influences should be encouraged

Table 23.3 The parental involvement continuum

Underinvolvement
Disinterested parent
Misinformed parent
Moderate involvement
The comfort zone
Overinvolvement
Excitable parent
Fanatical parent

Adapted from Lee (1993: 43)

Disinterested parents use sport as a babysitter, dropping the children off at a club to follow their own interests and activities. Misinformed parents are those that think getting involved would be interfering, so they stay away and leave the child without a family member to give them positive feedback. Excitable parents are those that get fully involved in everything the child does and become a screaming embarrassment on the sidelines, shouting abuse at officials or opponents.

Fanatical parents cause the greatest problems, as they celebrate every success as though it were a championship performance, criticise every failure and offer advice on how to put things right. They see their child as a reflection of themselves and live their lives through the child. This puts intense pressure on the child to perform well, and the child often plays sport because the parent has forced them to.

To improve parental involvement, hold a parent orientation meeting to outline what you expect from parents and what parents can expect from you.

Dos for parents
- Do attend games.
- Do encourage children to play by the rules.
- Do set an example by being friendly to other parents, opponents and officials.
- Do emphasise fun and enjoyment.
- Do praise effort and improvement.
- Do applaud good play from all participants.

Don'ts for parents
- Don't force children to participate.
- Don't abuse officials.
- Don't shout derogatory comments towards opposition children, parents and coaches.
- Don't interfere with the child's coaching decisions.
- Don't criticise the child's performance.

Increased motivation

Most children participate in sport because they are **motivated**. This motivation is usually a mixture of intrinsic and extrinsic motivation. Extrinsic motivation is where the child participates for some external reward such as medals, trophies, certificates or praise and recognition from others. Intrinsic motivation is where the child participates for fun, enjoyment and the pleasure they get from the sport.

A coach has a responsibility to promote and encourage participation for intrinsic not extrinsic rewards. Children who receive regular rewards for participation usually drop out when the rewards cease, because they forget why they participated in the first place. But extrinsic rewards are a very powerful motivator if they are used sparingly and when they are really deserved.

A particular problem for a coach when trying to encourage intrinsic motivation is that Sport England and other funding bodies, such as sponsors, will only issue funds on the basis of winning medals and trophies, and this contradicts some of the ethics of coaching.

Development of technical and tactical awareness

Children under age 12 should not specialise in a sport except for early-specialisation sports such as gymnastics, diving, figure skating and table tennis. Help children develop the **fundamentals** of movement and **physical literacy**, but keep to the basics on technical and tactical aspects. Later, when a child has chosen a sport for specialisation, they can concentrate on developing techniques and tactics.

This is quite difficult for a coach as competition demands some form of structure and positional sense. Yet making children stick rigidly to positions and patterns of play can stifle their development and cause them to become one-dimensional. A typical example is to put a tall, physical boy in the middle of a football defence and small, fast children on the wings. But children should be allowed to play and experience all positions, sometimes at the expense of team success.

Physiological effects

Improved general health and weight management

There are well-documented health benefits from being physically active in adulthood. Being physically active can help the prevention and treatment of many common but serious health conditions such as high blood pressure, obesity and some forms of cancer. There have been fewer studies on how physical activity affects health among children, and the results are inconclusive.

case study
23.2

Unfair tag

A mixed-sex under-9s rugby team had reached the semi-final of a tag rugby festival. Before the start of the festival the coach had agreed that all his squad should get equal game time. Near the end of the semi-final, the coach realised he had not played two of his weaker players for very long, so he quickly substituted them onto the field. While they were on, they conceded two tries and the team were knocked out of the competition. The parents of the other children had a go at the coach and the two weaker players, who seemed upset to be blamed for losing.

activity
INDIVIDUAL WORK

1. Was the coach right to substitute the two weaker players into the game?
2. What effect might the experience have on the two poorer players?
3. What might the coach say to the other children's parents?
4. What could the coach do differently to avoid the situation in future?

Anecdotal evidence suggests that less active children find it much harder than active children to manage their weight. According to the UK chief medical officer, juvenile obesity was increasing in 2002, when 2–15% of UK children were obese and 18.2–23.6% were overweight. Fatness in children has its own health problems as well as laying the foundations for problems later in life.

Unfortunately, physical activity on its own has little effect on reducing body fatness, but a bigger effect can be achieved by a combination of physical activity, nutrition and change in behaviour. A coach should incorporate nutritional advice and promote physical activity outside of sessions to reduce obesity in children and alleviate problems later in life.

Improved fitness

Strength

There has been controversy over resistance training for children. Investigators concluded that strength gains were not possible in prepubertal children and that strength training could cause irreversible injury to developing growth plates in bones. However, it is now established practice to include safe resistance training for children.

Strength is considered to be an important part of health-related fitness. It makes an important contribution to improved motor function, body image and athletic performance. When performed safely, it can help to reduce injuries.

The National Strength and Conditioning Association (NSCA) plus a number of sports medicine groups have recommended that strength training for prepubescent boys and girls is safe with proper programme design, instruction and supervision.

Here are the main principles of resistance training for young athletes:

1. Encourage children to participate in sports that require repetitive movements against an opposing force.
2. Do not allow children to perform competitive maximum lifting.
3. Focus on the development of proper technique.
4. Do not add resistance until a child has mastered the proper technique, then add the resistance gradually.
5. Use 8–12 repetitions for upper-body exercises and 15–20 repetitions for lower-body exercises.
6. Perform 1–3 sets of 8–10 different exercises.

7. Put in 1–2 min rest between exercises.

8. Have 2–3 sessions per week and allow at least a day's rest between sessions.

9. Follow the principle of progressive overload as the child gains in strength.

10. Use a wide range of exercises. Introduce specialisation later on.

11. Include a warm-up and a cooldown in every session.

Flexibility

Children are naturally flexible as the joint capsule is not fully developed and muscle mass and injuries do not restrict movement. However, as children grow, especially during the growth spurt, their flexibility rapidly decreases as the bone length outgrows soft tissue. Recommendations are to perform flexibility exercises 3–7 times a week using static stretching slightly beyond normal length and holding for 6–10 s three times for each muscle.

As the child develops, introduce **ballistic stretching**, assisted stretching and passive stretching plus **proprioceptive neuromuscular facilitation (PNF)**. To get children into good habits, it is a good idea to incorporate flexibility exercises into training sessions.

Sport-specific fitness

At early stages of development, the child doesn't require sport-specific fitness as some aspects of fitness cannot be fully developed until after puberty. The long-term athlete development model (LTAD), now adopted by most NGBs, is based on work by Istvan Balyi. He proposed that the physical development of children should be based on individual maturation and development, not chronological age.

He identified that during the development of a child there are optimal windows of trainability where accelerated adaptations can take place so the child can maximise its potential in that aspect of fitness.

The concept was soon grasped by many coaches that realised their early-developing athletes were not reaching their potential because they had to wait until the average age of maturity, and by this time they had missed the accelerated adaptation phase.

Figure 23.12 Base physical development on individual maturation

Puberty-related effects

Body composition

Physical activity decreases total body fat, increases fat-free mass and increases total body mass. The differences are greater after puberty. During puberty, child athletes do not experience the same increase in body fat as non-athletes of the same age and sex. Girl athletes experience a greater difference due to the larger increase in body fat after puberty compared with boys. The lower levels of body fat have a positive effect on health-related illnesses later in life and can enhance self-esteem and social status among their peers due to a socially appealing body image.

Menstrual dysfunction

There have been several studies into the effect of physical activity on **menstruation** and the effect of menstruation on sports performance. Athletic girls tend to experience **menarche**, or first menstrual period, at a later age than non-athletic girls, so people are concerned that intensive sports training could delay sexual maturation. However, it is possible that the later age of menarche in athletes simply reflects the fact that athletic girls have narrow hips, slender physiques, long legs and low levels of body fat, and that is why they experience a later menarche.

Figure 23.13 Adaptation to training and optimal trainability. Adapted from Stafford (2005)

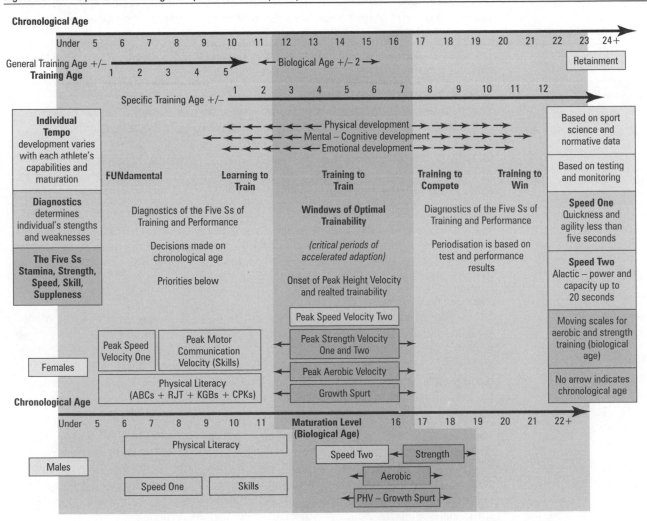

(ABCs = Agility Balance Coordination Speed + RJT = Run Jump Throw + KGBs = Kinaesthesis Gliding Buoyancy Striking w/object + CPKs = Catching Passing Kicking Striking w/body)

Secondary amenorrhea, or cessation of the menstrual cycle after menarche, can occur as a result of intense athletic training. If this continues, it may lead to **osteoporosis** due to a decrease in oestrogen secretion. An effective coach will know this and will try to educate the female athlete on improved nutrition and a decrease in training volume so their menstrual cycle can resume.

Participation during the menstrual cycle has no adverse effects, although girls suffering from premenstrual tension (PMT) will be in discomfort and this will probably affect their participation.

Injuries

Growth plate abnormalities

The **epiphyseal plates** at the ends of bones can be damaged because the cartilaginous plate is weaker than bone. This can lead to common fractures that interrupt normal ossification, affect growth and produce deformity.

A common area for epiphyseal damage is the anterior part of the vertebrae. Constant flexion through sitting incorrectly for long periods and inactivity in children can cause Scheuermann's disease, which causes the vertebrae to become wedge-shaped instead of rectangular.

Damage can also occur through overactivity, where the child regularly puts stress on a particular bone. Gymnasts can develop problems with their wrists through constant impact on the end of the radius. Throwers develop problems at the elbow and runners at the head of the femur.

Be aware of potential injuries when the child is in their rapid growth phase. Structure the training properly and put in rests between activities.

Tendon–bone attachment injury

The main tendon–bone attachments can be injury sites in children. Constant pulling of the tendon at the bone site can disturb **ossification** and the bone can become fragmented, a condition called **osteochondritis**. The injury usually occurs during the growth spurt when the length of the bone increases more than muscle length. The greatest risk occurs among active boys, because an increase in muscular strength adds extra stress to the tendon attachment.

Osgood–Schlatter's disease is a common osteochondritis injury where the attachment of the patella tendon to the tibial tuberosity just below the knee becomes swollen and tender. Another site is the attachment of the Achilles tendon at the heel. Be aware of localised pain experienced by adolescent children after a growth spurt and encourage a period of rest or reduced activity until the pain subsides.

Joint surface injuries

The surface of a joint consists of cartilage laid on bone. During repetitive jarring of the joint, the blood supply to an area of cartilage can cause it to die and separate from the bone, known as osteochondritis dessicans. The injury usually occurs at the knee, ankle and hip; it can also affect the elbow in throwers and gymnasts. If the child rests, the blood supply can re-establish itself at the fragment, which allows it to heal; otherwise the loose fragments must be removed or the joint could lock.

Stress injuries to the skeleton

Acute injuries of bones are easy to recognise and are usually caused by sudden impact. Stress or overuse injuries reveal themselves quite slowly. They could begin as a minor pain that gradually gets worse and may become difficult to treat if left too long. Be aware of possible stress injuries by monitoring the child during training. If the pain experienced by the child gets worse at each training session, it is probably due to a stress injury; stop the exercise immediately and seek medical help.

Skeletal growth and development

Children do not grow at a uniform rate throughout their development. There is a rapid increase in height, a growth spurt, during puberty. This is followed by a rapid increase in body mass.

There are four main phases of growth in humans. Growth is rapid in infancy and early childhood, followed by a relatively steady growth through middle childhood, rapid increase during adolescence and finally slow increases until growth stops when the child reaches adulthood. Figure 23.14 shows how this is different for girls and boys.

Istvan Balyi measured peak height velocity to establish the growth stage of individual children then used age-appropriate fitness activities to enable every child to reach their athletic potential.

A major difficulty of coaching children through puberty is that children of the same age have hugely different physical and mental maturity. Consequently, it is not very good practice to match children by age, although restrictions by NGBs do not allow early-maturing children to play in older age groups and late-maturing children to participate in younger age groups. This could lead to early developers missing out on their potential by being held back and late developers being pushed too quickly and suffering injuries or burnout.

Improved thermoregulation

Physical fitness enhances the body's ability to regulate temperature during exercise in the heat by lowering the temperature when sweating occurs. Recent evidence suggests that a fit person will also acclimatise to hot environments twice as quickly as a sedentary person. Children do not dissipate heat as efficiently as adults, because they have a lower sweat rate at rest and during exercise and they generate more heat during exercise. Children should not be exposed to extreme heat for long periods of time. Children do adapt but they take much longer to adapt than adults.

Improved immune system function

Participating in moderately intensive exercise has been linked to an improvement in the immune system. It is thought that regular, consistent exercise can lead to substantial benefits in immune system health over the long term. However, intense exercise seems to cause a temporary decrease in immune system function. Cortisol and adrenaline, known as the stress hormones, raise blood pressure and cholesterol levels and suppress the immune system. This effect has been linked to increased susceptibility to infection, particularly in endurance athletes after extreme exercise.

Children do not participate in many ultra-endurance events, so exercise should have a positive effect on the immune system, but take care with children who train long hours,

Figure 23.14 Humans have four main growth phases. Adapted from Robergs and Roberts (1997)

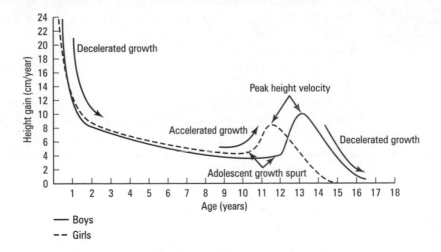

such as gymnasts and swimmers. If a child is already ill, their immune system will already be fighting the infection, and additional stress from intense training could undermine their recovery. The advice is that a runny nose and mild cold symptoms but without fever could benefit from exercise, but intense exercise will only make things worse and will probably extend the illness.

Improved coordination

Boys usually develop peak motor coordination velocity at ages 9–12 and girls at ages 8–11. The fundamental stage of LTAD enables the child to coordinate movements that are required for a variety of sports. If these are not mastered by the age of 11 or 12, the child will find it very difficult to reach their potential.

Children reach physical literacy when they have acquired four things:

- **ABCs** – agility, balance, coordination, speed.
- **Fundamentals of athletics** – running, throwing and jumping.
- **KGBs** – kinaesthetic sense, gliding, buoyancy and striking with an implement.
- **CPKs** – catching, passing, kicking and striking with a body part.

Physical literacy is the mastery of fundamental movement skills (FMS) with fundamental sports skills (FSS):

> Physical literacy = FMS + FSS

Children should try a variety of sports because, by age 11 or 12, it becomes very difficult to learn new skills and transfer old ones to new situations.

---

case study 23.3 — Troubled gymnast

The coach of an elite female gymnast, age 13, has recently noticed a decline in her performances. She has missed training with illness and regularly feels tired and lethargic. At the next training session, she complains of painful joints, particularly her wrists and knees.

activity
INDIVIDUAL WORK

1. What are the possible causes for the gymnast's symptoms?
2. What can the coach do to help the gymnast continue to train?
3. What other problems might a gymnast experience at that age?

---

activity
INDIVIDUAL WORK 23.2

P2

M2

A sports college has just come to the end of its first year as the focal point for a new school sports partnership. You have been the community sports coach working within the partnership's primary schools. As part of the evaluation and review process, you have been asked to contribute to a report for the partnership development manager (PDM).

Your report to the PDM should describe and explain how your activities have contributed to the children's social, psychological and physical development.

activity
INDIVIDUAL WORK 23.3

D1

For the report in Activity 23.2, including examples of how the sport has had a positive impact on the children's development and a negative impact on the children's development.

Good practice in the protection of children in sport

In all professions there are accepted and established codes of behaviour. Doctors conform to a professional code and organisations adopt customer charters such as the Patient's Charter. This ensures that the customer's rights are maintained and that, where possible, their needs are met. They safeguard the customer and protect the service provider from prosecution.

A code of ethics and conduct for sports coaches was originally drawn up by the British Institute of Sports Coaches and changed in 1995 by the National Coaching Foundation. Sports Coach UK revised it in 2001 and it became known as the Code of Practice for Sports Coaches.

Sports Coach UK

www.sportscoachuk.co.uk

The code of practice is not exclusive to coaches; it can apply to all people working with children, including parents, guardians, friends, peers, teachers, medics and the press.

Code of Practice for Sports Coaches

- **Rights** – coaches must respect and champion the rights of every individual to participate in sport.

- **Relationships** – coaches must develop a relationship with athletes and others based on openness, honesty, mutual trust and respect.

- **Personal standards** – coaches must demonstrate proper personal behaviour and conduct at all times.

- **Professional standards** – to maximise benefits and minimise the risks to athletes, coaches must attain a high level of competence through qualifications and a commitment to ongoing training that ensures safe and correct practice.

Key principles

General

- Provide choices for individual performers.

- Provide an environment in which children are free from fear or harassment.

- Recognise the rights of performers to be treated as individuals.

- Encourage performers to confer with other coaches or experts if the need arises.

- Promote the concept of a well-balanced lifestyle for performers within and outside sport.

Positive experience

- Treat all individuals with respect.

- Do not discriminate on the grounds of gender, marital status, race, colour, disability, sexuality, age, occupation, religion or political opinion.

- Do not condone or allow to go unchallenged any form of discrimination.
- Do not publicly criticise or engage in demeaning descriptions of others.
- Be discreet in conversations about performers, coaches or other individuals.
- Communicate with and provide feedback to performers in a manner which reflects respect and care.

Relationships

- Consider behaviour; do not engage in behaviour that constitutes any form of abuse.
- Promote the welfare and best interests of your performers, even if that means letting another professional take over.
- Avoid sexual intimacy with performers at all times and under any conditions, including immediately after the coaching relationship has ended.
- Empower performers to be responsible for their own decisions.
- Clarify the nature of the coaching services being offered to performers.
- Communicate and cooperate with other organisations and individuals in the best interests of your performers.

Responsibilities

- Set high moral and ethical standards throughout coaching practice.
- Be fair, honest and considerate to performers and others in your sport.
- Project an image of health, cleanliness and functional efficiency.
- Be a positive role model for performers at all times.

Basic rules

- **Appearance** – always project a professional image.
- **Fashion** – wear appropriate clothing and kit; parents won't thank you for recommending the latest gear.
- **Tattoos** – tattoos are not a good image to set others.

Figure 23.15 Wear appropriate clothing and kit

- **Jewellery** – remove or tape up jewellery during sport.
- **Language** – consider what you say and the way you say it; do not use foul and abusive language.
- **Alcohol** – do not drink alcohol while you are responsible for children, or immediately before.
- **Drugs** – take a firm stance against performance-enhancing drugs in sport.

Observation of behaviour

Observation of behaviour takes several years to master. Coaches need to observe the behaviour of children and recognise changes in behaviour that might indicate problems. Children regularly display behaviour that can be construed in several ways. In contact sports, they often go down clutching an injured part, waiting for assistance and reassurance, then moments later they are charging around again. Being quiet before a game may be pre-match nerves or it could be something more sinister.

Children seem to have a natural talent for imitating other people's behaviour and manipulating coaches and parents through behaviour. This makes it very difficult for a coach to decipher which behaviour requires further investigation.

Empowering children

One of the aims of any coach dealing with children is to improve the child's ability to make decisions for themselves. With beginners, coaches initially take a very authoritarian approach; they tell them what to do and how to do it. Children become used to this form of delivery as they are told what to do in most of their education and home life.

A good coach introduces children to decision making by offering them choices and providing alternative solutions. Children soon become independent learners and they get a sense of pride and satisfaction when they complete a task independently.

Developing relationships with agencies

Clubs or organisations should have a designated person who deals with all issues of child protection and child welfare. They should have a child protection policy and all the accompanying documents. They should be able to follow the process and they should be trained to deal with the situations. All NGBs are required to have child protection policies and a child protection officer or lead officer in child protection.

Local authority

In response to the Children Act 2004 and *Every Child Matters*, all local authorities have a statutory local safeguarding children board (LSCB) to coordinate children's welfare services.

> **remember**
>
> Follow up all observations that cause concern and seem out of character. This is a much safer approach than to ignore things and be found negligent.

---

case study 23.4　　**Fast and louche**

An experienced coach at an athletics club was busy warming up his athletes when a sports car skidded into the car park. Out stepped one of the new sprint coaches and declared that his athletes wanted to use the track. His breath smelled of beer, he wore a chain round his neck, his clothes were scruffy and he had a tattoo on his arm. His athletes greeted him with high fives and began their session. Later the experienced coach noticed two of the female athletes leave in the new coach's car.

activity
INDIVIDUAL WORK

1. What responsibilities is the new coach neglecting by his behaviour?
2. What actions may cause concern to the more experienced coach?
3. What action should be taken by the more experienced coach?

Social services have a statutory duty under the Children Act 1989, the Protection of Children Act 1999 and the Children Act 2004 to ensure the welfare and protection of children. They have a legal responsibility to investigate all situations where a child is suspected to be suffering or is likely to suffer abuse. They are the principal point of contact for any child welfare concerns.

The police have powers to enter premises and ensure the immediate protection of children believed to be suffering from or at risk of abuse. They work in conjunction with social services, but have child protection units that investigate cases of child abuse.

Here are some other organisations:

- Childline (0800 1111)
- NSPCC Child Protection Helpline (0808 800 5000)
- Education services
- Cultural and leisure services
- Health services
- Day-care services
- Probation services
- Prison services
- Youth justice services
- Voluntary and private sectors.

Guidance on the Children Act 2004

www.everychildmatters.gov.uk/strategy/guidance/

ACAP

Action on Children's Accidents Project (ACAP) schemes are set up by primary care trusts (PCTs) to help parents and carers make their homes safe for children. They supply equipment such as safety gates, fireguards and cupboard locks plus a visit from an expert on primary care in the home.

The scheme in Burnley, Pendle and Rossendale in Lancashire has seen a remarkable decrease in the number of accidents suffered by children under age 4 that are cared for at home.

Action on Children's Accidents Project

www.bprpct.nhs.uk/acap/acap_home.htm

> **remember**
>
> There is no excuse for individuals, clubs, organisations and local authorities that do not implement good practice in their coaching programmes.

Good practice policy

Clubs and organisations are required to develop a code of practice to provide a safe sporting environment for children. NGBs and employers should incorporate a good practice policy into their constitutions.

Staff

Pre-recruitment

Take all reasonable steps to prevent unsuitable people from working with children. Tell employment candidates what the club or organisation expects from its employees.

Checks

Check on the background of applicants. Obtain at least two character references, evidence of relevant qualifications and confirmation that the applicant has worked with children. Check their details with the Criminal Records Bureau.

Training

Send all new staff on a formal induction programme and train them in child protection awareness, first aid, working effectively with children, and child-centred coaching styles. Give current staff continuing professional development (CPD) to update their qualifications and skills.

Problems

Give all staff feedback on their performance that helps them identify training needs or that deals with issues which have arisen. Have a policy for dealing with complaints and a formal complaints procedure for staff and participants.

Concerns

Have a policy for dealing with concerns that arise. Deal with concerns in a calm and appropriate manner. It is usual to train a specific person to deal with concerns.

Whistle-blowing

Establish a procedure that allows employees and participants to raise any concerns confidentially and without upsetting others. Some possible ways are appraisal sessions, evenings for parents and guardians, and suggestion boxes. Work with the police and issue details of telephone help lines that people can ring anonymously.

Codes of conduct

Have a code of conduct that lays down good practice for volunteer coaches. Some possible directives are to maximise participation and enjoyment for all participants regardless of their ability, to teach and encourage participants to respect and accept the decisions of the match officials, and to give the same importance to honesty, effort and doing your best as the importance given to winning.

Legislation

Children Act 1989

The Children Act 1989 amended the law on children's homes, community homes, voluntary homes and voluntary organisations and made provisions on fostering, childminding and day care for young children and adoption.

Figure 23.16 Train new staff in child-centred coaching

Children Act 1989

www.opsi.gov.uk/acts/acts1989/Ukpga_19890041_en_1.htm

Protection of Children Act 1999

The Protection of Children Act 1999 added provisions to the Children Act 1989. The main additions were to require a list to be kept of persons considered unsuitable to work with children and persons suffering from mental health problems. It also extended the power to make regulations under Section 218(6) of the Education Reform Act 1988.

Protection of Children Act 1999

www.opsi.gov.uk/acts/acts1999/19990014.htm

Children Act 2004

The Children Act 2004 aims to encourage agencies to integrate their work with children through planning and delivery of services. This is to avoid duplication, increase accountability within the agencies and give local authorities considerable flexibility in how they implement their services.

Children Act 2004

www.opsi.gov.uk/acts/acts2004/20040031.htm

Convention on the Rights of the Child

The United Nations Convention on the Rights of the Child gives children and young people the right to express and have their views considered on all matters that affect them; the right to play, rest and leisure; and the right to be free from all forms of violence. All agencies that deal with the welfare of children use the convention to implement their policies and strategies.

Convention on the Rights of the Child

www.unhchr.ch/html/menu3/b/k2crc.htm

Common Core

The Department for Education and Skills (DfES), now the Department for Children, Schools and Families (DCSF), came up with a core of basic skills and knowledge needed by people, including volunteers, who work regularly with children, young people and families. They are grouped under six main headings:

- Effective communication and engagement
- Child and young person development
- Safeguarding and promoting the welfare of the child
- Supporting transitions
- Multi-agency working
- Sharing information.

It is expected that everyone working with children, young people and families will be able to demonstrate a basic level of competence in all six areas. They will form part of qualifications for working with children, young people and families and they will be a foundation for training and development programmes run by employers and training organisations.

Common Core

www.dfes.gov.uk/commoncore/

Agencies

Child Protection in Sport Unit

Founded in 2001, the Child Protection in Sport Unit (CPSU) is a partnership between the NSPCC and Sport England. Here are its roles:

- Be the first point of contact for sports organisations about child protection issues and individuals after sports organisations.
- Coordinate the production of child protection information and training for sports organisations.
- Commission research into a range of issues relating to child protection in sport.
- Develop and promote standards for child protection procedures and training in all sports.

Working with sport to keep children safe

www.thecpsu.org.uk/Scripts/content/Default.asp

NSPCC

The National Society for the Prevention of Cruelty to Children (NSPCC) aims to see a society where all children are loved, valued and able to fulfil their potential. It has four objectives:

- To mobilise everyone to take action to end child cruelty.
- To give children the help, support and environment they need to stay safe from cruelty.
- To find ways of working with communities to keep children safe from cruelty.
- To be, and be seen as, someone to turn to for children and young people.

National Society for the Prevention of Cruelty to Children

www.nspcc.org.uk/

Criminal Records Bureau

The Criminal Records Bureau (CRB) aims to help organisations in the public, private and voluntary sectors by identifying candidates who may be unsuitable to work with children or other vulnerable members of society.

Criminal Records Bureau

www.crb.gov.uk/

Children's Rights Alliance for England

The Children's Rights Alliance for England (CRAE) is an alliance of over 380 voluntary and statutory organisations committed to the full implementation of the Convention on the Rights of the Child.

Children's Rights Alliance for England

www.crae.org.uk/cms/index.php?option=com_frontpage&Itemid=1

UNICEF

UNICEF believes that every child should have clean water, food, healthcare, education and a safe environment in which to grow up. UNICEF upholds the UN Convention on the Rights of the Child and works to hold the international community responsible for their promises to children.

UNICEF

www.unicef.org.uk/

Save the Children

The UN Convention on the Rights of the Child underpins all of Save the Children's work. All children are equal and have human rights such as the right to food, shelter, healthcare, education and protection from violence, neglect and exploitation.

Save the Children

www.savethechildren.org.uk

---

activity
INDIVIDUAL WORK 23.4

You were recently appointed as the welfare officer at a local sports club with over 100 children under 16. As part of your role, you were asked by the committee to review all child protection policies at the club and to educate all employees and volunteers who come into contact with the children about good practice in child protection.

To fulfil this task, you produced for the club a new good practice policy in child protection.

---

activity
INDIVIDUAL WORK 23.5

M3

M4

After the release of the good practice policy that you produced in Activity 23.3, a number of employees and volunteers at the club questioned some of the practices and the impact on their coaching role. You have decided to address this by holding a meeting where you will make a presentation that describes and explains good practice in child protection then justifies the policies you have introduced.

Signs of potential child abuse and appropriate courses of action

All those directly or indirectly involved with children's sport have a responsibility to explore their own values and attitudes in relation to child abuse, and to be able to recognise signs and indicators of child abuse.

Abuse

Child abuse describes all ways in which children are harmed, usually by adults and by those they know and trust. It could be damage that has been done or may be done to a child's physical and mental health. An adult may abuse a child by inflicting harm or by preventing harm occurring. A child may abuse another child.

Neglect

Neglect occurs when an adult fails to meet a child's basic physical and/or psychological needs, resulting in the impairment of the child's health or development. Here are some examples:

- Failing to provide adequate food, shelter and clothing
- Constantly leaving children alone or unsupervised
- Failing to protect children from physical harm or danger
- Failing to ensure access to appropriate medical care or treatment
- Refusing to give children affection and attention.

An example in sport is failing to ensure children are safe and comfortable, or exposing them to undue cold or to unnecessary risk of injury.

Physical abuse

Physical abuse is when someone physically hurts or injures a child by hitting, shaking, throwing poisoning, burning, scalding, biting, suffocating, drowning or otherwise causing deliberate physical harm to them. Giving inappropriate drugs or alcohol can constitute physical abuse.

An example in sport is when the nature and intensity of the training and competition exceed the capacity of the child's immature and growing body. Drugs to delay puberty, control diet or enhance performance may also be regarded as physical abuse.

Sexual abuse

Sexual abuse is when adults or other children, male or female, use children to meet their own sexual needs. This could include full intercourse, masturbation, oral sex, anal intercourse or fondling. Showing children pornographic material (e.g. books, videos, pictures) also constitutes sexual abuse.

An example in sport is inappropriate physical contact between the coach and child, perhaps in gymnastics. Physical contact may occur in some sports, and videoing or photographing children doing swimming, gymnastics, etc., could be examples of sexual abuse.

Emotional abuse

Emotional abuse is emotional ill-treatment of a child resulting in severe and persistent adverse effects on their emotional development. Here are some examples:

- Imposing developmentally inappropriate expectations on them
- Making them feel worthless, unloved, inadequate or valued only insofar as to meet the needs of another person
- Making them feel frightened or in danger
- Shouting at, threatening or taunting them
- Overprotecting them or failing to give them love and affection they need.

An example in sport is constant criticism, name-calling, bullying, sarcasm, racism or unrealistic pressure to consistently perform to high expectations. Personal information in the wrong hands may cause emotional abuse that affects confidence and self-worth.

Bullying and harassment

Bullying is deliberate hurtful behaviour repeated over time. It can be verbal, written or physical, including actions of physical assault, name-calling, sarcasm, racist taunts, gestures and unwanted physical contact, graffiti, stealing or hiding personal items. Internet and mobile phone bullying have become more common among children.

Harassment is associated with bullying and occurs when the individual feels that they are subject to behaviour that is unacceptable to them. Usually name-calling or actions that annoy, upset or worry another child are examples of harassment.

Examples in sport are a parent pushing their child too hard, a coach who shouts or humiliates a performer, children who use sport as a way of making life difficult or unhappy for others.

It is difficult to detect bullying as bullies are crafty and usually bully people so they cannot be witnessed. The victim is reluctant to tell, and intervention without total closure can cause more problems. For clues about bullying, keep an eye on the victim's happiness and behaviour.

case study 23.5 — Push and boots

At the end of a coaching session, the coach returns to the changing rooms to find a number of parents waiting for their children. A young boy appears from the changing rooms and his mother, who looks hassled, hurries him to the car. When the boy realises that he's forgotten his boots, his mother forcibly pushes him back towards the changing rooms. The coach sees two other young children in the car and notices that they're crying. When the boy returns, he sheepishly gets into the back of the car and it speeds away. Next week the coach notices some bruises on the side of the boy's thigh.

activity
INDIVIDUAL WORK

1. Are there any signs that the coach should be concerned about?
2. What type of abuse might be occurring?
3. What action should the coach take?

Effects of abuse

Here are some effects of child abuse:

- Death
- Suffering pain and distress
- Developing behavioural problems
- Not fully developing physically, emotionally and mentally
- Developing low self-esteem
- Suffering depression, inflicting self-harm, attempting suicide
- Becoming introverted and withdrawn
- Suffering temporary or permanent injury.

activity
INDIVIDUAL WORK 23.5

P5

You are the child protection and welfare officer at a local sports club and have been approached by a coach who suspects that a child is being abused. They are unsure about the type of abuse and have asked you for help.

You realise that the child could be at risk. You immediately gain permission to produce a poster that could be displayed around the club so all users can identify the five kinds of abuse and their potential consequences.

Sport-specific abuse

Sport-specific abuse is where the coach and athlete are unaware that abuse is taking place as the abusive behaviour is a result of their desire to be successful and push the limits of performance.

Intensive training

Some athletes can become addicted to training and abuse their own bodies, but coaches can also put pressure on athletes to train extremely hard, believing that the harder the athletes train, the greater the rewards. But overtraining can damage an athlete's health and perhaps lead to serious illness, depression and withdrawal from the sport. Some coaches may put undue pressure on the athlete to compete when injured, which could be regarded as a more serious form of abuse.

Doping and drugs

Codes of conduct should cover drugs as drugs are an illegal and unethical way of gaining an advantage over other athletes. Drugs may cause health problems and an athlete may face punishment if they are tested and found guilty. Coaches who encourage or pressurise an athlete to use illegal substances could be accused of abuse. Even coaches that do not encourage the use of illegal substances may be accused of abuse if they discover it and then ignore it.

Signs of abuse

Neglect

Physical indicators

- Constant hunger, stealing food from others
- Untidy state, dirty, smelly, same clothes
- Loss of weight
- Inappropriate clothes for the weather conditions.

Behavioural indicators

- Being tired all the time
- Late for school, truancy
- Failing to attend appointments
- Few friends, little sign or relatives at events
- Regularly left alone and unsupervised.

Physical abuse

Sport and children's activity can lead to cuts and bruises, so it is difficult to know which were accidents and which were caused deliberately.

Physical indicators

- Unexplained or untreated injuries on parts of the body where accidents are not likely, such as face and thighs
- Bruises that reflect the pattern of hand marks or fingers from slapping, grabbing or pinching
- Bite marks
- Cigarette burns
- Broken bones
- Scalds.

Behavioural indicators

- Fear of parents
- Aggressive behaviour, anger

- Running away
- Fear of going home
- Flinching when approached
- Reluctance to get changed or show their body
- Wearing baggy clothes in hot weather
- Depression, withdrawn behaviour.

Sexual abuse

If a child reports sexual abuse themselves, then this makes the abuse much more likely. Abusers often threaten their victims not to tell anyone, so a child has to pluck up enormous courage to make a report.

remember

Get a medical expert to check the symptoms. Do not do this yourself.

Physical indicators
- Pain or itching in the genital area
- Bruising or bleeding in the genital area
- Sexually transmitted disease
- Vaginal discharge or infection
- Stomach pains
- Discomfort when walking or sitting down
- Pregnancy.

Behavioural indicators
- Sudden changes in behaviour, aggression or withdrawal
- Fear of someone
- Running away
- Nightmares
- Sexual knowledge beyond the child's age group
- Sexual drawings or language
- Bed-wetting
- Eating problems, overeating, anorexia
- Self-harm, mutilation, suicide attempts
- Saying they have secrets
- Substance abuse, drug abuse
- Unexplained sources of money
- Parental role at home
- Not allowed to have friends
- Acting in a sexually explicit way among adults.

Emotional abuse

Physical indicators
- Failure to thrive or grow
- Speech disorders
- Delay in development.

Behavioural indicators
- Neurotic behaviour, such as rocking, twisting hair, banging the floor
- Unable to play or unwilling to participate
- Excessive fear of making mistakes

- Self-harm or mutilation
- Fear of parents.

Bullying and harassment

Physical indicators

- Stomach aches or headaches
- Difficulty sleeping
- Bed-wetting
- Scratching or bruising
- Damaged clothes
- Bingeing
- Shortage of money
- Loss of possessions.

Behavioural indicators

- Poor concentration
- Withdrawn or depressed
- Clingy
- Emotionally up and down
- Reluctance to attend training and school
- Drop in performance in sport and school.

Courses of action

Respond to the child

- Control your own emotions.
- Reassure the child they are not to blame.
- Be honest; do not make promises you cannot keep.
- Explain that you will have to talk to others or write things down.
- Listen and believe the child, take them seriously.
- Keep questions to a minimum.
  - Do not ask closed questions.
  - Allow the child to describe what happened in their own words.
  - Do not ask them to elaborate and do not probe for more information.
  - Don't put words in their mouth.
- Do not be negative about the alleged abuser.
- Do not approach the alleged abuser.
- Ensure the child is picked up or collected.
- If the child is collected by the alleged abuser, you may seek help from the police.

Record the disclosure

Make an accurate written record immediately after speaking to the child. Include the details, time and location of the abuse. Sign it, date it and hand copies to the club's child protection officer or senior coach as required. Store all records securely until they are required.

An abused child will want to speak privately to someone they trust, such as a coach. To get this private time, you may need to arrive early or stay late. Listen carefully and consider all the evidence; this often takes a long time. If the meeting is before a coaching session, find someone to supervise the session, sort out equipment, etc. If the meeting is after a session, make sure doors are left open and that other people are around but out of earshot. Do not wait until the next day or the next session as it could be too late.

Deal with bullying

All clubs and teams should have a strict anti-bullying policy and promote it within their code of practice. Take all signs seriously and involve parents and carers. Listen, record, report, reassure and take appropriate action.

Share your concerns

After a disclosure it is usual for the coach to worry about what action they should take. They may know the family or the colleague. The child may be a storyteller or may tend to exaggerate things. But the main concern is the welfare of the child and the consequences if no action is taken.

If it turns out that there wasn't a problem, then friendships may have to be rebuilt. This can be upsetting for child and coach, but the feelings are much worse when the signs of abuse are ignored and a child suffers harm or death.

In most cases the person to contact is easy to identify; local authorities, schools, clubs and NGBs all have a child welfare officer or senior coach that deals with all child abuse situations. But if you take a voluntary position, such as on a Saturday morning, always find out who to contact when there are disclosures or suspicions of child abuse.

Share information with professionals

It is the responsibility of the child welfare officer to talk to the police or social services. If it becomes the coach's responsibility, then follow these guidelines:

- Inform the duty officer at social services or police and explain that it is about child protection. Give your name, role, address and telephone number. Give a clear and accurate record of the child's name, address and date of birth, and what you have observed, including the date, time and details of the child's behaviour and emotional state, what you have said and any action you have taken.

- Social services will advise on what to do next and how and when to involve parents and carers. They will also take responsibility for any investigations.

- If a child needs urgent medical attention, seek it immediately and tell social services.

- Carefully record everything that is heard, seen and done.

Allegations against others

Guardians

A child may come into greater risk if the coach shares their concerns with the parent or guardian as they may be the abuser or they may not be able to deal with the abuser appropriately. Therefore, report to the child protection officer, or if they are not available, report to the police and social services, who will advise on what to do.

- Maintain confidentiality on a need-to-know basis.

- Ensure the child welfare officer or person in charge follows up the situation with social services.

- Seek advice from social services about whether to involve the parents and carers.

Staff

There may be situations where allegations are made against a colleague. This can prove very difficult, especially if they are a friend or someone that has been a trusted colleague for a long time. Perhaps you feel guilty about reporting against other colleagues, but an organisation should have a policy and process that allows reports to be made confidentially.

remember Keep the child at the centre of all concerns; maintain their confidence, safety and security at all times.

case study 23.6

Touch judge

The coach of a local swimming squad was delighted when he had to take on another coach due to increased numbers. He split the squad in two but after a month in the new squads, two girls stopped attending. The coach rang their parents and was given excuses about the girls finding other things to do. When the coach bumped into one of the girls shopping in town, he asked how she was doing. She broke down and confessed that she hadn't been swimming because the other coach had touched her and a couple of other girls.

activity
INDIVIDUAL WORK

1. What action should the coach take?
2. What could the coach have done to avoid this situation?

Figure 23.17 A checklist for child abuse. Adapted from Lester (2006)

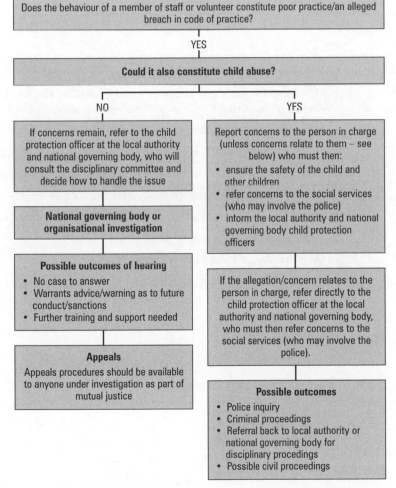

Does the behaviour of a member of staff or volunteer constitute poor practice/an alleged breach in code of practice?

YES

Could it also constitute child abuse?

NO

If concerns remain, refer to the child protection officer at the local authority and national governing body, who will consult the disciplinary committee and decide how to handle the issue

National governing body or organisational investigation

Possible outcomes of hearing
- No case to answer
- Warrants advice/warning as to future conduct/sanctions
- Further training and support needed

Appeals
Appeals procedures should be available to anyone under investigation as part of mutual justice

YES

Report concerns to the person in charge (unless concerns relate to them – see below) who must then:
- ensure the safety of the child and other children
- refer concerns to the social services (who may involve the police)
- inform the local authority and national governing body child protection officers

If the allegation/concern relates to the person in charge, refer directly to the child protection officer at the local authority and national governing body, who must then refer concerns to the social services (who may involve the police).

Possible outcomes
- Police inquiry
- Criminal proceedings
- Referral back to local authority or national governing body for disciplinary procedings
- Possible civil proceedings

If you do not know who to turn to for advice or are worried about sharing your concerns with a senior colleague, contact social services directly (or the NSPCC Child Protection Helpline on 0808 800 5000 or Childline on 0800 1111)

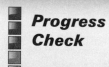

activity
GROUP WORK
23.6

P6

M5

After the posters in Activity 23.5 were put up around the club, two coaches approached you with concerns about a child. They had felt suspicions for a while but had been unsure what to do. You realise that you will need to follow up the poster with some workshops for employees and volunteers. The workshops will explain about child abuse and the appropriate action to take.

You decide to deliver a series of four workshops on four types of child abuse that may occur in sporting contexts, one type per workshop. Each workshop will set out a course of action to follow if that type of abuse is suspected.

activity
GROUP WORK
23.7

D2

Analyse the courses of action in suspected cases of child abuse of each type

Progress Check

1. What are the four needs of a child?
2. What are the rights of every child as stated by the UN Convention on the Rights of the Child?
3. Describe how sport can affect the social development of children.
4. Describe how sport can affect the psychological development of children.
5. Describe how sport can affect the physiological development of children.
6. Name the four key principles of good practice in sport.
7. Name four agencies that are involved in the protection of children.
8. What are the five types of child abuse?
9. Describe five effects of child abuse.
10. What is the main course of action if there is suspicion of child abuse?

Glossary

Accessibility
The ease with which somebody can participate in an activity.

Action plan
A tool used to aid a participant in planning for the future and meeting their goals.

Alzheimer's disease
A degenerative disease of nerve cells in the brain that leads to senility.

Amino acids
The building blocks of proteins. There are 10 amino acids that we are unable to make for ourselves; they are called essential amino acids.

Anthropometry
The scientific study of the measurements and proportions of the human body.

Antidepressant
A medication used to alleviate depression.

Antioxidant
A chemical that combines with free radicals and neutralises their effect on muscle cells.

Antioxidant vitamins
Antioxidant vitamins are beta-carotene, vitamin C and vitamin E; they are sometimes known as the ACE vitamins. They can help prevent damage to muscles and reduce post-exercise muscle soreness.

Anxiety
A negative emotional state characterised by nervousness, worry and apprehension and associated with arousal of the body.

Archimedes' principle
A body wholly or partially immersed in a fluid is subject to an upward force equal in magnitude to the weight of fluid it displaces.

Arousal
A participant's combined physiological and psychological response to motivation; usually influenced by the intensity of motivation.

Arthritis
Damage to joints that causes disability in people over age 55.

Atherosclerosis
A disease of the arteries where the artery walls harden and narrow, which restricts blood flow.

Attribution
The way people explain the outcome of an event; the reasons they give for success or failure.

Auditory learner
A person who learns best by talking and listening to explanations.

Ballistic stretching
A form of stretching that uses bouncing movements in a stretched position.

BMI
Body mass index; a person's mass divided by the square of their height.

Boccia
A sport similar to bowls for people with disabilities.

Branched-chain amino acid
An amino acid that helps to reduce fatigue by protecting the heart and the muscles.

Cheating
Breaking the rules of sport.

Cholesterol
A compound of the sterol type found in most body tissues. Cholesterol and its derivatives are important constituents of cell membranes and precursors of other steroid compounds but high concentrations in the blood are thought to promote atherosclerosis.

Chronic bronchitis
Inflammation of the bronchi that causes coughing and production of phlegm, or sputum.

Claudication
Pain in the thigh or calf after you have been walking for a while.

Clubmark
A cross-sport quality accreditation for clubs with junior sections.

COAD

Chronic obstructive airways disease.

Cognitive anxiety

Negative thoughts about performance that manifest themselves in a participant.

Cohesiveness

The degree of bonding between team members to produce a productive team.

Community sport network

A collection of people who have a desire to develop and promote sport and physical activity in their locality.

Congestive heart failure

Weakening of the heart muscle.

Connexions

An information and advice service for young people.

Coronary artery

One of several arteries that supplies blood to the heart.

CVA

Cerebrovascular accident.

DDA

Disability Discrimination Act 1995.

Deep vein thrombosis

A blood clot that forms in a deep vein, usually in the legs.

Desquamation

Removal of dead skin cells from the body; it can occur by friction of a masseur's hand against a person's skin.

Diabetes

A disorder of the metabolism causing excessive thirst and the production of large amounts of urine.

Diastolic blood pressure

The lowest blood pressure; it occurs during the resting phase of the cardiac cycle.

Disabled

Of a person, having a physical or mental condition that limits their movements, senses or activities.

EFA

Essential fatty acid; a fatty acid that cannot be made by the body and must be eaten as part of a diet, e.g. linoleic acid and alpha-linoleic acid.

Effleurage

Superficial movements used to apply a chosen massage medium such as oil or cream. Effleurage also accustoms the athlete to the masseur's touch; its long stroking movements usually follow venous return, i.e. towards the heart.

Emphysema

A disease of the lungs caused by long-term exposure to toxic chemicals.

Empower

To give power or authority to participants so they become responsible for their own actions.

Endorphins

Biochemical compounds that are released during pain, danger, stress or medium- to high-intensity exercise. They produce the feelings of exhilaration know as runner's high.

Enzyme

A substance produced by a living organism which acts as a catalyst to bring about a specific biochemical reaction. Examples are maltase, sucrase and pepsin.

Epiphyseal plate

The cartilage that contains an epiphysis, unites it with the shaft and is the site of longitudinal growth of the bone.

Epiphysis

A part or process of a bone that ossifies separately and later becomes joined to the main part of the bone; especially an end of a long bone.

Extrinsic motivation

A source of motivation that comes from outside a person, such as money and praise.

Extrinsic reward

A reward that comes from outside a person, such as money and praise.

Fair play

Treating opponents as equals and abiding by the rules of sport.

Formative assessment

Assessment that gives immediate feedback to a participant.

Free radical

A by-product of aerobic respiration that can damage muscle cells.

Frictions
A group of massage techniques which use the pads of the fingers or thumbs to apply deep pressure that loosens scar tissue.

Fundamentals
The second stage of LTAD where basic movement skills are taught to girls aged 6--8 and boys aged 6--9.

Gamesmanship
When players will do anything they can to overcome their opponent.

Goal setting
Devising targets or aims for a participant to achieve.

Growth plate
A cartilaginous plate in a bone that allows it to grow longitudinally.

Hazard
A potential source of harm.

Health
A state of complete physical, mental and social well-being and not merely the absence of disease or infirmity.

Hypertension
High blood pressure.

Immune system
A bodily system that protects the body from foreign substances that could cause infections.

Inclusive
Describes an activity that includes all participants or is accessible to everyone.

Inflammatory response
A response that leads to oedema at the site of an injury.

In loco parentis
Latin for 'in the place of a parent'; the legal responsibility of a person or organisation to take on the responsibilities of a parent.

Intrinsic motivation
A source of motivation that comes from inside a person, such as pride in performance.

Intrinsic reward
A reward that comes from inside a person, such as pride in performance.

IZOF
Individualised zone of optimum functioning; the point where anxiety and arousal elicit optimal performance.

Kinaesthetic learner
A person who learns best by practising actions and movements.

LDL
Low-density lipoprotein; bad cholesterol.

Leader-centred
A leadership style that focuses on the needs of the leader.

Learned helplessness
A psychological condition where a person has learned to believe they are helpless. They think that they have no control over the situation and that whatever they do is pointless.

Ligament sprain
Damage caused by a stretch or tear to a ligament.

LTAD
Long-term athlete development; a systematic approach to developing performers in sport based on work by Istvan Balyi.

Lymph
A straw-coloured fluid found in the lymphatic system; it contains proteins, fatty acids, glucose and hormones.

Lymphatic system
A system of lymph nodes (glands), vessels and fluid. It does not have a pump like the heart in the cardiovascular system. It removes bacteria and foreign materials, prevents infection and removes excessive fluid.

Macronutrient
A dietary component that is needed in large quantities; examples are fats, carbohydrates and proteins.

Menarche
The first occurrence of menstruation; it is usually experienced by a girl during puberty.

Menstruation
The process in a woman of discharging blood and other material from the lining of the uterus as part of the menstrual cycle.

Micronutrient
A dietary component that is needed in small quantities; examples are vitamins and minerals.

Motivated
Of a person, having the desire and direction to persist at something.

Motivation
Desire or willingness to do something.

Motor programme
A set of prestructured movement commands that are learned by practising skills.

Muscle strain
Damage caused by overstretching a muscle.

Myocardial infarction
A heart attack.

Non-insulin-dependent diabetes
See type 2 diabetes.

Notational analysis
Studies and records the movement patterns of officials in team sports.

OAP
Old-age pensioner.

Obese
Of a person, having over 27% body fat.

Oedema
A condition characterised by an excess of watery fluid collecting in the cavities or tissues of the body.

Ofsted
Office for Standards in Education.

Ossification
The process of bone formation from cartilage.

Osteochondritis
A painful swelling of the joint where some cartilage or bone has been damaged and become loose in the joint capsule.

Osteoporosis
A bone disease that reduces the bone's mineral density.

Participant-centred
A leadership style that focuses on the needs of the leader.

PCT
Primary care trust; controls all local healthcare. Its standards and performance are monitored by health authorities.

Peer
A person of the same age, status or ability as another specified person.

Pelvic floor
The muscular base of the abdomen, attached to the bony pelvis. The muscle fibres of the pelvic floor provide support for the intestines, bladder and uterus in women.

Percussion
A group of massage techniques that use light rhythmical movements, usually to stimulate and invigorate. Examples are hacking, cupping, beating and pounding.

Performance profiling
A way to evaluate the strengths and weaknesses of an official's performance. The strengths and weaknesses are used to plan training regimes and identify long-term goals.

Peristalsis
Contractions of the gastrointestinal tract that squeeze and push food in one direction.

Personality
A combination of characteristics that make a person unique.

Petrissage
A group of massage techniques that press and squeeze the tissues, such as kneading, wringing, picking up and skin rolling.

Physical literacy
The combination of fundamental movement skills and fundamental sports skills.

Pilates
A physical fitness system that uses the mind to control the core muscles; it is particularly used for posture.

PNF
Proprioceptive neuromuscular facilitation; a form of flexibility training where the participant isometrically contracts a muscle that is being stretched to facilitate increased range of movement.

Positive affirmation
Positive sentences that help a person to achieve their goals.

Post-natal
Relating to or denoting the period after childbirth.

Prenatal
Before birth; during or relating to pregnancy.

Primary damage
Tissue destruction at the site of an injury.

Private organisation
An organisation that is independently owned and usually run to make a profit.

Provision
An amount or thing supplied or provided, such as an activity, a programme of activities or a sports centre.

PSA
Public service agreement; used by the government to set targets for providers.

Psychological state
A person's state of mental well-being.

Public organisation
An organisation owned and run by the government.

Rapport
A close and harmonious relationship in which the people or groups concerned understand each other's feelings or ideas and communicate well.

Referred client
A client seen by one professional on the recommendation of another professional.

Ringelmann effect
A phenomenon which may be the cause of social loafing, whereby individual performance decreases with increasing group size.

Risk
For a given hazard, the likelihood that it will occur and the severity of the harm it will cause.

Risk factor
See hazard.

Secondary amenorrhea
Absence of the menstrual cycle after the menarche.

Sedentary
Inactive.

Self-concept
Knowledge and understanding of one's self.

Self-efficacy
Belief in one's ability to complete a task.

Self-esteem
A person's appraisal of themselves based on their successes and failures.

Self-fulfilling prophecy
A prediction that is bound to be proved correct or to come true as a result of behaviour caused by its being expressed.

Serotonin
A neurotransmitter found in the brain, platelets and gastrointestinal tract.

SMART
Describes goals that are specific, measurable, achievable, realistic and time-bound.

SMARTER
Describes goals that are specific, measurable, achievable, realistic, time-bound. exciting and recorded.

Social loafing
Describes the behaviour of players who seem to lack motivation in team situations.

Somatic anxiety
Changes in bodily function as a result of anxiety about performance.

Spinning
A form of intense exercise using a stationary bike.

Sports injury
An injury that results from acute trauma or repetitive stress associated with athletic activities. Sports injuries can affect bones or they can affect soft tissue, such as ligaments, muscles and tendons.

Sportsmanship
Conduct (as fairness, respect for one's opponent, and graciousness in winning or losing) becoming to one's participating in sport; conforming to the written and unwritten rules of sport.

Sportsmark
Sport England's accreditation scheme for secondary schools.

State anxiety
Anxiety that a person experiences during specific situations.

Stress
An imbalance between the demands of an activity and how a person perceives their ability to meet those demands plus the importance they attach to the perceived consequences of failure.

Summative assessment
Assessment that gives final feedback to a participant.

SWOT analysis
An analysis technique that looks at strengths, weaknesses, opportunities and threats.

Systolic blood pressure
The highest blood pressure in the arteries; it occurs at the end of the cardiac cycle.

Tangible reward
A reward that can be touched, such as a trophy or a certificate.

Trait anxiety
Anxiety that a person experiences; it is part of their core personality.

Trigger point
The result of an accumulation of waste products around a nerve receptor. Trigger points are painful when compressed and are often found in muscles that are overused or injured.

Tumble turn
A turn used by swimmers when they reach the side of a swimming pool. The swimmer flips their body over and pushes their feet against the side of the pool to propel themselves away. The turn reverses the swimmer's direction of travel, so they can swim the same length in the opposite direction.

Type 2 diabetes
A type of diabetes that usually occurs in adults and people suffering from obesity. It is caused by insufficient production of insulin in the pancreas or a resistance to the action of insulin in the body's cells, especially in muscle, fat and liver cells. It can cause increased blood sugar levels, or hyperglycaemia.

Unwritten rules
Values and ethics that are not written down but which all players are expected to follow; they are sometimes called the spirit of the game.

Varicose vein
A vein that has become enlarged and twisted where the blood pools; usually found in the legs.

Vibrations
A group of massage techniques that are normally used for their sedative effects. Examples are direct shaking and indirect movements; indirect movements are when one hand is placed over the other.

Vicarious experience
Experience gained by watching someone else perform a task.

Visual learner
A person who learns best by watching others perform skills and by using videos of their performance.

Volenti non fit injuria
When a person takes part in an activity accepting and fully aware of the risks, they cannot later complain or ask for compensation if they suffer an injury.

Voluntary organisation
An organisation that relies on donations and volunteers.

Well-being
A state of being healthy, happy and prosperous.

Bibliography

Balyi, I. (2001) Sport system building and long-term athlete development in Canada. *Coaches Report*, **8**(1) 25–28.

Bandura, A. (1977) *Social Learning Theory*. Prentice Hall, Englewood Cliffs NJ.

Bandura, A. (1997) *Self-efficacy: The Exercise of Control*. W. H. Freeman, New York.

Bean, A. (2003) *Fitness on a Plate*. A&C Black, London.

Brewer, B. W., Van Raalte, J. L., Petitpas, A. J., Sklar, J. H. and Ditmar, T. D. (1995) A brief measure of adherence during sport injury rehabilitation sessions. *Journal of Applied Sport Psychology*. **8**, S161.

Cale, L. and Harris, J. (2005) *Exercise and Young People: Issues, Implications and Initiatives*. Palgrave Macmillan, Basingstoke, Hants.

Carron, A. V. (1982) Cohesiveness in sport groups: interpretations and consideration. *Journal of Sport Psychology*, **4**, 123–138.

Cassidy, T., Jones, R. and Potrac, P. (2004) *Understanding Sports Coaching: The Social, Cultural and Pedagogical Foundations of Coaching Practice*. Routledge, London.

Chambers, D. (1997) *Coaching: The Art and the Science*. Key Porter Books, Toronto.

Chryssanthopoulos, C., Williams, C., Nowitz, A., Kotsiopoulou, C. and Vleck, V. E. (2002) The effect of a high carbohydrate meal on endurance running capacity. *International Journal of Sport Nutrition and Exercise Metabolism*, **12**(2), 157–171.

Cox, R. H. (1994) *Sports Psychology: Concepts and Applications*, 3rd edn. Brown & Benchmark, Madison WI.

Earle, C. (2003) *Coaching Young Performers*, 2nd edn. Coachwise, Leeds.

Earle, C. (2006) *How to Coach Children in Sport*. Coachwise, Leeds.

Ewing, J. A. (1984) Detecting alcoholism, the CAGE questionnaire. *Journal of the American Medical Association*, **252**, 1905–1907.

Gallahue, D. L. and Osmun, J. C. (2001) *Understanding Motor Development*. McGraw-Hill, Boston MA.

Gill, D. L. (2000) *Psychological Dynamics of Sport and Exercise*, 2nd edn. Human Kinetics, Champaign, IL.

Green, K. and Hardman, K. (2005) *Physical Education: Essential Issues*. Sage, London.

Griffin, J. (2001) *Food for Sport: Eat Well, Perform Better*. Crowood Press, Marlborough, Wilts.

Hanin, Y. L. (1980) A study of anxiety in sports. In *Sport Psychology: An Analysis of Athlete Behavior* (ed. W. F. Straub). Mouvement Publications, Ithaca NY.

Honeybourne, J., Hill, M. and Moors, H. (2000) *Advanced Physical Education and Sport*, 3rd edn. Nelson Thornes, Cheltenham, Glos.

Horn, T. (2002) *Advances in Sport Psychology*, 2nd edn. Human Kinetics, Champaign IL.

Jacobson, E. (1938). *Progressive Relaxation*. University of Chicago Press, Chicago IL.

Jones, R., Armour, K. and Potrac, P. (2004) *Sports Coaching Cultures: From Practice to Theory*. Routledge, London.

Kerr, A. and Stafford, I. (2004) *How to Coach Disabled People in Sport*. Coachwise, Leeds.

Lee, M. (1993) *Coaching Children in Sport: Principles and Practice*. Spon, London.

Lester, G. (2006) *Protecting Children: A Guide for Sports People*, 3rd edn. Coachwise, Leeds.

Malina, R. M., Bouchard, C. and Bar-Or, O. (2004) *Growth, Maturation and Physical Activity*, 2nd edn. Human Kinetics, Champaign IL.

Martens, R. (1997) *Successful Coaching*, 2nd edn. Human Kinetics, Champaign. IL.

McGrath, J. E. (ed.) (1970) A conceptual formulation for research on stress. In *Social and Psychological Factors in Stress*. Holt, Rinehart and Winston, New York.

McQuade, S. (2003) *How to Coach Sports Effectively*. Coachwise, Leeds.

Miles, A. (2004a) *Coaching Practice*. Coachwise, Leeds.

Miles, A. (2004b) *What Is Sports Coaching?* Coachwise, Leeds.

Morgan, W. P. (1979). Prediction of performance in athletics. In *Coach, Athlete, and the Sport Psychologist* (ed. Klavora, P. and Daniel, J. V). Human Kinetics, Champaign. IL.

Ochieng, B. M. N. (2006) Factors affecting choice of a healthy lifestyle: implications for nurses. *British Journal of Community Nursing*, **11**(2), 78–81.

Prochaska, J. O and DiClemente, C. C. (1983) Stages and processes of self-change of smoking: toward an integrative model of change. *Journal of Consulting and Clinical Psychology*, **51**, 390–395.

Purdy, D. A. and Snyder, E. E. (1985) A social profile of high school basketball officials. *Journal of Sport Behavior*, **8**(1), 54–65.

Pyke, S. P. (2001) *Better Coaching: Advanced Coach's Manual*. Human Kinetics, Champaign IL.

Ringelmann, M. (1913) Recherches sur les moteurs animés: travail de l'homme. *Annales de l'Institut National Agronomique*, **2**(12), 1–40.

Robergs, R. A. and Roberts, S. O. (1997) *Exercise Physiology: Exercise, Performance and Clinical Applications*. Mosby, St Louis MO.

Rowett, H. G. Q. (1988) *Basic Anatomy and Physiology*, 3rd edn. John Murray, London.

Sage, G. H. (ed.) (1974) *Sport and American Society*. Addison-Wesley, Reading MA.

Shephard, R. J. (1997) *Aging, Physical Activity and Health*. Human Kinetics, Champaign IL.

Smoll, F. L. and Smith, R. E. (1996) *Children and Youth in Sport: A Biopsychosocial Perspective*. Brown & Benchmark, London.

Sports Coach UK (2003a) *How to Coach Sports Safely*. Coachwise, Leeds.

Sports Coach UK (2003b) *The Successful Coach: Guidelines for Coaching Practice*. Coachwise, Leeds.

Stafford, I. (2005) *Coaching for Long-Term Athlete Development*. Coachwise, Leeds.

Steiner, I. D. (1972) *Group Process and Productivity*. Academic Press, London.

Tannenbaum, R. and Schmidt, W. H. (1973) How to choose a leadership pattern. *Harvard Business Review*, **May/June**, 162–180.

Tuckman, B. W. (1965) Developmental sequence in small groups. *Psychological Bulletin*, **63**, 384–399.

Tuckman, B. W. and Jensen, M. A. C. (1977) Stages of small group development revisited. *Group and Organizational Studies*, **2**, 419–427.

Weinberg, R. S. and Gould, D. (2003) *Foundations of Sport and Exercise Psychology*, 3rd edn. Human Kinetics, Champaign IL.

Wilmore, J. H. and Costill, D. L. (1999) *Physiology of Sport and Exercise*. Human Kinetics, Champaign IL.

Further reading

Brown, J., Rea, S. and Chance, J. (2003) *BTEC National in Sport and Exercise Science*. Hodder Arnold, London.

Dalgleish, J., Dollery, S. and Frankham, H. (2001) *The Health and Fitness Handbook*. Longman, London.

Heyward, V. (2002) *Advanced Fitness Assessment and Exercise Prescription*. Human Kinetics, Champaign IL.

Howley, E. T. and Franks, B. D. (2006) *Health Fitness Instructor's Handbook*. Human Kinetics, Champaign IL.

Jackson, A. W., Morrow, J. R., Hill, D. W. and Dishman, R. K. (2004) *Physical Activity for Health and Fitness*. Human Kinetics, Champaign IL.

Mahoney, C. (2005) *Managing People and Situations*. Coachwise, Leeds.

Norris, C. (2004) *The Complete Guide to Stretching*, 2nd edn. A&C Black, London.

Norris, C. (2005) *Complete Guide to Sports Injuries*. Perigee, New York.

Pegg, D. (2005) *An Introduction to Sports Officiating*. Coachwise, Leeds.

Shamus, E. (2001) *Sport Injury Rehabilitation*. McGraw-Hill, Maidenhead, Berks.

Sharkey, B and Gaskill, E. (2006) *Fitness and Health, Human Kinetics*, Champaign IL.

Two relevant journals

Peak Performance

Sports Injury Bulletin

Index